V&R

Schnittstellen

Studien zum östlichen und südöstlichen Europa

Herausgegeben von
Martin Schulze Wessel und Ulf Brunnbauer

Band 26

Boris Ganichev

Integrating Imperial Space

The Russian Customs System in the 19th Century

Vandenhoeck & Ruprecht

The printing of this book was made possible with support provided by the *Graduate School for East and Southeast European Studies* at Ludwig-Maximilians-Universität München.

Bibliographic information published by the Deutsche Nationalbibliothek:
The Deutsche Nationalbibliothek lists this publication in the Deutsche Nationalbibliografie; detailed bibliographic data available online: https://dnb.de.

Cover design: SchwabScantechnik, Göttingen
Typesetting: textformart, Göttingen
Printed and bound by ⊕ Hubert & Co, Göttingen
Printed in the EU

Vandenhoeck & Ruprecht Verlage | www.vandenhoeck-ruprecht-verlage.com

ISSN 2566-6592
ISBN 978-3-525-30208-8

Table of Contents

Acknowledgments

> You can't tie a knot with one hand.
> – Russian proverb

This book, based on my doctoral dissertation submitted to the Ludwig Maximilian University of Munich, would not have been possible without the hands or rather minds of many people who helped me tie this knot and at times untie the knot in my head.

I am deeply grateful to my two academic advisors. Martin Schulze Wessel has supported and challenged me since my first days at the Ludwig Maximilian University. His trust in me and my project allowed for invaluable academic freedom, his guidance and council helped me focus my research. Most of all I am thankful for having had the privilege to experience the unique and truly intellectual climate, which he has created at the Ludwig Maximilian University. To Jana Osterkamp I am greatly indebted for co-supervising my work and contributing her expertise on imperial formations. I owe much of the theoretic framework to conversations with her. Her personal support during the lows of academic research was invaluable.

I am extremely grateful to my dear friends and fellow researchers Matthias Golbeck, Max Trecker and Josef Prackwieser who have helped shape and sharpen my thoughts throughout the entire journey. The importance of their questions, comments and suggestions as well as their intensive reading of my manuscript cannot be overrated.

I also wish to thank a number of friends and fellow scholars who offered valuable insights, comments and advice: Martin Aust, Boris Belge, Ekaterina Boltunova, Ulf Brunnbauer, Franziska Davies, Adele Del Sordi, Lorenz Erren, Anastasia Fedotova, Guido Hausmann, Hubertus Jahn, Tatiana Kostina, Jan Kusber, Anton Liavitski, Marina Loskutova, Katja Makhotina, Christoph Neumann, Ekaterina Pravilova, Andreas Renner, Benjamin Schenk, Alexander Semyonov, Yuri Slezkine, Willard Sunderland, Ronald Suny, Alexander Turbin and Ricarda Vulpius. I also want to thank all library and archive staff without whom my research would not have been possible.

A special thank you goes out to Caroline Fricke and Christoph Hilgert who were the heart and soul of the Munich Graduate School for East and Southeast European Studies, did everything to accommodate complicated research plans and always had an ear for the graduates' concerns.

It has been a great pleasure working with Vandenhoeck & Ruprecht. The support and patience of Daniel Sander made this book possible. I would also like to extend my gratitude to Anna Katharina Thurn who meticulously proof-read my work. All remaining shortcomings are irrevocably my own.

Elionora Fedorovna Müller holds a special place in my heart. Without her this work would not have been possible at all. She has been the first from whom I had ever heard of Uzbekistan or the Fergana valley – long before these distant corners of the world would become the subject of my research. Foremost, I am immeasurably grateful to her for teaching me the Russian language through eleven years of painstaking private lessons. Her patience with me knew no bounds, the knowledge and abilities she bestowed upon me enriched me personally way beyond the mere ability to perform academic research in Russian. A pedagogue from the depth of her heart and mind, Elianora Fedorovna taught me to esteem the written word.

I am deeply grateful to my family: Olga Ganicheva, Sergey Ganichev and Daria Olden.

To my parents I owe everything. They taught me the value of curiosity, perseverance and walking one's own path. Their infinite support and unconditional love are my greatest assets.

My wife, Anja Reiter-Ganichev, supported me throughout the whole journey from the enthusiastic beginnings, through the valleys of despair until it was time to buckle down for the finale. Counting on her love, infinite patience and trust carried me through many difficult times – I strive to be equally supportive of her as she is of me. My beautiful daughter Sophia Ganichev did very little to further the development of this project, but her imminent birth had all the more to do with its swift completion.

This book is dedicated to you, Anja and Sophia, lights of my life.

Introduction

A fundamental change in the relationship between region and empire was hardly what Minister of Finance Mikhail Reitern expected when State Comptroller Samuil Greig submitted a report on the mundane issue of lax customs controls in the Transcaucasian region. The territory had been detached from the empire's core customs space and subordinated to the Caucasian Viceroy since 1847. Three decades later, however, growing complaints about smuggling activities called for revision. Rather than lingering over minor technicalities of border protection, Greig suggested the full reintegration of the Transcaucasian customs territory in his 1877 report. This reform appeared inevitable to him, as he argued that "[...] the financial history of other countries provides us with examples of the unification of the customs of different states under one administration. However, examples of several independent customs administrations within one state cannot be found anywhere."[1] What had once been designed as a bespoke solution to accommodate the region's peculiarities was now conceived as backwards and deviant. And it did not help that the construction of railways and telegraphs promising to shrink the empire spotlighted the non-uniformity of its many peripheral economic spaces.

Greig's lamentation on the deviation from a presumably normal developmental path is little surprising, and just one of many possible variations on the theme of Russia's "backwardness." Others had put an optimistic twist on it, hoping to skip over the pitfalls of modernization, which forerunner countries such as Britain experienced. And yet others, like economist Vasilii Vorontsov, advocated a developmental course altogether different from the European model.[2] Greig most likely bore in mind a comparison with the recently unified German Empire, which had developed from a customs union – the *Zollverein* – into a powerful political union, firmly positioning Germany within the concert of Great Powers.[3] Against this backdrop, Russia's

1 RGIA, f. 1152, op. 9, d. 84, "O preobrazovanii karantinno-tamozhennoi chasti na Kavkaze i v Zakavkazskom krae", l. 3ob.

2 For the many ways in which "backwardness" was interpreted by contemporaries throughout Russian history, see *Hildermeier, Manfred*: Das Privileg der Rückständigkeit. Anmerkungen zum Wandel einer Interpretationsfigur der Neueren Russischen Geschichte. In: Historische Zeitschrift, 244(3) (1987), 557–603. For Vorontsov's position in particular see 585–586.

3 From the vast body of literature on the Zollverein see the classic study by *Hahn, Hans-Werner*: Geschichte des Deutschen Zollvereins. Göttingen 1984. The more recent collection edited by Hahn presents fresh perspectives on a seemingly familiar subject, see *Hahn,*

fragmented customs system appeared as yet another archaism curtailing its pursuit of modernization, ignited by a devastating defeat in the Crimean War in 1856. The task of overcoming "backwardness" and debates over the empire's future development were ubiquitous. The ensuing phase, known as the "Great Reforms", saw almost every aspect of political, economic and social life in the Russian Empire put under scrutiny.

An overhaul of such significant scale, in a state so deeply steeped in autocratic political tradition as the Russian Empire, has attracted substantial scholarly interest. The static image of the empire was gradually revised, starting with the basic prerequisites for any reform – the reformers. Bruce Lincoln identified a group of "enlightened bureaucrats" as the driving force behind the Great Reforms of the 1860s and 1870s, establishing a continuity between the rule of Nicholas I and Alexander II, rather than reinforcing the idea of a radical and startling rupture.[4] As early as the 1840s, these distinguished state servants had identified serfdom as one of the most obstructive factors for the empire's development, yet reform was slow to come. It took the humiliating defeat in the Crimean War to embark on a sweeping reform program, the centerpiece of which was the abolition of serfdom in 1861. Alongside, the judicial and educational system had been reformed, institutions of local self-government were introduced, and the military was put on a new footing. The aim was an all-encompassing transformation from which the Russian Empire would emerge, strengthened both militarily and economically, ready to compete with other Great Powers.

This book contributes to the study of this transformative phase and the ensuing decades by tracing the development of the Russian Empire's customs system in the 19th century and exploring the junction between issues of economy, space and imperial rule. At its core, it tells the story of how the Russian Empire perceived and manipulated its imperial economic space throughout

Hans-Werner/Kreutzmann, Marko (eds.): Der deutsche Zollverein. Ökonomie und Nation im 19. Jahrhundert. Köln 2012. For a global perspective on the trade policies of the Zollverein see *Torp, Cornelius*: Die Herausforderung der Globalisierung. Wirtschaft und Politik in Deutschland, 1860–1914. Göttingen 2005. For the international impact of Friedrich List's ideas in general and particularly on Russia see *Wendler, Eugen*: Die List-Rezeption in Rußland. In: *Wendler, Eugen* (ed.): "Die Vereinigung des europäischen Kontinents." Friedrich List – Gesamteuropäische Wirkungsgeschichte seines ökonomischen Denkens. Stuttgart 1996, 473–490; *Barnett, Vincent*: D.I. Mendeleev, Russian Protectionism and German Political Economy. In: *Rieter, Heinz/Shirokorad, Leonid/Zweynert, Joachim* (eds.): Deutsche und russische Ökonomen im Dialog. Wissenstransfer in historischer Perspektive. Marburg 2005, 169–184.

4 *Lincoln, Bruce W.*: In the Vanguard of Reform. Russia's Enlightened Bureaucrats, 1825–1861. DeKalb 1982; *Lincoln, Bruce W.*: The Great Reforms. Autocracy, Bureaucracy, and the Politics of Change in Imperial Russia. Dekalb 1990.

the 19th century and what visions for its future can be read from the mundanity of customs regulations.

Late Imperial Russia's Economy

The interpretation of Russia's economic modernization as peculiar and deviant has not only been voiced by contemporaries such as State Comptroller Samuil Greig, but also made its way into scholarly work. Among the most influential was Alexander Gerschenkron's use of the Russian Empire as an example to theorize "economic backwardness" and extrapolate the specifics of belated development. He argued that the more backward an economy, the more important the role of the state in its developmental process and the larger the scale of production.[5] The elevation of "Great Men", most notably Sergei Vitte, went hand in hand with this statist interpretation.[6] Although persuasive in its elegance, Gerschenkron's thesis could not hold up to empirical scrutiny. Subsequent scholars discovered far greater ambiguity in the economic life of the late Russian Empire. While large-scale projects such as the Donbas coal and steel industrial zone were certainly of great importance, smaller industries like the Ural iron producers continued to exist in their slipstream and fared much better than previously assumed, adjusting flexibly to market conditions.[7] Close scrutiny of individual enterprises such as the Putilov works revealed a state that promoted the creation of large-scale enterprises, yet likewise suffered

5 *Gerschenkron, Alexander*: Economic Backwardness in Historical Perspective. A Book of Essays. Cambridge, Massachusetts 1962.

6 Vitte's interpretation as a great modernizer, popularized by von Laue, a contemporary of Gerschenkron, remains dominant and is in line with the latter's modernization theory approach. Francis Wcislo recently presented a more multifaceted reading of Vitte, contextualizing both him as a person as well as the Russian Empire within 19th century Europe, rather than perpetuating the narrative of a peripheral state of exception. Vitte has received much scholarly attention with Ganelin and Anan'ich presenting an in-depth account of his life and works. Other ministers of finance remain more obscure with only one substantial work on Nikolai Bunge written by Stepanov, who also produced a short outline on Mikhail Reitern. See *Von Laue, Theodore H.*: Sergei Witte and the Industrialization of Russia. New York 1963; *Wcislo, Frank*: Rereading Old Texts: Sergei Witte and the Industrialization of Russia. In: *McCaffray, Susan P./Melancon, Michael* (eds.): Russia in the European Context, 1789–1914. A Member of the Family. New York 2005, 71–83; *Wcislo, Francis William*: Tales of Imperial Russia. The Life and Times of Sergei Witte, 1849–1915. Oxford 2011; *Ganelin, Rafail/Anan'ich, Boris*: Sergei Iul'evich Vitte i ego vremia. Saint Petersburg 1999; *Stepanov, Valerii*: N. Kh. Bunge. Sud'ba reformatora. Moscow 1998; *Stepanov, Valerii*: Mikhail Khristoforovich Reitern. In: Russian Studies in History, 35(2) (1996), 8–41.

7 *Blanchard, Ian*: Russian Railway Construction and the Urals Charcoal Iron and Steel Industry, 1851–1914. In: The Economic History Review, 53(1) (2000), 107–126.

once it had to bail out conglomerates deemed too big to fail.[8] Neither did Gerschenkron's observations on the nature of the relationship between state and entrepreneurship in autocratic Russia hold true.[9] On the surface, many impediments to the emergence of interest groups and associations existed. Nevertheless, in practice, entrepreneurs succeeded in creatively circumventing limitations, and were able to develop a "proto-parliamentarian posture."[10] More often than not, the state failed to act upon its regulatory rhetoric, and economic activities were meddled with less than previously assumed. Limitations of the state's access even extended to vital areas such as the control of banking and speculation operations.[11]

These revisions do not mean to smooth over the peculiarities that existed in the Russian economic system, but rather challenge the notion of "backwardness" as such. Susan McCaffray and Michael Melancon argue that particular phenomena in Russia's development should not be unquestioningly read as "pathological deviance from a universal European norm" but taken seriously and situated within a field of "contested possibilities." Thus, "ideas that seem strange or doomed in retrospect seemed very much alive 150 years ago, and not just in Russia."[12]

While much of the backwardness theorem has been debunked, most studies on the economy of the late Russian Empire retained the geographical focus on the Western core regions of the empire inherited from the modernization-theory informed works of Gerschenkron and the likes. If modernization is understood narrowly as the creation of factories and railroads, then a look at any statistical map of the Russian Empire's industrial infrastructure justifies the neglect of territories such as the Transcaucasus, Turkestan and Siberia. Viewed from the center, they appear both geographically and economically peripheral.[13]

8 *Grant, Jonathan A.*: Big Business in Russia. The Putilov Company in Late Imperial Russia, 1868–1917. Pittsburgh 1999.

9 *Gerschenkron*: Economic Backwardness, 16–20.

10 *McCaffray, Susan P.*: The Politics of Industrialization in Tsarist Russia. The Association of Southern Coal and Steel Producers, 1874–1914. DeKalb 1996, 40.

11 *Anan'ich, Boris*: Banking Firms in the Russian Empire, 1860–1914. In: Russian Studies in History, 35(1) (1996), 6–61.

12 *McCaffray, Susan P./Melancon, Michael*: Introduction: A Member of the Family – Russia's Place in Europe, 1789–1914. In: *McCaffray, Susan P./Melancon, Michael* (eds.): Russia in a European Context, 1789–1914. A Member of the Family. New York 2005, 1–10, here 7.

13 The map of the Russian Empire's "industrial-enterprise-regions" included in the catalogue for the World's Columbian Exposition held in Chicago in 1893 went as far as fully omitting the territories east of Omsk. Only seven years later at the Paris World Fair in 1900, however, "Asiatic Russia" was already prominently featured as a land of opportunity only waiting to be invested in. For the map see *Il'in, A.*: Obshchaia karta fabrichno-zavodskoi promyshlennosti Rossiiskoi Imperii. In: *Mendeleev, Dmitrii* (ed.), Fabrichno-zavodskaia promyshlennost' i torgovlia Rossii. Saint Petersburg 1893. For the Trans-Siberian railway's

Nevertheless, the second half of the 19th century was particularly dynamic in the Russian Empire's east. While the end of the Caucasian Wars prompted debate on the region's future role in the imperial edifice, a bloody war was waged on the eastern side of the Caspian Sea to expand the empire further into Central Asia. Moreover, the construction of the Trans-Siberian railway made the realization of ambitious visions for Siberia more tangible than ever, and the Russian imperial space appeared to condense. However, only few industry-specific studies have ventured into these peripheries of the empire, though returning astounding results.

John McKay traced the protracted development of the Transcaucasian oil-pipeline to reveal the interplay of state and private interests, as well as the deep division between different departments and ministries over the issue. The close proximity to the border with the Ottoman Empire and Persia further heightened awareness for strategic considerations. However, the government lacked both funds and determination, leaving the project in limbo. The case can be read as a repudiation of the etatist interpretation of the late Russian Empire's economy. Likewise, it can serve as an example for the relationship of imperial center and periphery, in which a major project with the potential to alter regional hierarchies has been caught up between interdepartmental, military and regional interests.[14]

Similarly, grand schemes for the development of large-scale cotton production in Central Asia should not simply be dismissed as a story of imperial megalomania and inaptitude. Studies rather suggest that careful balancing of interests delayed the project. Local interests and customs had to be accommodated, strategic considerations outweighed economic ones, and international fundraising acquired a political dimension in this geopolitically sensitive region.[15] Thus, when analyzed for its imperial dimension and not along the

presentation in Paris see *Schenk, Frithjof Benjamin*: Das Zarenreich als Transitraum zwischen Europa und Asien: Russische Visionen und westliche Wahrnehmungen um die Jahrhundertwende. In: *Aust, Martin* (ed.): Globalisierung imperial und sozialistisch: Russland und die Sowjetunion in der Globalgeschichte 1851–1991. Frankfurt am Main 2013, 41–63. Russia's self-depiction in World Fairs is discussed by *Voerkelius, Mirjam*: Russland und die Sowjetunion auf den Weltausstellungen. In: *Aust, Martin* (ed.): Globalisierung imperial und sozialistisch: Russland und die Sowjetunion in der Globalgeschichte 1851–1991. Frankfurt am Main 2013, 207–224.

14 *McKay, John P.*: Baku Oil and Transcaucasian Pipelines, 1883–1891: A Study in Tsarist Economic Policy. In: Slavic Review, 43(4) (1984), 604–623.

15 *Joffe, Muriel*: Regional Rivalry and Economic Nationalism: The Central Industrial Region Industrialists' Strategy for the Development of the Russian Economy, 1880s-1914. In: Russian History, 11(4) (1984), 389–421; *Joffe, Muriel*: Autocracy, Capitalism and Empire: The Politics of Irrigation. In: The Russian Review, 54(3) (1995), 365–388; *Pravilova, Ekaterina*: River of Empire: Geopolitics, Irrigation, and the Amu Darya in the Late XIXth Century. In: Cahiers d'Asie centrale, 17/18 (2009), 255–287.

lines of modernization theory, economic activity in the Russian Empire's peripheral territories has far more to tell than its marginal role in the over-all process of industrialization would suggest. Rather than dismissing certain phenomena as deviant it should be asked how they developed, why certain approaches were deemed suitable, and how they relate to the specific conditions found within the Russian Empire. One such condition is indisputably the vastness and heterogeneity of its imperial space.

Russia's Imperial Space

The recent historiographic focus on Russia's heterogeneity was initially sparked by the study of the imposing ethnic and religious diversity found across its territory.[16] In order to avoid a fragmentation into disjointed regional studies Alexei Miller has suggested to approach the empire's heterogeneity using a "situational approach", focusing on a particular structural feature and trying to reconstruct the logic behind the actions and interactions of all involved actors. A thus widened perspective allows to transcend narrow regionalism by opening up comparative perspectives between the empire's various territories

16 Andreas Kappeler's now-classic study on Russia as a multinational empire coincided with the Soviet Union's dissolution, which was followed by an upsurge of works on the various ethnic and religious groups within the empire helping counterbalance the narrative of Russia as a nation-state. However, approaching the empire from its fringes – as it is even inscribed in the title of the series "Okrainy Rossiiskoi Imperii" – has also received criticism as implicitly operating with a center-periphery dichotomy, yet, shying away from defining the presumed "core." Proponents of the "new imperial history" suggest to use empire as a "context-setting category" and a phenomenon sui generis rather than measuring it against the nation-state and directing attention towards "imperial situations" analyzed for "languages of rationalization and self-description." See *Kappeler, Andreas*: Rußland als Vielvölkerreich. Entstehung – Geschichte – Zerfall. München 2008; For the "Okrainy Rossiiskoi Imperii" series see *Dolbilov, Mikhail/Miller, Aleksei*: Zapadnye okrainy Rossiiskoi Imperii. Moscow 2006; *Bobrovnikov, Vladimir/Babich, Irina*: Severnyi Kavkaz v sostave Rossiiskoi Imperii. Moscow 2007; *Dameshek, Lev/Remnev, Anatolii*: Sibir' v sostave Rossiiskoi Imperii. Moscow 2007; *Abashin, Sergei/Arapov, Dmitrii/Bekmakhanova, Nailia*: Tsentral'naia Aziia v sostave Rossiiskoi Imperii. Moscow 2008. For the "new imperial history" school's position towards the "imperial turn" see *Gerasimov, Ilya/Glebov, Sergey/Kaplunovski, Alexander/Mogilner, Marina/Semyonov, Alexander*: In Search of a New Imperial History. In: Ab Imperio, 1 (2005), 33–56; *Semyonov, Alexander*: Empire as a Context Setting Category. In: Ab Imperio, 1 (2008), 193–204; *Gerasimov, Ilya/Kusber, Jan/Mogilner, Marina/Semyonov, Alexander*: New Imperial History and the Challenges of Empire. In: *Gerasimov, Ilya/Kusber, Jan/Semyonov, Alexander* (eds.): Empire Speaks out? Languages of Rationalization and Self-Description in the Russian Empire. Leiden 2009, 3–32.

and highlighting both differences and administrative transfers.[17] Further, a situational rather than a territorial approach allows for better comparison with other imperial structures, firmly establishing Russian history within the field of empire studies.[18] Miller's approach has been fruitfully applied to questions of ethnicity and religion in the Russian Empire. Such questions, particularly with regard to traditional economic practice, certainly play a role in the study of the Russian Empire's customs system and will be addressed where appropriate. However, this book approaches the empire primarily via the category of space, analyzing *situations of economic territoriality* across the empire.

It builds on Jane Burbank and Mark von Hagen's argument for the "importance of differentiated space to imperial institutions and imaginations."[19] Of course, Russia's vastness is proverbial – so much so that the appeal seems to border on the banal. Yet it is not just the size of the imperial space they draw attention to but its heterogeneity that "became a habit of thought" and "profoundly affected the ways that rulers tried to govern the polity." Thus, they suggest analyzing the "intersecting roles of cultural assumptions, geographical knowledge, economic goals, and administrative practices in the extensions and attempted extensions of Russian state power over its enormous realm."[20] Such an approach promises a deeper understanding of the internal workings of the Russian Empire, as it avoids both centralism and regionalism. Rather than reducing the history of the empire to a national history of its core – however that would be defined – or counterbalancing the same with special regional studies, access via the category of imperial space presupposes the examination of the territory as a whole and the interrelations of its constituent parts. It

17 *Miller, Aleksei*: Imperiia Romanovykh i natsionalizm. Esse po metodologii istoricheskogo issledovaniia. Moscow 2006, 28–32.

18 Dominic Lieven's "The Russian Empire and its Rivals" is exemplary in attempting to resituate the Russian Empire amongst a broad range of imperial formations, see *Lieven, Dominic*: Empire. The Russian Empire and its Rivals. London 2000. Where Lieven's broad brushed approach can elicit criticism, other authors narrow down comparisons to other contiguous multi-ethnic empires, which are understood as facing similar challenges of modernization and nation-building as the Russian Empire see *Barkey, Karen/Von Hagen, Mark*: After Empire. Multiethnic Societies and Nation-Building. The Soviet Union and the Russian, Ottoman, and Habsburg Empires. Boulder 1997; *Brisku, Adrian*: Political Reform in the Ottoman and Russian Empires. A Comparative Approach. London 2017.

19 *Burbank, Jane/von Hagen, Mark*: Coming into the Territory: Uncertainty and Empire. In: *Burbank, Jane/von Hagen, Mark/Remnev, Anatolyi* (eds.): Russian Empire. Space, People, Power. 1700–1930. Bloomington 2007, 1–29, here 4; Remnev has earlier suggested the terminology "geography of power" – *geografiia vlasti* – to capture the dynamic territorialization of institutions and the shifting administrative hierarchy between center and periphery. *Remnev, Anatolii*: Rossiia dal'nego vostoka. Imperskaia geografiia vlasti XIX – nachala XX vekov. Omsk 2004.

20 *Burbank/von Hagen*: Coming into the Territory, 5, 7.

thus ties in with general reflections on the concept of territoriality and the management of space it entailed.

Territory, though often taken for granted by historians, was subject to constant reconceptualization and endowed with varying importance throughout history, as argued by Charles S. Maier. His seminal work "Once Within Borders" analyzes territory as "an underlying framework that makes states and economies possible", stressing that "territoriality is manifested less as a quality in its own right than as a property implicated with historical phenomena that change, whether frontiers, states, sovereignty, or economic resources." Thus, its evolving character can be traced by looking at "activities in which territory has a formative presence."[21] To situate specific activities, Maier outlines two ideal types of spatial imaginaries: the space of empires and the space of states.

The space of empire was marked by "unrest at the periphery" and an "uneven grip of central authority" that necessitated tolerance of "local autonomy" and entailed a proclivity towards ambiguous boundaries.[22] A notion reminiscent of Frederick Cooper's often-cited "long arms and weak fingers of empire-states", which suggests both a far outreach and the inability to permeate territory with power.[23] The opposite ideal type – the space of states – is characterized by an aspiration to stabilize frontiers and establish "a more direct, uniform, and pervasive administration at home." As ideal types, Maier acknowledges, they can hardly grasp reality; qualities of state and empire space can coincide, while self-descriptions as either empire or nation-state can be misleading.[24]

His model echoes Ronald Suny's argument that nation and empire, as ideal types, constitute two ends of a dynamic continuum within which a state is situated. The implied dynamism helps better explain how the challenges of modernity put empires under pressure to partially nationalize so as to match "the efficiencies of the new national states" by centralizing and unifying its "polycentric and differentiated polity."[25] Nevertheless, the typology provides a useful framework, particularly when thought of in conjunction with the growing technical potential to manipulate space through the rise of the railway,

21 *Maier, Charles S.*: Once Within Borders. Territories of Power, Wealth, and Belonging since 1500. Cambridge, Massachusetts 2016, 2–7.

22 Ibid. 15.

23 *Cooper, Frederick*: Colonialism in Question. Theory, Knowledge, History. Berkeley 2005, 197.

24 *Maier*: Once Within Borders, 15.

25 *Suny, Ronald Grigor*: The Empire Strikes Out. Imperial Russia, 'National' Identity, and Theories of Empire. In: *Suny, Ronald Grigor/Martin, Terry* (eds.): A State of Nations. Empire and Nation-Making in the Age of Lenin and Stalin. Oxford 2001, 23–66, here 29–30.

steamship, and telegraph in the 19th century.[26] If a polity, previously imagining its territory predominantly as a space of empire, acquired the technological means to saturate space with power, did its spatial imaginary then shift towards the space of the state? What tensions arose from the ambition to form a uniform and bounded space? Particularly, what can be learned about the self-imagination and envisioned developmental trajectory of the Russian Empire from the management of its economic space?

To be sure, the conceptualization of territoriality is not monolithic; competing approaches exist within particular situations and all the more across different spheres such as military, economy, religion, etc.[27] Thus, it appears appropriate to speak of *situations of economic territoriality*, particularly those relating to the manipulation of customs space and regulations, which will be isolated and treated in this book. To approach and grasp them, the focus is put on the "intersecting roles of cultural assumptions, geographical knowledge, economic goals, and administrative practices."[28]

The enormous potential that cultural assumptions and geographical visions could unfold was aptly demonstrated by Mark Bassin's study on Russia's expansion into the Far East. Despite a lack of geographical knowledge or even in defiance of it the Amur river had turned into a screen for personal and governmental aspirations. The prospect of fulfilling a national destiny had fueled imagination, yet ended in bitter disappointment.[29]

Similarly, cultural assumptions, availability or lack of specific knowledge, as well as visions of the empire's future in the Steppe regions, Central Asia and the Caucasus informed decisions in the imperial center and on the spot. Mapping – the production of "Herrschaftswissen" – constituted the basic operation underlying the claim to control territory.[30] Meanwhile, the coming of the railway age promised to deliver the tools to act upon it. Nevertheless, the technological possibilities were put to use with different – partly competing –

26 Maier devotes a chapter to the impact of railways on ideas of continentalism, the diminishing role of natural borders and the transformation of territory from "merely a container" to "a source of communal energy and self-realization", which elevated political territory to become the "underlying framework for industrial strategies" see *Maier*: Once Within Borders 185–232, here 191, 194.

27 I would like to thank Benjamin Schenk for a stimulating conversation about the multilayeredness and incongruence of imagined and administrative territorial units in the Russian Empire.

28 *Burbank/von Hagen*: Coming into the Territory, 5.

29 *Bassin, Mark*: Imperial Visions: Nationalist Imagination and Geographical Expansion in the Russian Far East, 1840–1865. Cambridge 1999.

30 *Sunderland, Willard*: Taming the Wild Field. Colonization and Empire on the Russian Steppe. Ithaca 2004, 5; *Weiss, Claudia*: Wie Sibirien "unser" wurde. Die Russische Geographische Gesellschaft und ihr Einfluss auf die Bilder und Vorstellungen von Sibirien im 19. Jahrhundert. Göttingen 2007.

visions of space in mind: some informed by geopolitical goals, others in the service of a mission civilisatrice, while others again followed economic goals.[31]

As an institution which – at least in its modern ideal type – operates on the state borders at the furthest distance to the imperial center, all these factors played an exacerbated role for the design of Russia's Asiatic customs space. Thus, the development of customs regulations reflects a growing belief in the malleability of geographic space, assumptions about the feasibility of bureaucratic and economic reforms on the empire's peripheries, as well as the limits for the implementation of plans drawn up in Saint Petersburg.

The tension between such visions and aspirations in the imperial center and their practical implementation on the spot can be best observed when closely scrutinizing administrative practices. The institution of Russian governors-general is a case in point. Though they formally existed in most peripheral regions of the empire at some point, their respective functions were distinctly divergent. Kimitaka Matsuzato argues, that "at the western peripheries governors-general manipulated ethno-social categories, whereas in Asiatic Russia they managed space." Strengthening the insular principle of government over a linear one, they "renewed the integrity of macro-regions"

31 For general observations on the impact of modern technologies on concepts of time and space as well as their role in managing territories see *Divall, Colin*: Railway Imperialisms, Railway Nationalisms. In: *Burri, Monika/Elsasser, Kilian T./Gugerli, David* (eds.): Die Internationalität der Eisenbahn. Zürich 2003, 195–210; *Kaschuba, Wolfgang*: Die Überwindung der Distanz. Zeit und Raum in der europäischen Moderne. Frankfurt am Main 2004; *Wenzlhuemer, Roland*: Connecting the Nineteenth-Century World. The Telegraph and Globalization. Cambridge 2013. On the role of telegraph lines in Imperial Russia's customs border protection see *Tovpeka, Andrei*: Razvitie sistemy sviazi i upravleniia v pogranichnoi strazhe Rossiiskoi imperii, 1827–1917 gg. Saint Petersburg 2014. For the role of the railway in Russia's modernization and restructuring of social space see *Cvetkovski, Roland*: Modernisierung durch Beschleunigung. Raum und Mobilität im Zarenreich. Frankfurt am Main 2006; *Schenk, Frithjof Benjamin*: Russlands Fahrt in die Moderne. Mobilität und sozialer Raum im Eisenbahnzeitalter. Stuttgart 2014; *Schenk, Frithjof Benjamin*: Mastering Imperial Space? The Ambivalent Impact of Railway-Building in Tsarist Russia. In: *Leonhard, Jörn/von Hirschhausen, Ulrike* (eds.): Comparing Empires. Encounters and Transfers in the Long Nineteenth Century. Göttingen 2011, 60–77; While the railway has received broad attention, the development of the road system and its imperial dimension have been researched less. Reinhard Nachtigal's substantial study fills the void for the Caucasus region, see *Nachtigal, Reinhard*: Verkehrswege in Kaukasien. Ein Integrationsproblem des Zarenreiches 1780–1870. Wiesbaden 2016. Similarly, Russia's merchant fleet awaits a renewed treatment taking into account recent paradigmatic shifts in historiography. Meanwhile the main works remain: *Konovalov, Iurii Petrovich*: Morskoi torgovyi flot Rossii v period promyshlennogo kapitalizma. 60-e - seredina 90-ch gg. XIX v. (na materialakh Chernomorsko-Azovskogo basseina). Odessa 1981; *Thomas, Ludmila*: Streben nach Weltmachtpositionen. Russlands Handelsflotte, 1856 bis 1914. Berlin 1995.

such as the "Far-East."[32] Hence, they simultaneously contributed to the consolidation of the administrative grip over remote areas and perpetuated their separation from the core space. Factors such as distance from the imperial center, lack of administrative resources, and the imperative to accommodate regional specifics necessitated the introduction of governors-general. However, a genuine tug-of-war with the central government accompanied the controversial institution throughout.[33]

Finances constitute one highly contested, yet understudied, field of conflict between regional and central administrations. Alleviating the general shortage of studies on the Russian Empire's finances, Ekaterina Pravilova's "Finansy imperii" analyzes the functioning and evolution of the imperial budget. Her work exceeds purely fiscal questions and rather uses the imperial budget as an entry-point to discuss larger issues of imperial rule. Instead of one unified budget, several existed for the respective peripheral territories (Poland, Finland, Transcaucasus and Turkestan) and thus could be analyzed as *situations of economic territoriality*. However, the 19th century saw increasing efforts to merge these budgets. Pravilova argues that the push towards uniformity was not so much part of a grand strategy to alleviate economic asymmetries within the empire but rather unfolded in a piecemeal fashion, mostly driven by political considerations and emerging nationalist notions of a unified Russia.[34]

Her study works precisely at the intersection formulated by Burbank and von Hagen, taking into account both cultural and economic factors and closely following administrative practices and shortcomings. Putting aside the Polish case, much of her analysis focuses on territories usually deemed economically marginal and thus neglected in economic histories of the Russian Empire. However, it is this comprehensive approach which allows to steer clear of a narrow quasi-national history of the Russian Empire's financial administration and which stresses the imperial moment. The bureaucratic infighting over the

32 *Matsuzato, Kimitaka*: Intra-Bureaucaratic Debate on the Institution of Russian Governors-General in the Mid-Nineteenth Century. In: *Uyaka, Tomohiko* (ed.): Asiatic Russia. Imperial Power in Regional and International Contexts. Abingdon, New York 2012, 83–101, here 86, 90, 95.

33 Matsuzato's attempt to theorize Russian imperial rule using a threefold model of core region and two types of peripheries has been criticized as overly static and "essentializing categories of geopolitics [...] and fixed national identities." Nevertheless, it provides a good frame of reference to situate the competition between linear and institutional logics in the management of the empire's peripheral territories. See *Remnev, Anatolii*: Stepnoe general-gubernatorstvo v imperskoi geografii vlasti. In: *Sugorova, Natalia* (ed.): Aziatskaia Rossiia: Liudi i struktury Imperii. Omsk 2005, 163–222, here 164–166; *Gerasimov/Kusber/Mogilner/Semyonov*: New Imperial History and the Challenges of Empire, 12–13.

34 *Pravilova, Ekaterina*: Finansy imperii. Den'gi i vlast' v politike Rossii na natsional'nykh okrainakh, 1801–1917. Moscow 2006.

role of peripheral territories and their budgets within the empire's financial system reveals the development of underlying concepts of territoriality.

Thus, an ideal object for the study of the relation of the empire towards its space would be one in "which territory has a formative presence"[35], that is of significant interest to both central and regional actors, and present along the many heterogeneous peripheries of the Russian Empire. Hardly any imperial institution qualifies as well as the customs institutions.

Customs in the Russian Empire

Customs constitute an often-overlooked hub of Russia's imperial finances, combining three central functions: fiscal, macroeconomic, and political. Second only to the alcohol excise, customs duties made up between 12,6 % and 29,7 % of total state revenue between 1860 and 1900.[36] The importance of indirect taxes had already begun to grow in the late 18th century. By the last decades of the 19th century, however, they dominated the imperial budget. Reasons for such a reliance on indirect taxes lie with a "combination of political pressure and administrative capacity." It was simply easier to indirectly tax consumption than to enforce direct taxes.[37] This prevalence of the fiscal function entailed a potential conflict with the second function of customs: macroeconomic regulation.

Against the backdrop of Great Britain's industrial dominance, most European countries resorted to protectionist policies. According to protectionist theories, customs tariffs were to foster the growth of domestic industries by both sheltering them from competing foreign produce and enabling cheap imports of raw goods and advanced technologies where necessary. Once domestic industries were deemed sufficiently well-established, tariffs could be maintained at a lower level to secure the market for domestic producers and eventually scrapped altogether. Despite a free-trade-inclined phase in the 1860s, initiated by the Cobden-Chevalier treaty, for most European countries protectionism was the norm rather than the exception in 19th century world trade relations. The 1870s already showed signs of disintegration in the complex network of bilateral trade treaties which had grown to become a sort of free-trade system by relating to each other via most-favored nation clauses. The Russian Empire followed these trends to a certain degree, but remained

35 *Maier*: Once Within Borders, 7.

36 *Sobolev, Michail Nikolaevich*: Tamozhennaia politika Rossii vo vtoroi polovine XIX veka. Tomsk 1911, 842–843.

37 *Gatrell, Peter*: The Russian Fiscal State, 1600–1914. In: *Yun-Casalilla, Bartolomé/O'Brien, Patrick K.* (eds.): The Rise of Fiscal States: A Global History, 1500–1914. Cambridge 2012, 191–212, here 204.

more protectionist throughout and eventually embarked on full-fledged high protectionism, even putting it ahead of the United States of America – the "mother country and bastion of modern protectionism."[38]

While protectionist ideas and rhetoric were wide-spread throughout the late Russian Empire, contemporary economists like Mikhail Sobolev criticized that in practice, fiscal rather than protectionist interests were paramount. Thus, in the Russian Empire, high tariffs were not the precise instruments of macroeconomic regulation protectionist theorists imagined them to be, but rather blunt measures to fill the state treasury. A lowering of tariffs, however, was not possible, as the low and only slowly increasing level of consumption could not have compensated for the loss of customs revenue.[39] Considering the heavy reliance of the state budget on customs duties, the reduction of tariffs would have been fiscally unbearable.

The third function of customs flows from the inherently transnational nature of the institution. Tariffs and border regulations cannot be regarded without the international and global context, be it general economic developments in the course of the first wave of globalization, the specifics of the bordering states, or geopolitical considerations. They could be used to reshape trade routes and geopolitical constellations or impact foreign economies and thus could serve as instruments of foreign politics. The most prominent example being the customs-war between the Russian and German Empires, lasting from 1893 to 1895, which was the peak of a decade-long customs-arms-race and eventually detrimental to both economies.[40] While Russia's Western borders were thus becoming increasingly restrictive, her Eastern borders remained significantly more permeable, allowing to maintain traditional cross-border relations and ambiguous boundaries, partially in order to exert influence beyond one's own state territory.

38 Cornelius Torp aptly demonstrates the interplay of economic ideologies, globalization, internal politics, foreign politics, and economic cycles, which resulted in the ephemerality of free-trade policies in the *Zollverein*. He thus provides more depth than Bairoch's economic history approach, though limited to the *Zollverein* only. Such a country-specific approach is particularly necessary for Russia, as can be seen from Bairoch's perfunctory treatment of the Russian Empire as compared with other European nations. He quotes the available data sets as "Incomplete information or difficult to classify" (19) or simply incomparable, as "numerous and important restrictions in importation of manufactured products [existed], which make all calculations of average tariff rates not significant." (40), see *Bairoch, Paul*: Economics and World History. Myths and Paradoxes. New York 1993, 16–40; *Torp*: Herausforderung der Globalisierung, 121–210.

39 *Sobolev*: Tamozhennaia politika Rossii, vi, 823.

40 On the Russian-German customs war see: *Torp*: Herausforderung der Globalisierung, 186–207; *Ivanov, Kirill*: Razvitie tamozhennogo dela v Rossii v kontse XIX-nachale XX veka: ot avtonomnogo zapretitel'nogo tarifa k torgovym konventsiiam. Saint Petersburg 2012, 177–232.

As customs issues touch upon a broad range of spheres, they were often accounted for as backdrop for the analysis of other political or economic processes, yet were rarely regarded as a standalone object of investigation in western historiography.[41] Russian historians have directed more attention to the functioning of the customs systems as such. Kislovskii has provided an overarching, albeit superficial, study of the Russian customs from 907 to the present.[42] Krikhunov studied both the ideological debates surrounding protectionism and free trade in the Russian Empire and attempted an evaluation of the protectionist system's efficiency.[43] Ivanov analyzed the development of Russian trade practice at the turn of the 20th century, with a focus on the conceptual shift from an autonomous tariff towards bilateral trade conventions.[44] Geographically, most of these studies retained a focus on the Russian Empire's core industrial region and trade with its western neighbors.

Only studies focusing on the junction between tariff policies and specific industries with an interest in eastern markets, such as the cotton industry, delved deeper into the discussion of the empire's customs policies in its eastern territories.[45] Further, customs issues have been productively used for regional studies. Be it either as a vivid source for the interaction of borderland populations with the state as demonstrated by Sören Urbansky, or as key issues for regional economic development, as shown by Nataliia Beliaeva's in-depth study of the Far-Eastern porto-franco.[46] Nevertheless, many aspects of the

41 Vincent Barnett's treatment of Russian economic thought and its impact on tariff policies forms a notable exception, see: *Barnett, Vincent*: Economics in Russia. Studies in Intellectual History. Aldershot, Hampshire 2008; *Barnett, Vincent*: M. Kh. Reutern and Tariff Reform in Russia. In: Œconomia. History, Methodology, Philosophy, 4(1) (2014), 17–27; *Barnett*: Russian Protectionism and German Political Economy.

42 *Kislovskii, Iurii*: Istoriia tamozhennogo dela i tamozhennoi politiki Rossii. Moscow 2004.

43 *Krikhunov, Vladimir*: Protektsionizm ili Fritrederstvo: vybor puti. Moscow 2002; *Krikhunov, Vladimir*: Tamozhennaia politika Rossii i ee ekonomicheskaia effektivnost', 1877–1914 gg. Moscow 1999.

44 *Ivanov*: Razvitie tamozhennogo dela v Rossii.

45 *Martin, Thomas*: Baumwollindustrie in Sankt Petersburg und Moskau und die russische Zolltarifpolitik (1850–1891). Eine vergleichende Regionalstudie. Giessen 1998; *Kuprianova, Liubov'*: Tamozhenno-promyshlennyi protektsionizm i Rossiiskie predprinimateli (40–80-e gody XIX veka). Moscow 1994.

46 *Urbansky, Sören*: Der betrunkene Kosake. Schmuggel im sino-russischen Grenzland (circa 1860–1930). In: *Aust, Martin* (ed.): Globalisierung imperial und sozialistisch. Russland und die Sowjetunion in der Globalgeschichte 1851–1991. Frankfurt am Main 2013, 301–329; *Beliaeva, Natal'ia*: Ot porto-franko k tamozhne. Ocherk regional'noi istorii Rossiiskogo protektsionizma. Vladivostok 2003. For customs policies in the Orenburg region prior to 1868 see *Solonchenko, Ekaterina*: Tamozhennaia politika na iugo-vostoke Rossii i ee realizatsiia v Orenburgskom krae v 1752–1868 gg. Orenburg 2007. For the Finnish border see *Katajala, Kimmo*: Cross-Border Trade in Karelia from the Middle Ages to the October Revolution 1917. In: *Lähteenmäki, Maria* (ed.): The Flexible Frontier. Change and Continuity in Finnish-Russian Relations. Helsinki 2007, 70–87; *Lähteenmäki,*

customs system in the empire's east remain understudied. This book aims to address this specific desideratum.

The readiness with which most accounts on Russia's financial system dismiss large parts of the empire's customs space partially stems from the very organization of the customs system. The Russian Department Customs Collection itself distinguished between "European" and "Asiatic" customs: Both with respect to the *tamozhennyi tarif* (customs tariff), which set the customs rate for each product, and with respect to the *tamozhennyi ustav* (customs regulations), the body of rules and regulations that defined the procedures of customs collection.[47] This division made it all too easy for researchers to dismiss the issue of "Asiatic" customs. Even contemporary economists such as Sobolev, a renowned expert on customs tariffs, opted to exclude "special tariffs, such as the Finnish, Transcaucasian and Asiatic, that had a limited scope of influence and were formulated under the influence of special local conditions."[48] Sobolev's understanding of the Asiatic customs as "special" echoes the deviance stated by State Comptroller Greig, quoted earlier. Since the inclusion of the Kingdom of Poland into the customs territory of the Russian Empire in 1851, the organizational form on the "western border" – meaning the border to the Kingdom of Prussia and the Habsburg Empire – had come to be considered the norm.

In practice, this meant that the "normal" customs border conformed to the state border and that the neighboring state shared a mutual understanding of economic and bureaucratic processes. Further, these customs institutions were subordinated to the Department of Customs Collection of the Ministry of Finance in Saint Petersburg. They were deliberately designed to be responsible to the central administration, circumventing local political institutions such as the Governor-general of Warsaw. In terms of material resources, the western border had a complex and dense network of both customs stations and border guards. The latter were administered by the civil ranks of the Department of

Maria: Cows, Guns and Bolsheviks: Smuggling in the Borderland Between South-East Finland and St. Petersburg. In: *Katajala, Kimmo; Lähteenmäki, Maria* (eds.): Imagined, Negotiated, Remembered. Constructing European Borders and Borderlands. Münster 2012, 119–140; *Suni, Lev*: Finliandsko-Russkie torgovye otnosheniia vo vtoroi polovine XIX veka, 1858–1885. Tartu 1963; *Kornilov, Genrikh*: Russko-Finliandskie tamozhennye otnosheniia v kontse XIX – nachale XX v., 1885–1914. Leningrad 1971. For the Habsburg border see *Adelsgruber, Paulus/Cohen, Laurie/Kuzmany, Börries*: Getrennt und doch verbunden. Grenzstädte zwischen Österreich und Russland 1772–1918. Wien 2011. For the Chinese border see *Noda, Jin*: Russo-Chinese Trade Through Central Asia. In: *Uyaka, Tomohiko* (ed.): Asiatic Russia. Imperial Power in Regional and International Contexts. Oxon 2012, 153–173; *Heller, Klaus*: Der russisch-chinesische Handel von seinen Anfängen bis zum Ausgang des 19. Jahrhunderts. Erlangen 1980.

47 For the development of this dualism see chapter 2.

48 *Sobolev*: Tamozhennaia politika Rossii, vi.

Customs Collection as well. Only in 1894 were they reorganized as *Otdel'nyi korpus pogranichnoi strazhi* (Independent Border Guards Corps), based on new military statutes and administered by military personnel; however, with the Ministry of Finance remaining the "head" of the Independent Border Guards Corps.[49] This costly border protection system was justified by the high turnover of the customs stations at the European border and the potential for smuggling that resulted from high tariffs. However, for the Asiatic border sections, protective measures had to be scaled down significantly.

Applying the above criteria, the other borders appear truly "deviant": The Grand Duchy of Finland constituted an economic territory of its own, separated from the empire by a de facto internal customs border and sporting several well-developed industrial branches, unlike many eastern peripheral regions. The Transcaucasian region bordered on the Ottoman Empire and Persia, which entailed differing economic and bureaucratic practices as well as foreign policy considerations. Similar considerations applied to the Transcaspian region and Turkestan, albeit additionally complicated by the on-going military expansion of the 1860s and 1870s and an unresolved demarcation of the state border to Afghanistan. With protectorates established in Bukhara and Khiva, any economic measures were additionally charged politically. In practical terms, the Caucasian and Central Asian borders were long and topographically challenging, with divergent economic traditions and practices. Meanwhile, the trade turnover of goods relevant for customs duties was limited, thus making border protection as dense as on the western border fiscally unreasonable.[50] In addition, complicated regional specifics challenged the introduction of a linear ministerial logic and called for an insular administrative organization with the subordination of the customs administration to the Viceroy or Governor-general. In the Russian Far-East, an enormous free-trade zone had been established in 1862, yet soon became a point of contention between local and central actors. While some of the special solutions remained in place until the end of the Russian Empire and a unified customs administration and territory had never been realized, the post-reform customs administration had

49 For a broad overview of the archival material on the Independent Border Guards Corps and its evolution see *Plekhanov, Aleksandr/Plekhanov, Andrei*: Otdel'nyi Korpus Pogranichnoi Strazhi na granitse Rossii, 1893–1919. Moscow 2012, 42–60.

50 In 1895, after the inclusion of Bukhara into the customs territory, the customs revenue levied on the Caucasian and Central Asian border sector constituted only 2,75 % or 5.101.000 credit rubles of a total of 185.477.000 credit rubles collected along all borders. Meanwhile the length of these border sectors accounted for 5.247 verst of a total 13.980 verst of protected customs border. In the "Asiatic" customs section only the Irkutsk customs generated significant incomes due its role as tea trading hub, see Obzor vneshnei torgovli Rossii po evropeiskoi i aziatskoi granitsam za 1895 god. Saint Petersburg 1897, 1, 9.

begun to adjust and modify its regulations, working towards a "normalization" of its economic space.

This book traces the development of these "deviant" customs regimes in the Russian Empire throughout the 19th century, reading customs as an institution delineating and creating economic and political spaces. Rather than being a work of economic history, it is an inquiry into the nature of the imperial space and its integration. It asks which logic – fiscal, macroeconomic or political – informed customs decisions at a given time in a specific region and how their relation shifted. Thus, the design of customs regulations allows for a better understanding of regional hierarchies, and the role ascribed to a specific territory within the Russian Empire at a given time, as well as its implied developmental trajectory. The latter assumed very different forms: from attempts to alleviate regional asymmetries to the consolidation of a subordinate role within the empire's economic structure.

Decision-making processes were shaped by cultural assumptions and spatial imaginaries that underwent significant changes with the advent of the railway and steamship age. This book connects these changing images to the development of Russia's customs space, analyzing the situations in which either uniform rules were enforced or special solutions were favored. Thus, it works along the stress line between the two concepts of territoriality outlined by Maier: the space of empires and the space of states. The underlying question is how the Ministry of Finance addressed its heterogeneous economic space, what motivated its manipulation, and in how far the history of the customs system supports the conceptualization of the late Russian Empire as a nationalizing empire.

Sources

This study inquires primarily how administrative elites, both in the central administration and in the regional administrations, perceived and shaped the imperial economic space. It thus considers archival sources of the Ministry of Finance, particularly the Department of Customs Collection, the Ministry of Trade and Industry, the Committee of Ministers, as well as the State Council located at the Russian State Historical Archive (Rossiiskii Gosudarstvennyi Istoricheskii Arkhiv, RGIA). Further, region-specific funds – the Caucasus Committee and the Minister-Secretary of State for Finland – at RGIA were consulted. Materials from the Asiatic Department of the General Staff provided insights into both the Transcaspian region and the Governorate-general of Turkestan and are located at the Russian State Historical Military Archive (Rossiiskii Gosudarstvennyi Voenno-istoricheskii Arkhiv, RGVIA). Consular reports from neighboring countries informed the central ministries' decisions on trade, while the correspondence of the Ministry of Foreign Affairs with its Political Agent in Bukhara illuminates the gradual encroachment on the economic independence of the protectorate of Bukhara. Both can be found in the Archive of the Foreign Policy of the Russian Empire (Arkhiv Vneshnei Politiki Rossiiskoi Imperii, AVPRI). The archival materials are complemented by published sources on issues of trade, industry, and transportation routes, voiced both by governmental institutions, individuals, as well as associations.

Chapter Outline

This book consists of seven chapters, which illuminate six different *situations of economic territoriality* across the Russian Empire's peripheries throughout the 19th century.

Chapter 1 "Russia's Trade and Tariff Policies in the 19th Century" provides a broad overview of the Russian Empire's customs policies throughout the 19th century and contextualizes Russia within a broader European development. The chapter analyzes key moments in Russia's customs politics, asks which personas and interest groups were considered in their shaping; how political and fiscal circumstances limited policy-options, and which politico-economy theories served as backdrop to policymakers.

The focus of this introductory chapter lies with Russia's "European" customs tariff and regulations, which are not discussed in-detail in the remaining book. However, the customs system on Russia's European borders constituted the point of reference against which the "Asiatic" customs system was measured by the imperial administration, and thus is of great importance for the understanding of the following case studies.

The chapter argues that, in many respects, Russia's trade policies on its "European" borders were not all that different from other European states and followed general world economic trends – even if usually less pronounced, due to certain specificities of the Russian Empire's economic and political composition. On the other hand, on its "Asiatic" borders – which are the primary subject of this book – the Russian Empire resorted to idiosyncratic solutions, tailored to the specific preconditions found in its southern and eastern peripheries. For the most part, these solutions were more laissez-faire and oftentimes contradictory to the policies implemented on the "European" border. However, the greater flexibility of the customs system on the "Asiatic" borders was never decoupled from developments in the "European" part of the empire, which either opened up or restricted the room for special solutions.

Chapter 2 "Expansion by Debordering: The Dissolution of the Orenburg Customs Line" looks closer into Russia's military expansion into Central Asia and the problems it presented for the customs administration. The piecemeal expansion of the state territory in the first half of the 19th century could hardly be ignored by the Ministry of Finance, as the preexisting Orenburg customs line was increasingly becoming an internal customs border, ridiculing its primary function. At the same time, the military expansion was a dynamic process, with territorial gains made in surges. Thus, the establishment of a customs border was nothing less than a moving target. Further, the new territories were marked by traditional Islamic economic practices, raising the question of whether it would be politically sensible or even possible to establish a "regular" customs regime, or whether adaptation to local conditions was preferable.

Thus, the challenge of managing the new Central Asian economic territories combined not only classic fields of customs policy such as fiscal and macro-economic considerations, but also implied issues of colonial rule. The chapter identifies the factors behind different models of customs space management proposed and traces the decision-making process which eventually led to the dissolution of the Orenburg customs line, rather than its relocation southwards. It argues that this radical measure partially owed to a transfer of administrative practices, previously implemented with the Far-Eastern porto-franco, and relied on the region's infrastructural weakness and the fragmentation of the imperial space. However, the decision proved short-lived as further military expansion and the consolidation of a military-civil administration reshuffled political and economic configurations in the region.

Chapter 3 "Closing the Gap: Bukhara's Loss of Trade Autonomy" addresses these shifts, with a particular focus on the inclusion of the Khanate of Bukhara into the Russian Empire's customs territory in 1894. Russia's expansion up to the Persian and Afghan borders and the subjugation of Bukhara as protectorate had sparked hopes for a quick development of Central Asia into both a profitable cotton production region and an outlet market for Central Russia's manufactured goods. However, due to poorly developed transportation networks, such plans remained paper tigers until the construction of the Transcaspian railway.

The chapter demonstrates how the railway line had inspired a new vision for the connectedness of Central Asia via the Caspian Sea to the core empire and urged for a quick enclosure of the macro-geographical region with a customs border. This opened up new possibilities for reshaping both its internal commercial geography and its position in the competition over trade hegemony in Persia vis-a-vis Great Britain by enabling export subsidization schemes. In lieu of traditional trade routes via Persia and Afghanistan, new alternative routes via the Far-East, Siberia and the Transcaucasus were promoted that had been made possible by the implementation of modern customs regulatory mechanisms in Transcaspia, Bukhara and Turkestan. Further, the chapter traces how issues of colonial rule played into the decision-making process as interests of local elites, border populations and the low administrative capacity of the empire had to be accounted for in the shaping of customs regulations.

Chapter 4 "Ob' and Enisei Porto-Franco: A Latecomer's Frustration" focuses on another infrastructural vision promising to reshape the Russian Empire's trade geography. A series of expeditions in the 1870s had proven the possibility of establishing the Northern sea route and connecting the estuaries of the Ob' and Enisei rivers to global trade currents. Despite the perils of such a route, the economic incentives of connecting the "treasury of Siberia" were considered sufficient by Russian and foreign entrepreneurs to further its development, if exemptions from import duties were granted. The Far-Eastern porto-franco established in the early 1860s had set the precedent for such a regional developmental measure. However, by the 1880s, when a Northern porto-franco came on the agenda, the political climate had changed and doctrines of national economics and protectionism had gotten the upper hand.

Despite pleas from merchant companies, regional industrialists, and city heads to grant free-trade privileges to the estuaries of Ob' and Enisei, the central government was now wary of granting long-term privileges as it was simultaneously caught up in the process of unwinding the Far-Eastern porto-franco. Moreover, the nationalist overtones introduced during the regency of Alexander III collided with the practical realities of navigation on the Northern sea route. Foreign expeditions were increasingly regarded with skepticism under the political climate, while Russian civilian shipping proved both disinterested and incapable of undertaking these risky ventures.

Meanwhile, the Trans-Siberian railway project pursued by the imperial government presented a competing vision for the infrastructural integration of Western Siberia, albeit orienting its trade currents inwards and using central distribution mechanisms, rather than connecting its regions directly to global trade currents. The issue of a Northern porto-franco was not dismissed altogether but rather regularly protracted by granting only short-time concessions, neither creating a secure business climate, nor closing the route altogether, and thus demonstrates the dynamic negotiation of regional hierarchies.

The chapter argues that the project of a Northern porto-franco shared many traits with the Far-Eastern porto-franco, which was cited as a model by its proponents; however, it had been brought forward too late, at a time when the governmental course had shifted from implementing flexible solutions towards the integration and unification of the customs space within the context of a nationalizing empire.

Chapter 5 "Insular Administration and the Economics Integration of the Caucasian Viceroyalty" analyzes the customs administration with regard to the competing linear and insular principles of government. The chapter traces the infighting surrounding the centralization and transfer of customs authority from the Caucasian Viceroy to the Ministry of Finance in the 1880s. It argues that the installation of an insular administrative system in the 1840s was initially motivated by a desire to accelerate the region's economic development to allow for a quicker integration, as earlier attempts at introducing all-imperial regulations in the Transcaucasus had failed. However, the central administration's distrust for the correct performance of customs procedures on the Caucasian border with the Ottoman Empire and Persia, as well as the deep entanglement of customs rights with the insular administrative organization of the Viceroyalty, ultimately perpetuated the region's exclusion from the core customs space – despite advancing legal and tariff convergence – rather than enabling a quicker integration. Eventually, the Ministry of Finance resorted to a transfer of practices, pushing for an integration based on the experience with the customs inclusion of the Kingdom of Poland in 1851. The issue of customs integration became a battleground over the Transcaucasus' role within the regional hierarchy of the Russian Empire and one of the first major steps towards a unification of the Russian Empire's customs space.

Chapter 6 "The Transcaucasian Transit: Stepping Stone to the World or the Empire's Backyard Market?" isolates and details one of the most contested issues in the Transcaucasian customs regime. In 1821, an international transit route from the Black Sea shores of the Transcaucasus to Northern Persia with significant customs privileges had been introduced. Throughout the following six decades, this import-regime experienced alternating phases of prohibition or governmental support until its final dissolution in 1883. Within this period, the Transcaucasian trade route had become a nexus for the negotiation of the region's role within the empire. Either it was to develop autonomously and mostly firewalled from the empire's core economic space, or reinterpreted as an internal market for Central Russian industries.

Decisions over the fate of the transit route were further informed by geopolitical considerations in the ruffle for influence over Northern Persia, following a logic in which trading goods were regarded as conduits for political influence. These geopolitical arguments received significant support after the conquest of the eastern shore of the Caspian Sea in the late 1860s and early 1870s. The altered geopolitical situation opened up new visions of connectedness, as the Transcaucasus ceased to be an appendix in the empire's south and was reinterpreted as a potential gateway into its recent Central Asian acquisitions.

The chapter traces the different stages in the transit route's history and the role the Transcaucasus was assigned within the context of the Russian Empire's economic system at different points in time. It argues that new visions of connectedness, the ascent of new interest groups, and an increasingly nationalist climate under Alexander III prompted its eventual prohibition and a tighter integration of the Transcaucasian region into the economic edifice of the empire.

Chapter 7 "The Finnish Customs Space: Nation-Building within a Nationalizing Empire" shifts the focus from Russia's southern and eastern peripheries towards the Grand Duchy of Finland. While most Asiatic territories were regarded as economically backward by the central administration and special concessions were granted based on this premise, Finland's separate status was grounded in its progressive economy and considerations of political stability, making it the "odd man out" within this study.

The Grand Duchy of Finland proved to be most persistent in the application of the insular principle and retained its status as separate customs territory until the decline of the Russian Empire. Nevertheless, beginning with Alexander III's rule, Finland's customs autonomy came under increased scrutiny, entailing decade-long debates about its role within the empire's economy.

The Finnish case introduces a set of factors which limited integration of Russia's imperial economic space and significantly differed from those found in the empire's "Asiatic" territories. The failed integration is read with regard to Finland's parliamentary system and its ongoing nation-building process against the background of the Russian Empire's increasing Russification policies.

The cases selected for this study by no means constitute a complete account of the Russian Empire's customs system and its many special regulations and idiosyncratic solutions. However, they were picked to represent both different decades as well as regions with varying political and economic settings. By reading these different *situations of economic territoriality* in conjunction with one another, customs issues are used as an entry-point to analyze the larger issue of territoriality in Russia's economic system. They highlight how specific imperial characteristics influenced economic policies and inversely, how economic imperatives under a modernization agenda retroacted on imperial rule. The administrative practices in each case are scrutinized, asking which factors informed the decision-making processes, how the underlying concepts of territoriality evolved, and how the Russian Empire proceeded with the integration of its imperial economic space.

1. Russia's Trade and Tariff Policies in the 19th Century

In the study of 19th century world economic development and processes of industrialization Great Britain, France and Germany still constitute the main subjects and role-models. The Russian Empire is often relegated to an "odd man out" position characterized by backwardness, imitation, and an awkward separate path. In many cases, this neglect is based on the difficulty of accessing Russian sources and contextualizing its internal debates, as well as the retrospective knowledge of its significantly deviant development in the 20th century.[1] This exclusion has been criticized by recent scholarship, with Susan McCaffray arguing that "Russia's experience was not atypical of Europe's as a whole" and that it "may be more fruitful to see Russians as responding to common European experiences than as perennially borrowing and imitating." She suggests to instead focus on the openness and contingency of mid-19th century transformative processes and thus "preserve the sense of rich possibilities that gripped Russian intellectuals, officials, and professionals in the nineteenth century, who were sometimes well informed about other countries, and who enthused about what could be learned from their failures as well as their successes."[2] Rather than reading the solutions chosen as inherently imitative or botched, attention should be directed towards the specific conditions – cultural, economic, geographic – which shaped Russian trade and customs policies.

1 Bairoch marks the available data sets for Russia as "incomplete information or difficult to classify" or simply incomparable, as "numerous and important restrictions in importation of manufactured products [existed], which make all calculations of average tariff rates not significant." *Bairoch*: Economics and World History, 19, 40; Pahre finds a peculiar spot between inclusion and exclusion for the Russian Empire by opening up the category of "the countries of developing Europe, plus Russia." His treatment of the Russian Empire is further to be regarded with caution, as his data sets often lack reliable citations and do not seem to hold up to archival evidence. For example, Pahre claims Russia's low reliance on customs for state revenue (10–15 %), which is clearly at odds with the much more plausible numbers extracted from Russian archives by Sobolev, who cites 20–29,7 % for the last 25 years of the 19th century. See: *Pahre, Robert*: Politics and Trade Cooperation in the Nineteenth Century. The "Agreeable Customs" of 1815–1914. Cambridge 2008, 58, 113; *Sobolev*: Tamozhennaia politika Rossii, 482–483.

2 *McCaffray/Melancon*: Russia's Place in Europe, 4–6.

The Russian Empire's peculiar position between the "East" and the "West" was arguably one of the most debated issues of the 19th century, serving as an inspiration to many unique projects. With regards to its customs space, the Russian Empire was conceptualized as split into two sections. Russia's "European" section was regarded as the norm by contemporaries and its development was primarily measured against the policies of Great Britain, France and Germany. The empire's "Asiatic" parts were understood to require distinctly different administrative tools and demonstrate well the adaptability and originality of solutions taken by the Russian administration.[3] The latter constitute the main focus of this book. In order to provide context and emphasize the idiosyncrasy of these solutions, this chapter aims to outline the main threads of Russian customs policy between the 1820s and 1900 in the "European" parts of the Russian Empire.

This chapter introduces the four most influential Ministers of Finance during this period and the specific system of trade regulations each stands for. While outwardly high tariffs had been one of the consistent features of the Russian Empire's economy, their justification and reasoning changed throughout the 19th century. Each phase will thus be analyzed, asking which aims specific policies pursued; which interest groups were considered in their shaping; how political and fiscal circumstances limited options, and which politico-economic theories served as backdrop to policymakers. Particular attention will be paid to the debate between "free-traders" and "protectionists" in the second half of the 1850s and the 1860s. It demonstrates well Russia's acquaintance with and involvement in contemporary European debates and created a fault line which remained relevant until the decline of the Russian Empire.

The chapter argues that the development of Russia's trade policies on its European borders was not all that different from other European states, but rather followed general world economic trends, albeit usually less pronounced, due to internal constraints. Meanwhile, customs policies in the "Asiatic" section of the Russian Empire presented idiosyncratic solutions to specific challenges of the empire's geography and heterogeneity. Nevertheless, their development was closely bound to trends in the "European" part of the empire, which either opened up or restricted the room for special administrative solutions, and thus provides a necessary context for the following chapters.

3 For the formation of the distinction between "European" and "Asiatic" customs see chapter 2.

1.1 Egor Kankrin and Prohibitionism

In terms of economic development, the reign of Nicholas I was characterized by a high degree of continuity, or, put more critically, tranquility and apathy, which spectacularly backfired with Russia's defeat in the Crimean War. The engineer behind this system of hesitation and economic conservatism had been Minister of Finance Egor Kankrin. Young Tsar Nicholas I inherited Kankrin as Minister of Finance, who had been appointed in 1823, but also kept him in this position until the latter's retirement in 1844. The duration of Kankrin's tenure in itself hints at the stable nature of economic policy under Nicholas I. The minister wielded a significant amount of power and with the transfer of the Department of Manufactures and Domestic Trade from the Ministry of Interior to the Ministry of Finance in 1819, the latter had begun to take shape as the super ministry which it would become over the 19th century, combining in itself both the domains of a ministry of finance and a ministry of economy.[4] Kankrin exercised a strong influence over the Tsar, and only by the end of his career had the Tsar begun to push forward economic projects on his own against Kankrin's cautioning. These late projects, such as the 1839 currency reform and railway construction projects, are among the most significant economic changes of Nicholas I's otherwise conservative reign.[5] Due to his preeminent role during this period, the following section will concentrate on Kankrin's views and policies.

Kankrin, who had been born in Hanau and studied in Gießen and Marburg, had initially built his career in the Russian Empire through service in the military, where he distinguished himself in matters of troop supplies. His transition into civil service and appointment as Minister of Finance partially owed to the publication of his politico-economic treaty "Weltreichthum, Nationalreichthum und Staatswirthschaft, oder Versuch neuer Ansichten der politischen Oekonomie" in 1821 and to the protection of Count Aleksei Andreevich Arakcheev.[6] Although he regularly published on politico-economic matters, he was never a serious academic theoretician and did not present a coherent theoretical framework. If anything, his "guiding principle was the extent to which a given policy contributed to the strength of the state as an independent entity, separate, not only from other states but from the welfare or happiness of the population itself."[7] While this preoccupation with

4 On the Department of Manufactures and Domestic Trade see *Blackwell, William L.*: Beginnings of Russian Industrialization, 1800–1860. Princeton 1968, 163–168.

5 *Pintner, Walter M.*: Russian Economic Policy under Nicholas I. Ithaca 1967, 18–19, 121–122.

6 Ibid. 15, 28; *von Cancrin, Georg*: Weltreichthum, Nationalreichthum und Staatswirthschaft, oder, Versuch neuer Ansichten der politischen Oekonomie. Munich 1821.

7 *Pintner*: Russian Economic Policy under Nicholas I, 20.

the vigor of the Russian Empire would suggest a close proximity to the ideology of "Official Nationality", the latter was never induced with economic content by Kankrin. Pintner argues that under Nicholas I the regime had no general theory of economic policy.[8] Nevertheless, the main traits of the economic action of the state can be explained by Kankrin's personal outlooks.

If Kankrin did not present a coherent politico-economic theory, then his views are best carved out ex-negativo. He was acquainted with Smithian Liberalism, and while it had gained ground in the Russian Empire among scholars such as Heinrich Friedrich von Storch, as well as statesmen such as 1810–1823 Minister of Finance Count Dmitrii Gur'ev, Kankrin starkly rejected Smith's theory.[9] With regard to the generation of wealth, Kankrin continued Russia's mercantilist tradition, maintaining "that total wealth of the world is a virtually fixed quantity and one nation can increase its share only at the expense of another."[10] As for the integration into a global system of division of labor, he perceived national self-sufficiency as paramount for reasons of national security.[11] With this outlook, Kankrin seemed to be the right candidate for the post of the Minister of Finance in 1823, as Russia was bouncing back from a short-lived and failed economic experiment with tariff liberalization, which had wrought havoc on its industries.

The traditional cameralist and mercantilist outlooks of the 18th century had been challenged by new liberal politico-economic ideas after the ascension of Alexander I. Due to the Napoleonic Wars and Russia's involvement in the Continental Blockade, liberal beginnings, however, were not implemented in trade policy on Russia's European borders. Rather, under the war strains, the Russian Empire resorted to even higher tariffs in 1811.[12] After the Vienna Congress, debate erupted between so-called "free-traders" and "protectionists" over the reform of Russia's economy after the war. The two terms by no means signified clear-cut camps, but rather the ends of a continuum of politico-economic visions concerned not only with foreign trade policy, but also with the necessity to industrialize and the ensuing issues of serfdom.[13] Despite a significantly different starting position, similar debates on free trade and protectionism took place in Great Britain at the same time, demonstrating that the

8 Ibid. viii.

9 Ibid. 23; For a good overview over politico-economic debates between free-traders and protectionists as well as the industrialization debate in the early 19th century see *Blackwell*: Beginnings of Russian Industrialization, 123–148. For the earliest engagement with Adam Smith in Russia see *Taylor, Norman W.*: Adam Smith's First Russian Disciple. In: The Slavonic and East European Review, 45(105) (1967), 425–438.

10 *Pintner*: Russian Economic Policy under Nicholas I, 21.

11 Ibid. 21

12 For a closer examination and particularly the Asiatic dimension see chapter 2.

13 *Blackwell*: Beginnings of Russian Industrialization, 172–173.

Russian Empire was not out of step with the international politico-economic developments of the time.[14]

Eventually, not these debates but the Vienna treaty and subsequent agreements with Prussia in 1818 and 1819 proved crucial to Russia's commitment to opening its trade. In 1819 a significantly lowered tariff had been issued, which could well be regarded as the most liberal tariff of 19th century Russia. However, its disastrous results seemed to prove the protectionist camp right, as the Russian market was quickly flooded with foreign-manufactured goods, leading to the ruination of many Russian manufacturers. To salvage what was left by 1822, a new tariff with strict prohibitionist beginnings had been introduced.[15] Again, a regress to strict tariff limitations was not exceptional for the time, the phase between 1815 and 1825 is best described as an "Ocean of protectionism surrounding a few liberal islands" for the European continent.[16] The failure of the first experiment with free-trade policies contributed to the dismissal of the liberal Count Dmitrii Gur'ev from his post as Minister of Finance, and brought Kankrin into office, who would tinker with the tariff over the following decades, but never deviated from its prohibitionist beginnings.

It is thus little surprising that after this crisis, Kankrin had earned a reputation as protector and sponsor of industrial enterprises. However, much of this perception owed to Kankrin's adherence to high tariffs and his self-fashioning at the end of his career, promoted by a memorandum given to the Tsar.[17] Quite the contrary, Pintner's in-depth study of economic policy under Nicholas I demonstrates well that the 1820s constituted the only period in Kankrin's tenure in which a genuine attempt to make the economy more productive could be observed, with a promotion of technical education, journals on technical and commercial issues and industrial exhibitions.[18] With the Polish uprising of 1830/31, which put the imperial budget under extreme strain, and the minister's increasing skepticism towards the negative consequences of industrialization, Kankrin's initial momentum to reform slowed. The last significant measure to support Russian industrialists had been the erection of a substantial tariff wall between the Kingdom of Poland with its further developed textiles industry and the core customs space of the Russian Empire.[19]

14 *Bairoch*: Economics and World History, 18.

15 *Blackwell*: Beginnings of Russian Industrialization, 172–173.

16 *Bairoch*: Economics and World History, 18.

17 *Blackwell*: Beginnings of Russian Industrialization, 141. The interpretation of Kankrin's tariff policies as primarily motivated by concerns for industrial development continues to circulate, see e.g. *Kislovskii*: Istoriia tamozhennogo dela, 171, 198.

18 *Pintner*: Russian Economic Policy under Nicholas I, 28, 48–54.

19 Ibid. 83, 92.

Foremost, Kankrin was concerned with balancing the heavily strained budget and limiting expenditures. The high customs tariff was thus primarily a source of revenue and an instrument to ensure a positive balance of trade, rather than a macroeconomic mechanism to support nascent industries. Although the toolset suggests a similarity to the principles of Friedrich List's *Nationalökonomie*, which would subsequently inform the high tariff policies of Sergei Vitte, ultimately Kankrin fundamentally disagreed with List's focus on industrialization.[20]

This does not mean that the high tariffs did not inadvertently develop protectionist effects. Those, however, were met with skepticism on the side of the Minister of Finance. Particularly the sugar beet industry profited from the high tariff of 1822. The high duties on raw cane and a prohibition on the importation of refined sugar were initially aimed at increasing customs revenues. In conjunction with a grain crop failure, they stimulated the growth of Russian sugar beet farming and processing factories. Eventually, this undermined fiscal intentions as the import of sugar and subsequently customs revenue dropped. The Ministry of Finance attempted to compensate for the losses by increasing sugar tariffs, which only further stimulated the growth of the sugar industry.[21] Far from being delighted with a successful protectionist measure, Kankrin bemoaned that the "beet-sugar industry is one of the most illfounded projects of the Russian gentryman."[22] Ultimately, the possibilities of tariff manipulation reached their limits, and an excise tax had to be introduced on the manufacturing of sugar in 1848 to compensate for revenue losses.[23] With this, the Ministry of Finance accepted the fact that it had inadvertently bred an industry it never wanted and whose existence and subsequent crises it would have to support.[24]

Although the initial prohibitionist tariff of 1822 had seen nine revisions under Kankrin's tenure, it maintained its basic tenets and was mostly concerned with establishing a sweet spot between maximum revenues and a minimum incentive to smuggling.[25] It is little surprising that the high tariffs caused smuggling on the Russian Empire's Western border to flourish. The empire responded with the increase, professionalization, and militarization of its border protection. The system created under Nicholas I would serve as

20 Ibid. 22.

21 *Smith-Peter, Susan*: Sweet Development. The Sugar Beet Industry, Agricultural Societies and Agrarian Transformation in the Russian Empire 1818–1913. In: Cahiers du monde russe, 57 (2016), 101–124, here 106–107.

22 *Pintner*: Russian Economic Policy under Nicholas I, 223–224.

23 Ibid. 225.

24 For the sugar industry and its relation to the customs policies in Russia's south-eastern peripheries see chapter 3.

25 *Pintner*: Russian Economic Policy under Nicholas I, 237–238.

the model for decades to come. The Border Customs Guard (Pogranichnaia tamozhennaia strazha) was introduced on the Western border in 1827 and renamed into Border Guard (Pogranichnaia strazha) in 1832. It was developed as a hybrid of a militarized institution under the civil control of the Department of Foreign Trade (Departament vneshnei torgovli) and subsequently of the Department of Customs Collection (Department tamozhennykh sborov). Over the following decades it continued to grow, creating a tight-knit net of customs stations and checkpoints on the Western border, but always at odds with smuggling activities, therefore lucrative on a border with high tariffs. Only in 1893 did it see a major reform, as the border guard was reorganized as Separate Corps of Border Guard (Otdel'nyi korpus pogranichnoi strazhi), and put under the direct control of the Minister of Finance. It was further militarized and increasingly understood as a military unit stationed permanently on the border for the event of war.[26]

The customs system on Russia's European border under Kankrin can be summed up as conservative, yet, not for its political content but for its guiding principle: the conservation of the status quo. Its main aim was the generation of substantial revenues and the maintenance of a positive balance of trade, continuing the mercantilist tradition of the 18th century. Protectionist considerations did play a role, however, mostly in order to secure existing industries, not as part of an elaborate industrializational plan. While the Russian Empire was increasingly closing down its Western borders and locking out the Kingdom of Poland from its economic space in a protectionist effort, on its south-eastern border, the Ministry of Finance proved more willing to experiment with trade deregulation during this phase.[27]

1.2 The 1850s Tariff Revisions and Liberalization

While Kankrin's persona looms large as one of the most influential Ministers of Finance in the 19th century, his successors Fedor Vronchenko and Petr Brok are primarily remembered as pale bureaucrats who had internalized bureaucratic routines and mostly continued Kankrin's system. Konstantin Fisher, Head of the Railway Department, finds little flattering words for both. Describing the gallery of past ministers in the hallway of the Ministry of Finance, he remarks: "Behind Kankrin [we see]: Vronchenko, Brok, Kniazhevich – bureaucrats [chinovniki]. They neither have intellect [just as Kankrin's

26 *Adelsgruber/Cohen/Kuzmany*: Getrennt und doch verbunden, 110–112. For details on smuggling on the Galician border see also 113–123.
27 See chapter 2.

predecessors], but one can see a bureaucrat's self-satisfaction, with the exception of Kniazhevich may be, whose face does not show self-satisfaction, but simply satisfaction."[28] This snarky depiction may be biased; however, it is true that the first significant tariff reform since 1822 – the tariff of 1850 – owed little to Minister of Finance Vronchenko, but was primarily the work of the economist Liudwig Tengoborskii[29], who proved instrumental to the loosening of the tight prohibitionist framework.

The initial impetus for tariff reform had come from a memorandum submitted by a merchant named Popov in 1844. Less concerned with issues of state revenue or the protection of Russian industries, he advocated an expansion of Russian foreign trade. His suggestions included the improvement of trading infrastructure, the abolition of export duties, and a complete tariff revision.[30] The petition came at an opportune moment. With Kankrin gone as a powerful and stubborn minister, a window for debate and renewal had opened.

Simultaneously, the concept of free trade was gaining momentum as a policy. Great Britain began lowering its tariffs in 1842 under Prime Minister Robert Peel, and subsequently repealed its Corn Laws in 1846, opening its market for foreign grain. Peel had hoped that tariff liberalization would inspire other states to follow Britain's example; however, the opposite came true. Initially, this seems counter-intuitive given how received wisdom assumes that tariff wars spiral upwards while reciprocal concessions spiral downwards. To explain this counter-intuitive effect, Robert Pahre offers his "reaction hypothesis", which takes into account internal political support as a factor. He argues that with country A lowering its tariffs at home, it did not only increase its imports, but also "spurred competitive sectors to export more, inciting protectionists abroad." With this disturbance of its political equilibrium, country B would have attempted to satisfy its domestic interest groups by increasing protection.[31]

In the case of Great Britain, its significant lead in industrial development exacerbated this effect, as other European states came to realize their industrial backwardness and reacted with "defensive mercantilism" or better called "protectionism" in an attempt to secure and nurture their industries.[32] Britain's liberalization put the Russian Empire into a political predicament: As an important exporter of grain, the Russian Empire profited significantly from

28 *Fisher, Konstantin*: Zapiski Senatora K. I. Fishera. Chast' 1. In: *Shubinskii, Sergei Nikolaevich* (ed.): Istoricheskii vestnik. Tom CXI. Saint Petersburg 1908, 43–70, 66.

29 Tengoborskii is the Russian transliteration, accommodating the "ę" in the original Polish spelling Ludwik Tęgoborski. Oftentimes he is spelled as Tegoborski, particularly in German and French transliterations.

30 *Pintner*: Russian Economic Policy under Nicholas I, 238–239.

31 *Pahre*: Politics and Trade Cooperation, 179–181.

32 *Bairoch*: Economics and World History, 20.

this liberalization, and reciprocal acts of trade liberalization were called for.[33] At the same time, its home industries would not have stood a chance in open competition, and a remake of the disaster with the 1819 tariff needed to be avoided. With regard to Pahre's thesis on internal political support, it could be argued that the political weakness of Russian entrepreneurs as interest groups in the 1840s provided the Russian financial administration with more leeway to implement tariff reduction than it would have had in other states with stronger interest group opposition.[34] Eventually, diplomatic reasons prevailed, leading to the first significant tariff revision since 1819.

Russia's new European tariff of 1850 was by no means an out-and-out free-trade tariff. However, it was a substantial departure from the Kankrin system, doing away with the indiscriminately high duties of prior tariffs, which primarily followed a fiscal logic, even taxing goods, that were not manufactured in the Russian Empire at all. The new tariff was to introduce a more balanced and target-oriented system of tariff protection. Such an elaborate revision required in-depth statistical knowledge, and thus it is little surprising that Polish-born economist Ludwig Tengoborskii had become the main engineer of the 1850 tariff.

Tengoborskii had worked in Vienna as Plenipotentiary Commissioner (polnomochnyi kommissar), where he was charged with re-negotiating the rights of the Republic of Krakow in the aftermath of the 1830/31 November Uprising. Further, he conducted the negotiation of the 1846 trade- and navigation treaty between Austria and Russia.[35]

Besides these official diplomatic functions, Tengoborskii also distinguished himself as an economist, publishing analyses on the Austrian economy, which had had been translated to German and widely discussed.[36] Tengoborskii's work was praised for its "clarity, resoluteness and thoroughness" approaching the topic "purely from a standpoint of comparative statistics and financial inquiry, avoiding any political tinge." This praise was, on the one hand, a rebuttal of prior reviews, in which Tengoborskii's qualification to write on Austria's economy was questioned, as he was neither an Austrian, nor an economist

33 *Pintner*: Russian Economic Policy under Nicholas I, 239–240.

34 On the development of entrepreneurs as a politically potent interest group beginning in the 1850s see *Rieber, Alferd J.*: The Moscow Entrepreneurial Group: The Emergence of a New Form in Autocratic Politics. In: Jahrbücher für Geschichte Osteuropas, 25(1) (1977), 1–20.

35 See Tengoborskii's entrance in the Russian biographical dictionary: Russkii biograficheskii slovar'. Volume 20. Saint Petersburg 1912, 466–468.

36 *Tęgoborski, Ludwik*: De l'instruction publique en Autriche, par un diplomate etranger: qui a long-temps résidé dans ce pays. Paris 1841; *Tęgoborski, Ludwik*: Des finances et du crédit public de l'Autriche de sa dette, de ses ressources financières et de son système d'imposition. Paris 1843.

in the narrower sense, but a diplomat.[37] At the same time, the emphasis on the scientific merit of his work reflects the irreconcilable politico-economic debates of the time, which often took the form of colliding "belief systems" with "almost religious claims to truth."[38] Breaking up Russia's long-established prohibitionist system required an outsider – not home-grown under Kankrin's rule – yet someone with more than just idealistic reform vigor. Tengoborskii's long service abroad, his statistical sure-footedness and economic expertise recommended him as Head of the Tariff Commission for the full revision of the Russian European tariff.[39]

Indeed, most of the revision had been pushed through against the will of Minister of Finance Vronchenko, who attempted to maintain the status quo. Tengoborskii and Count Aleksei Orlov had been the main driving forces behind the significant tariff revision, although the resulting 1850 tariff was by no means a clear break with the old beginnings, but rather an incremental development.[40] Described as a "convinced free-trader" in his outlooks, Tengoborskii believed in division of labor between nations, however was realistic rather than dogmatic in his approach. He did not oppose protectionist measures, yet only saw them as justifiable for those industries that had potential under Russia's natural conditions.[41] Neither did he entertain ideas of national self-sufficiency and isolation, as Kankrin had. Thus, many prohibitions had been removed from the tariff and protectionist provisions kept in place only where necessary. Unlike Kankrin's system, the new approach was more target-oriented, and did away with indiscriminate high tariffs, rather than with high tariffs as such.

37 *Herz, Johann*: Noch ein Wort über Tęgoborski's Werk: Die Finanzen, der öffentliche Kredit, die Staatsschuld, und das Besteuerungssystem des österreichischen Kaiserstaates, mit vergleichendem Hinblick auf Preussen und Frankreich. Vienna 1844, 7; For these critical points against Tengoborskii see *Wiesner, Adolf*: Russisch-politische Arithmetik. Streiflichter auf was Werk des russischen Geheimrathes M-L. von Tegoborski: Ueber die Finanzen, den Staatskredit, die Staatsschuld, die Hülfsquellen und das Steuersystem Oesterreichs. Leipzig 1844.

38 *Etges, Andreas*: Wirtschaftsnationalismus: USA und Deutschland im Vergleich (1815–1914). Frankfurt/Main 1999, 35–38.

39 It appears that he had laid out his reform intentions soon after his appointment in an 1848 work titled "Expositions des motifs concernant la révision du tarif." The work is regularly cited and re-cited, however, the author was unable to trace a copy. The work is referred to in *Nikol'skii, Sergei*: O vneshnikh tamozhennykh poshlinakh. Moscow 1865, 155. It appears that the passage was copied from there to *L. V.*: Svobodnaia torgovlia i pokrovitel'stvennaia sistema v Rossii. Doklad Moskovskomu Otdeleniiu Obshchestva dlia sodeistvia Russkoi Promyshlennosti i Torgovle. Moscow 1891, 62. It seems to have also been used for Tengoborskii's entry in the Polovtsov biographical dictionary.

40 *Pintner*: Russian Economic Policy under Nicholas I, 239–240.

41 *Sobolev*: Tamozhennaia politika Rossii, 9–11.

Apart from macroeconomic regulation, political motives played into the tariff revision. Next to the aforementioned political pressure emanating from Great Britain's liberalization, the lowering of tariffs also had internal political reasons. Against the background of the 1848 revolutions, the closer integration of the Kingdom of Poland into the Russian Empire had acquired special significance.[42] Economically, the separateness of the Kingdom of Poland manifested itself not only in the existence of a customs border with the Russian Empire's core customs space, but also in the existence of its own sophisticated banking institutions and a separate currency. The higher economic development of the peripheral region complicated its integration into the core imperial economic space. Nevertheless, since the 1830s, first symbolic steps towards introducing a uniform currency had been made, and with the introduction of the silver standard in 1841, both currencies were linked closer together.[43]

With the new tariff, the customs barrier between the Kingdom of Poland and the Russian Empire had been removed, taking effect on January 1, 1851, and signified an even closer merging of both economic spaces. It had been of particular importance to Tsar Nicholas, who specifically pushed for a quicker unification of the two customs spaces.[44] This integration in turn effected a general lowering of the imperial tariff, as preexistent lower tariffs of the Kingdom of Poland had to be accommodated to avoid disrupting its industrial basis.[45] Thus, the special solution which the imperial administration had chosen for its peripheral territory earlier turned out to limit its options, once it came to the homogenization of its economic space.

The 1850 tariff was the first significant change to the prohibitionist system established in 1822. It departed from indiscriminate high duties, which were fiscally motivated initially, but eventually incentivized smuggling, and raised costs for consumers. Further, it accommodated some principles of free trade departing from the siege mentality under Kankrin. Foreign and domestic political motives played an important role in its conception, proving Russia's participation in the politico-economic trends of the time. The new tariff had demonstrated that a politico-economic reorientation was underway and sparked a new public debate between "free-traders" and "protectionists" in the 1850s, which laid the foundation for economic policies during the Great

42 *Pintner*: Russian Economic Policy under Nicholas I, 239–240.

43 For the history of the Polish Zloty in the 19th century see *Pravilova, Ekaterina*: From the Zloty to the Ruble: The Kingdom of Poland in the Monetary Politics of the Russian Empire. In: *Burbank, Jane/Von Hagen, Mark/Remnev, Anatolyi* (eds.): Russian Empire: Space, People, Power, 1700–1930. Bloomington 2007, 295–319, particularly 304–310.

44 *Pintner*: Russian Economic Policy under Nicholas I, 240. For a detailed account of the 1850 tariff commission with a focus on cotton tariffs see *Martin*: Baumwollindustrie und die russische Zolltarifpolitik, 40–51.

45 *Pintner*: Russian Economic Policy under Nicholas I, 240

Reforms. Again, Tengoborskii had been instrumental, as his study "Sur le forces productives de la Russie" provided the starting point for debate.[46]

1.3 "Free-Traders" Versus "Protectionists"

Tengoborskii's four-volume study, published between 1852 and 1855, presented the first all-encompassing work on the Russian economy. With a delay of only two years, it had been translated into Russian by economics professor Ivan Vernadskii and made available to a broader Russian audience. Taking into account the geographic preconditions of the Russian Empire, Tengoborskii argued that agriculture should remain the main basis for the empire's economy, with industrial production playing only a secondary role. Simply said, in many industries Russia did not have the potential to be competitive, no matter how much protection they received. From this he drew the conclusion that Russia should not strive to produce everything on her own, but limit herself to industrial branches suitable to her geography and resources. Such a specialized economy could be more productive, while a shift towards free trade would ensure the country benefitted from the division of labor between nations. More liberal tariffs would have lowered consumption costs for the Russian population and production costs for both agriculture and industry. Eventually, this would lead to both more spending capacity within Russia as well as more trade turnover benefitting the export of agricultural goods.[47] The underlying assumption here was one of peacetime and international trade cooperation as normal conditions, rather than the siege mentality under Kankrin. The devastating defeat in the Crimean War had demonstrated the failure of Russia's existing economic structure and opened up debate on its reconceptualization.

Debate on future trade policies was sparked by Ivan Vernadskii's article "O vneshnei torgovle" (On Foreign Trade) published in "Russkii vestnik" (Russian Herald) in 1856. He interpreted foreign trade as the main source for the success of Great Nations.[48] Further, he attributed a peace-promoting function to international trade, arguing that "much blood and energy could have been saved in Europe without the miserable [zhalkoe] striving for so-called

46 *Tęgoborski, Ludwik*: Études sur les forces productives de la Russie. Volume 1. Paris 1852; *Tęgoborski, Ludwik*: Études sur les forces productives de la Russie. Volume 2. Paris 1852; *Tęgoborski, Ludwik*: Études sur les forces productives de la Russie. Volume 3. Paris 1853; *Tęgoborski, Ludwik*: Études sur les forces productives de la Russie. Volume 4. Paris 1855.

47 *Pintner*: Russian Economic Policy under Nicholas I, 241–243.

48 *Vernadskii, Ivan Vasil'evich*: O vneshnei torgovle. In: Russkii vestnik, 2 (1856), 603–624, 603–604.

industrial independence, blessed/consecrated by mercantilism."[49] Vernadskii argued that trade restrictions hurt foreign merchants and manufacturers, leading them "to join the ranks of irreconcilable enemies of the country, that caused their loss."[50] He further argued free and self-regulating trade benefitted the internal economy and stabilized prices. He also dismissed the high hopes invested by some parties into Russia's "Asiatic markets" in the late 1850s, which were supposed to absorb overpriced Russian manufactured goods, arguing that no significant influx of capital could be expected on these borders and a concentration on trade with Europe was imperative.[51]

Vernadskii was surely on the extreme end of a debate led by "free-traders" and "protectionists" at the time. The bipolar juxtaposition of these two labels is owed to the polemic nature of the debate and somewhat glosses over the finer differentiated positions in between, as many authors labeled "free-traders" were by no means calling for full deregulation of trade and often supported moderate tariffs both as source of fiscal income and protectionist measure. Vernadskii had not only been the most outspoken "free-trader", but beginning in 1857 he also published his own journal "Ekonomicheskii ukazatel'" (Economic Guide) and its supplement "Ekonomist" (Economist), promoting liberal economic doctrines and particularly free trade. Despite a general loosening of censorship in the post-war period, Vernadskii's journals were subject to an above-average number of interventions from censors due to their radical and harshly articulated positions on Russia's economy.[52]

The outreach of Vernadskii's publications unsettled the opposite camp of "protectionists." Ushinskii directly criticized him, complaining that in the "battle of simple, healthy Russian reason against one of the most tempting and deceitful utopias that has dizzied many learned and smart heads in Europe" Vernadskii's journals contributed to "the reading public devoting itself to wrong preconceptions against the protectionist system and the manufacturing industries of Russia supported by it."[53] Free trade, one of the main protectionist objections read, "draws up a mute map of the world on which all differences between nations and governments are destroyed," populated "only by citizens of one indivisible republic, who, not thinking of their national benefits, care only about the reduction of distances between each other, about the facilitation and the cheapening of communications, about the expansion of mutual

49 Ibid. 611.

50 Ibid. 611.

51 Ibid. 609, 616; For Russia's export ambitions on its south-eastern borders see chapter 2.

52 *Surnina, Irina*: Tsenzura i "Ekonomicheskii ukazatel'" I. V. Vernadskogo 1857–1861 godov. In: Filologicheskie nauki. Voprosy teorii i praktiki, 2(80) (2018), 244–249.

53 *Ushinskii, A.*: O znachenii manufakturnoi promyshlennosti v Rossii i ob okhrannoi sisteme, s izlozheniem mnenii raznykh pisatelei v zashchitu-i-protiv ucheniia o svobodnoi mezhdunarodnoi torgovle. Saint Petersburg 1858, i-ii.

relations and the removal of material and moral boundaries, erected between states by politics."[54] Politically, Ushinskii understood free trade to "hide in itself the heavy chains of foreign political dependency, which is political slavery, servitude."[55] This polemic captures well the main accusations brought up against liberal economic ideas gaining ground after the Crimean War: They were accused of being theoretical or utopian rather than grounded in Russian realities and cosmopolitan in their outlook, putting national interests at risk.

In reality, many contributors grouped under "free-traders" were much more moderate in their suggestions and well aware of Russia's specificities. Economics professor and future Minister of Finance (1881–1886) Nikolai Bunge positioned himself "on the side of the followers of free trade", however, he cautioned that the protectionist system "cannot be suddenly sacrificed for the common good" and that he was "far from the idea that free trade presupposes the full absence of customs lines and duties from the consumption of imported goods: there can be no talk of such an order in Europe."[56]

Bunge's main point of contention was the inefficiency of an economic system oriented towards self-sufficiency. He argued that the low rates of foreign consumption registered in Russia were by no means an indicator of self-sufficiency, but rather of high prices distorted by the prohibitive system and a lack in buying power. Citing the example of the United States of America, which had significantly lowered their tariff between 1846 and 1861, Bunge argued that the enormous size of their territory, their multiple climate zones, and many resources reminiscent of Russia did not impede active participation in world trade, with both exports of agricultural products and manufactured goods.[57] Thus, he concluded, that "the reasons for our backwardness lie partially in the limited means of the large mass of the population, which in an economic sense constitutes an almost closed world, and partially in the ancient high tariff."[58]

Similar sentiments were uttered by entrepreneur and active publicist Vasilii Kokorev, who argued that Russian industries "developed artificially and exist forcibly, supported not by natural direction, not by the requirements of things, not by the life [byt] of the people, but by tariff stimulation."[59] He criticized the

54 Ibid. 2.

55 Ibid. 15.

56 *Bunge, Nikolai Kh.*: Promyshlennost' i ee ogranichenie vo vneshnei torgovle. (Stat'ia vtoraia) Obshchee obozrenie vneshnei torgovli Rossii. In: Otechestvennye zapiski, June (1857), 473–508, 473–474.

57 Ibid. 478–479. For the temporary lowering of US tariffs see *Bairoch*: Economics and World History, 34–35.

58 *Bunge*: Promyshlennost' i ee ogranichenie, 478–479.

59 *Kokorev, Vasilii A.*: Vzgliad Russkogo na evropeiskuiu torgovliu. In: Russkii vestnik, 14 (1858), 29–64, 46.

heavy dependence of the state on customs as revenue, arguing that the artificial rise in prices it created impeded the development of true wealth, which would generate other sources of fiscal income.[60] Customs, most authors of the free-trade persuasion agreed, were a welcome source of revenue as long as they were set moderate enough not to interfere with market forces. Lower duties and simpler customs procedures could even increase total customs revenue if they stimulated the growth of trade turnover, as Bal'tazar Kalinovskii argued, referring to the American example as well.[61]

In the post-Crimean War phase, liberal politico-economic ideas were noticeably gaining ground in public discourse. The authors were well accustomed to both Western politico-economic theories as well as avid observers of economic policy developments abroad. Some authors like Kokorev even placed Russia next to England in its openness towards the idea of free trade, attesting that "France, Germany and Belgium are lagging behind in the understanding of this issue."[62] In fact, it would be more accurate to say that the Russian discourse was in line with a general European trend, which in the 1850s saw the assertion of free-trade theory in the political public, with proponents of free trade succeeding in "stigmatizing protectionist tariffs as reactionary."[63]

The tariff revision of 1857, again conducted under the auspices of Tengoborskii, confirmed the impression that change was underway, as it was conceptualized as the logical continuation of the 1850/51 revision following the same underlying principles. The commission deemed the reductions of 1851 not decisive enough to take full effect, and further saw itself obliged to react to the lowering of tariffs in other states, such as Austria and the United States, in order not to further damage its foreign trade relations after the Crimean War. In its final statement, the State Council's Department of Economics reiterated that the 1857 revision was yet another step in dismantling the old prohibitionist system and a step towards moderate protectionism.[64]

The late-1850s polemics between free-traders and protectionists differed from early 19th century debates, as they were conducted much more publicly. Further, neither side challenged the necessity for modernization, debating only the appropriate means to achieve it. Lastly, practical experience with free-trade policies abroad provided a new point of departure. These heated debates opened up a fault line which would regularly reemerge over the following decades, testing economic policies for their "cosmopolitan" or

60 Ibid. 46.

61 *Kalinovskii, Bal'tazar Fomich*: O razvitii i rasprostranenii idei svobodnoi torgovli i o primenenii ikh k polozhitel'nym zakonodatel'stvam v glavnykh zapadno-evropeiskikh gosudarstvakh. Saint Petersburg 1859, 44–45.

62 *Kokorev*: Vzgliad Russkogo na evropeiskuiu torgovliu, 46.

63 *Torp*: Herausforderung der Globalisierung, 125.

64 *Martin*: Baumwollindustrie und die russische Zolltarifpolitik, 68–71.

"national" intentions and asking to which degree Russia was exposing itself to international dependencies. At least for the coming decade, it appeared that the free-trade camp would prevail as the Cobden-Chevalier treaty rang in a Europe-wide cascade of trade liberalization, and Russia's economic future was remolded by Mikhail Reitern, its most liberal Minister of Finance until then.

1.4 Mikhail Reitern and Tariff Liberalization during the Great Reforms

Reitern's predecessor, Aleksandr Kniazhevich, had long served in the Ministry of Finance under Kankrin and had been rumored as his likely successor, yet ultimately had been superseded first by Vronchenko and then by Brok. His turn to rule the ministry came only in 1858, at the age of 66. Although he attempted to implement reforms, he was dismissed from his post for a lack of reform vigor. It can be argued that his most significant contribution to economic reform had been a substantial replacement of the senior staff of the Ministry of Finance with younger, able men.[65] Mikhail Reitern would become their undisputed leader, coming into office as Minister of Finance in 1862, in the hot phase of the Great Reforms.

Reitern, like many other "enlightened bureaucrats", had been educated at the prestigious Tsarskoe Selo Lyceum and began his career on the empire's peripheries, contributing information from the Baltic, Tauride and Kherson provinces. With his election to the Russian Geographic Society, the focal point of progressive thought in late Nicholean Russia, he had caught the attention of its liberal-minded president, Grand Duke Konstantin Nicholaevich. The latter appointed Reitern as "official in charge of special assignments" to his Naval Ministry, where a nucleus of young reform-minded bureaucrats was forming, often referred to as "Konstantin's eagles." Reitern undertook research trips to Prussia, France, England, and the United States of America, studying their economic systems, and eventually presented a plan of action of his own.[66]

65 *Shepelev, Leonid E.*: Sud'by Rossii. Problemy ekonomicheskogo razvitiia strany v XIX-nachale XX vv. Dokumenty i memuary gosudarstennykh deiatelei. Saint Petersburg 2007, 105; See entrance on Kniazhevich in the Russian biographical dictionary: Russkii biograficheskii slovar'. Volume 9. Saint Petersburg 1903, 5–10.

66 *Stepanov*: Mikhail Khristoforovich Reitern, 10–14; For the concept of "enlightened bureaucrats" and their prototypical career paths see *Lincoln*: Vanguard of Reform, 41–76. For the importance of the Russian Geographic Society as focal point of progressive thought see ibid. 91–101; For Konstantin Nicholaevich and his circle see *Stadelmann, Matthias*: Großfürst Konstantin Nikolaevič. Wiesbaden 2012.

In his writings prior to his assignment as Minister of Finance, Reitern distinguished himself as a follower of laissez-faire doctrine, blaming state overregulation and Russia's restrictive estate order for smothering private initiative and causing economic underperformance. He promoted freedom of trade and suggested cutting expenses on the state apparatus, reforming the tax system, partially privatizing state properties and centralizing the state budget in the hands of the Ministry of Finance to counter the obscurity of monetary flows in the different branches of state administration.[67] Once he had become Minister of Finance, practical and political limitations watered down this "wish list." Yet, Reitern was no dogmatist and proved successful at adapting and implementing substantial changes to Russia's financial administration and economic system. Jacob Kipp aptly described Reitern's actions in office as a "special mutation of 'liberalism' that reformist bureaucrats came to champion – the association of the ideal of 'freedom' and an open society with the overriding motives of Realpolitik, national regeneration, and the strengthening of state power."[68] In contrast to the Nicholean period, "national power" was reinterpreted by Reitern "to include economic growth and called on the state to make this a goal of national policy" rather than focusing on its military power and territorial extent.[69]

With regard to foreign trade policy, Reitern's tenure fell into one of the most liberal phases in 19th-century Europe. It had been initiated by the 1860 Cobden-Chevalier treaty. Primarily aimed at reducing the risk of war between Great Britain and France, the treaty reciprocally lowered import tariffs to promote interdependence in trade. While Great Britain had actively promoted its free-trade doctrine since 1846, the majority of the French parliament maintained a protectionist outlook. Eventually, the treaty had been decreed directly by Napoleon III, circumventing the parliament, yielding it critique as "coup d'état."[70]

Its effects were indeed significant and by no means confined to the two signatories. Based on a most-favored-nation clause, any trade rights and tariffs offered by France or Britain to a third party automatically extended to the signatories of the Cobden-Chevalier treaty as well. With the use of most-favored-nation clauses in further trade treaties, bilateral trade agreements quickly became integrated into an interreferential network. France's turn towards free trade initiated a downward spiral in average European tariff

67 *Stepanov*: Mikhail Khristoforovich Reitern, 14.

68 *Kipp, Jacob W.*: M. Kh. Reutern on the Russian State and Economy: A Liberal Bureaucrat during the Crimean Era, 1854–60. In: The Journal of Modern History, 47(3) (1975), 437–459, here 439.

69 Ibid. 447.

70 *Bairoch*: Economics and World History, 22–23.

levels. Though it had not been designed as an all-European framework, by the mid-1860s most Western and Central European states had become part of a large-scale free-trade zone referred to as the Cobden-Chevalier network.[71] This sort of international tariff disarmament conformed with Reitern's liberal political-economic outlook, and yet the Russian Empire never entered the network.

At the end of the 1850s, the Russian Empire had been in a dire fiscal situation, grappling with the aftermath of the Crimean War on the one hand, and facing structural challenges such as monetary reform and the imminent serf emancipation on the other. Costly military expeditions on the empire's peripheries further strained the budget. Reitern evaluated the situation in 1859 as "*without parallel* in the complexity of [its] causes" and Russia's system of taxation left only little leeway to increase incomes. Apart from the tax on alcohol, the most important taxes – the soul tax, the salt monopoly and the tariff – appeared to be non-elastic.[72] Customs incomes constituted a too important pillar of the state budget to risk their decrease by whole-heartedly following continental Europe's drastic tariff reductions through entering the Cobden-Chevalier network.

At the same time, neither did an increase of the tariff promise higher revenue. The tariff's underperformance owed not to it being set too low, but on the contrary to it being too high. In a memorandum on tariff revision from 1867, Reitern acknowledged that the tariff revisions of 1850 and 1857 had been important steps away from prohibitionism, although it failed to increase customs revenues. Tariffs had remained high enough to incentivize large-scale smuggling, while "the immense extent of the land frontier of Russia renders it impossible to increase vigilance to an extent that will entirely prevent smuggling [...]." As sealing the border was fiscally unreasonable and administratively impossible, Reitern proposed combating smuggling with economic instruments – by lowering the smugglers' margin of profit.[73] With the general trend towards tariff-lowering in Europe and a reform spirit within Russia, the moment seemed opportune for a major tariff revision. The challenge was to design a tariff which would both have lower customs rates and generate more revenue by increasing trade volume and incentivizing legal imports.

Soon after his appointment, Reitern had already introduced the first partial changes to the customs system, abolishing almost all export duties in 1863. While this step indicated an opening towards global trade, he was well

71 Ibid. 22–23; *Torp*: Herausforderung der Globalisierung, 121–123.

72 *Kipp*: Reutern on the Russian State and Economy, 449.

73 *Reutern, Mikhail Kh./Barnett, Vincent*: Memorandum on Tariff Reform in Russia (1867). In: Œconomia. History, Methodology, Philosophy, 4(1) (2014), 29–34.

aware that caution was called for with regards to Russia's industries, which still required "a somewhat considerable amount of protection."[74] Thus, an involvement in the Cobden-Chevalier-network by means of trade treaties with most-favored-nation clauses was undesirable, as it would have automatically pushed tariffs lower, stripping the Russian financial administration of the ability to exercise an autonomous – if necessary protectionist – tariff policy.[75]

Nevertheless, the tariff of 1868 followed the general European trend of trade liberalization. Customs rates on 217 items were significantly lowered. Though rates on 169 items were simultaneously increased, these were only small raises. All things considered, the reductions clearly outweighed any increases. Particularly raw materials and semi-manufactured goods were heavily discounted, indicating the importance attributed to industrial development in the new tariff. Juxtaposing the aims and results of the 1868 revision, Barnett comes to the conclusion that Reitern was successful in increasing both import volume and customs revenues despite lowering tariff rates, while also increasing Russia's total exports over the 1870s.[76] On its European border, Russia thus followed – albeit less pronounced – general European trends: from a gradual popularization of free-trade ideas in the 1850s to their concrete implementation in trade policy in the 1860s.

Russia's reluctance to join the Cobden-Chevalier-network can be explained both by continuing fears for its domestic industries' inability to compete globally and its deep budgetary crisis. On its Asiatic peripheries, however, these factors and the reformist climate of the 1860s played out differently than on the European border, spawning a number of special regimes. In its Far-Eastern region, an enormous porto-franco regime had been established in the early 1860s, stretching from Irkutsk to the Pacific Ocean, which would become emblematic for the empire's heterogeneous approach to regulating its economic space.[77] In the late 1860s, the Ministry of Finance considered it a successful administrative model and drew on this experience when dissolving its south-eastern customs border in Central Asia to both save costs and expand its influence and access to new markets.[78] Similarly, the 1860s meant a second bloom for the Transcaucasian transit route, which successfully filled the treasury without causing many administrative costs.[79] Both the reform climate and the international trend towards free trade, as well as the Ministry of Finance's agenda to discard any unprofitable expenditures – most prominent

74 Ibid.
75 *Barnett*: Reutern and Tariff.
76 Ibid.
77 See chapter 4.
78 See chapter 2.
79 See chapter 6.

with the sale of Alaska in 1868[80] – benefitted the creation of deregulated economic spaces on the Russian Empire's peripheries, making the 1860s the heyday of experimental territorialized laissez-faire customs arrangements.

Reitern's reformist course was not met with support from all sides. Financial shake-ups resulting from the 1863 Polish insurrection had first damaged his reputation, while an assassination attempt on Alexander II in 1866 ushered in a conservative turn calling into question the success of the recent liberal reforms. Nevertheless, Reitern managed to retain his post. He was irreplaceable as a financial expert, and his interpretation of "liberalism" – a combination of the dynamism of national economic growth through private initiative and the conservation of the existing monastic order – allowed him some flexibility in dealing with the conservative fraction. Beginning in 1867, the national economy began to improve and the railroad boom appeared to vindicate Reitern's trust in private entrepreneurship, despite indications of speculation and abuses. The Ministry of Finance began replenishing the Russian metal reserves, striving for a monetary reform. This optimistic mood persisted as Russia survived the 1873 economic crisis relatively unscathed.[81]

Much of the economic success story was, however, built on international capital. When a "crisis of overproduction" hit the Russian Empire in 1875, international trust in Russia's economy was seriously disturbed, causing a drainage of foreign capital and dragging the ruble rate downwards. As if that were not enough, the prospect of war with the Ottoman Empire loomed large in 1876. Reitern saw his reforms as endangered and urgently warned Alexander II against military confrontation, but to no avail.[82] Despite his protests, it was for the Minister of Finance to locate the necessary funds to finance the campaign. Tinkering with the customs tariff seemed to be the only viable option to generate the necessary income and cushion the drop in the currency rate.

In the Committee of Ministers, Reitern sketched out the main dangers of the economic slump. Russia had taken up large credits abroad, which it would soon be unable to service, as the influx of new capital was receding. Over the past decade, Russia's foreign obligations had grown substantially, while its balance

80 The sale was part of a larger reevaluation of Russia's assets and its overstretch. It was not so much the day-to-day operational unprofitability of the Alaskan colony as its potential to result in large strategic expenses, which prompted the decision to sell see *Vinkovetsky, Ilya*: Russian America: An Overseas Colony of a Continental Empire, 1804–1867. Oxford 2011, 181–188.

81 *Stepanov*: Mikhail Khristoforovich Reitern, 26–35.

82 Ibid. 26–35. The concept of a "crisis of overproduction", used by Stepanov, is strongly associated with the economic theories of J. C.L. de Sismondi and Karl Marx. The possibility of "overproduction" as such is regarded critically by contemporary economists see *Simpson, Brian P.*: Money, Banking, and the Business Cycle, Volume II: Remedies and Alternative Theories. New York 2014, 9–13. For a critical discussion of the term see chapter 3.

of trade had tipped into the negative, essentially draining metallic currency. Reitern thus suggested switching the collection of customs from credit rubles to gold currency. The customs incomes would then be decoupled from the volatile ruble rate and could be used directly to service foreign credits without exchanging them into rubles and back again, and thus would reassure foreign creditors. At the same time, the change in the mode of customs collection, if performed at the nominal rate without adjusting it to the low ruble rate, would mean a significant increase of customs rates without making changes to the tariff. This, the minister hoped, would curtail imports and positively influence Russia's balance of trade.[83]

The collection of customs in gold currency was already practiced in Austria, Italy, and the United States of America, convincing the Committee of Ministers of its usefulness. However, the conversion of the existing customs rates to gold caused doubt among its members. State Comptroller Samuil Greig argued that it would be more sensible to apply the average exchange rate of credit rubles to gold over the past two years, rather than adopting the nominal value. Considering the weakness of the credit ruble, the latter would have meant an effective increase in customs rates by 30 %. The tariff of 1868 proved to be the "most complete" Russia ever had, Greig argued, and should not be distorted by a flat-rate increase of customs rates. Neither did he believe that it would successfully curtail imports, as they would continue at approximately the same level, only now as contraband. Further, such a large increase in tariffs would send a negative political signal to other governments.[84]

Although Reitern agreed with Greig's latter objection, he argued that being able to reliably fulfill credit obligations was the more important foreign political signal. Further, this would allow to increase customs revenues so important to the war effort while simultaneously reducing import volume to achieve a more favorable balance of trade. Eventually, the Committee of Ministers approved Reitern's proposals, seeing that the impending war required quick action, and agreed that with January 1, 1877 customs would be collected in gold currency at nominal value.[85] Despite formally retaining the 1868 tariff, the switch to customs collection in gold currency altered its balanced and free-trade-inspired character, giving it a protectionist twist. This emergency measure foreshadowed the return of protectionism as a dominant doctrine – not only in Russia, but Europe-wide.

A number of other emergency measures saved the Russian Empire's economy from collapse during the Russo-Ottoman War, but by its end the state finances were in deep distress. Reitern resigned in 1878, leaving a "testament" to his

83 RGIA, f. 563, op. 2, d. 232, "O vzimanii tamozhennykh poshlin zolotom", l. 2–5.

84 Ibid. l. 7–10ob.

85 Ibid. l. 15–16.

successor, Greig, in which he bemoaned the effects of economic liberalization and advised for a more protectionist course, further increases in customs and the curtailing of imports. The failure of his liberal economic vision vis-a-vis the political realities ushered in a roll-back to more state interventionism and stricter regulation of the economy.[86] Despite being caused by a crisis in Russia, Reitern's renunciation of free-trade ideas and promotion of protectionist measures corresponded with an international shift towards protectionism. With the German tariff of 1879, protectionist ideas began to gradually gain ground across continental Europe. By 1892, Europe's "free-trade interlude" was definitely over as France – once instrumental to the opening of European trade – introduced the protectionist Méline tariff.[87]

During the period of the Great Reforms, Russia's customs policy loosely followed international trends. The 1850s saw a popularization of free-trade ideas in public discourse, which was carried over into political practice by young "enlightened bureaucrats" in the 1860s. Internal constraints such as the fiscal crisis and the weakness of domestic industries, however, prevented the Russian Empire from fully committing itself to continental Europe's tariff disarmament. If regarded on an international scale, Russia's brief flirt with free trade appears reluctant. Compared to its own previous and future customs policies, however, the 1860s and early 1870s clearly stand out as a liberal phase. It was against this ideological backdrop that many idiosyncratic solutions to ordering the heterogeneous imperial economic space discussed in this book could be conceived.

1.5 Nikolai Bunge: A Liberal in Conservative Waters

Just as Reitern had predicted, the Russo-Ottoman War shattered his prior efforts to reform and stabilize Russia's economy, which he took as "a personal tragedy." With the signing of the Berlin Treaty in 1878, his immediate duties of maneuvering the empire's economy through the war effort were fulfilled and Reitern resigned as Minister of Finance. However, it was not a final farewell from high politics as he remained on important posts as Chairman of the Committee of Ministers and other committees in the 1880s.[88] Within the Ministry of Finance, bureaucratic inertia maintained Reitern's spirit, as the new minister, former State Comptroller Samuil Greig, was not a financial

86 *Stepanov*: Mikhail Khristoforovich Reitern, 37–39.

87 *Bairoch*: Economics and World History, 24–25; *Torp*: Herausforderung der Globalisierung, 154.

88 *Stepanov*: Mikhail Khristoforovich Reitern, 36–37.

expert and hardly left an imprint.[89] The appointment of Aleksandr Abaza in 1880, who belonged to a group of liberals surrounding Count Mikhail Loris-Melikov, indicated a continuation of Reitern's liberal agenda. However, with the assassination of Alexander II and the failure of Loris-Melikov's "constitution" the political climate changed dramatically. The Manifesto of 29 April 1881, issued by the new Tsar Alexander III, indicated a conservative turn. In an unprecedented display of political dissent, the liberal ministers surrounding Loris-Melikov resigned from their posts following the Manifesto. Despite upholding the political conventions and citing other reasons as a pretense for their resignation, the signal was clear. The departure of Abaza left the position of Minister of Finance open for an expert on economics to move up from the second row. Though of liberal persuasion, his successor was not compromised by too close association with Loris-Melikov: his deputy minister, Nikolai Bunge.[90]

Before entering the Ministry of Finance in 1880, Bunge had already made a career for himself as professor of economics and advisor to the government. Bunge belonged to the same age cohort as Mikhail Reitern and had developed his liberal outlook while teaching at the Prince Bezborodko Lyceum in Nezhin in the 1840s. In his early economic views, he had been influenced by Western political economy and particularly laissez-faire doctrine. By the mid-1850s he had become a professor teaching at the St. Vladimir Kiev University and was active in debates on reform, contributing regularly to "Russkii vestnik", "Otechestvennye zapiski" (Patriotic Notes) and "Ekonomicheskii ukazatel'" (Economic guide). While he clearly self-identified as an adherent of the free-trader camp in the 1850s, Bunge nevertheless shied away from extreme positions, maintaining that the uniqueness of Russian statehood should be accounted for. Despite his theoretical inclination towards free trade, he advocated a transitional phase of protectionism and the maintenance of customs as a source of income.[91] Paradoxically, 25 years later as Minister of Finance, he would be the one to roll-back prior tariff liberalization, preparing the late-19th century protectionist course in Russia and making disproportionate use of customs as source of fiscal income.

89 *Andreeva, E. A.* (ed.): Upravlencheskaia elita Rossiiskoi Imperii. Istoriia ministerstv, 1802–1917. Saint Petersburg 2008, 338.

90 *Taranovski, Theodore*: Alexander III and his Bureaucracy: The Limitations on Autocratic Power. In: Canadian Slavonic Papers/Revue Canadienne des Slavistes, 26(2/3) (1984), 207–219, 215; *Stepanov, Valerii*: Nikolai Khristianovich Bunge. In: Russian Studies in History, 35(2) (1996), 42–72, 54–56; *Polunov, Aleksandr Iur'evich*: Russia in the Nineteenth Century. Autocracy, Reform and Social Change, 1814–1914. Armonk, N. Y. 2005, 174–189.

91 *Stepanov*: Nikolai Khristianovich Bunge, 45–48; For Bunge's views on foreign trade in the 1850s see *Bunge*: Promyshlennost' i ee ogranichenie.

By the late 1860s, Bunge had moderated many of the positions on Russia's economy he had held in the late 1850s. Russia's infrastructural weakness and poor spending power required more state intervention than he had previously acknowledged.[92] His definitive turn towards protectionist tariff policies in the 1880s, however, was conditioned by dire fiscal needs. The budgetary crisis caused by the Russo-Ottoman War demanded higher revenues and a stabilization of the ruble rate, both tasks traditionally tackled by tariff manipulation. At the same time, the ascension of Alexander III empowered two new voices in the shaping of economic policies, which both actively propagated protectionist policies: the conservative press and entrepreneurial interest groups.

The most pervasive voice of the conservative press had been "Moskovskie vedomosti" (Moscow News), with its infamous editor Mikhail Nikiforovich Katkov. Already in the wake of the Polish insurrection of 1863, "Moskovskie vedomosti" had achieved immense outreach and began redefining Russian politics. Katkov's earlier career in the 1850s had seen him as an outspoken advocate of English liberalism; thus he is often interpreted as having "reversed himself completely" in an "opportunistic switch" to the camp of conservative supporters of autocracy in the 1860s.[93] Under closer scrutiny, Renner argues, it becomes obvious that his "nationalism is intrinsically linked to the liberalism of its day" and was not incompatible with the reforms he had previously proposed. Rather, he appears as a supporter of autocracy, as an implementer of reform-from-above, with a concept of nationalism comprised of "a modern, unified state, whose responsibility for the rule of law lay with a politically aware civil society."[94] Renner argues that Katkov's success was founded not in the "winning of arguments" but in "the supply of argumentative categories." By fusing competing concepts, Katkov created a unique and unavoidable language to which other authors were forced to react.[95] He "invented", as the censor Nikitenko noted, "a new method of 'patriotizing' ['sposob patriotizirovaniia'] thoughts and actions."[96] Much of Katkov's critique crystallized around questions of the empire's peripheries. In terms of foreign trade and customs organization, both protectionist policies and the reduction of territorial special regimes did lend themselves particularly well to "patriotizing" and became focal points of polemics on the national interest and the empire's unification.

92 *Stepanov*: Nikolai Khristianovich Bunge, 52–53.

93 *Pyziur, Eugene*: Mikhail N. Katkov: Advocate of English Liberalism in Russia, 1856–1863. In: The Slavonic and East European Review, 45(105) (1967), 439–456, 456.

94 *Renner, Andreas*: Defining a Russian Nation: Mikhail Katkov and the 'Invention' of National Politics. In: The Slavonic and East European Review, 81(4) (2003), 659–682, here 660–661, 670.

95 Ibid. 672–674, 676, 681.

96 Cit. Ibid. 676.

The second party which had gained importance over the 1860s and 1870s, and was able to fully assert itself under the rule of Alexander III, was dubbed the "Moscow Entrepreneurial Group" by Alfred Rieber. He had identified a group of Moscow-based merchants, industrialists and entrepreneurs, which had formed in the aftermath of the Crimean War and played a "pioneering role as the first political interest group outside the court and the bureaucracy to influence in any significant way the making of policy within the autocracy."[97] Taking advantage of the more open publishing climate after the Crimean War, this group actively employed print media to further its agenda. Though economic issues were at the heart of their publications, they were not dealt with as mere technicalities, but framed within "the light of Great Russian national aspirations." With this wider claim, they carved out a niche within the autocratic system for themselves which allowed them to criticize the bureaucracy, while maintaining loyalty towards the autocracy and "endow[ing] their economic activities with a moral and political purpose" which elevated their social status.[98] Similarly to Katkov's method of "patriotizing", the Moscow Entrepreneurial Group refracted any economic issues it brought forward through the national lens.

Nevertheless, their success throughout the 1860s had been limited, as their patriotic appeals often failed against the economic rationale of Minister of Finance Reitern.[99] While many of their larger demands for Russia's economic renewal were of no immediate consequence to their business operations, tariff revision directly affected entrepreneurs and became the issue around which the group developed new organizational forms to increase its impact. Rumors of a secret trade agreement with the German Customs Union led to the formation of a permanent committee to lobby on tariff questions in 1864. Despite their ability to exert pressure on the government, the Moscow Entrepreneurial Group still found itself side-lined during the consultations for the 1868 tariff revision. They were given the chance to participate but were outnumbered by bureaucrats and delegates from the empire's peripheries who favored tariff reductions. Ultimately, the Moscow Entrepreneurial Group was hardly able to implement any of its demands for the tariff revision of 1868. Even if they lost out short-term, the group was successful in acquiring a more valuable long-term asset. In the background of the consultations, Ivan Kondrat'ev Babst

97 *Rieber*: Emergence of a New Form in Autocratic Politics, 2.

98 Ibid. 2–3, 17–18; For the involvement of individual entrepreneurs in publishing see *Laverychev, Vladimir*: Russkie kapitalisty i periodicheskaia pechat' vtoroi poloviny XIX v. In: Istoriia SSSR, 1 (1972), 26–47.

99 *Rieber, Alfred J.*: The Moscow Entrepreneurial Group: The Emergence of a New Form in Autocratic Politics: II. In: Jahrbücher für Geschichte Osteuropas, 25(2) (1977), 174–199, 178.

had gained the trust and support of Tsesarevich Aleksandr Aleksandrovich, future Tsar Alexander III, and sensitized him to the importance of tariffs and protectionist policies.[100]

Thus, when Nikolai Bunge had been appointed Minister of Finance in 1882, three factors came together which limited his leeway in shaping economic policies: a strong conservative press successful at placing its topics, a well-organized entrepreneurial interest group with a national underpinning, and a new Tsar willing to carry out a conservative rollback and at times overrule decisions of the State Council.[101] Facing both public pressure and a deep budgetary crisis, it is little surprising that the economist Bunge, known for a liberal outlook, was forced to resort to quite conservative economic policies as Minister of Finance.

By the end of the Russo-Ottoman War the Russian Empire's state debt had grown to 6 billion rubles, requiring in 1881 alone 239,9 million rubles for debt repayment – this equaled 34 % of the state budget.[102] Already in 1878, the first changes to customs were made in a scramble to stem the budgetary crisis. First the cotton tariff had been raised in 1878; then a flat rate increase in tariffs by 10 % followed in 1880.[103] Thus, tariff increases under Bunge only continued an existing trend. Though he shied away from a general tariff revision, sweeping increases were introduced in 1882, followed by more raises in 1884, and a comprehensive 10–20 % raise in 1885. By 1886 the average ad valorem customs rate in the Russian Empire had grown from 16,5 % in 1881 to 27,8 %. As contemporaries reported, Bunge – a self-proclaimed free-trader in the 1850s – himself joked about maxing out protectionism, yet remained skeptical about its negative consequences.[104]

Still, Bunge was not a conservative convert, but rather operated under the conditions at hand. In many fields, he re-interpreted the role of the Ministry of Finance to go beyond narrow fiscal goals and include a social agenda. He introduced Russia's first factory legislation regulating child labor and workers' rights.[105] The increase in customs rates was part of a general reform of Russia's taxation system as well. Bunge had hoped to shift the tax burden away from the peasantry by relying more on indirect taxation rather than direct taxation. Along with customs, other indirect taxes such as the alcohol excise were continuously increased, while the poll tax (podushnaia podat')

100 Ibid. 183–186.

101 Alexander III increasingly made use of his right to overrule decisions of the State Council, see *Mosse, W. E.*: Aspects of Tsarist Bureaucracy: The State Council in the Late Nineteenth Century. In: The English Historical Review, 95(375) (1980), 268–292, here 283–285.

102 *Stepanov*: Sud'ba reformatora, 110.

103 *Sobolev*: Tamozhennaia politika Rossii, 427–431.

104 *Stepanov*: Sud'ba reformatora, 164–168.

105 *Stepanov*: Nikolai Khristianovich Bunge, 59.

was abolished.[106] Stepanov aptly describes Bunge as a "confirmed liberal and sixties man" who was the "'Last of the Mohicans' in Alexander III's reactionary government."[107] In many regards, his work in the 1880s was driven by pressure from the public sphere.

By the 1880s, protectionism began replacing free trade as the dominant politico-economic doctrine across Europe.[108] In the Russian Empire, Katkov's "Moskovskie vedomosti" was the spearhead of this shift, calling for a course of "national economy" echoing Friedrich List's famous work.[109] For the Russian Empire's economic policy, this constituted a tectonic shift. While national considerations had played a role before, Gatrell and Anan'ich contend that for the most part "economic policy reflected non-national or supra-national purposes" as the dynastic state prioritized the maintenance of "domestic and external security."[110]

Under Alexander III and a state-led policy of Russification, the interests of groups claiming to speak on behalf of "national interests", such as the Moscow Entrepreneurial Group, gained ground. Unlike in the 1867 tariff committee, where they were counterbalanced by a liberal bureaucracy and voices from the periphery, Russia's bureaucracy for the most part in the 1880s supported the new "national course." The State Council, which had absorbed most of the former liberal ministers, acted as the last liberal stronghold, and a counterbalance, however, was frequently overruled by Alexander III.[111] Bunge found himself "besieged from all sides", both from within the government and by press campaigns against him.[112]

In this climate, debates on the cost of the empire intensified in the 1880s, with individual regions branded as disproportionate beneficiaries of the empire.[113] Special customs regulations introduced for peripheral regions in previous decades came under scrutiny and were refracted through the nationalist lens, asking: Cui bono? The empire as a whole? A peripheral region? Foreign

106 *Stepanov*: Sud'ba reformatora, 127; *Gatrell*: Russian Fiscal State, 201–202.

107 *Stepanov*: Nikolai Khristianovich Bunge, 68.

108 *Bairoch*: Economics and World History, 24–25; *Torp*: Herausforderung der Globalisierung, 154.

109 *Stepanov*: Sud'ba reformatora, 121–122.

110 *Gatrell, Peter/Anan'ich, Boris*: National and Non-National Dimensions of Economic Development in Nineteenth- and Twentieth-Century Russia. In: *Teichova, Alice/Matis, Herbert* (eds.): Nation, State and the Economy in History. Cambridge 2003, 219–236, 222.

111 *Taranovski*: Alexander III and his Bureaucracy, 213–219; *Mosse*: Aspects of Tsarist Bureaucracy, 283–285.

112 *Taranovski*: Alexander III and his Bureaucracy, 218; *Stepanov*: Nikolai Khristianovich Bunge, 60–61.

113 For an overview over Russia's history in evaluating the costs and benefits of its imperial expansion see *Pravilova, Ekaterina*: 'Cena' Imperii: centr i okrainy v Rossiiskom biudzhete XIX- nachala XX vv. In: Ab Imperio, 4 (2002), 115–144.

manufacturers? As will be discussed in the following chapters, demands to establish a porto-franco regime in the Ob' and Enisei estuaries paralleled and specifically referred to the Far-Eastern porto-franco established in 1861; but the time for the introduction of special custom-zones – a popular instrument in the 1860s – had passed.[114] The demands for a modern unified state also put the Transcaucasian transit route in question, as it was accused of operating both at the cost of central Russian manufacturers to the benefit of foreign manufacturers and of furthering the separateness of the Transcaucasian region. Abolished in 1883 – against Bunge's recommendation – the special transit regime had been one of the first victims of a strong press campaign spearheaded by Katkov.[115] Further, Finland's quasi-autonomous position in foreign trade came under criticism, with the relation and loyalty of the Grand Duchy to the Russian Empire being questioned.[116]

On an international scale, the 1880s saw a spread of protectionism coming to replace the dominance of liberal trade doctrines established in the 1860s. The Russian Empire followed this trend, both anticipating a positive effect on its industrial development from higher tariffs and in dire need for additional sources of state revenue. Despite being of a liberal outlook and at best a moderate protectionist Minister of Finance Bunge found himself in a constellation in which he became the forerunner for Russia's high protectionist phase in the 1890s. The rise of nationalist rhetoric and strong public voices furthered the ideal of a unified state, discrediting regional idiosyncratic solutions. Flexible customs regimes established in the 1860s and 1870s were accused of fragmenting the imperial space and harming all-imperial interests, serving only regional or international actors. With its unificatory agenda, the imperial administration stripped itself of flexible options, which in the past had allowed to keep administrative costs down in remote areas or served to balance regional economic differences. The analysis of this transition forms the core of this book.

1.6 Sergey Vitte: Towards an Integrated Empire

Ultimately, the press campaigns against Bunge had been successful and he was forced to resign his post as Minister of Finance in 1886. He was succeeded by Ivan Alekseevich Vyshnegradskii, a successful engineer and businessman with a stellar career, however, lacking the usual track record within govern-

114 See chapter 4.
115 See chapter 6.
116 See chapter 7.

mental service. Vyshnegradskii had been Mikhail Katkov's and Vladimir Meshcherskii's favored candidate for the post. He had received protection from both, as well as from Alexander III. Since 1883–1884 he had been a contributor to "Moskovskie vedomosti", sharing many of Katkov's views on economic policy. Prior efforts to place him in high positions within the Ministry of Finance had failed against Bunge's resistance, but eventually Katkov's and Meshcherskii's persistent lobbying for Vyshnegradskii's appointment convinced Alexander III. His background promised to replace Bunge's academic approach and introduce a businessman's perspective into the office, and he was expected to be generally more in line with the governmental course. Nevertheless, Vyshnegradskii's appointment was not broadly welcomed by the public at first.[117]

Unlike Bunge, who designed financial policies with a keen eye on their social repercussions, Vyshnegradskii followed a narrow "finansism" treating state finances as a business. In many ways, his tenure constituted a transitional phase between Nikolai Bunge and Sergei Vitte. Vyshnegradskii put in place numerous initiatives designed under Bunge, such as the preparation of a monetary reform and the vast statization of railroads. On the other hand, he followed the program propagated by "Moskovskie vedomosti", further increasing customs duties and suggesting a reintroduction of alcohol and tobacco monopolies. His measures prepared the ground for Vitte's later success, particularly for the introduction of the gold standard in 1897.[118]

Despite initial doubts, he was soon celebrated by the public as a talented financial administrator. However, much of Vyshnegradskii's success owed to Bunge's policies, which began to unfold their potential, as well as to external factors: between 1887 and 1889, harvests had been abundant and his tenure coincided with the end of a prolonged industrial recession. Analogously, crop failures in 1891 brought Vyshnegradskii down. Fearing a negative effect on Russia's balance of trade, he had failed to stop grain exports in time, resulting in a catastrophic famine. He was succeeded by "one of his own creations" – Sergei Vitte – who had made a career for himself as a railroad expert.[119]

117 *Stepanov*: Nikolai Khristianovich Bunge, 60–61; *Stepanov, Valerii*: Ivan Alekseevich Vyshnegradskii. In: Russian Studies in History, 35(2) (1996), 73–103, 82–85.

118 *Stepanov*: Ivan Alekseevich Vyshnegradskii, 86, 90, 99.

119 Ibid. 80, 91, 97; For the origins of the 1891–1892 crop failures see *Simms, James Y.*: The Crop Failure of 1891: Soil Exhaustion, Technological Backwardness, and Russia's 'Agrarian Crisis'. In: Slavic Review, 41(2) (1982), 236–250. Simms argues that the actual economic impact of the famine on Russia's economy and its trade as a whole was lower than usually assumed. However, the perception of the gravity of the crisis cost Vyshnegradskii his post, see *Simms, J. Y.*: The Economic Impact of the Russian Famine of 1891–92. In: The Slavonic and East European Review, 60(1) (1982), 63–74, 69–74.

In terms of trade and customs policies, Vyshnegradskii continued Bunge's protectionist course, but distinguished himself from the latter by motivation. While Bunge had introduced protectionist tariffs out of shear necessity, Vyshnegradskii was a staunch protectionist.[120] Bunge never undertook a full general tariff revision, introducing raises in piecemeal fashion, which gave them an air of emergency and temporariness. Vyshnegradskii systematized the change of course towards protectionism by conducting the first general tariff revision since 1868. The resulting general tariff of 1891 maxed out protectionism and was without match in a European context, where protectionism was entering a new high phase, putting Russia on a collision course with Germany.

The engineer of this new tariff had been the famous chemist and industrial adviser Dmitrii Ivanovich Mendeleev.[121] Beginning with the 1880s, Mendeleev had developed an interest in questions of economic development, and particularly in ways to industrialize the Russian Empire. His reputation as a brilliant scientist and the compatibility of his protectionist suggestions with Vyshnegradskii's outlook recommended him for the tariff commission. His proposals both for the general principle of tariff reform and his detailed elaborations of individual tariff rates became the basis for the 1891 tariff.[122] Rates for half of all product groups, mostly those increased prior, in the 1880s, were kept at the same level, whereas half of the product groups received substantially higher rates. Only 21 product groups out of 530 received lower rates.[123] In 1892, Mendeleev published an accompanying work titled "Tolkovyj tarif" (Explanatory Tariff), in which he laid out his economic premises and the interrelation between industrial development and customs tariffs.[124]

Mendeleev drew substantial inspiration from the German political economy and clearly positioned himself against free-trade doctrine, comparing it to the scientifically discredited Phlogiston-theory.[125]

The teachings of free trade might be logical, rational, and beautiful. But this does mean that they are right. "Phlogiston" was logical, rational and beautiful, but did not stand experimental testing and transformed into something completely different, to a

120 *Stepanov*: Ivan Alekseevich Vyshnegradskii, 99.

121 For an account of Mendeleev's involvement in governmental economic policies see: *Gordin, Michael D.*: A Well-ordered Thing. Dmitrii Mendeleev and the Shadow of the Periodic Table. New York 2004, 145–172.

122 *Barnett*: Russian Protectionism and German Political Economy, 170, 180.

123 *Sobolev*: Tamozhennaia politika Rossii, 698.

124 *Mendeleev, Dmitrii*: Tolkovyi tarif, ili issledovanie o razvitii promyshlennosti Rossii v sviazi s ee obshchim tamozhennym tarifom 1891 goda. Saint Petersburg 1892.

125 *Barnett*: Russian Protectionism and German Political Economy, 169; For an overview over the influence of the German Historical School in Russia see *Sheptun, Alla*: The German Historical School and Russian Economic Thought. In: Journal of Economic Studies, 32(4) (2005), 349–374.

degree, that all of chemistry once was called "anti-phlogistonian teaching." It has to be acknowledged, that the economic teachings of "nationalists", "sociologists" and the "historical school" have long snapped free trade at its root, and that modern economic science has to, for clarification, be called "anti-free-tradism." This should be known to all deciding to speak about economics in the name of science.[126]

Beyond theoretical influences, the actual German experience with industrialization constituted an important point of reference for Mendeleev. He frequently paralleled Russia's situation with that of Germany, arguing for the necessity of protectionist policies.[127] Although Mendeleev himself did not explicitly refer to Friedrich List's "National System", Barnett evaluates his work and policies as "the most extreme expression of List's general approach to economic development witnessed in Europe at the end of the nineteenth century."[128]

List's ideas had been known in the Russian Empire; yet neither were they compatible with Kankrin's skepticism towards industrialization, nor could they develop a significant force in the 1850s debates on free trade and protectionism. He had found sympathizers among Slavophile thinkers, particularly Iurii Fedorovich Samarin, who embraced List's concern for national historical specificities and his repudiation of laissez-faire policies.[129] The late 1880s and early 1890s then saw a popularization of Listean thought in Russia, first with Sergei Vitte's 1889 brochure "National Economy and Friedrich List" (Natsional'naia Ekonomika i Fridrikh List),[130] followed by Konstantin Vasil'evich Trubnikov's translation of List's "Nationalökonomie" into Russian in 1891 – the same year the new high protectionist tariff had been issued.[131] Vitte's appointment as Minister of Finance in 1892 practically declared the "National System" state doctrine – not only with protectionism as core policy, but also with the goal of creating an integrated economy. Unsurprisingly, given Vitte's career path in railroad administration, integration was to be achieved via the expansion of the railroad network.

Sergei Vitte was born in Tiflis in 1849 as the son of a state official working for the Department of State Property under the Caucasian Viceroy (Kavkazskii Namestnik). His university studies of mathematics took him from the Trans-

126 *Mendeleev*: Tolkovyi tarif, ix.

127 *Barnett*: Russian Protectionism and German Political Economy, 169, 174–175.

128 Ibid. 180.

129 Ibid. 176; *Wendler*: List-Rezeption in Rußland, 477; Most prominently, Kalinovski devoted a whole chapter to refuting List's theory. *Kalinovskii*: O razvitii i rasprostranenii idei svobodnoi torgovli 35–88.

130 *Vitte, Sergei*: Natsional'naia ekonomika i Fridrikh List. Kiev 1889.

131 *Barnett*: Russian Protectionism and German Political Economy, 178.

caucasus to Odessa.[132] It could be argued that his first-hand experience at various peripheries of the empire was constituent to an "imperial biography" and shaped his later political thinking.[133] But it was not only the encounter with heterogeneity which coined Vitte, but as much his acquaintance with railroad technology, which promised the ability to alter the imperial space. Instead of an academic career, Vitte had made a career for himself first with the Odessa railways, later as manager of operations of its larger successor, Southwestern railways. His position granted him access to networks, including Katkov's and Vyshnegradskii's, promoting his stellar rise in state service, first as director of the Department of Railroad Affairs in 1888, then as Minister of Ways and Communications in 1892, quickly followed by him replacing Vyshnegradskii as Minister of Finance.[134]

He had particularly made a name for himself as an expert on freight rates with the publication of his 1883 book "Printsipy zheleznodorozhnykh tarifov po perevozke gruzov" (Principles of Railroad Freight Rates), which distinguished itself by the principle that freight rates should not be shaped by market forces, but fixed, in order to achieve specific goals of national economic development. This "offered an alternative vision" which "made explicit the connections between the commercial topography that surrounded him and the capacity of railroad technology to transform it." Intentional manipulation of freight rates, Vitte argued, would allow the integration of regional markets into a larger imperial market, leading to general economic growth.[135] In Vitte's vision, Russia had to grow together in order to develop economically, and this grand transformation could not be left to the whim of free entrepreneurship, but had to be guided from above. Beyond the freight rate issue, which Vitte had developed based on his practical work at the Southwestern railways, he found a theoretical underpinning for his program in List's "National System."

Vitte had contributed to the popularization of List's ideas with his brochure titled "Natsional'naia ekonomika i Fridrikh List."[136] It was, at its core, a best-of List, sparsely annotated by Vitte and stripped of any notions unsuitable to his agenda. Wortman describes the brochure as an example of the "nativization of a Western idea." The liberal aspects of List's text identifying representative institutions as prerequisites for national economic growth were incompatible with Vitte's support for autocracy and had been omitted. In essence, it was

132 *Ganelin/Anan'ich*: Sergei Iul'evich Vitte i ego vremia, 8–11.

133 For the concept of imperial biographies see: *Rolf, Malte*: Einführung: Imperial Biographien. Lebenswege imperialer Akteure in Groß- und Kolonialreichen (1850–1918). In: Geschichte und Gesellschaft, 40 (2014), 5–21.

134 *Ganelin/Anan'ich*: Sergei Iul'evich Vitte i ego vremia, 11–14.

135 *Wcislo*: Rereading Old Texts, 75–80; *Vitte, Sergei*: Printsipy zheleznodorozhnykh tarifov po perevozke gruzov. Kiev 1883.

136 *Vitte*: Natsional'naia ekonomika i Fridrikh List.

reduced to a treatise against free trade and in favor of protectionism, with a specific emphasis on the role of railroads.[137] A such curtailed reading of List and its popularization provided Vitte with the theoretical and historical underpinning to promote an interventionist state-led process of industrialization under autocratic conditions.

With regard to the European tariff, Vitte had inherited the new 1891 tariff with its high protectionist rates from Vyshnegradskii, which was certainly to his liking. However, he was also forced to handle a major customs war with Germany early in his tenure. With the global rise of protectionism and the disintegration of the Cobden-Chevalier network in 1892, Germany, which heavily relied on global exports, was forced to secure its trade relations through individual treaties. These usually included a lowering of Germany's agricultural tariffs, while the other party lowered its tariffs on German-manufactured goods.[138] Russia's extremely high tariff of 1891, which even exceeded the American McKinley tariff of 1890, proved particularly problematic. Continuing the creeping tariff-armament-race between both countries in the 1880s, German Chancellor Leo von Caprivi followed a confrontational course.[139]

Germany had lowered agricultural tariffs for other states with a number of treaties in 1892; however, no agreement could be found with the Russian Empire, as it was not willing to offer sufficient reductions on its new high-protectionist tariff. Thus, Russia remained the only important grain exporter to be excluded from an otherwise broad lowering of agricultural tariffs in Germany. The Russian Empire retaliated with the introduction of a maximum customs tariff – 20–30% higher than the protectionist tariff of Mendeleev – which was specifically tailored for and applied singularly to Germany. The tariff war quickly escalated, causing large damage to both countries' economies. Reciprocal retaliation measures spiraled up over the next two years. The good harvests of 1893 in the Russian Empire increased the pressure, as Germany was an important market. Similarly, German representatives of trade and industry pressured for a quick end to the economic war. Eventually, a trade and shipping treaty was concluded in 1894, which granted Germany the same rights and conditions as other nations. Despite this confrontation and the severe economic pressure it endured, the Russian Empire was able to uphold its new highly protectionist course.[140]

137 *Wortman, Richard S.*: Scenarios of Power: From Alexander II to the Abdication of Nicholas II. Princeton 2000, 267–268; *Wendler*: List-Rezeption in Rußland, 489; *Von Laue*: Sergei Witte and the Industrialization of Russia, 56–64.

138 *Torp, Cornelius*: The Challenges of Globalization. New York 2014, 114–116.

139 Ibid. 129–132.

140 Ibid. 129–132.

The 1890s were characterized by a systematic combination of outward protectionist policies and internal infrastructural integration. The construction of the Trans-Siberian railway was emblematic of the promise of a shrinking empire. The transformation of the Imperial space – both physical and on the administration's mental maps – caused by new infrastructural projects made the inherent conflicts between parallel, heterogeneous economic spaces increasingly tangible. The Far-Eastern porto-franco, once far removed, now threatened to disrupt the new protectionist system. Similarly, petitions for a free-trade zone in the Ob' and Enisei estuaries, which promised to link Western Siberia to global trade currents, but weaken the empire's internal cohesion, lost any prospects.[141] Two autonomous regions, albeit with diametrically opposite relations to the Russian Empire, came under pressure to be integrated into the Russian customs space. The Khanate of Bukhara was stripped of its vested economic autonomy in order to create a continuous customs border in Russia's south-east for the first time since 1868. This abandonment of prior laissez-faire customs arrangements signified the changing role of Russia's Central Asian territories within the economic topography of the empire.[142] At the same time, the Grand Duchy of Finland came under increased scrutiny, as its autonomous and globalized foreign trade policy distanced it from the Russian Empire and went both against the all-imperial protectionist turn and the unificatory rhetoric. Unlike with Bukhara, a potential integration of the partially industrialized Finland threatened to introduce strong internal competition to the core empire's industries, which the Ministry of Finance sought to protect, disclosing a contradiction between "economic nationalization" and "political nationalization."[143]

1.7 Conclusion

This survey of Russia's European trade and customs policies in the 19th century demonstrates that while outwardly, the Russian Empire appears to have maintained high tariff levels throughout, it did indeed follow all-European trend patterns. Russian statesmen and economic publicists were well-aware of European developments in politico-economic theory and attempted to apply or adapt them to their specific situation. However, continuous budgetary strains regularly limited the leeway for tariff manipulation. The fiscal function of customs, even when disguised as protectionist concern for native indus-

141 See chapter 4.
142 See chapter 3.
143 See chapter 7.

tries, played a critical role throughout the 19th century. Be it Kankrin's high protectionism or Reitern's liberalization, the aim of the Ministry of Finance was revenue generation – even if the tools used were diametrically opposed.

This fiscal preoccupation was two-sided. For the European section, it came with a positive prefix, asking: How can revenues be maximized? For its Asiatic sections, the Russian financial administration operated with a negative prefix, asking: How can administrative expenditures on trade regulation be minimized? The unprofitability and inability of administratively saturating its eastern peripheries gave birth to idiosyncratic solutions, often in opposition to policies effective on the European border. Contrived within the financial administration, they were mostly the result of a cost calculation and largely devoid of ideological underpinnings.

While the liberalization phase in the 1860s prompted the spread of territorialized special regimes to the management of Russia's economic space, it also empowered new interest groups, which began exerting influence on the shaping of customs policies. Paradoxically, these new entrepreneurial interest groups opposed the idiosyncratic and heterogeneous solutions put in place to regulate the imperial space and politicized issues of customs regulation. With the consolidation of a national-course under Alexander III, the Ministry of Finance found it increasingly difficult to isolate its traditional cost calculation approach from ideologically motivated demands for administrative unification. The vision of an imperial economic space integrated via railway eventually elevated the unificatory agenda to state doctrine in the 1890s, ringing in the end for a heterogeneous customs space. Once celebrated as efficient tools for the structuring of a heterogeneous imperial economic space, the idiosyncratic solutions discussed in this book eventually began to be perceived as "non-normal" and a reminder of unwanted deviance and backwardness vis-a-vis unified nation states. The technological possibilities of modernity were quick at altering visions of space, while the actual administrative permeation of the imperial space lagged behind.

2. Expansion by Debordering: The Dissolution of the Orenburg Customs Line

The south-eastern steppe border was the scene for the most dynamic territorial changes in the 19th century Russian Empire, confronting the imperial administration with grand challenges – both military and administrative. With regard to the customs administration, the territorial changes prompted a full reconceptualization of the modus operandi previously established on the Steppe customs line.

The fortified Orenburg line, which had been completed in the 1740s, had remained the Russian Empire's main south-eastern military frontier until the 1840s, when military advances into the Kazakh steppe and the establishment of new fortifications began pushing the line south. By 1853, General Vasilii Alekseevich Perovskii had established Fort No.1 (Kazalinsk), Fort No.2 (Karmakchi) and conquered Ak-Mechet, renamed into Fort Perovskii. Though further expansion was temporarily suspended by the Crimean War, by the 1860s military confrontation with the Khanate of Kokand had picked up again. It culminated in the capture of Tashkent in 1865, the creation of the Turkestan Governorate-general in 1867 and the defeat of the Khanate of Bukhara in 1868.[1] While the military dynamically expanded the territory it controlled, the economic border did not match the pace and remained stable. Almost 1500km of linear distance separated Tashkent, the capital of the new Turkestan Governorate-general, from the Orenburg customs line, which followed from Gur'ev along the outer border of the Orenburg and the Tomsk governorates.

The quick expansion had created a situation in which the outside economic border was so far removed from the state border that the State Council found it fitting to speak of "all the disadvantages [neudobstva] of an internal customs border"[2], supposedly abolished since the Shuvalov reforms of the 1750s. By the mid-1860s, the situation was considered anachronistic and undesirable, and a quick fix was sought. Despite a consensus between different administrative branches on the necessity of relocating customs institutions south,

1 For an overview of Russia's engagement with the Kazakh steppe see *Olcott, Martha Brill*: The Kazakhs. Stanford 1995, 28–53. For the conquest of Central Asia see: *Soucek, Svat*: A History of Inner Asia. Cambridge 2000, 195–200.

2 RGIA, f. 1152, op. 7, 1868, d. 172, "Ob uprazdnenii Orenburgskoi i Zapadno-Sibirskoi tamozhennykh linii", l. 2.

the process dragged on. Eventually, it ended with the full dismantling of the Orenburg customs line in 1868, without substitution. A vast de-facto free-trade zone had been created, yet, unlike with the Far-Eastern porto-franco, it was never labeled as such.[3] This measure was the extreme continuation of a new trade policy on the empire's south-eastern borders, which had been developed since the beginning of the 19th century.

This chapter seeks to first outline the changes in the Russian Empire's customs and trade regulations, which began with the accession of Alexander I in 1801. The "European" regulations are put in relation to those on the "Asiatic" border section, and the latter's distinct logic is demonstrated, arguing that fiscal and protectionist considerations took a back seat in favor of trade intensification. This was to be achieved through simplification and deregulation of trade, entailing side-effects not acceptable under prior mercantilist doctrine. It is argued that the tumultuous foreign political situation of the Napoleonic wars strongly influenced the reforms of "European" border regulations, leading to their uneven development. Meanwhile, the reorganization of trade on the "Asiatic" borders was followed through more consistently. Ultimately, the "Asiatic" customs tariff and body of customs regulations of 1817 are discussed as a first attempt to unify and systematize trade on the various sections of the empire's south-eastern borders.

The second part examines the debates surrounding the relocation of the Orenburg customs line. The issue is placed within the context of the military conquests and economic trends of the 1860s. It takes into consideration the practical aspects and functions of border control on the empire's periphery. It is argued that ultimately the deregulation of trade and economic debordering were not a renouncement of the empire's claim to sovereignty over its territory, but rather served to exude influence beyond the state border. Both the application of a solution forgoing border controls and the coexistence of diametrically opposed systems to the ordering of economic space within one empire were only possible due to the infrastructural weakness and fragmentation of the imperial space.

3 For the changing semantics of the term "porto-franco" in the Russian discourse see *Turbin, Aleksandr*: Dal'nevostochnyi porto-franko v iazykakh i praktikakh modernizuiushcheisia imperii. In: Ab Imperio, 1 (2019), 45–78, here 46–48.

2.1 18th Century Tariff Policies on the Empire's South-Eastern Borders

One of the most striking peculiarities of 19th century Russia's customs system was the separation of both its tariff and its customs regulations into a "European" and an "Asiatic" section. Legally, this separation was first codified with the 1817 "Asiatic" *tamozhennyi tarif* (customs tariff) and *tamozhennyi ustav* (body of customs regulations).[4] This implied a fundamentally different approach towards the functioning of customs and the management of economic space than on the "European" border. Though this division into two halves of the empire suggests a separation, it was indeed a first, if curtailed, step towards unification. Prior, in the second half of the 18th century, the south-eastern border sections of the Russian Empire had been subject to different tariffs and regulations tailored to each specific situation. They were to accommodate the specificities of "Asiatic trade", a term already in use in the 18th century. However, the term was not yet used to conceptualize a distinct system, but rather to accentuate deviance as such and the plurality of special situations. With the 1817 reform the designation "Asiatic" had come to describe a system distinct from the "European" model, and thus introduced a second parallel standard.

Before the 1817 reform, trade across the Caspian Sea had been governed by the Astrakhan tariff of 1754. It had significantly higher stakes than those of the land-based customs stations of Orenburg and Troitsk, through which trade with the Kazakh steppe and the Central Asian khanates was conducted, and which operated based on the 1752 Orenburg tariff.[5] Both tariffs were introduced in the course of Petr Ivanovich Shuvalov's general customs reform of 1753–1757, which removed internal customs in the Russian Empire and increased customs on its outside borders and ports in order to compensate fiscal losses by increasing the taxation of foreign trade.[6] Further east, trade on the Russian Empire's long border with China was governed by the bilateral Kiakhta agreement of 1727 and its subsequent revisions.[7] Even after the

4 Tamozhennyi ustav po aziatskoi torgovle. Saint Petersburg 1817. For both European and Asiatic tariffs prior to 1830 see: Polnoe sobranie zakonov Rossiikoi Imperii. Tom 14. Kniga tarifov. Saint Petersburg 1830.

5 On the Orenburg customs tariff and its development in the 18th century see: *Solonchenko*: Tamozhennaia politika na iugo-vostoke Rossii, 50–67.

6 *Kislovskii*: Istoriia tamozhennogo dela, 149–150.

7 For Russia's Kiakhta trade see: *Heller*: Der russisch-chinesische Handel; *Heller, Klaus*: Der russisch-chinesische Handel in Kjachta: Eine Besonderheit in den außenwirtschaftlichen Beziehungen Rußlands im 18. und 19. Jahrhundert. In: Jahrbücher für Geschichte Osteuropas, 29(4) (1981), 515–536; *Paine, Sarah C. M.*: Imperial Rivals. China, Russia, and their Disputed Frontier. Armonk 1996, 31–32.

introduction of the "Asiatic tariff" of 1817, which aimed at unifying Russia's south-eastern trade regulations, Russo-Chinese trade remained distinct and regulated by bilateral agreements. Thus, the Chinese section is explicitly excluded from the discussion of the south-eastern border in this chapter.

Throughout the second half of the 18th century, the Russian government had only reluctantly adjusted the various tariffs on its southern-eastern borders, protracting revisions and creating anachronisms. The guiding economic doctrine, just as in the European parts of the empire, had been mercantilism, and thus the main aim of the customs policy was to ensure a positive trade balance with exports exceeding imports. Thus, it is little surprising that the long-overdue 1777 revision of the 25-year-old Orenburg tariff included a prohibition on the export of gold and silver and prohibited "Asiatic merchants" – meaning non-Russian subjects from neighboring khanates – from conducting trade within the Russian Empire. It was feared that these merchants would sell their goods on the internal fairs not in exchange for Russian export goods, but for metallic currency. The returning unladen caravans would carry away gold and silver, thus devaluing the assignation ruble. The revised regulations made sure foreign merchants had to conduct their business in the border cities of Orenburg and Troitsk, as they were the main customs stations on the steppe border, and barter trade of raw materials from Central Asia against finished goods from Russia was facilitated. However, these measures could not sufficiently curtail the drain of precious metals from the Russian Empire along the steppe border.[8]

The mercantilist rationale of a positive trade balance at all cost was only challenged with the accession of Alexander I in 1801, which heralded fundamental changes to Russia's trade policies and particularly to trade on the south-eastern border. The reforms found their culmination in the introduction of the 1817 "Asiatic tariff", which attempted to systematize the way trade on the empire's south-eastern borders was conducted, by creating a preferential regime with simpler regulations.

2.2 Trade and Customs Reform Initiatives under Alexander I

Foreign trade policies under Alexander I were characterized by a fluctuation between residual mercantilist principles, new ideas of free trade, and protectionist counter-measures. This unsteady course was to a large degree dictated by the foreign political situation. The onset of his regency, however, had promised a decisive departure from the mercantilism of his predecessors.

8 *Solonchenko*: Tamozhennaia politika na iugo-vostoke Rossii, 65–68.

Quite symbolically, it was the new Tsar himself who had ordered the first Russian translation of Adam Smith's "Wealth of Nations", published between 1802 and 1806. Smith's ideas had previously circulated in educated circles, but now quickly rose to have a significant impact on government representatives.[9]

In this spirit, one of the first measures of Alexander I was the immediate revocation of his predecessor's export ban on Russian goods, which had been aimed at curtailing the expansion of British sea trade.[10] A liberal and free-trade-inclined agenda was formulated by his first Minister of Commerce[11], Nikolai Petrovich Rumiantsev, in his 1802 trade program:

> Three rules constitute the care for the abundance of trade: 1) the decrease of import goods not by means of any prohibitions or inhibitions, but by producing the same kind of goods within the state; 2) the increase of export goods, which cannot be achieved other than by the removal [otvrashcheniem] of internal inconveniences and impediments and by exploring in which foreign country a new field [poprishche] can be discovered for them, and 3) the expansion of transit.[12]

Nevertheless, Rumiantsev remained realistic about Russia's economic condition and cautioned, in an 1803 memorandum to Alexander I, that a transition to full free trade was not feasible for the Russian Empire:

> Admittedly, if such a turn was possible, then of course only when the state gives itself a new essence [bytie], after having been exposed towards all sorts of development [obrazovaniiu]. But we are not in this position.[13]

These restrictions led him to propose maximum import tariffs of 20 percent – prior certain products had been taxed with 50, 100 or 130 percent – so as to allow for moderate protectionism of Russia's nascent manufacturing industry. This, he argued, would suffice unless the "own production of the same kind is built on an irrational calculation [bezrasshchetnaia vykladka] and therefore the government should not save it."[14]

9 *Barnett, Vincent*: A History of Russian Economic Thought. New York 2005, 20; *Lodyzhenskii, Konstantin N.*: Istoriia russkogo tamozhennogo tarifa. Cheliabinsk 1886, 160; For the pre-history of Adam Smith's arrival to Russia see *Taylor*: Adam Smith's First Russian Disciple.

10 *Zlotnikov, Mikhail F.*: Kontinental'naia blokada i Rossiia. Leningrad 1966, 127–128; *Lodyzhenskii*: Istoriia russkogo tamozhennogo tarifa, 159.

11 The ministry was first established in 1802 and incorporated the Collegium of Commerce. Only in 1810 was it reorganized as Ministry of Finance.

12 *Ekspeditsiia zagotovleniia gosudarstvennykh bumag*: Ministerstvo Finansov. 1802–1902. Volume 1. Saint Petersburg 1902, 127.

13 *Rumiantsev, Nikolai Petrovich*: Zapiska ministra kommertsii o razume tarifa. In: Arkhiv Gosudarstvennogo Soveta. Tom 3. Chast' 1. Saint Petersburg 1878, 369–380, 371.

14 Ibid. 373.

As for export duties, these were only to be levied on products solely Russia could provide. Meanwhile "everything without which the foreigner can get by should not be burdened, so as to expand the space of the market."[15] These measures, Rumiantsev warned, would not guarantee a further growth of customs revenues, as had been recorded since 1790, nor would the current level of customs incomes be necessarily upheld. However, such a tariff would serve as "a spring for the animation of the national economy [narodnoe khozaistvo]."[16] Rumiantsev's proposal was a clear departure from the fiscally motivated tariff policies of 18th century mercantilism, which he dismissed as a "rich and ready branch of state revenue [...] inherent to decrepit and declining states."[17] He embraced the basic premises of liberal trade, albeit adjusted to the specific situation of the Russian Empire and enriched by protectionist elements.

2.3 The Continental Blockade and Russia's Trade Policies on its "European" borders

The new regency of Alexander I promised fundamental reforms to the customs policies of the Russian Empire on both its European and its Asiatic borders. However, the new beginnings were soon halted by foreign policy considerations. Between 1806 and 1814, Napoleon I's Continental Blockade shaped trade in Europe and constituted an "important 'bridge era' between the prosperous but bitterly competitive eighteenth-century mercantile economy and the instability of rapidly shifting markets, mechanization, consumer demand and calls for free trade in the first half of the nineteenth century."[18] For the Russian Empire's economy, joining the Continental Blockade under the 1807 Treaties of Tilsit had become a watershed moment. Great Britain had been its main trading partner and could not simply be replaced by more exchange of goods with France. Most of Russia's bulk export goods could not be shipped via land economically, whereas Britain's naval domination blocked the sea route. Eventually, the loss of British trade sent the ruble rate downward,

15 Ibid. 376–377.

16 Ibid. 379.

17 Ibid. 369.

18 *Aaslestad, Katherine B.*: Introduction. Revisiting Napoleon's Continental System. Consequences of Economic Warfare. In: *Aaslestad, Katherine B./Joor, Johan* (eds.): Revisiting Napoleon's Continental System. Local, Regional and European Experiences. Houndsmill, Basingstoke 2015, 1–22, here 2.

brought the Russian economy into a deep crisis, and plummeting customs revenues aggravated Russia's budgetary crisis.[19]

By 1810, the Russian government began to extricate itself from the restrictions of the Continental Blockade and undertook steps to stabilize its currency by adjusting trade regulations. While France had not proven to be a suitable outlet market for Russian bulk products under the circumstances of the Continental Blockade, it was a significant source of imports that contributed to Russia's negative trade balance and the weakness of the ruble. Thus, the Economic Department suggested a comprehensive program to correct the balance of trade. The new 1811 tariff, prepared by Mikhail Speranskii and implemented unusually quickly, practically banned the import of foreign goods into Russia and particularly penalized luxury goods, many of which were of French origin.[20]

Further, regulations for "neutral shipping" were reviewed, so as to make clearance procedures quicker and simpler for neutral vessels. The "neutral committees", installed to monitor compliance with Continental Blockade regulations, were criticized for their slowness in verifying vessels' neutral status. Under the new regulations, this decision could be made by Russian customs services on the spot, less documentation was required, and the nationality of a ship's crew was not inquired anymore. The new regulations formally upheld the Continental Blockade of England, however, the French government suspected them to be a backdoor to smuggling. It is hard to gauge in how far such accusations were justified, but numerous cases of dubious or sub-standard inspections of ships' neutrality are documented, and a large increase in transit goods from Russia into Western Europe has been recorded. Although Alexander I attempted to appease Napoleon's discontent, Russia's new trade policies contributed to the souring of relations, soon to turn into military confrontation.[21]

Both joining the Continental Blockade and the prohibitionist tariff of 1811 constituted significant departures from the economic agenda formulated in the early years of Alexander I's reign. Issuing the 1811 tariff, the Tsar accounted for this by supplementing the new regulations with a manifesto conjuring up the population's willingness to suffer under the expected price increases. He emphasized the exceptionality of the measure, as "under normal trade conditions prices of goods are set solely by their consumption [potrebnost']",

19 *Tchoudinov, Alexandre*: Russia and the Continental System: Trends in Russian Historiography. In: *Aaslestad, Katherine B./Joor, Johan* (eds.): Revisiting Napoleon's Continental System. Local, Regional and European Experiences. Houndsmill, Basingstoke 2015, 56–68, here 57–60, 62–63.

20 *Zlotnikov*: Kontinental'naia blokada i Rossiia, 226–235.

21 Ibid. 244–252.

and "We consider any constraint of this against the true logic [razumu] of a well-established [blagoustroennaia] governmental economy."[22]

The tumultuous foreign policy situation decisively shaped the Russian Empire's customs policy on its European border in the first two decades of the 19th century. The reordering of Europe at the Vienna Congress of 1815 promised a return to stability that would allow a more autonomous trade policy as well. Russia's first post-war "European" tariff of 1816, however, was still markedly prohibitionist, as the empire was struggling to repair its state finances. Nevertheless, projects dating from before the Continental Blockade and the Patriotic War soon received a new impetus, most visibly with the declaration of Odessa as porto-franco.

The idea to strengthen the port city's position as a transit hub had already been put forward by the Duke of Richelieu in 1806, but was protracted by the foreign political situation. After the Vienna Congress, it was returned on the agenda, and by 1817 Odessa was declared a free-port, becoming fully operational by 1819. In the same year, the "European" tariff also received a major revision, departing from the prohibitionist beginnings of the 1816 tariff and introducing one of the lowest and most liberal tariffs of 19th century Russia. It allowed the import of almost all foreign goods into the Russian Empire, doing away with the restrictive wartime bans.[23] Further, the highly privileged Transcaucasian transit route had been established in 1821, carrying on the spirit of Rumiantsev's 1802 agenda for fostering transit trade.[24]

However, this short respite from protectionist policy ended quickly. The tariff of 1819 was broadly criticized for undermining Russia's manufacturing industries by letting in cheap foreign produce, while other states themselves did not pursue free-trade policies. Despite his generally liberal outlook, Minister of Finance Dmitrii Aleksandrovich Gur'ev had to concede to the necessity of re-introducing import bans.[25] The short-lived free-trade intermezzo was renounced with the issuing of the 1822 tariff, which returned the Russian Empire on a strictly protectionist course, a turn embodied by the new Minister of Finance, Egor Kankrin, appointed in 1823 and remaining in this post until 1844. Under his auspices, the "European" tariff would be revised every few years, but the general protectionist outlook was maintained. Customs constituted one of the main tax revenues necessary to balance the fragile state

22 Polnoe sobranie zakonov Rossiikoi Imperii s 1649 goda. 1810–1811. Volume 31. Saint Petersburg 1830, no. 24464.

23 *Kislovskii*: Istoriia tamozhennogo dela, 189–190.

24 See chapter 6.

25 *Strakhova, Natalia P.*: Rossiiskii tamozhennyi tarif 1822 goda. In: Vestnik Volgogradskogo gosudarstvennogo universiteta. Seriia 4: Istoriia. Regionovedenie. Mezhdunarodnye otnosheniia, 11 (2006), 15–22, here 15–19.

budget, as Kankrin was "determined to avoid any inflationary measures."[26] The maintenance of a positive trade balance contributed to the stabilization of the ruble, eventually enabling the monetary reform of 1839.[27]

Throughout the first two decades of the 19th century, customs policies on the Russian Empire's "European" borders fluctuated significantly. New liberal economic ideas of free trade received upwind under Alexander I; however, the foreign political situation precluded their implementation. The post-1815 period was marked by an overlap of protectionist measures to stabilize state finances and a return to earlier free-trade-inspired projects. Ultimately, the on-going financial crisis and the reaction to other states' protectionist policies brought about a clear break with liberal trade ideas in the 1820s and turned Russia's western border into a protectionist bulwark. On the empire's south-eastern borders, however, neither the Continental Blockade, nor protectionist considerations played a major role, and thus trade policy there developed with less interruptions and in a distinctly different way.

2.4 New Departures in "Asiatic Trade" under Alexander I and the "Asiatic tariff" of 1817

The protectionist considerations, which Rumiantsev pointed out in his 1802 program, played only a minor role on the south-eastern borders. Asiatic-manufactured goods were not considered to be in direct competition with Russian-manufactured goods. Rumiantsev's primary agenda for Asiatic trade was the increase of trade volume by simplifying customs procedures and by developing Russia's role as a trade intermediary with routes through the Caspian Sea, Orenburg and Troitsk, as well as from the Irtysh river heading towards Tashkent. These routes, Rumiantsev hoped, would allow a link up to the trade hub of Bukhara and thus unlock the "gates to Persia and Northern India, and on the other side to Tibet, Kashgar and Kashmir, reaching into China."[28]

First steps towards intensifying trade on the south-eastern border and developing Russia's future role as a transit link between Europe and Asia were

26 *Pintner, Walter M.*: Government and Industry during the Ministry of Count Kankrin, 1823–1844. In: Slavic Review, 23(1) (1964), 45–62, 58–60.

27 The reform, often labeled "Kankrin reform", was engineered primarily by Mikhail Speransky, see: *Sheptun, Alla*: Russian Monetary Reformers: Speransky, Mordvinov and Bunge. In: *Barnett, Vincent/Zweynert, Joachim* (eds.): Economics in Russia: Studies in Intellectual History. Abingdon 2016, 41–56, 42–45.

28 Cit. *Khalfin, Naftula A.*: Rossiia i khanstva Srednei Azii. Moscow 1974, 33–34.

Figure 1: Map of Steppe customs stations and Central Asian khanates.

taken in 1803. By increasing the number of customs stations, new trade routes into the Russian Empire were opened. Prior, Orenburg and Troitsk had been the only customs stations on the steppe border with the rights to clear caravans and conduct large-scale trade operations. The next customs border station was Kiakhta, located 3000km eastwards by a direct line, which regulated trade with China. Incoming caravans that followed through the eastern part of the steppe in the direction of the Irtysh river would have thus been forced to take long detours to declare goods. In order to tap into existing trade currents in the Kirghiz steppe, particularly towards Tashkent, and link them to the internal fairs in Irbit and Eniseisk, it was suggested to grant customs stations on the Irtysh river in Western Siberia broader competences.[29] Rather than drafting up new provisions, the existing clearing rights and regulations of the Orenburg station were taken as a model and simply extended to the Bukhtarma customs station first and soon to the Petropavlovsk and Semipalatinsk stations as well.[30]

29 *Ekspeditsiia zagotovleniia gosudarstvennykh bumag*: Ministerstvo Finansov, 128–129.

30 Polnoe sobranie zakonov Rossiikoi Imperii s 1649 goda. 1802–1803. Volume 27. Saint Petersburg 1830, no. 20739 and no. 20821.

Simultaneously, the Russian Empire had made significant territorial gains on its Caucasian border, and as early as 1803 the regulations of the Astrakhan tariff were extended to the newly annexed Georgian territories of the Russian Empire. However, unresolved border demarcation with Persia and the persistence of rented-out *rakhdar* fees, levied by local potentates, complicated the implementation. By 1807, the measure was deemed premature and imperial customs scrapped altogether in the Georgian territories.[31]

Both above measures demonstrated a willingness in governmental circles to restructure trade on the south-eastern borders however, the traditional separation between customs regulations tailored to Steppe trade and those to Caspian Sea trade was still maintained. Rumiantsev's vision to turn the Russian Empire into a trade intermediary between Europe and Asia, outlined in his 1804 "Zapiska Ministra kommercii o razume tarifa" (Note of the Minister of Commerce on the Reasoning of the Tariff), however, would require fundamental changes to the existing system of trade regulation:

> Apart from the existing transit between Odessa and Radzivilov I envision the possibility of the same trade: 1) between the Black and the Caspian Sea, by which the Levante will be connected to Persia, India and Bukhara, and this region, by an interlinked chain with the Baltic sea; 2) by thus receiving goods through the Caspian Sea and transferring them to Orenburg or further to the Ishim line [Ishimskuiu liniu] and reciprocally from there as well, the riches of Bukhara, Tashkent, Tibet and China can be connected through Russian confines. The benefit from this flow [pereliv] is, that the goods, by passing through the interior of the state, will disseminate on their way traces of unprecedented profits.[32]

Facilitating trade across such vast spaces required major revisions of the complicated old tariffs and regulations with which Kamerger Aleksei Vasil'evich Vasil'chikov and State Councilor Nikolai Petrovich Lobri had been tasked. In 1804, they presented a project departing from the traditional separation of Steppe and Caspian Sea trade, suggesting equalizing the tariffs on the Astrakhan and Orenburg lines. Primarily, this implied a lowering of the Astrakhan tariff, which had significantly higher rates; the project thus pushed towards a more uniform management on the south-eastern border. This proposal anticipated the later differentiation between a "European" and an "Asiatic" system of trade regulations, formally introduced in 1817. Further, tariff rates were to be lowered across all product ranges, while the import of Asiatic raw materials

31 RGIA, f. 560, op. 45, d. 76, "Ob inostrannom tranzite cherez Zakavkaz'e v Persiiu", l. 84–85; RGIA, f. 40, op. 1, d. 31, "Vysochaishe utverzhdennyi Zhurnal Osobogo komiteta po voprosu o Zakavkazskom tranzite ot 19 aprelia 1879g.", l. 140. See also chapter 6.

32 *Rumiantsev*: O razume tarifa, 378.

and goods necessary for the Russian manufacturing industries, such as silk, cotton, and wool, as well as the export of Russian-manufactured goods, was to be freed from duties altogether.[33] Fiscal concerns, which had been a priority on the south-eastern border in the 18th century, moved into the background, as only little customs revenue could be expected from the remaining set of goods still subject to duties. With the removal of import duties on the main bulk of goods, the project also departed from the mercantilist preoccupation with maintaining a positive trade balance – at least for the Asiatic border section – as no equivalent volume of exports could be expected in the near future.

Further, Vasil'chikov and Lobri suggested transitioning the process of customs collection from the ad valorem principle to the specific rate principle, which would make levying duties easier and quicker in practice.[34] The latter system is based on a specific predefined sum of duties, which are levied per unit of quantity. Thus, it does not take into account price fluctuation, and does not require an estimation of dutiable goods' value by an official on the spot. The ad valorem principle, on the other hand, was more intricate to apply and came with inherent complications, as pointed out in Rumiantsev's commentary to the project. To function correctly and maintain a correct percentage of customs, ensuring the comparability of customs rates to the general tariff, price estimations had to be adjusted regularly and expertise in assessing the value was required.

In the case of Astrakhan, real prices and estimations had already drifted apart dramatically in the late 18th century and distorted the percentage and sum total of customs collected. By 1804, the valid Astrakhan tariff appeared to have impressively high customs rates of 26 % for imports and 27 % for export goods. However, these rates were still based on 50-year-old price valuations from 1754. If converted to the real prices of 1804, the actual rates were closer to 8 ⅓ % and 12 ½% respectively.[35] Thus, Rumiantsev's suggestion to set the new import tariffs to 7 % and export tariffs to 4 % appeared to be a drastic reduction only at first glance. First and foremost, the case demonstrated the difficulty of comparing the general tariff and the old Astrakhan tariff caused by neglecting it for five decades. It is an inherent problem of the ad valorem system that it requires regular, accurate price estimations and profound product knowledge. The specific rate system, on the other hand, is more transparent, makes for easier comparisons of tariff rates, and requires nothing of the customs clerk but to weigh the goods and multiply the result with a predefined rate. For Rumiantsev's plans to intensify Asiatic trade, it was paramount to simplify

33 *Rumiantsev*: Razum proektov Astrakhanskogo i Orenburgskogo tarifov, 385–387.

34 Ibid. 385–387.

35 Ibid. 385–389.

transactions as much as possible, limiting both administrative costs and friction losses during trade transactions.

Trade on the Asiatic border was further complicated by a layer of additional fees, which were not part of the main tariff, but had accumulated through supplementary regulations over time. These included fees for the alimentation of the Persian consul in Astrakhan or additional 10 % duties which were not part of the *tariff*, but added later through the backdoor, by including them in the regulatory framework – the *ustav*. Navigating through this thicket of dues required higher administrative efforts, slowed down trade transactions, obscured the actual level of customs rates, and ultimately deterred merchants. In the new spirit of Asiatic trade, Rumiantsev dismissed these fees as "ancient [starinnye]" and suggested disposing of them so that the "stamp of uniformity will be applied to the whole body of the customs administration."[36]

Rumiantsev's proposal marked a new quality in trade and space management on the south-eastern border. He suggested to do away with the piecemeal fashion in which trade regulations on the south-eastern border had grown and conceptualized it as one economic space which required fundamentally new and uniform regulations. Without explicitly labeling it as such, he anticipated many of the provisions of the "Asiatic tariff" introduced in 1817.

The proposed measures aimed at a maximum simplification of the process of customs collection with lower overall fees and a duty-free regime for the circulation of raw-materials from the neighboring Asiatic territories and manufactured goods from Russia. The remaining products were to receive lower tariff stakes, so as to suit "trading peoples, who should be attracted by the modesty [of the tariff] and the poor [skudnye], who are not able to pay."[37] Rumiantsev acknowledged that the underlying principle deviated from the approach formulated for European trade with its protectionist provisions, but concluded that "different trade requires different fees."[38] Further, for trade on the south-eastern border, fiscal loss was not only anticipated but also easily swallowed, as the sum total of customs revenues on the Astrakhan and Orenburg sections was only marginal to the overall state income. The total fees collected on this vast border in 1803 constituted 324.000 rubles.[39] In comparison, Saint Petersburg customs alone collected up to 535.000 rubles annually.[40]

36 Ibid. 388.
37 Ibid. 388.
38 Ibid. 388.
39 Ibid. 388.
40 O dokhodakh i raskhodakh S.-Peterburgskoi stolitsy. In: ibid Arkhiv Gosudarstvennogo Soveta. Tom 3. Chast' 1. Saint Petersburg 1878, 142–144, here 142.

The ambitious program, however, soon faded into the background against the larger foreign political situation and the quickly deteriorating economic situation of the Russian Empire under the Continental Blockade. Thus, the propositions made by Vasil'chikov and Lobri were not implemented. However, unlike on the "European" border, trade on the "Asiatic" border was neither affected by international treaties, nor by fluctuating political-economic trends, and simply remained unchanged. While the 1810 tariff, with which the Russian Empire attempted to extricate itself from the restrictions of the Continental Blockade, equated to a prohibitionist import ban, later followed by the liberal 1819 tariff and eventually zig-zagging back to high protectionism in the 1820s, the restructuring of "Asiatic" trade simply picked up where it had left off.

In 1811 Mikhail Fedorovich Verigin, Governor of Orenburg, had been appointed "Head of Asiatic customs", a new office indicating the trend towards the unification in the customs management on the south-eastern border. Minister of Finance Dmitrii Aleksandrovich Gur'ev provided him with an initial instruction spelling out the contemporary governmental outlook on Asiatic trade:

> 1. The importance of Asiatic trade, particularly that conducted through the Caspian Sea and the Orenburg line, always attracted the government's special attention and thus its expansion and its facilitation [oblegchenie] by removing all restraints to trade relations with the neighboring peoples populating the interior of Asia, constitutes the main goal of your appointment. 2. Difficulties in the Asiatic trade can stem from two reasons. First: When the issued rules for the conduct of trade with such diverse peoples are not in accordance with their education [prosveshchenie], customs, habits and laws, and thus oppose a big vitalization of trade relations. Second: when the indulgence of the local administration allows for abuses [zloupotrebleniia] and weaknesses [pristrastiia] of various kinds, against the issued rules, to creep in in customs stations [tamozhni] and crossing points [zastavy] in which trade is conducted.[41]

After being initially rejected by the State Council, a new reworked *tarif* and *ustav* were introduced in 1817, which replaced the former Astrakhan and Orenburg tariffs of 1754 and 1777, respectively. The body of regulations was intended to be universally valid along the empire's south-eastern border, with the exception of the Chinese border, furthermore governed by the Kiakhta treaty.

It was referred to as "Asiatic" *tarif* and *ustav*, and thus for the first time introduced the systemic distinction between "European" and "Asiatic" regulations, which continued to exist into the 1900s. The new tariff allowed duty-free imports of raw materials, with semi-finished products being taxed as low

41 Cit. *Khalfin*: Rossiia i khanstva Srednei Azii, 28.

as 2%. Only manufactured goods and luxury goods received customs rates between 10% and 25%, accommodating protectionist provisions. The export of Russian products received a flat rate of 1%. The multitude of additional payments and fees, which had accumulated over time, were removed as well, only leaving quarantine and port fees in place.[42]

The protectionist 1816 "European" tariff had been an obvious breach with the new beginnings in trade policy proclaimed at the beginning of Alexander I's reign. On the contrary, the new "Asiatic" tariff implemented many provisions spelled out 15 years earlier. Customs rates were set low enough to increase trade turnover and trade regulations were simplified, also establishing regulatory uniformity across the south-eastern border.

The 1817 reform also marked the Russian Empire's second attempt at introducing imperial customs in its Transcaucasian territories. However, the new "Asiatic" regulations were introduced for Baku only. Tiflis received its own "Georgian tariff", thus creating an exception while conducting a unifying measure. In any case, the "Asiatic tariff" did not remain valid in the Transcaucasus for long, as it was superseded by the broad trade privileges granted to the region in 1821.[43] The Turkmanchai treaty of 1828 and its corresponding trade treaty further fixed the bidirectional customs fees on the Russian-Persian border to 5%, supplanting the "Asiatic tariff" by a bilateral agreement.[44] Thus, after only four years, the new regulations, which were intended to unify "Asiatic" trade, were merely valid for the Astrakhan and Orenburg sections. Nevertheless, they were considered the new standard against which deviant regimes such as the Transcaucasian transit were measured thenceforth and acquired importance as points of reference.[45]

The regency of Alexander I had given impetus to the reform of trade on the Russian Empire's south-eastern border. Fiscal income and the achievement of a positive trade balance, so important to 18th century mercantilism, took a backseat in favor of trade intensification on this border section. In order to incentivize trade relations, customs procedures were simplified and fees and duties lowered overall. The instruments selected made trade with the Russian Empire more profitable, thus attracting foreign merchants. At the same time, the simplified procedures allowed for a minimum of administrative expenditures, yet maintained the customs border's function of excluding foreign merchants from trading within the Russian Empire. The reform efforts

42 *Ekspeditsiia zagotovleniia gosudarstvennykh bumag*: Ministerstvo Finansov 148–149.

43 RGIA, f. 560, op. 45, d. 76, l. 84–85. See also chapter 6.

44 Polnoe sobranie zakonov Rossiikoi Imperii s 1649 goda. 1689–1699. Volume 3. Saint Petersburg 1830, no. 1795.

45 RGIA, f. 560, op. 45, d. 76, l. 84–85.

introduced a new quality to the conceptualization of the many special customs regimes introduced on the various sections of the empire's south-eastern border. They were now regarded in conjunction with one another, transitioning from a bunch of deviant regimes towards a distinct system of "Asiatic trade." This system was first codified with the 1817 "Asiatic" *tarif* and *ustav*, which constituted a parallel standard to "European" customs and trade regulations. Whereas the latter fluctuated frequently and were subject to both foreign relations and politico-economic trends, "Asiatic" regulations developed more consistently. The direction taken with the 1817 reform was carried on throughout the 1820s and 1830s, with further deregulation that aimed at intensifying trade on the steppe border. As the Russian Empire expanded militarily into the steppe, the relevance and function of a customs border drifting further into the interior came under increased scrutiny.

2.5 The Steppe Conquest and Trade Deregulation

The Russian Empire's engagement with the Kazakh steppe dates back to the 16th century; however, initially limited efforts were invested, as the advancement into Siberia and its fur trade were of paramount interest throughout the 16th and 17th centuries.[46] It was not until the early 18th century that the Russian Empire began to show serious interest in its south-eastern boundaries and fortified lines were erected. The creation of the Irtysh line had begun under Peter I with the construction of the fortresses of Omsk (1717), Semipalatinsk (1718) and Ust'-Kamenogorsk (1720) and was completed in 1752. West of it, the fortified line of Orenburg was begun in the 1730s and stretched from Gur'ev on the Caspian Sea through Orenburg to Troitsk. It was completed under Orenburg Governor Ivan Ivanovich Nepliuev (1744–1758). Both lines were eventually linked by the Uisk line in 1739, establishing a continuous fortified frontier. The Small and Middle Hordes beyond these lines had sworn loyalty to the Russian Empire in the 1730s and 1740s, however, their territories were not considered to have been annexed and were depicted as being beyond the empire's border on 18th century maps.[47] Nevertheless, the Russian Empire exerted significant indirect influence beyond its borders by forging alliances with local khans and meddling with power constellations.[48] By the 19th century, however, "the internal rule of the khans had all but disintegrated" and

46 *Olcott*: The Kazakhs, 28.
47 Ibid. 30–33.
48 See for this ibid. 31–53.

raids on caravans posed an increasing danger to Russia's trade to the steppe and beyond, to the Central Asian khanates and Persia.[49]

The destabilized situation led to a number of Russian military missions into the steppe throughout the 1820s and 1830s and the creation of new military outposts further south. This new push found its preliminary peak with the military expedition of Orenburg Governor-general Perovskii against the Khanate of Khiva in 1839. What promised to be an easy victory against a weak enemy ended in an embarrassing defeat and set off the creation of two new fortified lines: one running from Lake Aral along the Syr-Darya river and the other southward from Semipalatinsk.[50] By 1853, Fort No.1 in Kazalinsk, Fort No.2 in Karmakchi, and Fort Perovskii, prior known as Ak-Mechet, marked the new southern frontier of Russia's militarily controlled territory. The customs line, however, continued to run along the old Orenburg and Irtysh fortified lines, thus gradually drifting into the interior.

For the better part of this expansion period, Egor Kankrin had served as Minister of Finance (1823–1844). His tenure marked the rollback from the last remaining free-trade ideas introduced by the 1819 tariff and quickly set the course for a highly protectionist tariff policy on the European border. Customs were to serve as an instrument to stabilize the ruble, as they both allowed to regulate the outflow of metal currencies securing the Russian assignats, and to regulate export and import, thus ensuring a positive trade balance. However, on the empire's south-eastern border, his policies were diametrically opposed to this restrictive approach and continued the deregulatory measures of the 1810s.

Trade on the steppe border during the 18th century had been legally restricted to Orenburg and Troitsk and the export of metallic currency had been prohibited, thus creating a framework allowing for barter trade only.[51] In the 1820s, this mercantilist logic had been dismissed for the south-eastern border, and both restrictions had been lifted to intensify trade contacts. In 1826, Asiatic merchants were granted the right to conduct wholesale trade on Russia's internal fairs within the period of one year without paying guild fees. If they wished to extend this period, they had to pay the same guild fee as Russian merchants.[52] This arrangement put foreign-subject merchants in a beneficial position vis-a-vis their Russian-subject counterparts interested in conducting trade with the khanates. Four years later, the prohibition on exporting metallic currencies on the south-eastern border had been overturned as well.[53] In

49 Ibid. 57–58.
50 Ibid. 72–73.
51 *Solonchenko*: Tamozhennaia politika na iugo-vostoke Rossii, 65–68.
52 Ibid. 72.
53 Ibid. 75–76.

conjunction, these two measures opened up the potential for an explicitly negative trade balance on the steppe border, with foreign merchants selling their products on Russia's internal fairs in exchange for metallic currency without exporting Russian goods for the equivalent sum.

The underlying rationale of the Ministry of Finance was to make trading with the Russian Empire more attractive for merchants from the Central Asian khanates, and thus create a stable channel for the export of Russian-manufactured products. The goal was to increase the total export of Russian-manufactured goods and gain access to the markets of the Central Asian khanates and beyond, even if this meant an excess of imports and the acceptance of a negative trade balance. It was a continuation of the policies introduced in the previous decade, which aimed to intensify trade on the south-eastern border by making it more attractive through the simplification of regulations and the reduction of trade fees. The importance attributed to trade intensification becomes evident in the debates surrounding the unequal trade conditions under which Russian subjects involved in trade with the Central Asian khanates and foreign merchants – referred to as "Asiatic" – operated.

The latter's exemption from trade fees on Russia's internal fairs had not escaped the attention of Russian-subject merchants. The 1836 visit of the Bukharan envoy Kurbanbek Ashurbekov to Orenburg presented the Orenburg merchantry with a welcome opportunity to voice their complaints, passed on to the Asiatic Committee by Orenburg Military Governor Perovskii in March 1837. The merchants claimed that while trade fees for local Muslims in Bukhara accounted for 10 percent, non-Muslim Russian subjects faced trade fees of 40 percent when trading in the Khnanate of Bukhara.[54] The fourfold divergence might well have been an exaggeration on the side of the petitioners, but they clearly were in a disadvantaged position trading in the khanates. The ziaket fee collected in marketplaces and caravanserais was indeed 2,5 % for Muslims and doubled for non-Muslims. Further, the rift between total trade fees might have stemmed from additional fees or the lack of local knowledge and networks in conducting trade. The Orenburg merchants further complained about arbitrary price estimates on which their taxation was based. Meanwhile, merchants from the khanates enjoyed privileges trading within Russia introduced in the 1820s.

The Orenburg merchantry demanded not only to equalize trade fees and introduce a Russian consular representation in Bukhara, but also to re-introduce the prohibition for Asiatic merchants to trade on Russia's internal fairs.[55] This new trope of unequal treatment of Russian and non-Russian subjects,

54 *Khalfin*: Rossiia i khanstva Srednei Azii, 256–258.
55 Ibid. 259.

introduced here, persisted well through the 1870s, without much being done about the situation. Only in the climate of growing national sentiment in the 1880s did Russian officials begin to seriously problematize the loss of prestige of Russian subjecthood conveyed by the disadvantageous trade rights of Russian subjects. Ultimately, they sought a solution by integrating the autonomous Bukhara into Russian customs territory and thus equalizing all trade rights.[56]

Though the Minister of Finance accepted the desirability of some of the demands, his verdict was that little could be done. The "main goal of Asiatic trade should be the sale [sbyt] of our products [proizvedenii]", Kankrin reasoned, which was best facilitated by "Asiatic" merchants, as Russian merchants were subject to constraints in the khanates. He was pessimistic that anything could be done about these, as the principles of trade taxation were religion-based. Meanwhile, prohibiting "Asiatic" merchants from trading within Russia would have given a trade monopoly to Orenburg merchants, who lacked the capacity to conduct trade on the necessary scale.[57] Kankrin prioritized unobstructed trade flow, the increase of trade volume, and thus the ability to export more Russian goods to the Central Asian khanates. The price he was willing to pay was accepting both a negative trade balance and the discontent of Russian-subject merchants.

These policies were diametrically opposed to his prohibitionist agenda on the empire's western border. There, the Russian Empire bordered with European empires that shared the same baseline understanding of trade regulations and reacted in predictable ways to changes in Russia's trade policies. On its south-eastern border, Kankrin accepted the otherness of trade practices in the khanates as an invariable factor. If little could be done to change the situation of Russian merchants in the khanates, then it would be in the empire's best interest to increase trade turnover by improving trade conditions for foreign merchants in Russia.

The measures quickly began to take hold, with both the total trade turnover and the exports on Russia's steppe border consistently growing since the second half of the 1820s (see Graphic 1). The share of manufactured goods in Russia's eastern exports also grew from 27 % in 1825 to about 60 % in the 1840s, somewhat substantiating the hopes set in the new markets.[58] However, the trade balance developed as predicted, and throughout the 1820s to the mid-1860s imports on the steppe border clearly exceeded Russian exports (see Graphic 2).

56 See chapter 3.

57 *Khalfin*: Rossiia i khanstva Srednei Azii, 259

58 *Sokolov, A.Ia.*: Torgovaia politika Rossii v Srednei Azii i razvitie Russko-Afganskikh torgovykh otnoshenii. Tashkent 1971, 46.

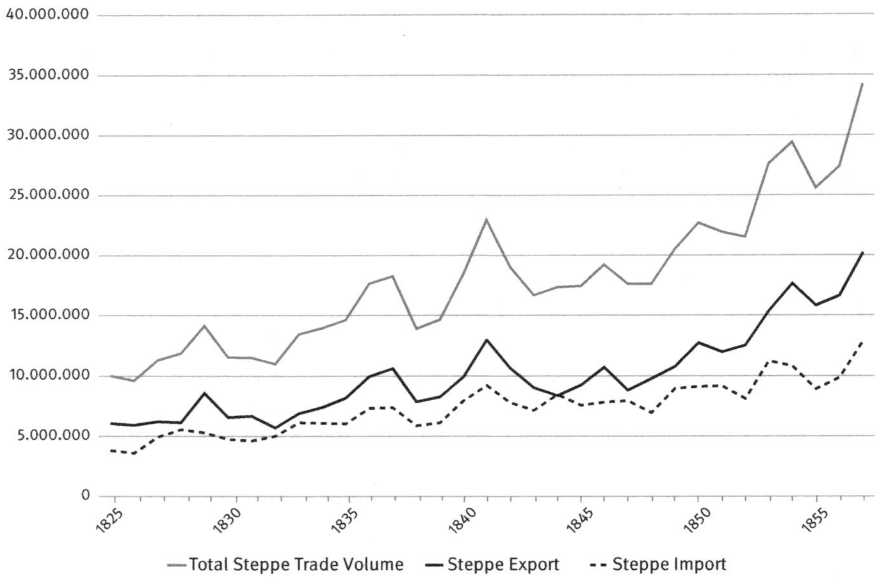

Graphic 1: Total volume of steppe trade (1825–1857) subdivided into import and export volume.[59]

With the exception of few customs stations in very remote regions such as Arkhangel'sk, most customs stations on the European border recorded a positive trade balance, in line with Kankrin's policy of strengthening the ruble. Meanwhile, on the south-eastern border the situation was inverted, as almost all customs stations recorded a negative balance of imports versus exports.[60] Graphic 2 draws a comparison between the all-imperial trade balance and the trade balance on the steppe border. With the value 1.0 signifying a balanced proportion of exports to imports, it becomes clear that the all-imperial trade balance was consistently balanced or positive, with the exception of the Crimean war years. Meanwhile, trade balance on the steppe border was negative throughout. Even more so when adjusted for the export of metallic currency, allowed since 1830, which was listed separately in "Gosudarstvennaia vneshniia torgovlia v raznykh ee vidakh" (The National Foreign Trade in

59 Data extracted from the annual reports of the Ministry of Finance, which were published under the name of "Gosudarstvennaia vneshniia torgovlia v raznykh ee vidakh" (The State's Foreign Trade in various views) and later as "Vidy vneshnnei torgovli Rossii" (Views on Russia's Foreign Trade).

60 The ministerial surveys listed all customs stations and their respective profitability; for an example see Gosudarstvennaia vneshniaia torgovlia v raznykh ee vidakh za 1859 god. Saint Petersburg 1860, section II.

its Various views) but included in the total exports value by the Ministry of Finance's statisticians. This allowed somewhat to sugarcoat the negative trade balance; a practice which was criticized from the periphery by Orenburg Governor-general Perovskii, as it obscured the actual balance of trade, as the value became increasingly distorted since 1838.[61]

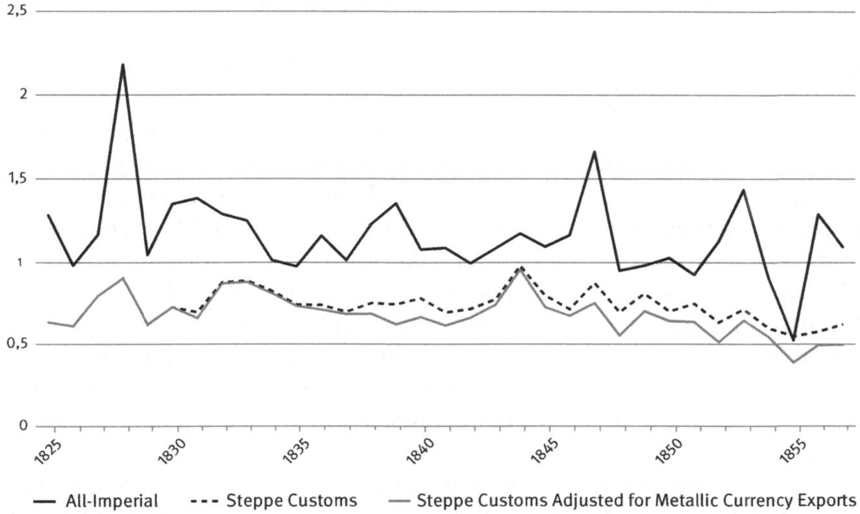

Graphic 2: Proportion of exports to imports in the Russian Empire and on the Steppe customs border (1825–1857).[62]

Nevertheless, the impact on the overall trade balance was tolerable, as the overall share of exports on the Asiatic border, including the Transcaucasian section, never exceeded 11,9 % –the only exception being the Crimean War years – of the Russian Empire's total exports.[63]

Through deregulation and incentivization of trade, the goal of increasing trade volume was achieved, and the steppe territories and the Central Asia khanates were drawn closer economically to the Russian Empire. Russian merchants increasingly used Kazakh middlemen as proxies to conduct trade with the khanates, who, being Muslims, were not subject to higher fees in the khanates.[64] The Russian Empire's military outreach into the steppe and the establishment of outposts also improved the safety of caravan routes, a

61 *Khalfin*: Rossiia i khanstva Srednei Azii, 188.

62 Data extracted from the annual reports of the Ministry of Finance.

63 *Rozhkova, Mariia K.*: Ekonomicheskie sviazi Rossii so Srednei Aziei, 40–60-e gody 19. veka. Moscow 1963, 56–57.

64 Ibid. 42.

long-standing issue already addressed by Rumiantsev, who in 1803 had suggested the assignment of Cossack troops to convoy caravans, splitting the costs with the merchants, but ultimately never solved the issue to satisfaction.[65]

Despite these achievements, the issue of unequal trade conditions remained a major point of contention as the Russian Empire expanded its influence over the steppe, transitioning from single outposts to the creation of a continuous fortified line along the Syr-Darya river in the 1850s. Once again, the critique came from the Orenburg Governor-general Perovskii, backed by Vasilii Vasil'evich Grigor'ev, Head of the Frontier Expedition (Nachal'nik pogranichnoi ekspeditsii), in two reports from 1856. Grigor'ev argued that it was time to enforce equal trade rights and, if necessary, to do so by applying pressure on merchants from Bukhara, Kokand and Khiva, inciting them to protest as they "very well understand that it is not Russia that requires trade with Central Asia, but Central Asia that requires trade with Russia."[66] The situation was undesirable, both the Ministry of Foreign Affairs and the Ministry of Finance agreed, however, they did not share Grigor'ev's bold claim about the ease with which the Russian Empire could surrender Central Asian markets. The Ministry of Foreign Affairs feared that a prohibition for Asiatic merchants to trade within the Russian Empire could lead to a rupture of relations with the Central Asian khanates.[67]

The late 1850s were characterized by an increased perception of competition between Russia and Great Britain, retrospectively and quite ineptly labeled "The Great Game." Newer scholarly literature persuasively argued that "cotton hunger" and the conquest of new markets were not the decisive driving factors for the conquest of the Central Asian khanates in the 1860s.[68] Nevertheless, the fear of missing out in a global race for markets, paired with a wide-spread sense of industrial inferiority, did play a role and put the Russian Empire's diplomats on the back foot with regards to the equalization of trade rights. In an 1857 correspondence with Foreign Minister Aleksandr Mikhailovich Gorchakov, Colonel Nikolai Pavlovich Ignat'ev argued that Central Asia "was the only field left for our trade activities and that the development of our industry is too weak to enter into a successful competition with Britain, France, Belgium, America and other states."[69] One year later, he embarked on a diplomatic mission to the khanates of Khiva and Bukhara. Inquiring whether he could use the withdrawal of trade privileges for the local merchants as a bargaining

65 Polnoe sobranie zakonov s 1649 goda. Vol 27, no. 20821.

66 *Khalfin*: Rossiia i khanstva Srednei Azii, 362–363.

67 Ibid. 365.

68 *Morrison, Alexander*: 'Nechto Eroticheskoe', 'Courir Après L'ombre'? – Logistical Imperatives and the Fall of Tashkent, 1859–1865. In: Central Asian Survey, 33(2) (2014), 153–169, 155.

69 Cit. *Khalfin*: Rossiia i khanstva Srednei Azii, 370.

chip, he was warned by Gorchakov of uttering "a clear threat, which we could not fulfill without harm to our own trade."[70] Eventually, no privileges were withdrawn at all, but rather expanded as a sign of good-will instead.[71]

After the return of Ignat'ev's mission, the Ministry of Foreign Affairs coordinated with the Ministry of Finance which further privileges could be granted to Bukharan merchants. Minister of Finance Kniazhevich argued that while the import of cotton and raw silk was already duty-free, it was still subject to a quarantine fee, which could be removed along with the 1 % added-fee on Russian exports. The suggestions were put into law in 1859 and continued the logic of trade expansion through deregulation, as Kniazhevich pointed out that the expected increase in trade turnover would be to the benefit of both states.[72]

Unlike previous privileges, this was not a universally valid adjustment to the tariff but a bilateral agreement. However, Russian customs had no provisions to verify the origin of imported goods or the actual destination of exports. Soon rumors spread that goods from other khanates were falsely declared as originating from Bukhara to avoid the quarantine fees, and Bukhara was specified as the destination for most export goods, in order to circumvent the 1 %-export fee. A newspaper article from the "Orenburgskie gubernskie vedomosti" (Orenburg Gubernia News) making these claims suggested extending the privileges to all khanates, so as to avoid that "the regulations on dues and quarantine fees become a pure formality" and pursue a "general liberation of this trade from restraints and barriers inhibiting its development."[73] Regardless of the validity of these rumors, this could only be a minor concern to the Ministry of Finance, as the de-facto deregulation was in line with its program for the intensification of economic exchange on the south-eastern border through deregulation, while the potential political gains from a bilateral agreement with Bukhara had already been reaped.

The goal of intensifying trade on the empire's south-eastern border was not only conceived as an economic necessity for Russia's growing manufacturing industry, but as part of a mission civilisatrice. This contemporary view is well demonstrated by Pavel Ivanovich Nebol'sin's "Ocherki torgovli Rossii s stranami Srednei Azii" (Sketches of Russia's trade with the countries of Central Asia), published in 1856. The monography constituted the most comprehensive resource on trade and economy in the Central Asian khanates available to contemporary Russian readers and received many accolades, including the Demidov prize of the Russian Academy of Sciences. Nebol'sin was praised for

70 Cit. Ibid. 373.

71 Ibid. 369–373.

72 Ibid. 382.

73 *K-shev, M.*: Sredneaziatskaia torgovlia v 1859 godu. In: Orenburgskie gubernskie vedomosti, 9, 27.2.1860, 39–41, here 41.

conducting original research on the spot, traveling along the Orenburg customs line, and questioning hundreds of local merchants in 1850.[74] However, it was his particular achievement, the reviewer of the Demidov committee Grigor'ev argued, that his work did away with "widely circulating ideas about the splendor and education of the Asiatic peoples, and presented in true light the pitiful societal, economic and moral state of the domains of Bukhara, Khiva, and Kokand in our time."[75] Russia's encounters with the Ottoman Empire had produced similar sentiments of disenchantment and can be seen as part of a discursive carving-out of Russia's self-positioning between East and West.[76] The simultaneous self-perception of economic inferiority vis-a-vis highly industrialized western states and superiority on its south-eastern borders drove the enlightenment rhetoric in Russian debates on trade management.

Indeed, the introduction of Nebol'sin's monography on trade is a textbook example of Eurocentric condescension, as he understood the "[…] Bukharan, as any Asian" to be "uneducated, dirty, deceitful and due to the eastern system of rule, eastern customs and habits and the Asiatic way of reasoning, deprived of clear concepts of law and lawfulness, and nothing but a steppe Kirgiz, only that he is not a nomad […]."[77] The reviewer's take-away from Nebol'sin's observations was that for the khanates of Khiva, Kokand, and Bukhara, due to the "impossibility of regenerating on their own because of the Mohammedan belief, the only escape from their current pitiful situation, and the only comforting future, can be to come under the rule of any Christian power [derzhava], which would introduce order and peace."[78] Nebol'sin himself did not propose conquest, but made a clear case for the necessity for a "true merchant" to get involved in Central Asian trade. This, he argued, could only be an ethnically Russian merchant from "the core Russian people", dismissing the many Muslim merchants who were Russian subjects and already actively involved in trade on the south-eastern border.[79] This notion of superior European rationality versus Asiatic lawlessness and irrationality was not only to apply to a reorganization of trade, but trade itself was understood as a conduit of cultural and political influence and a tool for the mission civilisatrice.

74 *Grigor'ev, Vasilii Vasilievich*: Razbor sochineniia P. I. Nebol'sina: Ocherki torgovli Rossii s Srednei Aziei. In: *Veselovskii, Konstantin Stepanovich* (ed.): Dvadtsat' piatoe prisuzhdenie uchrezhdenykh P. N. Demidovym nagrad. 26 Maia 1856 goda. Saint Petersburg 1856, 109–182, 116–117.

75 Ibid. 118.

76 For this argument regarding Russia's encounters with the Ottoman Empire see: *Taki, Victor*: Tsar and Sultan. Russian Encounters with the Ottomann Empire. London and New York 2016.

77 *Nebol'sin, Pavel I.*: Ocherki torgovli Rossii s stranami Srednei Azii, Khivoi, Bukharoi i Kokanom: so storony Orenburgskoi linii. Saint Petersburg 1856, 3.

78 *Grigor'ev*: Razbor sochineniia P. I. Nebol'sina, 181.

79 *Nebol'sin*: Ocherki torgovli Rossii s stranami Srednei Azii, 19–20.

Reviewing the trade development with the Central Asian khanates for 1859, the "Orenburgskie Gubernskie vedomosti" pointed out that the benefits gained from the increased trade turnover were not only of economic nature and could hardly be quantified. The "Asiatic neighbors" received above the "material profits more important moral benefits, the amount of which no bookkeeper would be able to put a number on."[80] The demand to pursue a "general liberation of this trade from restraints and barriers inhibiting its development", expanding Bukhara's 1859 privileges to other khanates, was thus not only framed in terms of capturing new markets, but also as a civilizational measure. The article positioned itself explicitly against the thesis of Grigor'ev, abovementioned reviewer, that the "[...] development of Central Asia's natural resources could not be achieved other than by it coming under the control of any European Great Power [...]"[81], and argued for a soft power approach.

> With the facilitation of communications, Russia will, of course, have more influence on Central Asia; the light of civilization will pour faster, and with it will come ideas of the necessity of labor, all kinds of improvement, comfort in life, and ultimately true wealth. All this can be achieved by peaceful means, without force, and not infringing upon foreign independence at all. "Civilization as a magnet", as is said in a French newspaper, "spreads its beams beyond its borders. Russia is a rich, strong and benevolent country; why should it not attract Central Asia?" [...] Who of us Russians would not want a solution to this challenge by peaceful means, without shedding a single drop of blood.[82]

Ultimately, Russian influence did expand militarily and with great bloodshed, albeit not driven primarily by economic or civilizing considerations. But the notion of trade as a conduit of political influence beyond the state border and deregulation as a mechanism of trade stimulation remained in the imperial repertoire.

Throughout the 1840s and 1850s, the privileges granted to foreign merchants remained contested between the Governor-general of Orenburg and the central administration. Nevertheless, the main course of tying both the steppe and the Central Asian khanates closer to the Russian Empire through further deregulation of trade was maintained. The reduction of border formalities and trade barriers was interpreted as a way to exude Russian influence beyond the borders in the form of Russian-manufactured goods. With the abolition of customs duties on the most important commodities the fiscal function of customs on the south-eastern border had been clearly subordinated to both the

80 *K-shev*: Sredneaziatskaia torgovlia v 1859 godu, 40.

81 Ibid. 41.

82 Ibid. 42.

political functions of extending the empire's zone of influence and the long-term macroeconomic goal of strengthening market ties. The measures taken were deemed without alternative by the Ministry of Finance, as the functioning of trade management on the south-eastern border was understood to distinctly deviate from that on the European border. External limitations to trade were mostly accepted as invariable, even if they entailed negative side-effects such as the discontent of Russian-subject merchants and the outflow of metallic currency, which would have been unacceptable on the empire's western border. Eventually, the military advance into the steppe and the further deregulation of the late 1850s created a situation in which the customs border was far removed from the new and still-changing state border, while its very reason for existence was increasingly dismantled. The debate on the reform of Russia's south-eastern economic space unfolding in the 1860s, however, initially did not question the necessity of a customs borders and maintained the concept of a clearly demarcated economic space.

2.6 The First Debate on the Customs Border Relocation

The first debate on the relocation of the Orenburg customs line southward had been initiated by the Governor-general of Orenburg in 1862. Joined by the Ministry of Finance and the Head of the Orenburg customs *okrug*, the possible costs and benefits of such a relocation as well as its symbolic necessity were explored. As the newspaper "Severnaia pchela" (Northern Bee), an unofficial governmental outlet, pointed out, the border trade was considered "unnormal." It urged for the relocation of the customs line to "the true borders of the state, from the southern border of the Orenburg gubernia to the southern borders of the Orenburg krai on the Syr-Darya river", thus bringing the economic territory into alignment with the state territory. For Nikolai Aleksandrovich Leont'ev, Head of the Orenburg customs *okrug*, this was also an issue of revenue maximization, as the whole steppe population remained outside the Russian economic territory and deprived the state treasury of 30.000 rubles in potential customs incomes. But it was as much a symbolic issue: the customs institutions were not to be relegated to the hinterland anymore, but placed on the "natural border" of the empire, as Leont'ev referred to the Syr-Darya fortified line.[83] The message was that the conquests of the 1850s were no

83 *Solonchenko, Ekaterina A.*: Preobrazovanie Orenburgskogo tamozhennogo okruga v 1862–1868gg.: ot reformirovaniia k rasformirovaniiu. In: Reformy i reformatory v Rossii. Orenburg 2003, 72–93, here 72–74.

longer provisional, and it was time to integrate the steppe into the imperial economic space.

However, both the practical implementation and the use of this large-scale restructuring of border institutions remained questionable. Leont'ev himself pointed out that the Orenburg merchantry would be unwilling to move their operations to the scarcely developed steppe frontier, and that the creation of new infrastructure for customs and merchants – such as warehouses, checkpoints, and staff quarters – could outweigh potential increases in revenue. Neither was the workaround proposed in 1863 by his successor, Brilevich, implemented. He had suggested to keep all existing *skladochnye tamozhni* (storage customs) with their complex infrastructure in place, merely placing *zastavy* (customs outposts) on the Syr-Darya river.[84] The benefit of such a solution could only be symbolic, as *zastavy* were merely checkpoints without the rights and personnel necessary to clear goods and collect duties. Their function within the customs system was to check transports on lesser-used routes, to register and seal the load, allowing it to temporarily enter the customs territory. Only once it was cleared at a customs station could the goods go into circulation. This system was sensible if the next significant trade hub was not too far removed from the border. In Brilevich's proposal, the clearance would have still been conducted in Orenburg or Troitsk, almost a thousand verst from the Syr-Darya line, thus doing little to enhance the status of the settlements on the southern border.

If such a workaround was already a setback for the plan of establishing a regular customs line on the new state border, then non-cooperation on the side of the Western Siberian Governor ultimately undermined the endeavor. The plan for the new Orenburg customs line saw it stretching eastwards from Lake Aral, along the Syr-Darya river and the Chu river, until the southern tip of Lake Balkash. The territory west of Lake Balkash, however, fell under the responsibility of the Western Siberian Governor. Without equivalent customs control in this section, a corridor would have been created along the lake's western shore, allowing a circumvention of the newly established customs line. Both the Orenburg and Samara Governors-general attempted in vain to persuade the Western Siberian Governor to either relocate his customs institutions south or agree on creating an additional customs line, separating the steppe territories under Orenburg jurisdiction from those under the Western

84 Ibid. 75–77. Brilevich's first name and patronymic are not specified in the sources. Neither can he be found as Head of the Orenburg customs *okrug* in the 1863–1864 "Adres kalendar'. Obshchaia rospis' nachal'stvuiushchikh i prochikh dolzhnostnykh lits po vsem upravleniiam v Rossiiskoi imperii" – the published register of state servants. As the position was frequently reassigned in the 1860s, his tenure was likely too short to be considered in the printed version of the register. The only other Brilevich who can be found in earlier versions of the register is Vasilii Semenovich Brilevich.

Siberian Governor's jurisdiction. The latter deemed a relocation too costly and dismissed the second option, as it was bound to disrupt the interaction of the steppe population.[85] From being united, yet outside the Russian customs territory, the steppe would have gone to being split between two different economic zones. This issue was one more variation of the general debate on policies concerning the steppe, stemming from a vacillating and indeterminate political situation.

The initiative had come mostly from the Orenburg Governor in 1862, and despite a general agreement on the desirability of a border relocation, the central administration did not decisively further the cause. The question was not whether the economic border should match the state border, but where exactly the latter would eventually be located. It was the "indeterminacy of our border with the Khanate of Kokand" – or, plainly put, the potential for further territorial expansion – which had stalled the project.[86] Both the terms "true state border" and "natural border", as used by proponents of the relocation of the customs border above, obscured that the empire "did not have a definite state border"[87] in Central Asia, as War Minister Dmitrii Miliutin acknowledged.

Alexander Morrison argues that with "the Syr-Darya line, the Russians had chosen the worst possible place to try to build a frontier [...] which was too expensive and difficult to maintain, precisely because it lay midway between the limits of Russian settlements to the north and the riverine oases to the south."[88] It was more for these practical considerations, and less for the commonly cited "Great Game" or "cotton hunger" lines of argumentation that further conquest was considered. The in-between situation created the dilemma of either retreating to the former Orenburg line and facing a loss of face, or expanding further and capturing the city of Tashkent. The latter option allowed the connection of the Syr-Darya line to the Western Siberian line and Fort Vernyi through fertile regions, making the border more profitable and sustainable. Both proposals for retreat and advance had already been floated in the late 1850s and found supporters in governmental circles.[89] When discussion on the relocation of the customs border began in 1862, the future of the southern frontier was still far from decided.

The new Minister of Finance Mikhail Reitern, who had inherited a state budget in deep disarray, positioned himself clearly against any further advances in Central Asia, pointing to the difficulty of "attracting manpower and capital

85 Ibid. 76.
86 RGIA, f. 1263, op. 1, d. 3210, "Prilozhenie k zhurnalam zasedanii maia 1866g.", l. 348.
87 Miliutin quoted in *Morrison*: Nechto eroticheskoe, 161.
88 Ibid. 165.
89 Ibid. 156, 165.

to the new regions" and arguing that they would "divert these forces from the heart of Russia."[90] One of the subordinate arguments for capturing Tashkent had been that it presented an ideal trade hub for long-distance trade to China, the other khanates, Persia, and India. However, at the beginning of the 1860s the facilitation of such long-distance trade had already been developing satisfactorily.[91] From the perspective of the Ministry of Finance, it was hardly reasonable to strain the state budget with a large-scale military campaign, if its policy of trade deregulation, pursued over the past decades, was already successfully incentivizing Russia's trade exchange in the region. Neither did the costly relocation of customs institutions to the Syr-Darya line make fiscal sense, if its location were to change again. As Reitern was part of an 1863 interministerial special Central Asia Committee debating the further course of action on the Syr-Darya line, he was well aware of the possible changes to the position of the frontier lingering in the near future.[92]

The proceedings of the committee show that in 1863, the opinions of its members were split on further action. However, an easy victory obtained at Suzaq by General Mikhail Grigor'evich Cherniaev eventually tipped the scale towards a determined military advance.[93] It was quickly followed by the capture of Turkestan, Auli-Ata, and Chimkent over the course of the summer of 1864. This new constellation urged the Ministry of Finance to seriously look into the issue of the Orenburg customs line relocation, and two special interdepartmental commissions including the Governor-general of Orenburg and members from the War Ministry and the Foreign Ministry were organized. Both commissions "came to the conviction that a relocation of the customs border south was useful and timely."[94]

The new customs line suggested by the ministerial commission in 1864 was to run from the Caspian Sea, along the shores of Lake Aral and the Syr-Darya river, through the newly captured Turkestan and Auli-Ata to Vernyi, ending at either the existing Semipalatinsk customs station or the Bukhtarma *zastava*.[95] The plan, however, was short-lived, as it was quickly rendered obsolete by further military advances. In 1865 the city of Tashkent was captured, an incident often explained as an instance of "disobedience and deceit by Russia's 'man on the spot', General Cherniaev, in defiance of St. Petersburg's orders."[96] Morrison argues that this narrative was used to deflect responsibility from

90 *Stepanov*: Mikhail Khristoforovich Reitern, 21.
91 *Morrison*: Nechto eroticheskoe, 159.
92 Ibid. 163.
93 Ibid. 163–165.
94 RGIA, f. 1263, op. 1, d. 3210, l. 349.
95 Ibid. l. 349.
96 *Morrison*: Nechto eroticheskoe, 154.

state officials for the advance and that ultimately the idea of capturing Tashkent had been circulating since the late 1850s and was supported by many officials.[97] Nevertheless, for the members of the customs border commission, the new push towards Tashkent had come as a surprise, as they already had considered the previous frontline sufficiently stable to resolve the relocation of the Orenburg customs border. Once again, the Ministry of Finance found itself pressured to react and reorient itself in Central Asia in view of the changing situation created by the military.

Despite the continuing changes to the frontline, the Committee of Ministers, which addressed the issue in 1866, seemed determined to go through with the customs relocation. The question was only whether the new customs line should be placed north or south of Tashkent. Both the Orenburg merchantry and an 1865 expedition, commissioned to explore feasibility on the spot, argued for including Tashkent into the empire's customs territory.[98] Meanwhile, the protraction of the issue had caught the attention of the press, with "Sibirskie vedomosti" (Siberian News) complaining that the "customs, which at some point had been on the border, now had become internal and – contrary to the *ukaz* abolishing internal customs – continued to exist."[99] The *ukaz* referred to dated from 1753, thus highlighting the anachronism constituted by the Steppe customs border.[100] Increasingly, the situation on the south-eastern economic border was understood as unbearable and requiring comprehensive reform, not only with regards to the "internal border", but to the Asiatic tariff and customs procedures as well.

2.7 The 1867 "Asiatic" Tariff Revision

The "Asiatic" *tariff* and *ustav* of 1817 had initially been designed to introduce uniform rules on Russia's Asiatic borders and was shaped to be more lenient than the European regulations. By 1867, both of these characteristics had vanished. Apart from minor corrections, little had been done over the course of 50 years to update the main body of regulations. Some fees and procedures long abolished on the European border persisted. Meanwhile, ever more exclusions and special regional regulations had been introduced, undermining uniformity. The relocation of the customs border, the Ministry of Finance

97 Ibid. 153–155.

98 RGIA, f. 1263, op. 1, d. 3210, l. 351; *Solonchenko*: Preobrazovanie Orenburgskogo tamozhennogo okruga, 85–88.

99 *Sokolov*: Torgovaia politika Rossii v Srednei Azii, 67.

100 Polnoe sobranie zakonov Rossiikoi Imperii s 1649 goda. 1689–1699. Volume 13. Saint Petersburg 1830, no. 10164.

argued, could not be tackled until new rules, upon which future trade on the Asiatic section of the customs system was to be based, were decided upon.[101]

The general outlook was to return to the original spirit of the tariff by lowering rates, as some customs rates set for the Asiatic border and once considered lenient, were now higher than those on the European border.[102] Further, trade procedures were to be simplified and administrative costs reduced by declaring a large array of commodities duty-free. Of 133 product groups listed in the 1817 tariff, only 13 generated revenues exceeding 1.000 rubles annually. All the other goods still required elaborate inspection, with some still cleared according to the ad-valorem principle, which had already been found unsuitable for trade on the south-eastern border in 1803. This complicated system slowed down trade procedures, led to frequent quarrels between merchants and customs officials, but did not generate relevant revenue.[103] By declaring all but the most important commodities duty-free, significantly less personnel and storage space would have been necessary to ensure an effective functioning of customs controls.

The suggested measures had previously been successfully tested on the Chinese border when its main customs station had been transferred from Kiakhta to Irkutsk in 1862. Trade statistics had shown that customs revenues derived mostly from the tea trade, while all other commodities constituted only an impalpable fraction. They were primarily consumed by the indigenous borderland population and "did not only not find their way into Russia, but not even into Western Siberia."[104] Thus, protectionist measures taken on the European border would not be undermined by deregulating trade on the Chinese border, and no harm was to be expected for the internal market of the imperial core. The arduousness of transportation across the imperial space allowed to simultaneously retain restrictive tariffs on one border, while almost fully removing trade barriers on the other. Meanwhile, both the border population and the general trade intensity would profit from reduced controls. Thus, all commodities legal for import, except for tea and spirits, were declared duty-free. These experiences from the Chinese border section were to be transferred and applied to the reform of the general Asiatic tariff. It was to be "guided by these very principles, which is even considered necessary, so as to ensure as much universalization or at the least harmonization of the varying tariff regulations on Asiatic trade as possible."[105] The 1867 reform promised an opportunity to fulfill the 1817 plan for a uniform system of "Asiatic"

101 RGIA, f. 1152, op. 7, 1867, d. 597, "O proekte novogo Aziatskogo tamozhennogo tarifa", l. 8.

102 Ibid. l. 7.

103 Ibid. l. 7ob, 8ob., 10ob.

104 Ibid. l. 9.

105 Ibid. l. 9–9ob.

trade management in its own right by transferring successful concepts and accommodating bilateral trade agreements, instead of treating them as an exclusion to the regular system.

Following this logic, the rates for the remaining products not declared duty-free on the future Central Asian customs line, were to be equalized with those on the Persian and Ottoman borders. On the Persian border, the Asiatic tariff of 1817 had never applied, as the customs rate was fixed at a flat 5 % by the 1813 treaty of Gulistan and the 1828 treaty of Turkmanchai. The Ministry of Finance argued that 50 years of experience on the Persian border with "the import of goods absolutely similar to the Central Asian ones with said rate did not have any palpable impact on the internal sales of domestic products." Considering that the steppe route was even more hazardous and thus transport costlier than through the Caspian Sea or the Transcaucasus, there could be no objections to extending the 5 % flat rate tariff to the steppe border sections.[106] Instead of canceling existing bilateral treaties, which offered the advantage of being able to limit the other party's scope of action, the provisions of the treaties were incorporated into the general "Asiatic" tariff and expanded to other border sections. The proposed tariff revision was thus not only a necessary step to prepare for the relocation of the Orenburg and Western Siberian customs border. It was, much in the spirit of the Great Reforms, to be a major overhaul of the legal framework originally designed to unify "Asiatic" trade, which promised a modern, uniform and budget-friendly solution.

It had not been the first attempt to reform the old "Asiatic" trade regulations in the 1860s. Kniazhevich, Reitern's predecessor, had already addressed the State Council in 1861, suggesting the creation of a new tariff which would unite the regulations for Astrakhan, Orenburg and Western Siberia, as well as the Kiakhta customs on the Chinese border. However, the project had been stopped due to "new views on free trade in Eastern Siberia" – namely the establishment of the Far-Eastern porto-franco under Mikhail Reitern.[107] Reforming the baseline legal framework while establishing a vast territorialized free-trade regime was simply too much to coordinate. By 1867, the first operating experience had been collected with the free-trade zone, customs had been reorganized as its own department of the Ministry of Finance, suggesting a professionalization, and the ministry considered a general revision of the Asiatic tariff timely and necessary in preparation for the relocation of the Steppe customs border. Reitern submitted a draft law to the State Council in April 1867. By the time he received a reply in September, recommending coordinating the revision of the "Asiatic" tariff with the revision of the "European" tariff being undertaken by a special commission at the same time, a radical

106 Ibid. l. 11–11ob.
107 Ibid. l. 6ob. See also chapter 4.

new suggestion had come from the Orenburg Governor-general. Nikolai Andreevich Kryzhanovskii proposed fully dismantling the existing customs border without creating a new line on the southern frontier at all.[108]

2.8 The Dissolution of the Steppe Customs Border

Two months later, Reitern submitted a finished proposal for the full dismantling of the Steppe customs border to the State Council.[109] It argued that the "chaos from all the contradictory regulations" had a negative effect on regional trade in general and particularly burdened the "empire's new Tashkent subjects" who had to pay customs when trading through Orenburg and Troitsk, whereas "the merchants from hostile Bukhara, with whom we have been at war for two years [...] do not pay anything."[110] Although the Ministry of Finance was well aware that the 1859 privileges granted to Bukharan merchants were claimed by others as well, the letter of the law still penalized subjects of the Russian Empire and rewarded foreign hostile subjects. Removing customs barriers altogether promised to solve the problem of unequal trading rights.

The second consideration that tipped the scales towards dissolution rather than relocation was fiscal. The initial costs of building the necessary infrastructure for a new customs line would have been very high due to the length of the new border, and a doubling of the running budget allocated to the Orenburg customs section would have been required as well. However, customs revenues were expected to drop significantly, as the revised "Asiatic" tariff removed additional fees, declared many goods duty-free, and introduced a fixed 5% rate for the remaining goods.[111] The Orenburg and Western Siberian customs lines had already previously operated at a narrow margin, as their operation cost about 97 thousand rubles in 1867, while the average of pure customs revenues for the years 1860–1863, before military actions affected regional trade, amounted to 298 thousand rubles. With the tariff revision, a decrease of 130 thousand rubles was expected. The expected remaining fiscal profit of 70 thousand rubles was negligible and the narrow margin problematic to operate with.[112] Meanwhile, the dissolution appeared as the logical continuation of the general policies taken on the eastern border:

108 Ibid. l. 33–34ob.
109 RGIA, f. 1152, op. 7, 1868, d. 172, l. 1.
110 Ibid. l. 2ob.
111 Ibid. l. 4.
112 Ibid. l. 12.

All measures taken by the government with regard to the tariff and customs relations on the eastern border of our state were for the most part directed not so much towards the increase of the state's customs income, but towards the development of trade relations with our Asiatic neighbors. [...] Under such a steady direction, the purely fiscal side cannot have an important role in the question on the removal of the Asiatic customs line, and hardly any difficulties can be found with it.[113]

Although the cited passage referred specifically to the recent changes made to the Kiakhta tariff and the removal of duties on Central Asian cotton, it also captured the general spirit of the Russian Empire's customs and trade policies in its eastern section since the beginning of the 19th century, and particularly since the introduction of the 1817 "Asiatic" tariff.

The only remaining objection to a border dissolution could be the penetration of products into the empire's core economic space, which could undermine the protectionist system in place on the western border. The manufactured products of Bukhara and Khiva, the ministry argued, could not compete in quality and thus did not pose a threat to the empire's industries. On the contrary, the removal of trade barriers would increase trade turnover and serve to boost the sale of Russian-manufactured goods and the import of Central Asian raw materials, particularly cotton, required for the metropole's industries.[114] As for the import of European-manufactured goods, a large part of the draft proposal was devoted to an analysis of the various trade routes via which they were traded to the Khanate of Bukhara and Russian Turkestan. Each route – through the Black Sea, the Suez Canal, the Persian Gulf, or via land route from India – was analyzed for its duration, safety and additional expenses such as customs fees levied en route.[115]

The verdict was that foreign goods played a negligible role and could hardly be found on Turkestan's market and not at all beyond the Kirghiz steppe. The report argued that Russia's "steppe pack-saddle transportation has been organized a long time ago, and correctly, while English caravans are not safe from robberies and pay the doubled ziaket to any petty lord whom they pass."[116] Russia, on the contrary, had managed – through conquest and deregulation – to create an economic space in which the exchange of goods was incentivized. By the time competing European products reached this space, their advantage of lower production costs had been nullified. The cost-intensive steppe transportation precluded them from penetrating the empire's main economic space, and there was little prospect they could endanger the empire's

113 Ibid. l. 11ob.-12.
114 Ibid. l. 4ob.
115 Ibid. l. 5ob-7.
116 Ibid. l. 12ob.-13.

core domestic market and undermine the protectionist barriers erected on the western border. The topography and infrastructural fragmentation of the imperial space came to replace conventional methods of border protection. The deregulation of trade, meanwhile, allowed for an extension of the sale of Russian goods, which were seen as a conduit of political influence, beyond the empire's borders.

2.9 Conclusion

By July 1868, the old Orenburg and Western Siberian customs border had been dismantled and "full free trade" introduced. The Russian Empire had thus created a vast free-trade zone on its south-eastern border, albeit never outright labeling it such. As long as infrastructural fragmentation provided sufficient protection against the import of European products, this system constituted a solution with minimal administrative costs and conducive to the intensification of trade relations. Although practical and fiscal considerations did play a role, it was by no means a renouncement of the empire's claim to sovereignty over its territory, but rather served to exude influence beyond the state border. The full border dissolution was the extreme continuation of a new trade policy for the empire's south-eastern borders, which had been developed since the beginning of the 19th century. Since 1817, "European" and "Asiatic" customs constituted two distinct systems, following different logics. On the "European" borders, protectionist measures and the maintenance of a positive trade balance were of paramount importance and were shaped against the example of the neighboring states. In contrast, "Asiatic" customs were guided by an agenda to increase trade turnover and expand political influence by deliberately blurring the borders of the Russian Empire. The unobstructed coexistence of two diametrically opposed approaches to the management of economic space was guaranteed by the infrastructural fragmentation of the imperial space. As long as the south-eastern borders remained remote, vast territorialized free-trade regimes did not undermine the protectionist bulwark on the western border. Only with changing political and infrastructural constellations in Persia, Russia's later conquest of the Transcaspian region, and the construction of the Transcaspian railway in the 1880s did calls for the reintroduction of a fixed customs border reappear. The new railway technology promised a quick route to the empire's metropole and introduced new visions of a deeper integration of the imperial space, which put the system of free trade on the south-eastern border under pressure, as will be discussed in the following chapter.

3. Closing the Gap: Bukhara's Loss of Trade Autonomy

Taking a sovereign state's control over a vital source of income and its choice of trade routes and partners should never come easy. Yet, it was precisely the ease and routineness with which the Khanate of Bukhara had been absorbed into the Russian Empire's customs territory in 1894 – meaning the loss of its economic independence – that baffled and frustrated Anton Frantsevich Gubarevich-Radobyl'skii:

The project, which was not sufficiently harmonized to merge the interests of the two governments on site, however, went the usual way of any law. Namely, it was fully reviewed in the customs department and examined routinely in the State Council, which mainly touched upon issues of staffing and not its local governmental significance [mestnoe gosudarstvennoe znachenie]. And thus, the deep side of the issue, which had interested the government during its first consultation, somehow fell away by itself: the project was developed as if we were placing cordons on our territory in the Caucasus, rather than claiming the first and quite substantial indirect tax from the khanate.[1]

Gubarevich-Radobyl'skii had served in Central Asian customs since they were first put under the control of the Ministry of Finance in 1886. After joining the newly opened Samarkand customs office in 1887, he worked his way up to Head of the Turkestan Customs District by 1904.[2] He published extensively on issues of economy and trade in Central Asia and was certainly an expert in the dealings of "his" periphery.[3] And just like many "men on the spot", he was

1 *Gubarevich-Radobyl'skii, Anton*: Ekonomicheskii ocherk Bukhary i Tunisa. Opyt sravnitel'nogo issledovaniia dvukh sistem protektorata. Saint Petersburg 1905, 170.

2 Nachal'nik Turkestanskogo Tamozhennogo Okruga was the highest regional post in the customs administration. For Gubarevich-Radobyl'skii's service record see RGIA, f. 21, op. 4, d. 214, "Gubarevich-Radobyl'skii, Anton (lichnoe delo)", l. 232–234.

3 Apart from various reports, he published four monographies on Russia's south-eastern economic space: *Gubarevich-Radobyl'skii*: Ekonomicheskii ocherk Bukhary i Tunisa; *Gubarevich-Radobyl'skii, Anton*: Chai i chainaia monopolia. Opyt issledovaniia osnov oblozheniia chaia v Rossii. Saint Petersburg 1908; Two appeared as volumes in the Cotton Committee's series "Materialy dlia izucheniia khlopkovodstva": *Gubarevich-Radobyl'skii, Anton*: Znachenie Turkestana v torgovle Rossii s sopredel'nymi stranami Azii. Saint Petersburg 1912; *Gubarevich-Radobyl'skii, Anton*: Kakie dorogi sleduet stroit' v Turkestane i v Zakavkaz'e. Saint Petersburg 1914.

left with the feeling of not being sufficiently heard and valued in the imperial center.[4] His pleas to be transferred to Saint Petersburg as regional expert after 23 years of service in Central Asia went unheard, just as the 1894 law project had been rushed forward against more cautious voices from the periphery.[5]

For a man with his first-hand knowledge of the local peculiarities and administrative pitfalls, the hurried expansion of the Russian customs territory to the borders of Persia and Afghanistan was truly incomprehensible. Was the Khanate of Bukhara not a sensitive region which required a particularly cautious approach, as practiced by the Ministry of Foreign Affairs with its non-interventionist policy?[6] Should such a significant expansion of the imperial economic space not generate more debate? The apparent routineness of the process appears surprising, considering that Bukhara's integration had already been brought forward and forgotten prior. How had the constellation changed and which factors hastened the decision-making process?

This chapter first introduces the project of trade development with Central Asia suggested by the Society for Aid to Russian Industry and Trade (Obshchestvo dlia sodeistviia Rossiiskoi Promyshlennosti i Torgovle) in 1868/69. The complex protectionist program and its claim for spatial reconfiguration is then contrasted with the fragmentary nature of the Russian-dominated Central Asian economic space. The varying operational modes of customs that existed in parallel in different territories are outlined, and the underlying logics of each configuration and the functions attributed to customs are shown.[7] It is then argued that the construction of the Transcaspian railway fundamentally altered the spatial visions of decision-makers in the imperial center. The changing perception of the macro-region contested its hitherto fragmented arrangement, serving as a catalyst for administrative unification. The extension of the empire's economic regulatory mechanisms to this vast new space is understood as a process of territorialization that opened up new possibilities for reshaping both the empire's internal commercial geography

4 Particularly with regard to trade in the Pamirs see *Golbeck, Matthias*: (Selbst)beschreibungen vom Rand des Imperiums. Die Briefe des russischen Beamten und Amateurwissenschaftlers N.F. Petrovskij aus dem Generalgouvernement Turkestan und Kaschgar 1870–1895. In: *Aust, Martin/Schenk, Frithjof Benjamin* (eds.): Imperial Subjects. Autobiographische Praktiken in den Reichen der Romanovs, Habsburger und Osmanen. Köln 2015, 291–323.

5 RGIA, f. 21, op. 4, d. 214, l. 213, 245, 260, 267, 270.

6 Becker suggests that "St. Petersburg did the inescapable minimum to protect and promote Russian private interests in the khanates", prioritizing the "foreign ministry's policy of nonintervention." See *Becker, Seymour*: Russia's Protectorates in Central Asia: Bukhara and Khiva, 1865–1924. London 2004, 150.

7 With regard to customs regulations, a subdivision into the Governorate-general of Turkestan, the Transcaspian region, and the Khanates of Khiva and Bukhara applied until 1894.

and Central Asia's role in global trade. It is scrutinized against the background of Russia's global economic situation, its predominant economic thought, and geopolitical implications.

3.1 Central Asian Space and Early Economic Visions

The four territories, each a customs space of its own[8], discussed in this chapter came under the influence of the Russian Empire in piecemeal fashion throughout the 1830s-1880s. Each of these incremental steps left behind a specific mode of trade and customs regulations, which were unified – and then only partially – by the 1894 law. The analysis of the specific sets of regulations and their evolution informs us about the changing functions ascribed to each territory within the context of the empire.

The Governorate-general of Turkestan, discussed in detail in the previous chapter, had been the result of numerous military advances from the 1830s onward. By 1868 it bordered the Khanate of Bukhara and a military-civil administration under the auspices of the Ministry of War, and its first Governor-general, Konstantin Petrovich Kaufman, had been installed. The bordering Khanate of Bukhara had been defeated as well, however it received the status of a protectorate under the temporary treaty of 1868. The treaty itself left Bukhara's state sovereignty intact and granted trade rights for Russian subjects. Despite this face-saving approach, the relationship was one of dependency from Russia.[9] The defeat of the Khanate of Khiva in 1873 resulted in the establishment of a protectorate as well, however, with considerably less rights than Bukhara.[10]

The last substantial territorial gains made by the Russian Empire in Central Asia were the areas along the eastern Caspian shore, labeled Transcaspian oblast', conquered between 1879 and 1885 by the Generals Nikolai Pavlovich Lomakin, Mikhail Dmitrievich Skobelev, and Mikhail Nikolaevich Annenkov. The military expansion drove the empire's borders up to Persia and Afghanistan and incidentally solved a long-disputed issue: the construction of a Central Asian railway. It was for military necessity, not commercial interest, that the route from Uzun-Ada (later moved to Krasnovodsk) towards Ashkhabad had been chosen, and it was military needs that ensured its financing and swift

8 An even finer differentiation of customs territories could be made for the Turkestan Governorate-general, which is not necessary at this point.

9 *Becker*: Russia's Protectorates in Central Asia, 32–33.

10 For a discussion of the 1873 Russo-Khivan and Russo-Bukharan treaties see ibid. 58–61.

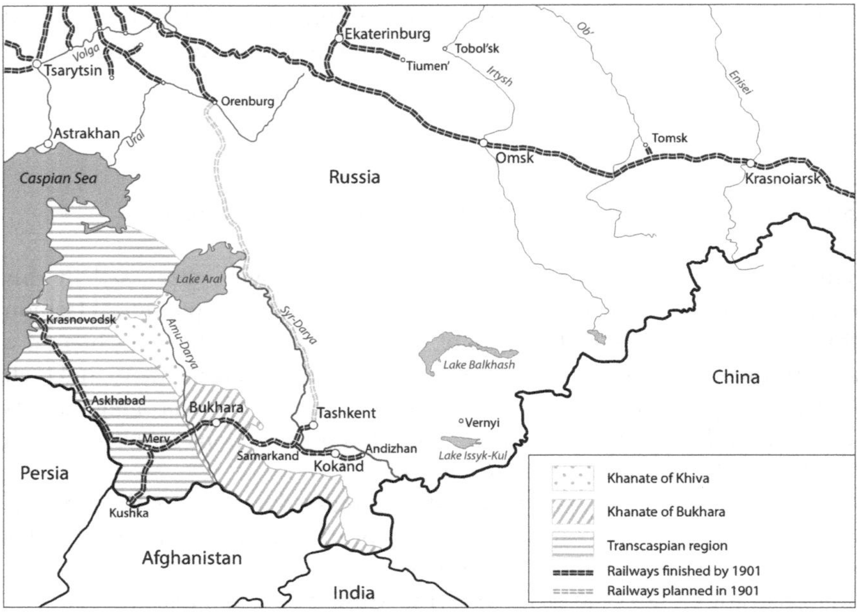

Figure 2: Map of Central Asian khanates with Trans-Caspian railway.

construction. Nevertheless, the new railway line also answered economic demands, which would consequently gain importance.[11]

Economic interest in Central Asia had existed within Russian governmental and entrepreneurial circles long before the 19th century conquest. Since Peter the Great, it had been linked with visions of geopolitical expansion and grand infrastructural undertakings. Lured by rumors of great riches, Tsar Peter I entertained thoughts of conquering the Central Asian khanates and altering their geographic and political configuration by straightening the Oxus river (Amu Darya river) so it would flow into the Caspian Sea. This, he hoped, would allow for direct trade from Moscow through Central Asia to the Indian Mughal Empire. His visions were buttressed by action when Peter dispatched Aleksandr Bekovich-Cherkasskii on an expedition to conquer Khiva and Bukhara in 1716. Although the undertaking ended in a definitive defeat, the episode remained in Russia's historical memory and was regularly cited.

By the turn of the century, Tsar Paul I – in a Russo-French Alliance against the British Empire – orchestrated a new attempt to conquer the Central Asian khanates and advance towards the Indian dominions. The hastily dispatched Cossack regiment only made it as far as the Aral Sea before news of the

11 Ibid. 136.

emperor's assassination prompted its retreat.[12] It was not until the 1830s that the Russian Empire, despite numerous drawbacks, began to expand and consolidate itself successfully in its south-east. In a mix of strategic arguments, personal military ambitions, and an imperial reflex, justifying expansion by a need for secure borders, the conquest gained momentum.[13] By 1853 the Syr-Darya-line had been established. By 1868 the major cities of Tashkent and Samarkand had been conquered and the Khanate of Bukhara defeated. The fulfillment of Tsar Peter's vision at last seemed tangible.

3.2 Economic Visions of the 1860s and Limits of Implementation

Charged with renovating the empire's ramshackle finances, Minister of Finance Mikhail Khristoforovich Reitern was certainly not a man to endorse this military extravaganza. To fix the growing budgetary deficits he had embarked on a severe austerity policy across all ministries, which was particularly abhorred by the Ministry of War. Reitern pointed out the financial insanity of further expansion into Central Asia, as neither manpower nor capital could be easily attracted to the new regions.[14] Yet, expansion continued and when put before the fact of having to delineate a vast and distant newly annexed economic space, Reitern opted for a policy of minimal governmental intervention entailing virtually no administrative costs by basically declaring a porto-franco regime, yet, stopping short of calling it such.[15]

Paradoxically, it was the new politico-economic climate of Reitern's reforms that simultaneously nourished grand schemes for the transformation of Central Asia's economy among industrialists and merchants. Reitern had embarked on an "integrated economic plan that combined banking, tariff, and budgetary reform together with railroad construction" complemented by a new policy of glasnost'.[16] In 1862, the state budget had been disclosed for the first time, and Reitern was the first Minister of Finance to "consult

12 *Schimmelpenninck van der Oye, David*: Paul's Great Game: Russia's Plan to Invade British India. In: Central Asian Survey, 33(2) (2014), 143–152.

13 For a critical evaluation of the various motives for the expansion see *Morrison, Alexander*: Introduction: Killing the Cotton Canard and Getting Rid of the Great Game: Rewriting the Russian Conquest of Central Asia, 1814–1895. In: Central Asian Survey, 33(2) (2014), 131–142.

14 *Stepanov*: Mikhail Khristoforovich Reitern, 21.

15 See chapter 2.

16 *Rieber, Alfred J.*: The Imperial Russian Project. Autocratic Politics, Economic Development, and Social Fragmentation. Toronto 2017, 165.

entrepreneurs and to invite them to discuss various bills."[17] Apart from individual invitations, he supported the establishment of a novel advisory body of industrialists and merchants in 1867: the Society for Aid to Russian Industry and Trade (Obshchestvo dlia sodeistviia Rossiiskoi Promyshlennosti i Torgovle).[18] The organization was the first of its kind and was vested with the right to petition the government, adding weight to its publications.[19] Inspired by the recent defeat of Bukhara and the unfurling railway craze, the society dedicated one of its first publications to the issue of Central Asian trade routes and the means to capitalize on the new territories.

Individual petitions to further trade with Central Asia had been put forward since the 1850s. Cotton manufacturers showed particular interest in Bukhara's raw cotton, exacerbated by a supply crisis caused by the American Civil War. However, the Russian government showed little support for these propositions, and economic motives were not the driving force behind the conquest.[20] Once the war dust had settled and the political constellation seemed more favorable, the Society for Aid to Russian Industry and Trade was quick to make use of its right to petition and put forward a series of publications, urging for a complex program to secure the Central Asian markets. In an 1868 addendum to the newspaper "Deiatel'nost'" the society sketched out the luring potentials of a "huge population of nomadic and settled peoples in Central Asia, that do not produce anything of their own apart from rough (handmade) textiles, called *daba*, and thus naturally would have a necessity for the produce of Russia."[21] Though it would require "the most substantial assistance" to build suitable transport routes and thus "retain this market for us", the society felt confident that the benefits of drastically reduced shipping rates would compensate for the investment.[22]

Their proposal, directed at the highest governmental authorities, would have been an unremarkable call for governmental protectionism, if it were not for the scope of action proposed. The text dismissed plans for a connection of the northern Caspian Sea through Russian-controlled territory to the Aral Sea and the Syr-Darya river altogether and instead suggested connecting Krasnovodsk on the south-eastern Caspian coast to the Amu Darya river and

17 *Stepanov*: Mikhail Khristoforovich Reitern, 20, 23.

18 *Rieber*: The Imperial Russian Project, 187.

19 For the statute of the society see Ustav Obshchestva dlia sodeistviia russkoi promyshlennosti i torgovle. Saint Petersburg 1867.

20 *Becker*: Russia's Protectorates in Central Asia, 16–18.

21 *Obshchestvo dlia sodeistviia russkoi promyshlennosti i torgovle*: Zapiska obshchestva dlia sodeistvia russkoi promyshlennosti i torgovle, o torgovykh putiakh v Sredniu Aziiu. Saint Petersburg 1868, 1.

22 Ibid. 2, 5.

the city of Bukhara.[23] This direction would later be picked for the Transcaspian railway in the 1880s. In 1868, however, this territory was not yet under Russian control. The society's vision for Russia's dominance on the Central Asian markets anticipated both the conquest of the Transcaspian region and the creation of a railway, which the society suggested would "be built in just time."[24] This pretense to manipulate trade geographies on a large scale has to be read against the background of a quickly unfolding railway sector in the Russian Empire and the completion of the Suez Canal that very year, which made such grand projects appear tangible.[25] It was feared that "Europe [could] both flood the Persian and Central Asian markets with its goods through the Caucasus and the Hindukush and heavily derail our trade and manufacturing industry", if measures to secure these markets were not urgently pursued, as Podpolkovnik Aleksandr Ivanovich Glukhovskoi expressed in a meeting of the society.[26]

His statement was part of the larger follow-up publication "Materialy po voprosu o torgovykh putiakh v Sredniiu Aziiu" (Materials on the Subject of Trade Routes in Central Asia), in which the society collected the voices of merchants, industrialist and military figures with first-hand experience of Central Asia, such as Glukhovskoi. The delicate nature of suggesting significant extraterritorial infrastructural measures did not escape the assembly, as Kiakhta-based tea merchant Ivan Andreevich Noskov, backed by other members, duly noted that "we will have to petition not for the exploration of the territory [between Krasnovodsk and the Amu Darya] but for its conquest. The society does not claim this right."[27] Yet, the eventual petition of the society deemed the establishment of the Krasnovodsk-Amu Darya trade route without alternative and found an open ear with the Ministry of War. It was certainly a coincidence, and not due to the petition, that Russian troops landed in Krasnovodsk only five weeks later.[28] Yet the timing was fortunate, as furthering Russian trade interests in Central Asia could serve as one more justification for the expansion.

23 Ibid. 3–4.

24 Ibid. 5.

25 Ibid. 7. The completion of the Suez Canal also prompted discussions on its impact on cotton trade in Central Asia as found in "Turkestanskie vedomosti", 23.8.1871, no. 30, 121 and 20.9.1871, no. 34, 137.

26 *Obshchestvo dlia sodeistviia russkoi promyshlennosti i torgovle*: Materialy po voprosu o torgovykh putiakh v Sredniiu Aziiu. Saint Petersburg 1869, 15.

27 Ibid. 56

28 *Khalfin, Naftula A.*: Obshchestvo dlia sodeistviia russkoi promyshlennosti i torgovle i Sredniia Aziia. In: Voprosy Istorii, 8 (1975), 45–63, 54; *Solov'ev, A. G./Sennikov, A. A.*: Rossiia i Turkmeniia v XIX veke. Ashkhabad 1946, 31.

The territorial vision put forward by the society was not limited to regarding the space east of the Caspian Sea in isolation either. The society supplemented its argument with a brochure – sent to its members, leading periodicals, and the Caucasus Namestnik – linking the Transcaucasian territories to the Transcaspian region and Bukhara. They accused the Transcaucasian transit route, used to transport European goods to Northern Persia, of jeopardizing Russia's claim to the Central Asian markets. They argued that the transit route, particularly after the construction of the Tiflis-Baku railway, which was rumored at the time, would serve a "severe blow to Russian trade in Central Asia" by bringing Bukhara's markets closer to France and Britain than to Moscow, thus putting Russian manufacturers in a disadvantaged position "on those very Central Asian markets, on which, qua the geographic location of this region, it would be in our hands to fully eliminate foreign competition."[29] Only a shutdown of the transit, they argued, would ensure sole dominance. Their demand became a bone of contention between the War Ministry, the Ministry of Finance, and the Caucasus Namestnik throughout the 1870s. However, the opposing interests of the parties and their differing conceptualizations of the relation between the territories of the empire prevented the closure. Only after Reitern's departure as Minister of Finance in 1878 and the strengthening of protectionist thought in governmental circles would the transit route be closed in 1883.[30]

Similarly, the society's program for a Southern Caspian trade route did not find support across all ministries. The Ministry of Finance was occupied with the realities of a budgetary crisis grave enough without embarking on a multimillion ruble infrastructural project in yet unchartered territories. Meanwhile, the Ministry of War seemed at least supportive of a trade reconnaissance mission conducted by Glukhovskoi in 1873, who suggested that urgent measures, such as the immediate construction of a railway and the inclusion of the Khanates into a "customs union", should be taken[31] – a maneuver substantiating the recent conquest of Khiva. Nevertheless, the governmental approach towards Russian merchants' interests in Central Asia in the 1870s and 1880s was one of neglect.[32] There simply was no coordinated developmental program and none would emerge until the 1890s, when the interests of the involved ministries began to converge.

29 *Obshchestvo dlia sodeistviia russkoi promyshlennosti i torgovle*: Dopolnitel'naia Zapiska o torgvykh putiach v Sredniiu Aziiu i o vliianii na nashu sredneaziatskuiu torgovliu sushchestvuiushchego tranzita tovarov chrez Kavkaz. Saint Petersburg 1869, 1–3; *Khalfin*: Obshchestvo dlia sodeistviia russkoi promyshlennosti i torgovle i Sredniia Aziia, 59.

30 See chapter 6.

31 *Khalfin*: Obshchestvo dlia sodeistviia russkoi promyshlennosti i torgovle i Sredniia Aziia, 56–57.

32 *Becker*: Russia's Protectorates in Central Asia, 135

To be sure, the program put forward by the Society for Aid to Russian Industry and Trade was not the first to suggest a railway link between the newly annexed territories. The idea had existed since 1854, and "by 1880 over forty different projects had been submitted", however, with the "majority favoring the Orenburg-Tashkent route along the Sir-Darya", which the Society for Aid to Russian Industry and Trade categorically dismissed. Neither was it the most ambitious, as Suez Canal-builder Ferdinand de Lesseps suggested a railway linking Calais to Calcutta via Turkestan in 1873.[33]

The idea of a zero-sum game for Central Asia's markets kept occupying Russian publicists and economists.[34] Nevertheless, the program proposed by the Society for Aid to Russian Industry and Trade in 1869 is remarkable. Put forward right after the defeat of Bukhara and in the year of the Suez Canal opening, it suggested both urgency and feasibility. Against the general climate of Reitern's free-trade-inspired agenda of the 1860s, most visible in the establishment of the Far Eastern Porto-Franco in 1862, the society presented a complex alternative vision, conceptualizing the integration of space through infrastructural permeation in conjunction with protectionist regulations directed against outside competition, reminiscent of Friedrich List's "Nationalökonomie." Paradoxically, it did so by making use of the liberal glasnost' reforms introduced by Reitern. Though the society did not explicate the creation of a unified customs space, both their claim to sole dominance on the Central Asian markets as well aspiration to lower shipping expenditures within the empire's economic space would suggest the removal of internal and the creation of external trade barriers. The reality of Central Asian customs spaces, however, was one of complicated fragmentation.

3.3 Fragmented Customs Regulations on the Periphery

Until the 1894 customs unification, which will be discussed in the last part of this chapter, the Central Asian economic space was subdivided into the Governorate-general of Turkestan, the Transcaspian oblast', and the Khanates of Khiva and Bukhara with regard to trading regulations. Each of these territories had vastly varying pre-conditions, favoring specific operational

33 Ibid. 99–100.

34 For prominent examples see *Shavrov, Nikolai*: Put' v Tsentral'nuiu Aziiu po napravleniiu ukazannomu Petrom Velikim. Saint Petersburg 1871; *Terent'e v, M.A.*: Kak ustranit' torgovoe sopernichestvo anglichan v Srednei Azii? In: Trudy obshchestva dlia sodeistviia russkoi promyshlennosti i torgovle. Volume 2 (1873), 154–186; *Terent'ev, M.A.*: Rossiia i Angliia v bor'be za rynki. Saint Petersburg 1876; *Subbotin, A.P.*: Rossiia i Angliia na Sredneaziatskikh rynkakh. Saint Petersburg 1885.

modes. In the following, these are outlined, highlighting the underlying logics of each configuration and the functions attributed to customs in each territory.

The Governorate-general, discussed in detail in the previous chapter, was initially subject to the highest degree of deregulation, after spatially defined trade barriers had been disposed of in 1868. Since 1817, the empire's customs line had stretched from the northern Caspian shore along the eastern border of the Orenburg Governorate-general until the Zverinogolovskaia *zastava*[35] following further to Semipalatinsk. However, the southward military expansion under Nicholas I and Alexander II had rendered it an internal customs line, putting its usefulness into question, as it hampered trade relations with the new Kirghiz subjects. Beginning in 1862, the relocation of the customs border to the Syr-Darya frontline had been discussed between the Orenburg Governor-general, the Ministry of Finance, and the Ministry of War. However, already in his 1866 annual report to the Committee of Ministers, Governor-general Kryzhanovskii was forced to concede that military expansion had outpaced the planned reform. Russian troops had moved forward and now stood between Bukhara and Kokand. A further relocation of the customs border would be too costly, annulling any potential fiscal gains, he suggested. Meanwhile, protectionist measures would not be necessary, as Anglo-Indian manufactured goods – the only threat to Russia's internal market – could not be imported cost-efficiently due to the low quality of transportation routes. On the other hand, deregulation would enliven trade relations to the newly annexed territories and facilitate the sale of Russian-manufactured goods.[36]

His position was well in line with the general tendency towards free trade under Reitern, and particularly towards "Asiatic" trade, the regulation of which was not primarily governed by fiscal considerations, as exemplified by the removal of customs on Chinese goods (with the notable exception of tea). In an understanding of trade as a conduit of political influence, deregulation further served the broadening of Russia's influence in its own Central Asian territories and in the neighboring Khanates. The proposal was formed into a legislative act granting "at least temporarily, full freedom to Asiatic trade."[37] By September 1, 1868, the vast Orenburg and Western-Siberian customs line had been fully dismantled.

This claim, however, did not stand as absolute. Though convinced that foreign goods could not penetrate the Russian economic space, Reitern nevertheless promptly informed Turkestan Governor-general von Kaufman that European goods, which included, and in this case particularly meant,

35 Minor customs checkpoint, usually guarded by a toll gate only, without extensive rights to clear goods.

36 RGIA, f. 1152, op. 7, 1868, d. 172, l. 2–3.

37 Ibid. l. 2–3.

Anglo-Indian products, should be considered as forbidden to import. In the absence of any customs institutions, local *ziaket*[38] collectors were charged with enacting the ban. It is doubtful whether the *ziaket* collectors actively enforced the ban, however, by 1875, their position had been made obsolete in the Syr-Darya oblast' and the Zerashanskii *okrug* anyway, as the *ziaket* was replaced by a trade fee tailored after the "Obshchee polozhenie o poshlinakh za pravo torgovli i promyslov" (General Imperial Trade and Business Regulations) of 1865, thus ushering in the process of legal harmonization with the core empire.[39]

This effectively disposed of any customs control in large parts of the Turkestan Governorate-general. It was deemed sufficient to retain one post on the main trade route from Bukhara, manned with an overseer and horsemen from the indigenous population, to prevent the smuggling of tea, as alternative routes were considered not safe from raids anyway. Duties on trade with Khiva had been removed under paragraph 9 of the 1873 Gendemian treaty.[40] Only the Eastern parts of Turkestan were not yet deemed ready to implement imperial regulations and retained *ziaket* collectors, who also served to regulate the tea trade. Thus, making use of the arduousness and costliness of transportation through Peshaver or Kabul, and the limited access routes to Turkestan, the administration of the Governorate-general decided to save on administrative costs.

Simultaneously, the removal of the *ziaket* in Turkestan created a future fault line. Additional fees such as a trade fee were not covered under the 1873 Russo-Bukharan treaty signed in Shaar, which explicitly stated in paragraph 6 that no "third, additional fees on top of the ziaket will be levied" and thus would not apply for Bukharan subjects.[41] By removing the *ziaket* unilaterally, the Russian government thus implicitly granted the Bukharan-subject merchants full free trade to Turkestan, while the Russian subjects were now double-burdened: by an imperial trade fee in Turkestan and by a 2,5 % *ziaket* they had to pay in Bukhara.

38 The *ziaket* was often misunderstood or equated to customs by Russian authorities. However, it was a religiously founded trade fee of 2,5 %, collected at the place of trade and intended for charitable use. Thus, it does not imply either the protectionist function of customs nor does it share the concept of customs spaces.

39 RGVIA, f. 400, op. 1, d. 770, "Ob uchrezhdenii tamozhennogo nadzora v Turkestanskom krae", l. 1–2.

40 Gendemianskii mirnyi dogovor mezhdu Rossiei i Khivoi. In: *Sazonov, A. A./Gerasimova, G. N./Flushkova, O. A./Kisterev, S. K.* (eds.): Pod stiagom Rossii: Sbornik arkhivnykh dokumentov. Moscow 1992, 347–352, here 350.

41 Dogovor mezhdu Rossiei i Bukharoi. Shaar, 28 sentiabria/10 oktiabria 1873g. In: *Adamov, E. A.* (ed.): Sbornik dogovorov Rossii s drugimi gosudarstvami. 1856–1917. Moscow 1952, 135–139, here 136.

The situation remained one of little to no control and only improved slightly when the administration of the Governorate-general was urged by the State Comptrol to introduce stricter protective measures in 1881. Particularly the issue of protectionism towards Russian tea merchants was brought forward. It was argued that Russian merchants' sales of Kiakhta tea to Turkestan were not developing well, as the pacification of internal turmoil in Afghanistan meant that more tea was transported to the Central Asian khanates from the south.[42] These teas, subject to high customs fees upon entering Turkestan, appeared to be smuggled via new paths from Khiva into Turkestan, further evidenced by a slump in customs incomes.[43] However, the lack of reliable statistical data on trade turnovers and on smuggling in general put the fiscal sensibleness of any major overhauls into question. It was decided to upgrade the protection to four overseers with 17 horsemen, and charge them with levying data on the caravan trade. Further, the use of these caravan routes was prescribed, and the import of Persian, Turkish and Indo-European goods forbidden, with the exception of tea, indigo, and muslin – goods not produced in Russia.[44]

These cost-efficient measures were a far cry from the dense cordons on the empire's western border and not executed by professionally trained border guards and customs clerks. Such were not available either, as customs control in Turkestan was beyond the reach of the Ministry of Finance, whose customs department organized customs protection on the European border. In Turkestan, trade regulation was solely the domain of the Governor-general. However, by 1883, the State Council had come to the conclusion that a regular customs organization for Turkestan was becoming necessary.[45] A first step towards this goal was taken in 1886, when the administration of Turkestan was reformed and a departure from the insular principle in favor of the ministerial principle began, and a special official from the Ministry of Finance was attached to the local administration in order to professionalize the customs protection. Though not coordinated within one program or commission, these first steps signaled a departure from the policy of attracting the trade of the khanates by deregulation as practiced since the second quarter of the 19th century. Regarded in conjunction with the closure of the Transcaucasian transit in 1883, this development indicated a turn towards a protectionist and territorialized organization of the empire's economic space.

42 RGVIA, f. 400, op. 1, d. 770, l. 2ob.
43 Ibid. l. 44–44ob.
44 Ibid. l. 3, 13–15.
45 RGVIA, f. 400, op. 1, d. 979, "Ob ustroistve tamozhennogo nadzora na granitse s Persiei i Srednei Azii. O sodeistvii komandirovannomu v Zakaspiiskuiu oblast' po ministerstvu finansov general-maioru Baevu dlia issledovaniia voprosa", l. 1.

In the period between 1868 and 1886, the economic space of Turkestan was barely regulated. The paramount motivation behind the regulations was to reduce trade impediments between Turkestan and the Central Asian khanates. Though protectionist measures against European goods following through Bukhara were always part of the equation, the measures taken were hardly significant. This can be attributed both to cost-saving considerations and to an understanding of the region as infrastructurally so weak that topography and shipping expenditures would safeguard the imperial core economic space from contraband. This approach bore striking similarities to the Far-Eastern Porto-Franco. There, the existence of a free-trade zone on the empire's periphery did not appear problematic, as long as the territorial fragmentation of the empire made sure that it could not challenge the system of tariffs established for the European border. The debate surrounding the Transcaucasian transit in 1882–1883 already outlined a new understanding of cohesion between the Transcaucasus, Transcaspia, Bukhara and Turkestan; however, it would not be until 1891 that the integration of these territories into one economic space was put on the way.

One of the reasons for the changing vision of the Central Asian space around 1890 was Russia's rapid military expansion in the Transcaspian region, accompanied and made possible by the construction of the Transcaspian railway. By 1877, a military station had been established in Kizyl Arvat, halfway between the Caspian shore and the Bukharan border. The first attempt at pushing southeastward to conquer the fortress of Geok Tepe under General Nikolai Pavlovich Lokamin in 1879 ended in Russian defeat. Among other reasons, a shortage of supplies was cited. To avoid repeated humiliation, the construction of the Transcaspian railway, led by General Mikhail Nikolaevich Annenkov, had been begun in 1880. The railway, initially constructed for strategic, not economic considerations, contributed to the conquest of Geok Tepe in 1881 under General Mikhail Dmitrievich Skobelev.[46] By 1884, the oasis of Merv had been taken; in 1885, the Pandjeh incident brought Great Britain and Russia on the verge of war. As a result, the northern Afghan border was negotiated between the two empires – without Afghan participation – and Russia's expansion southeastward was stopped.

Its last substantial push for territory had brought the space between the Caspian Sea and the Khanates of Bukhara and Khiva under Russian control. Though the preconditions for an integrated economic strategy for

46 For a good overview over the history of the construction of the Transcaspian railway see *Stadelbauer, Jörg*: Bahnbau und kulturgeographischer Wandel in Turkmenien: Einflüsse der Eisenbahn auf Raumstruktur, Wirtschaftsentwicklung und Verkehrsintegration in einem Grenzgebiet des russischen Machtbereichs. Berlin 1973, 85–107, here 92; *Becker*: Russia's Protectorates in Central Asia, 136.

Russian-dominated Central Asia appeared more favorable than ever before, the fact remained, that while the Governorate-general of Turkestan and the Transcaspian oblast' were both full constituents of the Russian Empire, both Khiva and Bukhara remained protectorates. As such, particularly the latter enjoyed extensive rights concerning its internal organization. It looked back at a century-old history as a regional trade hub and separated the two Russian territories of the Governorate-general of Turkestan and the Transcaspian oblast' like a wedge.

Nevertheless, the Ministry of Finance quickly went about exploring the new economic opportunities of the Transcaspian region. In 1885, they commissioned General-Major Mikhail Georgievich Baev to explore Transcaspia's border with Persia and Afghanistan, particularly with a view to its economic situation, as previous studies had neglected this aspect. Baev, a military man of Ossetian descent, was serving as officer for special assignments on customs issues in the Caucasus[47] and had previously served at the Prussian customs border. As such, he was familiar with "the existing foundations [osnovaniia] of the customs protection, on both European and Asiatic borders."[48] Baev traveled as far as the Persian city of Meshkhed, capital of the Khorasan region, to evaluate trade potentials.

His report, also published monographically in 1888, attributed to the Transcaspian region the role of a transit space. Local consumption of Russian goods was limited to the Russian forces and as such the region was not seen as an important market for Russian goods, the way Turkestan and Bukhara were. Rather, it was intended to facilitate transit trade from Persia to Bukhara and allow the flow of raw materials into the Russian Empire, and in return the sale of Russian-manufactured goods to the Bukharan and northern Persian markets.[49] As such, enclosing the region could hardly serve any fiscal benefits. However, customs control gained importance as an instrument of macroeconomic regulation. Just as the Transcaspian could serve as a corridor for Russian exports, it could also be a dangerous gateway for Anglo-Indian and European goods to enter the Bukharan market. The Transcaspian railway, Baev warned, could "significantly ease the access of European goods into Central Asia through the Transcaspian region, particularly if trade routes in Persia were to be improved", and thus suggested that immediate protective measures were to be taken. Further, the establishment of customs protection on Transcaspia's

47 Chinovnik osobennykh poruchenii po tamozhennym delam na Kavkaze.

48 RGVIA, f. 400, op. 1, d. 979, l. 3ob.-5ob.

49 *Baev, Mikhail Georgievich*: Otchet chinovnika Ministerstva Finansov General'nogo Shtaba General-Maiora Baeva po komandirovke dlia issledovaniia nashei granitsy s Persiei i Avganistanom v predelakh Zakaspiiskoi oblasti. Saint Petersburg 1888, 73.

outside border would allow for the "free flow of Central Asian goods through the Transcaspian region to the internal markets of the empire."[50]

To this point, goods following from the Transcaspian across the Caspian Sea were subject to customs control in either Baku or Astrakhan, established with the aim of "preventing the duty-free import of similar Persian products."[51] Baev thus pointed to the necessity of both, integrating the Central Asian peripheries into the Russian imperial economic space and blocking access to their markets for European goods. Similarly to the debate around the Transcaucasian transit route, the new infrastructure, which promised to shrink the space, was supposed to be used to the benefit of Russian manufacturers and merchants only.

The aspiration to integrate the newly annexed Transcaspian territory into a monolithic imperial economic space, however, was limited by fiscal considerations and the political status of Bukhara. This becomes most visible in Baev's discussion of appropriate tariffs for green tea, a main staple for the population of the Transcaspian region. If these tariffs were set too high on the Persian border, tea would be imported into Bukhara instead, thus beyond Russian customs authorities' reach. The danger would be that they then could be smuggled into Transcaspia, as no customs control existed between the two territories. Thus, either a costly and fiscally unbearable border control between the Russian Empire and Bukhara was needed, or the inclusion of Bukhara into Russia's Central Asian customs line, removing the unwanted bridgehead wedged between Turkestan and Transcaspia.[52]

Both options were dismissed by Baev, who instead suggested a cost-efficient mode of control adjusted to local conditions. "The existing foundations of border protection for the European and Transcaucasian borders, if applied to the Transcaspian region, absolutely do not match the local conditions of the region and the local necessities of protection."[53] These foundations implied the creation of a customs territory delineated by a linear border, manned with both forces of the border guard and customs stations of different rank with different levels of clearing rights. Instead, he proposed to adopt the local practice of *ziaket* collection[54], levying customs inland in the places of trade, rather than on the border. This would allow to save expenditures on border guards along a vast and topographically challenging border and would not be as burdensome to the local population, who were accustomed to such a system of trade fees. In addition, local horsemen (dzhigity), who would not require

50 Ibid. 106–107.
51 Ibid. 106.
52 Ibid. 107–110.
53 Ibid. 111.
54 *Ziaket* in Afghanistan and Bukhara or *badzh* in Persia.

a translator either, could be recruited with little expenditures and deployed to patrol against smugglers.[55] The proposed strategy showed parallels to the decision to retain *ziaket* fees in Turkestan, which had been valid until 1875.

Baev's proposals were not implemented until 1889, thus, between 1885 and 1889, the Transcaspian region de-facto remained a porto-franco outside the empire's customs space. The establishment of a customs regime was simply not deemed necessary yet.[56] These new regulations were, however, not to remain valid for a long time, as in 1891 a lively debate surrounding the arrangement of Central Asia's economic space began, which ended with the inclusion of Bukhara into the Russian Empire's economic space. A decision which baffled the observant customs official Gubarevich-Radobyl'skii, cited at the beginning of this chapter. How had the constellation changed, causing the acceleration of the integration process?

3.4 The Integration of Central Asian Economic Space

It is argued that by 1891 a number of factors had converged: A global economic crisis had hit Russia in the mid-1880s, leading to an often-cited "crisis of overproduction" and a shift in its economic policies even further towards high-protectionism.[57] Russian political influence in Bukhara had grown through the stationing of a Political Agent in Bukhara and the ascent of the young Emir Said Abd al-Ahad Khan. Finally, the Transcaspian railway had been extended until Samarkand, thus creating a link between Turkestan and the Transcaspian. These factors brought the Ministry of War, the Ministry of Finance and the Ministry of Foreign Affairs to sit down at one table and design a profound change to the arrangement of the Central Asian economic space.

The European free-trade phase that had been ushered in by the Cobden-Chevalier system and to some extent influenced Russia's customs policy in the 1860s and early 1870s had definitely ended by the late 1870s, with a global reversal towards protectionist policies on the way. Its origin lay with the 1873 depression that had affected all major industrialized countries due to an increasing degree of globalization.[58] Russia was no exception to this

55 *Baev*: Otchet po komandirovke dlia issledovaniia nashei granitsy s Persiei i Avganistanom, 114–115.

56 RGIA, f. 1152, op. 11, 1893, d. 222, "Ob ustroistve tamozhennogo nadzora v Zakaspiiskoi oblasti", l. 2.

57 The notion of a "crisis of overproduction" is brought forward by Stepanov. However, it is more apt to speak of a "crisis of regulation" or a "crisis of political clientelism" as discussed below. *Stepanov*: Mikhail Khristoforovich Reitern, 34.

58 *Torp*: Herausforderung der Globalisierung, 147–148, 154, 173–174, 176.

trend, only that its reversal was milder, as it had not fully embraced free-trade policies in the first place.[59] Minister of Finance Nikolai Bunge (1881–1886) had further inherited a state budget deeply disturbed by the Russo-Turkish War of 1877–1878, and thus fiscal interests, next to the protection of Russian industries, played a significant role in the formation of tariffs, even though Bunge's own views partially contradicted this.[60] The 1880s were marked by a customs arms-race, particularly between the Russian Empire and the German Empire.[61]

The persistent economic crisis further led to what has been described as a "crisis of overproduction." The sugar industry was particularly affected. However, modern economists reject the concept of overproduction which had been put forward by 19th century thinkers such as J. S.L. de Sismondi and Karl Marx arguing that it is "based on the belief that the need and desire for goods is limited and the rapidly expanding production in a capitalist society inherently leads to the supply of goods outstripping the limited need and desire." However, it is argued that "the only sense in which there can be an overproduction of goods is in a partial or relative sense: there can be an overproduction of some goods in the economy; however, this implies a corresponding underproduction of other goods."[62] In theory, a market would self-regulate, productive forces would be redistributed, and thus economy-wide overproduction or a "crisis of overproduction" constitutes a misleading description.

In the case of the Russian Empire, it is more apt to speak of a "crisis of regulation" or a "crisis of political clientelism" caused by sectional overproduction. The Russian sugar industry had initially developed due to unintentional governmental protectionism, as discussed earlier. Overproduction was thus not a failure of market mechanisms, but of state regulation. Further, the Ministry of Finance harbored a political interest in warding off too heavy a drop in sugar prices, which would be detrimental to a large number of manufacturers. The sugar industry was to a large degree in the hands of members of the gentry; with both factory owners who had entered the business in the foundational decades of the industry as well as new-comers from the gentry in the late 19th century.[63] The conservative rule of Alexander III relied on the gentry's

59 For an account of the competition between free-trade and protectionist positions in late 19th century Russia with a focus on the western border see *Krikhunov*: Protektsionizm ili Fritrederstvo.

60 *Stepanov*: Nikolai Khristianovich Bunge, 59.

61 *Torp*: Herausforderung der Globalisierung, 198. For an overview of the Russian Empire's trade policies see chapter 2.

62 *Simpson*: Money, Banking, and the Business Cycle, Volume II: Remedies and Alternative Theories, 9–12.

63 *Munting, Roger*: The Russian Beet Sugar Industry in the XIXth Century. In: The Journal of European Economic History, 2 (1984), 291–309, here 293, 299–302.

support, and thus the re-regulation and bailout of the sugar industry followed primarily a political or clientelist logic.

Thus, in order to create an additional market for the surplus sugar, the Russian government set export incentives by offering the return of excise fees (production fees) when sugar was exported abroad, to avoid a plummeting of prices within the Russian Empire. The export to Asiatic markets was further subsidized by an additional payment of one ruble per pud.[64] The basic problem lay in the combination of Russia's relatively high production costs for its manufactured goods compared to other industrialized countries, and the increasing walling-off of European markets. Russia's manufactured goods simply could not be sold to Europe. For branches such as the sugar industry and the textile industry, the Asiatic markets gained importance during the crisis.

Looking towards the competitors, Russia's Political Agent in Bukhara, Nikolai Valer'evich Charykov, identified two possible approaches in 1887: "In Western Europe, with the onset of the current commercial and industrial crisis, two main measures are taken that can ensure an increased demand and the necessary increase in prices. Those have been: cutting down production and opening up new markets."[65] The first option was deemed the English solution and considered to burden the working class and exacerbate the social question[66]; a notion the Ministry of Finance was becoming increasingly sensitive to under Minister of Finance Nikolai Bunge.[67] The second suggestion was to follow the German example of securing new markets in Africa, the Pacific and China.[68]

For Russia, such were considered to be its Central Asian territories and protectorates, as well as Persia, north and north-western Afghanistan, and Kashgar. Apart from the establishment of a branch of the Russian State Bank in Bukhara, the Political Agent suggested that the quickest possible continuation of the railway to Bukhara and a coordination of means of transportation across the Caspian Sea, the Volga, the Transcaucasian railway, and the Black Sea, allowing also to access the Odessa-Moscow railway, were necessary. A such integrated market would allow for faster turnover of capital and goods and serve to support Russian merchants.[69]

64 Ibid. 303–304.

65 AVPRI, f. 147, op. 485, d. 1344, "Delo ob okhrane Sredne-Aziatskoi granitsy, tamozhennom nadzore, komandirovanii Baeva, o vkliuchenii Bukharskogo khanstva v Russkuiu chertu, o poshline na Indiiskii chai", l. 43ob.

66 Ibid. l. 43ob.

67 *Stepanov*: Nikolai Khristianovich Bunge, 62.

68 AVPRI, f. 147, op. 485, d. 1344, l. 43ob.

69 Ibid. l. 46–46ob.

His report was a reaction to growing complaints about the disadvantaged position Russian subjects found themselves in after the removal of the *ziaket* in Turkestan in 1875, which had undermined the principle of trade parity between Bukhara and the Russian Empire. Under the duress of the global economic crisis, this pre-installed fault line began to crack. Sectional overproduction had led Moscow manufacturers to sell their goods, granting most favorable credits with a duration of 18–20 months, which were often not paid back, or outright selling their produce below production costs, speculating on an increase in market prices in the future.[70]

In March 1886, the trade company N. Kudrin and eleven other companies had petitioned Turkestan Governor-general Nikolai Ottonovich Rozenbakh for the removal of the *ziaket* in Bukhara. He considered the timing good to propose this delicate issue to the Emir and asked permission from the Ministry of Foreign Affairs to negotiate with Bukhara through the new Political Agent.[71] Political Agent Charykov generally supported the notion that increased exchange of goods with Bukhara should "lead to the establishment of uniformity of laws, regulating the rights and duties of trade in both dominions. The Russian laws are more suitable to modern trade and industries than the Muslim law operating in Bukhara."[72] However, he warned that the *ziaket* was a staple of the Emir's budget, and freeing Russian merchants from paying it would significantly cut state income. He feared that the Emir would find himself "forced to increase direct taxes to compensate the deficit, whereby the moral responsibility for the new burden on the Khanate's population would fall on the Russian government."[73] This would undermine the "peaceful increase of the sale of Russian goods in Bukhara, which is only possible by retaining the Emir's prestige and order within the Khanate, and with the increase in the wealth and buying power of the mass of the indigenous population."[74]

Taking the trade data from 1883, which stated an import of Russian goods worth 15 million rubles, *ziaket* revenue would have constituted 375 thousand rubles. With an additional 225 thousand rubles of *aminana*, a Bukharan export tax which would have been removed as well to ensure parity, the Emir's deficit would have been a substantial 600 thousand ruble.[75] The Political Agent thus suggested a middle way: the *aminana* could be retained, as from a Russian perspective it would serve as a protectionist measure, once the railway link to

70 Ibid. l. 38ob.–39.
71 Ibid. l. 11–11ob. For a similar petition from Grigorii Lukin Konovokh (10.12.1886) see ibid. l. 30–34ob.
72 Ibid. l. 14ob.
73 Ibid. l. 17ob.
74 Ibid. l. 18.
75 Ibid. l. 18.

Turkestan was finished. Goods following from Bukhara would have to pay the *aminana*, whereas goods transited from Turkestan through Bukhara would be exempt from the fee, thus canceling out the advantage Bukharian merchants enjoyed over their Turkestan counterparts due to the shorter transport route from Bukhara to Moscow.[76] The *ziaket* could be replaced by a 1st guild fee under the all-imperial regulations for large-scale Russian merchants, whereas merchants with a small-scale turnover could continue to pay *ziaket* profiting from its low 2,5 % ad valorem stakes.[77] The thus much smaller deficit in the Emir's income would be compensated by the stimulation of trade and resulting higher turnover.[78] The establishment of a political agency had strengthened Russia's position within Bukhara and constituted the basis for the discussion of a possible introduction of imperial regulations in Bukhara.

Nevertheless, the Asiatic Department of the Ministry of Foreign Affairs did not support the notion and, pointing to the primacy of supporting the Emir's prestige and independence, stuck to its policy of non-intervention. Further, the Bukharan administration could neither bear the transition to the Russian system of trade fees, nor would it serve Russian trade interests in the bordering countries. The proposed adjustment would privilege large Russian merchants, weakening smaller competition. However, political interests demanded favoring the Bukharan merchants in particular, as it was them who facilitated trade to Persia, where Russian merchant companies were hardly present.[79] Further, it was argued that the Bukharan markets were protected sufficiently, as the import-ban on European goods to Turkestan had the side effect of lowering their import volume into Bukhara in general.[80]

Apart from the Governor-general of Turkestan and the Political Agent in Bukhara, both "men on the spot", as well as the naturally interested party of Russian merchants, the Ministry of Finance as well contacted the Ministry of Foreign Affairs on the issue. The new Minister of Finance Ivan Alekseevich Vyshnegradskii suggested to Foreign Minister Nikolai Karlovich Girs on March 11, 1887 to reconsider the inclusion of Bukhara into the Russian customs line. He was reviving an initiative of his predecessor, Bunge, who had made the suggestion while considering the establishment of Transcaspian customs in 1885. Vyshnegradskii proposed to establish a customs line on Bukhara's border with Afghanistan, linking it to the Turkestan Governorate-general's

76 Ibid. l. 17–17ob.

77 The annual guild fee in 1887 was set at 750 rubles; thus any merchant trading under 30.000 rubles annually would benefit from paying the *ziaket* rather than the fee. This particularly applied to indigenous merchants from Turkestan, legally considered Russian subjects, yet having an operation very different from large trade companies.

78 AVPRI, f. 147, op. 485, d. 1344, l. 18ob.

79 Ibid. l. 26ob.-29.

80 Ibid. l. 36.

line. The tariffs would be set by the Russian authorities, however, in order to compensate the Emir's loss of *ziaket* revenues, a fixed sum from the customs incomes could be transferred to the Emir.[81]

This proposal technically implied the abolition of Bukhara's trade autonomy and an inroad into its internal finances inconsistent with the principles of the 1873 treaty. Vyshnegradskii's proposal was motivated by Britain's construction of a railway to Quetta and Pishin, destined to reach Kandahar (which it never did).[82] Despite these concerns, Vyshnegradskii's proposal was rejected by the Foreign Ministry, citing that it was neither fiscally reasonable due to the large and topographically challenging space that would have to be secured, nor necessary, as trade was developing to the benefit of Russia anyways.[83] Eventually, the Transcaspian region received only a provisional customs control in 1889, as explicated in the previous section.

Throughout the 1880s, political interests, stability in Bukhara, and a policy of non-intervention had been paramount for the Ministry of Foreign Affairs, thus foreclosing substantial action coordinated with other ministries in order to re-organize the Central Asian economic space. Impulses, including the regulatory harmonization of Bukhara with the Russian Empire, had come both from regional representatives such as the Turkestan Governor-general and the Political Agent in Bukhara, as well as from the Ministry of Finance in the imperial center. Under the pressure of an ongoing global economic crisis and the general shift towards protectionist policies in the 1880s, the integration of a large prospective market and the state-led elimination of foreign competition seemed only logical. The on-going construction of the Transcaspian railway constituted the foundation for such a reinterpretation of the Central Asian space. A territorial vision, which had already been formulated by the Society for Aid to Russian Industry and Trade as early as 1869, now appeared both infrastructurally tangible and matching the economic spirit of the time, and thus began seeping into governmental circles.

Nevertheless, during Baev's expedition in 1885 the Transcaspian railway was still little more than a military supply line, a cul-de-sac ending in Bami, hardly 294 verst of railway tracks from the Caspian Sea station Uzun-Ada. It lacked 1049 verst of railway lines to link it to Samarkand.[84] It had already reached Merv by 1886, and Bukhara by February 1888. By May 1888, Samarkand had been added to the line. As it was expanding, the new railway rendered the recent adjustments to the regulation of customs space obsolete. The strategy of low-cost customs collection based on local practice and indigenous collectors,

81 Ibid. l. 50.
82 Ibid. l. 50ob.-51.
83 Ibid. l. 52–53ob.
84 Entrance "Bami" in Entsiklopedicheskii slovar' Brokgauza i Efrona, Tom II (1891), 867.

transferred from Turkestan to Transcaspia, was challenged by the improved infrastructural situation, as no provisions against smuggling on the railway existed. Meanwhile, developing the full trade potential of the new railway would require a minimum of trade barriers between Samarkand and Moscow. Neither complicated customs formalities at the Caspian Sea, separating Transcaspia from the core empire, nor the crossing of Bukhara, a foreign territory in terms of customs, could be acceptable anymore.

In 1891, only two years after customs regulations in Transcaspia had been put in place, Vyshnegradskii returned to his proposal from 1887 to include Bukhara into the Russian customs line, arguing towards the Foreign Ministry that the circumstances had changed substantially. Samarkand had been linked to the Transcaspian railway; meanwhile, political unrest in Afghanistan had led to a rerouting of Anglo-Indian goods imported by Bukharan merchants. Rather than following through Afghanistan, they were now shipped to the Persian Gulf, went north towards Meshkhed, and covered the last section via the Transcaspian railway. The attraction of new goods certainly benefitted the railway's profitability, but it indicated the potential danger of losing dominance on the Bukharan market. Further, petitions from Bukharan merchants, backed by the Emir, had been handed in, proposing an improved trade route for tea importation. The merchants petitioned for permission to conduct transit trade from Batum on the Black Sea across the Transcaucasian region, the Caspian Sea, and eventually into Bukhara.[85] A such designed shipping route would cut over-land transportation to a minimum, relying solely on overseas shipping and the Russian railway, and could thus dramatically reduce prices for tea.

Considering the lack of any customs control between the Transcaspian region and Bukhara, as well as the weak protection on the Turkestan border, the intrusion of foreign produce into imperial Russia's economic space from Bukhara could hardly be fended off if the new route created a sufficiently substantial price difference to incentivize smuggling.[86] The scenario outlined by Vyshnegradskii thus pointed to the ambivalence of the new railway: it had the potential to reshape global trade routes, but without proper customs protection it could just as well become a gateway for uncontrollable imports, which would spread along the railway network into the empire's core economic space. Thus, he saw the time as ripe for the inclusion of Bukhara into the Russian Empire's customs territory.

Unlike in his previous attempts to further this cause, Vyshnegradskii anticipated the Foreign Ministry's objection concerning the Emir's prestige and suggested leaving the *ziaket* in place. The Minister of Finance argued that the entrepreneurial security which an inclusion of Bukhara into the

85 AVPRI, f. 147, op. 485, d. 1344, l. 61–64.
86 Ibid. l. 61–64.

Russian customs zone would offer to Russian merchants would be a sufficient incentive to expand their operation, thus creating larger storage facilities and increasing turn-over. Meanwhile, the Bukharan population would profit from an increased capital flow as well, and in addition parts of the customs incomes could be used for socially useful projects such as the development of regional infrastructures.[87]

Unlike the Minister of Finance, the Political Agent in Bukhara, though agreeing with the observation on an increase in Anglo-British imports, did not see any imminent danger. In his opinion, only a British-Afghan trade settlement could sufficiently alter the regional trade and create a threat. Nevertheless, he pointed to another flaw in the customs system, caused by the weak customs border protection and Bukhara's exclusion. In order to attenuate the effects of sugar overproduction and facilitate exports, sugar exported into Asiatic countries, including Bukhara, was granted a premium. The exported sugar was thus significantly cheaper than sugar on the domestic Russian market. However, if exported sugar cleared of excise-fees was reimported into the imperial economic space, it would put pressure on domestic prices and nullify the intended price-stabilization-effects.[88] As long as re-importation remained arduous due to a weak infrastructural connection between the Russian Empire's south-eastern border regions, this export-oriented protectionist instrument functioned as intended. The new railway, however, significantly increased the danger of a wider dissemination of reimported sugar within the empire's core customs space.

Against the backdrop of a general reform of the tariff system towards high protectionism, with the tariff of 1891, an airtight sealing of the Russian customs space was mandatory – such an obvious leak undermining the protectionist system being unacceptable. Thus, within just one and a half months, first the export premium of 80 kopeek per pud was abolished by the State Council, followed by the abolition of the excise-fee return in 1892. The latter, however, only applied to exports via the Transcaspian land border to Persia, not for export via the Caspian Sea and the Transcaucasian land border, as they did have tighter customs protection. As a result, sugar exports to Persia plummeted.[89]

The contradictions of the existing regime did not escape the first Head of the Transcaspian Region (Nachalnik Zakaspiskoi Oblasti), Aleksei Nikolaevich Kuropatkin, either, as he pushed for a quick introduction of a new customs regime:

87 Ibid. l. 61–64.

88 Ibid. l. 66–75ob.

89 RGVIA, f. 400, op. 1, d. 1474, "O vkliuchenii Bukhary i Khivy v tamozhennuiu chertu i ob ustroistve tamozhennogo nadzora v Zakaspiiskoi oblasti. Chast' 2", l. 104ob.-105ob.

> [...] it is hard to argue that the abolition of excise returns on sugar and the non-extension of the return of customs duties for cotton and other foreign [raw] materials for the manufactured goods of domestic [otechestvennaia] production, if exported to Persia on the land borders of the Transcaspian region, were a mistake. The faster this mistake is corrected, the better. Each month of further hesitation constitutes a sharp contradiction to the general customs practice on our western border, based on the recognized [soznannoi] idea of national economy and aimed at the stimulation of the domestic [otechestvennoi] factory industry [zavodsko fabrichnoi promyshlennosti] [...] Every month of further hesitation gives England new chances for success in the battle with us for the markets of Khorasan.[90]

This specific type of export subvention and external protectionism required an airtight linear system of customs control, not the market-place-based system of *ziaket* collection, which was in place.

The issue made it obvious that while better infrastructural integration of the Russian Empire's Central-Asian domains did promise new markets and a release valve for domestic overproduction in certain industries, it also increased the pressure to homogenize trade regulations on the periphery with imperial regulations. The deregulation strategy pursued since the first quarter of the 19th century was reaching its limits, with economic activities on the south-eastern periphery showing increasing repercussions in the imperial center. The coexistence of high protectionism and de-facto free trade within the imperial edifice was no longer secured by territorial fragmentation. It is hard to gauge in how far the concerns of a significant reimport of excise-cleared sugar and the ensuing negative economic effects were truly substantiated in 1892, however, the debate demonstrates that the perception of the imperial economic space's cohesion had shifted within the imperial administration, prompting a shift towards regulatory integration.

However, in the case of Bukhara, it was not as simple as issuing a new set of regulations for any Russian border province, but a politically delicate endeavor. Pavel Mikhailovich Lessar, Political Agent in Bukhara, warned that an inclusion of Bukhara would not be easy to negotiate with the Emir, whose support was crucial to the success of the project, as only he could ensure the cooperation of local authorities in Bukhara. Further, the drawing of a customs line in eastern Bukhara would have been tantamount to the acceptance of the Afghan border line, not yet fully settled with Great Britain. Neither was he supportive of Vyshnegradskii's suggestion to allocate customs incomes for infrastructural development, as these long-term measures would hardly serve to pacify the local population, faced with increased prices if they were included

90 Ibid. l. 149–149ob.

into the Russian customs zone. He concluded that the integration of Bukhara was not necessary at this point.[91]

Nevertheless, an interministerial preparatory meeting had been called in and decided in favor of pursuing the integration of Bukhara. Despite the skepticism of its Political Agent in Bukhara, present at the meeting as well, the Asiatic Department of the Foreign Ministry had distanced itself from its 1880s policy of non-intervention. Apart from the general economic argument, it was particularly worried about the disturbed parity between Turkestan's and Bukhara's indigenous population.[92] Count Dmitrii Alekseevich Kapnist, director of the Asiatic Department, argued that:

> [...] Bukharan and Khivan products such as cotton, rice, wool, lambskin and the like are imported into Russia duty-free and freely compete on our internal markets with similar Turkestan products. Meanwhile tea, indigo and some other products not produced in Russia are subject to a substantial duty upon import into the Turkestan region and thus our subjects, of the same tribe as the Bukharans [odnoplemennye Bukhartsam] and neighbors of the latter, while not enjoying any advantages to the sale of their own products, pay a tax, which the subjects of the Bukharan Emir do not know. Such a situation is obviously not normal and not desirable.[93]

In a further council on June 15, 1892, the details of the arrangement were negotiated between the Ministry of Finance, the Ministry of War and the Foreign Ministry. A pressing question was how to inform the Emir of Bukhara about the plans. However, as the *ziaket* was supposed to be retained, the inclusion would not encompass an "outward decrease of the importance and power of the Emir in his relationship to his subjects", nor would his revenues be decreased. Thus, "if put correctly", the closer connection established with the Russian Empire through the customs inclusion could be framed as mutually beneficial, greatly diffusing the delicacy of the issue. Thus, it was deemed adequate to inform the Emir during his planned visit to Saint Petersburg.[94]

Further issues included the delineation of the eastern Bukharan customs border, the retention of the local currency, ten'ga, before a monetary integration could be discussed at a later stage, as well as the allocation of customs incomes for infrastructural measures in Bukhara.[95] The Ministry of War objected to the latter, as the integration of Bukhara did not serve a fiscal goal and possible surpluses were not foreseeable. Meanwhile, the Bukharan Emir was not losing any revenue and thus should not be compensated additionally. The council, however, rejected the motion, arguing that the introduction of

91 AVPRI, f. 147, op. 485, d. 1344, l. 66–75ob.

92 Ibid. l. 77–81.

93 Ibid. l. 78–78ob.

94 Ibid. l. 110ob.

95 Ibid. l. 112ob.-114.

previously unknown customs in Bukhara, particularly on the staple product of green tea, would increase consumer prices. Investing into infrastructure development would compensate the disadvantages by putting Bukhara's population into labor and thus raising their wealth and purchasing power.[96] The tariffs for foreign goods, valid in Turkestan since 1886, were to be extended to Bukhara.[97]

On August 7, 1892, the decision of the council had been approved by Tsar Alexander III.[98] During his visit to Saint Petersburg, on January 15, 1893, the Emir had been instructed about the planned changes.[99] The drawing of the new customs line had been treated as an urgent matter and by June 4, 1893, a reconnaissance party under General-Major Baev, who had already led the 1885 expedition into the Transcaspian region, had been dispatched.[100] Baev, who had suffered a stroke [udar] on August 22 in Kalai Khuve, had been temporarily replaced by German Karlovich Kaizer, Head of the Turkestan Customs District.[101] A second expedition led by Nikolai Antonovich Usov, Head of the Kalish Customs District, was dispatched on September 30. On October 29, 1893, Usov met with the Emir of Bukhara to present his findings and the proposed setup of the customs border and received the Emir's permission.[102] By June 6, 1894, the law had passed the State Council and been ratified by the Tsar. Customs were to open on January 1, 1895.[103]

The integration of Bukhara and the homogenization of customs regulations in Transcaspia, Bukhara, and Turkestan marked a significant departure from the prior approach to managing economic space on the Russian Empire's south-eastern border. The prior flexible situative approach often assumed the shape of deregulated trade. This was partially conditioned by a lack of administrative resources, partially by a narrower regional focus of the local administration, and definitely facilitated by administrative and infrastructural separation. With customs and trade regulation moving from the domain of the Governor-general of Turkestan into the domain of the Ministry of Finance, the insular logic of administration was replaced with a linear one. The Ministry of Finance, which had in the late 1880s embarked on a nationalist and protectionist course in its economic doctrines, introduced a stronger

96 Ibid. l. 112ob.-113ob.
97 Ibid. l. 114–114ob.
98 Ibid. l. 115.
99 Ibid. l. 120.
100 RGIA, f. 21, op. 12, d. 31, "Ob ustroistve tamozhennoi chasti v Srednei Azii", l. 36.
101 RGVIA, f. 400, op. 1, d. 1473, "O vkliuchenii Bukhary i Khivy v tamozhennuiu chertu i ob ustroistve tamozhennogo nadzora v Zakaspiiskoi oblasti. Chast' 1", l. 193.
102 RGIA, f. 21, op. 12, d. 31, l. 36ob.-37.
103 Polnoe sobranie zakonov Rossiikoi Imperii. Sobranie 3. Volume 14. Saint Petersburg 1898, no. 10774.

all-imperial macro-economic perspective into the management of Russia's Central Asian economic space. Abandoning the flexible approach, it pushed for an increased homogenization of trade regulations. In this respect, the 1890s restructuring of customs in Central Asia marked a departure from an imperial management of space, characterized by slow negotiation processes between a multiplicity of institutions and actors and a reliance on decentralization, towards a nation-state inspired homogenization and centralization of spatial management aimed at a "Durchstaatlichung" – the state's administrative permeation of space – which was to secure the competitiveness of the empire in the future.[104]

Ten years after Minister of Finance Bunge's first proposal, Transcaspia, Bukhara, Khiva, and Turkestan were encircled by a unified linear customs line.[105] The trade regulations for Russian Central Asia were mostly uniform, although particular exceptions such as the retention of the *ziaket* in Bukhara persisted. The Turkestan tariff, as well as the 1886 ban on the importation of European and Anglo-Indian products – with the existing exceptions on tea, indigo and muslin – was extended to Bukhara. The export premiums previously abolished due to the lack of customs control could now be reinstated as well, as the danger of re-importation was considered to be dispelled.

The construction of the Transcaspian railway had significantly altered the spatial vision in the imperial ministries, contesting the co-existence of heterogeneous customs regimes and prompting administrative homogenization. But railway technology also promised to become a powerful tool in restructuring internal and global trade currents. Against the backdrop of the economic crisis of the 1880s and a turn towards protectionism, this power for reshaping economic constellations, as well as Russia's increasing political influence and ambitions in Bukhara, resulted in a convergence of interests between various ministries. For the first time, a coordinated interministerial approach towards Central Asia's economic integration into the Russian imperial space was attempted.

104 *Ganzenmüller, Jörg/Tönsmeyer, Tatjana*: Einleitung: Vom Vorrücken des Staates in die Fläche. Ein europäisches Phänomen des langen 19. Jahrhunderts. In: *Ganzenmüller, Jörg/Tönsmeyer, Tatjana* (eds.): Einleitung: Vom Vorrücken des Staates in die Fläche. Ein europäisches Phänomen des langen 19. Jahrhunderts. Köln/Weimar/Wien 2016, 7–31, 16–17.

105 For topographic reasons, the customs line was nevertheless partially positioned inland and not directly on the state border.

3.5 Shaping Global Trade Currents

This new coordinated, interministerial approach was institutionalized with the establishment of the Permanent Council on Matters of Trade with Persia and on the Asiatic Border (Postoiannoe soveshchanie po delam o torgovle s Persiei i po sredneaziatskoi granitse). The impulse had come from the Department of Trade and Manufacture of the Ministry of Finance, which suggested in April 1893 that issues of trade in the region could not be resolved without prior coordination and agreement with other departments of the Ministry of Finance as well as representatives of the Ministry of War and the Ministry of Foreign Affairs.[106] The goal of the council was to facilitate the harmonization of political and macroeconomic interests of Asiatic trade, as seen from the example of tea transit to Bukhara.

One of the main concerns expressed by the Emir of Bukhara in the run-up to the customs integration was the stabilization of the price for green tea, as it constituted a main staple of the Bukharan population. The existing *ziaket* of 2,5 % ad valorem constituted fees of around 1 ruble per pud of tea. However, the Turkestan tea tariff, which was to apply to Bukhara after its inclusion in the customs territory, had stakes of 14 rubles 40 kopeks for higher quality green teas and 6 rubles per pud for lower quality green teas.[107] If the retail price for tea was to remain stable, only two options were possible: reducing the tariff or compensating for the tariff differential by lowering the product cost of imported tea. The latter was only possible by significantly reducing the costs of shipping. As discussed above, a petition to open up an alternative, significantly more cost-efficient tea trade route had already been put forward by Bukharan merchants in the late 1880s, yet had been rejected for fear of creating an uncontrollable gateway to the empire's core economic space. With the inclusion of the Khanate of Bukhara into the Russian customs zone, this objection lost its validity. The administrative and infrastructural unification with the Russian Empire allowed the opening of a new trade route to Bukhara, which benefitted from both the Suez Canal and the railway system constructed in the Transcaucasus and the Transcaspian regions.

Prior tea had been imported into Bukhara mainly by two routes. Either by land from Peshaver through Kabul, Tashe-Kurgan and Kelif into Bukhara. Or it was shipped from Bombay to the port of Bender-Abbas, and then transported overland through Meshkhed, to Dushak or Ashkhabad, and then into Bukhara.

106 RGIA, f. 20, op. 7, d. 183, "Ob obrazovanii postoiannogo soveshchaniia po delam o torgovle s Persiei i po sredneaziatskoi granitse", l. 80–82.

107 RGVIA, f. 400, op. 1, d. 1475, "O vkliuchenii Bukhary i Khivy v tamozhennuiu chertu i ob ustroistve tamozhennogo nadzora v Zakaspiiskoi oblasti. Chast' 3", l. 159.

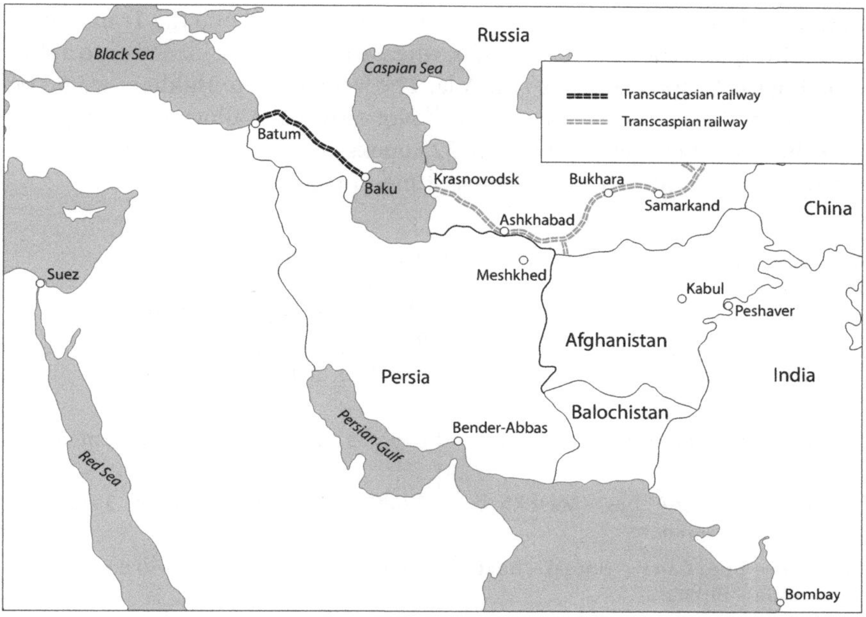

Figure 3: Map of Asia indicating important trade hubs.

The first route through Afghanistan was significantly quicker. The second route through Persia took almost double as long, however, with significantly reduced shipping costs.[108] A transit route through the Suez Canal and the Transcaucasus promised to be both cheaper and quicker. However, considering that until 1895 Bukhara-subject consumers were already in an undesirably preferential position compared to the Russian-subject consumers in Turkestan, it was not in the interest of the Russian Empire to facilitate a quicker and cheaper route, as had been proposed in the petition of the Bukharan tea merchants. Such a route would have made Bukharan tea with its ad valorem clearance incredibly cheap, whereas the fixed and relatively high tariffs in Turkestan would have created such a significant price differential that an upsurge in smuggling would have been inevitable. With the new integrated space, however, the Ministry of Finance was now in a position to permit the transit of tea from Batum to Bukhara, as it would not constitute a preferential treatment of Bukharan subjects anymore while simultaneously meeting the demand of the Emir of Bukhara for stable tea prices.

This new trade route was both significantly faster and cheaper than the previous options. Indian teas could now be shipped from Bombay through the

108 Ibid. l. 157–157ob.

Suez Canal to the Black Sea port of Batum, then loaded onto the Transcaucasian railway and transported to Baku, where they would be loaded onto a ship crossing the Caspian Sea to Uzun-Ada. The last stretch to Bukhara would be covered by the Transcaspian railway.[109] Not only did it allow to cut shipping costs by a sum between 5 rubles and 52 kopeks and 9 rubles 94 kopeks; it also allowed significantly shorter turnover times, further reducing prices.

Table 1: Cost and duration of tea transportation to Bukhara.

Trade route	Shipping costs per pud	Duration
Peshaver – Kabul – Tashe-Kurgan – Kelif – Bukhara	12 rubles 80 kopek	75 days
Bombay – Bender-Abbas – Meshkhed – Dushak – Bukhara	8 rubles 38 kopeks	Approx. 5 months
Bombay – Bender-Abbas – Meshkhed – Ashkhabad – Bukhara	8 rubles 61 kopeks	Approx. 5 months
Bombay – Suez Canal – Batum – Baku – Uzun-Ada – Bukhara	2 rubles 86 kopeks	45–50 days

Data extracted from: RGVIA, f. 400, op. 1, d. 1475, "O vkliuchenii Bukhary i Khivy v tamozhennuiu chertu i ob ustroistve tamozhennogo nadzora v Zakaspiiskoi oblasti. Chast' 3", l. 157ob.

The expansion of a customs system based on a territorial and linear logic, as practiced on Russia's western border, instead of the dotted logic of the *ziaket* collection practice in the Central Asian khanates, allowed for the implementation of this protectionist regulatory measure. It was very much in the logic of the Minister of Finance Sergey Vitte's promotion of a *Nationalökonomie* program. Before his rise to the ministerial post, he had served as head of the Railway Department of the Ministry of Finance and had already formulated the necessity of harmonizing/adjusting railway tariffs to the state's macroeconomic necessities. Thus, he "offered an alternative vision and in doing so made explicit the connections between the *commercial topography* that surrounded him and the capacity of railroad technology to transform it."[110] Vitte had been the first to popularize the ideas of Friedrich List to a non-German-speaking readership by publishing "Natsional'naia ekonomiia

109 Ibid. l. 157ob.
110 *Wcislo*: Rereading Old Texts, 80.

i Fridrich List" in 1889 – basically a Vitte-annotated collection of List texts, tailored and partially curtailed to support Vitte's agenda.[111]

The introduction of the new trade route ticked multiple boxes at once: both railway lines and the Caspian Sea shipping company "Kavkaz i Merkurii" would receive more cargo, making them more profitable, and tea trade could be brought under the control of Russian merchants, wringing it from Peshaver merchants.[112] This basically would solve the longstanding problem of supporting Russian tea trade from Kiakhta to Turkestan, which was one reasoning for the tea tariffs on its Bukharan borders. Even Russia's maritime fleet could be fostered if these customs exemptions were only granted to teas shipped under the Russian flag to Batum.[113]

Shortly after Bukhara's integration into the Russian Empire's customs territory and the ensuing establishment of this transit route, an additional political aspect became apparent. The Brothers K. and S. Popov tea trading company (tovarishchestvo chainoi torgovli i skladov Brat'ia K. i. S. Popov) pointed to the fact that only Indian teas were eligible to benefit from the transit route.[114] An arrangement which would seem only logical, considering that both trade routes transported tea from Bombay. However, these teas, the Popov brothers argued, were often of Chinese origin and only repackaged in Bombay, thus giving them the appearance of Indian teas. They themselves had attempted direct imports from China successfully, yet, customs authorities in Baku had denied granting the lower tariff stakes set for teas transited to Bukhara, as these only applied to Indian teas. The company thus petitioned for an adjustment of the rule, seeing that:

> [...] there are no gains, nor goals in impeding this natural direction [of direct trade from China] and forbidding the transit of Chinese green tea bought by Russian merchants on the market in Shanghai first-hand and support, by this ban, the market in Bombay to the benefit of foreigners and the detriment of Russian entrepreneurs, forcing them, no matter what, to buy Green tea not first-hand in Shanghai, if they wanted to use the transit, but even from third-hand of foreigners in Bombay.[115]

Further, even the head of the Baku customs and quarantine office himself confirmed that it would require a "very fine connoisseur" to distinguish between

111 *Vitte*: Natsional'naia ekonomika i Fridrikh List; *Wortman*: Scenarios of Power, 267–268; *Wendler*: List-Rezeption in Rußland, 489; *Von Laue*: Sergei Witte and the Industrialization of Russia, 56–64.

112 RGVIA, f. 400, op. 1, d. 1475, l. 156ob.

113 RGVIA, f. 400, op. 1, d. 1474, l. 1–1ob. For Russia's maritime fleet see *Thomas*: Russlands Handelsflotte.

114 RGVIA, f. 400, op. 1, d. 1475, l. 143.

115 Ibid. l. 144–45.

Chinese and Indian high-quality tea.[116] The meeting of the joint council held on October 11, 1895, also with the presence of major tea merchants such as Wogau and Co., concluded that Chinese teas should be allowed for transit as well. Particularly the vice-director of the Asiatic Department endorsed the notion, considering that "it would surely put the tea trade into Russian hands, ending the activities of Indian merchants in Bukhara, strengthening the importance and influence of the Russian colony in Wuhan[117] and will provide Russian steamship lines with income." The "development of trade with China, replacing Central Asian trade with India, appears [...] desirable from a political point of view" as well.[118]

By the mid-1890s, the interests of the different ministries pursuing their own agendas in Central Asia began to converge and a coordinated program towards the economic space of Central Asia began to develop. The new organization of economic space further allowed to apply protectionist mechanisms, creating favorable trade routes limited to Russian merchants as well as thus shaping global trade currents. The increasing importance of trade in Central Asia and the region's new role in Russia's system of protectionism and the entanglement of economic policies with political considerations reinforced the relative importance of the Ministry of Finance, which was continuously encroaching on the domains of the Ministry of War and the Foreign Ministry.

3.6 Conclusion

Visions for the economic integration of the Central Asian space through a Transcaspian railway had been put forward by industrial circles before the territory in question had even come under Russian control. However, throughout the 1870s such proposals found little governmental support under a free-trade-inspired economic policy applied to Russia's eastern peripheries. The Central Asian economic space was marked by fragmentation and the coexistence of different economic regimes. The maintenance of low administrative costs was paramount, and even under the increasingly protectionist climate of the 1880s, this approach changed only slowly, as expenditures for a territorially conceptualized customs regime would have been fiscally unbearable for such a vast space. Only with the construction of the Transcaspian railway and the link to Samarkand, the reshaping of the Central Asian economic space appeared tangible. The new vision of connectedness challenged the old

116 Ibid. l. 147.

117 A center of Chinese tea production in eastern China.

118 RGVIA, f. 400, op. 1, d. 1475, l. 156, 161.

principles of flexible, fragmented, low-cost customs protection. From a statist and protectionist viewpoint, the new infrastructure would either become captured by foreign merchants or fully integrated into the new program of the national economy and thus action was required. The increasing convergence of interests between the various involved governmental branches facilitated a coordinated approach, and by 1895 the Russian-dominated economic space in Central Asia had been unitized, even though only partially. The new logic of economic space management unlocked hitherto unavailable regulatory mechanisms which allowed to shape global trade currents and increasingly oriented the Central Asian economic space towards Russia as trading partner. Bukhara's traditional tea trade connections to Persia and Afghanistan had been challenged by a more efficient connection to global trade currents, albeit increasingly facilitated by large Russian trade companies. The customs system thus served as an instrument of territorialization for the Russian Empire, facilitating "the exclusion of alternative claims on political or economic [...] outcomes" in a contest for "finite global space."[119] Although the eventual implementation of Bukhara's integration had taken place quickly and with seemingly little resistance, as Gubarevich-Radobyl'skii had remarked, it was the result of a three-decade-long process during which the empire's space and its manipulation had been fundamentally reinterpreted.

119 *Maier, Charles S.*: Transformations of Territoriality. 1600–2000. In: *Budde, Gunilla/ Conrad, Sebastian/Janz, Oliver* (eds.): Transnationale Geschichte. Themen, Tendenzen, Theorien. Göttingen 2006, 32–55, here 34.

4. Ob' and Enisei Porto-Franco: A Latecomer's Frustration

The construction of the Trans-Siberian railway was arguably the grandest infrastructural project of the late Russian Empire, promising to connect its remote eastern regions to the imperial center and reshape the political and economic space of the empire. Yet, for many actors in Western Siberia, these promises either read as an encroachment on local autonomy or simply as the wrong tool for the development of their region. In an extraordinary general assembly of the Tobol'sk City Duma on April 30th 1907, Aleksandr Aleksandrovich Dunin-Gorkavich, forester of Samorovo[1] in the Tobol'sk Gubernia and active explorer of the region, stated his frustration with the lack of a positive economic effect of the railway, and proposed to seriously re-consider alternative administrative and infrastructural tools to develop his region economically:

> The construction of the Siberian railway mostly enlivened the space adjacent to the railroad tracks, having only a quite weak impact on the more distant and isolated regions. As a result, the economic condition of Western Siberia today, as before the construction of the railway, is developing weakly. […] At the current time, when the question of raising the economic situation of the empire's population is coming up in all its power, the regional question of the development of productive forces in Siberia has to be discussed in all its broadness. But in order to fulfill these cultural needs, large spending and means are required, which the population cannot provide and the government does not have. Foreign capitals have to be attracted to develop the productive forces of Siberia, which is only possible by instituting a porto-franco.[2]

Dunin-Gorkavich urged to introduce a free-trade regime for the estuaries of the Siberian Ob' and Enisei rivers, creating a Northern Siberian porto-franco, which would make trade along the dangerous Northern sea route more lucrative to foreign shipping companies. He conceded that it was a "radical measure", yet:

> It is accepted that in countries on a low stage of economic development, and particularly in isolated regions, a porto-franco can sometimes be the only means of creating a

1 Today's Khanty-Mansiisk.

2 *Dunin-Gorkavich, Aleksandr Aleksandrovich*: Neobkhodimost' otkrytiia porto-franko v ust'iach reki Obi i Eniseia. Tobol'sk 1907, 1.

new artery for international trade exchange and a mighty lever of economic elevation. This opinion is well applicable to Western Siberia as a land which is on a low stage of economic development in an isolated region, currently devoid of the possibility of using cheap sea routes to access markets. The only such route for Western Siberia is the Northern sea route through the Kara Sea.[3]

Dunin-Gorkavich's proposal in the Tobol'sk City Duma was by no means new. It drew on prior demands to establish a stable free-trade regime for the Ob' and Enisei rivers and prior experience with temporary free-trade concessions for ships on the Northern sea route. After a series of successful expeditions in the late 1870s and 1880s, which proved that the establishment of a regular steamship connection along the Northern sea route was technically possible, the route began to be discussed as a viable option to exploit the economic potential of Western Siberia. This chapter traces the development of the idea of a porto-franco on the estuaries of Ob' and Enisei and examines which factors impeded its implementation. The initiatives are put in relation to previous territorialized free-trade regimes in the Russian Empire, the increasing nationalization of economic policy debates, and the competing vision of an empire integrated via a central railway.

The chapter argues that unlike other large territorialized free-trade regimes established in the 1860s, such as the Russian Empire's Central Asian territories and the Far-Eastern porto-franco, the concept of a porto-franco on the estuaries of the Ob' and Enisei rivers[4] was a late-comer and only became a viable option in the late 1880s and early 1890s, when navigation on the Northern sea route became more reliable. By this time, the organization of the Russian Empire's economic space had shifted towards an approach of integration and centralization. Heterogeneous customs regimes in peripheral economic spaces, which allowed these regions relatively autonomous foreign trade relations, were increasingly regarded with suspicion by the central administration. The resolute 1898 decision against a stable porto-franco regime for the Ob' and Enisei rivers – which in the 1860s would probably have been the go-to administrative tool – owed in large part to a strategy of re-orienting the economic activity of Western Siberia (and other peripheral regions) through the imperial center, and precluding the region's direct interaction with world trade currents.[5]

3 Ibid. 5.

4 Most contemporary sources use the geographically descriptive nomenclature "porto-franko v ust'iakh rek Obi i Eniseia" (porto-franco in the estuaries of the Ob' and Enisei rivers). Sometimes it is referred to as "Northern porto-franco" as well.

5 A similar process can be observed with the integration of Bukhara into the imperial customs territory, as described in chapter 3.

The first section introduces the Far-Eastern porto-franco as a seminal concept. While the older Odessa porto-franco had been the most prominent example for the use of territorialized free-trade regimes in the Russian Empire, the preconditions and motivations in Western Siberia in the 1880s much closer resembled those of the Far-Eastern porto-franco. There, a series of singular free-trade regulations had fallen together to form a vast free-trade zone, ranging from Lake Baikal to the Pacific Ocean in the early 1860s. It was in part designed as a regional developmental measure, in part born from a necessity to supply a distant periphery of the empire. This Far-Eastern porto-franco would later become an important point of reference in the argumentation for a free-trade regime in the Ob' and Enisei estuaries.

However, the Far-Eastern porto-franco had developed during the liberal phase of the early 1860s. By the time it was cited as a positive example by proponents of a Northern porto-franco, the political climate had begun to change and territorialized porto-franco regimes were increasingly understood as a deviant and problematic form of structuring the empire's economic space. It is argued that the protracted fights over the continuation of free-trade privileges in the Far-East and the discursive devaluation of the term "porto-franco" negatively impacted efforts to establish a Northern porto-franco.

This chapter's second section focuses on the exploration of the Northern sea route since the 1860s. It traces the early exploratory phase as well as the first phase of commercial seafaring between Great Britain and Western Siberia via the Northern sea route. It explores the interplay of private entrepreneurial and governmental interests both on the Russian and the British side. It demonstrates how the establishment of free trade on the estuaries of Ob' and Enisei was interpreted as an issue of both center-periphery relations and foreign politics. The institution of an economic tool became politicized within an increasingly nationalist climate. The section demonstrates that a porto-franco in the estuaries of Ob' and Enisei constituted an alternative vision of structuring the economic space of the empire, competing with the Trans-Siberian railway, and identifies the factors which conditioned the termination of free-trade rights in 1898.

The last section picks up on the recurrence of the porto-franco idea in the last years of the Russian Empire. It argues that the disappointment with the transformative power of the Trans-Siberian railway for certain regions, as articulated by Dunin-Gorkavich, led to a reevaluation of the Northern sea route. Eventually, it was the prospect of servicing the Northern sea route without the assistance of foreign companies that tipped the scales in favor of renewed subsidies for the Northern sea route, right before the First World War compelled the Russian government to resort to foreign service of the route in order to ensure supply lines.

4.1 The Far-Eastern Porto-Franco: From Seminal Concept to National Nuisance

The Far-Eastern porto-franco was not the first experience of the Russian administration with establishing territorialized free-trade zones. Earlier, the city of Odessa had been the prime example of development through territorialized free trade, as it had grown and prospered based on its rights as porto-franco.[6] In other cases, duty-free importation had been employed in remote regions such as Kamchatka. The Far-Eastern porto-franco, however, was by far the largest and longest-lasting free-trade territory. The description as a free port is in so far misleading as it stretched from Irkutsk on Lake Baikal to the Russian Empire's Pacific coast. This vast expansion of the free-trade zone, the high degree of difficulty in connecting the Far-East with the Russian Empire's European parts and the relative economic underdevelopment and scarce population of the Russian Far-East are traits shared by the Western Siberian regions adjacent to the Ob' and Enisei rivers. The Far-Eastern porto-franco thus constituted on the one hand a seminal concept and model for imitation for regional actors in Western Siberia, who drew parallels to their own situation, as well as a cautioning experience for the central administration on the other hand, as the Far-Eastern porto-franco soon fell from grace with the surge of nationally-charged debates on economic policy. It is against this backdrop that the fate of the Ob' and Enisei porto-franco had been decided.

The nomenclature "Far-Eastern porto-franco", which had already been used by contemporaries, suggests a deliberately created system. However, what is described as Far-Eastern porto-franco was in no way monolithic, being "not a unified regime, but a set of practices, a compounded, fragmented phenomenon", which had grown incrementally.[7] Duty-free trade had already been implemented in Kamchatka in 1828. But the first significant step towards the creation of a large territorialized free-trade regime came after the Crimean War in 1856, with the extension of the Kamchatka regulations to the Priamur ports. The initial initiative had come from U. S. entrepreneurs who petitioned Eastern Siberian Governor-general Nikolai Nikolaevich Murav'ev for duty-free trade rights on the Amur river. Having consulted with the Ministry of Finance and the Ministry of Foreign Affairs, duty-free trade was introduced in the ports of the Priamurskii krai as well as on Sakhalin. The main motive was to ensure a stable supply in order to quickly populate the region – Russian-subject merchants were simply not prepared to fulfill this role. Neither did a Russian merchant fleet exist yet, which could have enabled quick and stable trans-

6 *Herlihy, Patricia*: Odessa: A History, 1794–1914. Cambridge, Massachusetts 1986, 21–48.
7 *Turbin*: Dal'nevostochnyi porto-franko, 73.

portation from Russia's European to its Pacific ports. In 1860, these customs privileges were extended to the Primorskai oblast' with a stepwise introduction of duty-free trade in all its ports – most notably in Vladivostok in 1862.[8]

These initial trade privileges applied to ports only. The emergence of the territorially expansive porto-franco was the result of two additional separate adjustments. The 1862 regulations on Russo-Chinese land trade, which were to complement the Beijing treaty, established a 50-verst wide duty-free border zone on each side of the border between the Russian Empire and China.[9] Further, the Eastern Siberian Governor-general Murav'ev initiated the relocation of the Kiakhta customs to Irkutsk, as it was an infrastructural nodal point and thus more convenient for customs collection. He was aware of the consequences, as he conceded that "this way, all of the Transbaikal krai, including Irkutsk, will become a porto-franco..." In part, Murav'ev pursued economic stimulation through these liberal reforms, regardless of whether economic activity in the region was conducted by Russian or foreign subjects. In part, it was also a concession to the fact that effective customs control would not have been possible anyway due to a lack of administrative resources.[10]

These measures were well in-line with the general liberalization of the Russian Empire's customs policies which had begun in the late 1850s, as well as the aversion of the Ministry of Finance to invest into costly administrative structures in the empire's peripheral regions in the early 1860s. The Far-Eastern porto-franco experience was deemed so successful initially that its mechanism was transferred to other regions as well. When the Ministry of Finance made the decision to fully dissolve the Steppe customs border in 1868, creating a vast de-facto free-trade zone, the Far-Eastern porto-franco was explicitly cited as a good-practice example.[11]

In the Far-East, the creation of a vast free-trade territory de-facto also introduced an internal customs border within the empire, with the two economic zones not even matching the administrative partitioning of Siberia. However, this was not regarded as problematic by the central administration but rather as a "fitting administrative decision." Neither was it understood

8 *Beliaeva*: Ot porto-franko k tamozhne, 12–16. On the Russian merchant fleet see *Thomas*: Russlands Handelsflotte. The first steamship of the Russian voluntary fleet reached Vladivostok from Odessa in 1879. A regular connection was introduced in 1880 see *Thomas, Ludmila*: Ein deutsches Unternehmen im russischen Fernen Osten (1864–1921). Zwänge und Grenzen der Anpassung. In: *Dahlmann, Dittmar/Scheide, Carmen* (eds.): '... das einzige Land in Europa, das eine große Zukunft vor sich hat.' Deutsche Unternehmen und Unternehmer im Russischen Reich im 19. und 20. Jahrhundert. Göttingen 1998, 611–635, 22.

9 *Skach'kov, Petr Emel'ianovich*: Russko-kitaiskie otnosheniia, 1689–1916. Moscow 1958, 42–45.

10 *Turbin*: Dal'nevostochnyi porto-franko, 50–54.

11 See chapter 3.

Figure 4: Map of Siberia with Trans-Siberian railway.

to be disruptive, but framed as part of a national policy, which would accelerate Siberia's integration into the empire.[12] In this regard, the Far-Eastern porto-franco shares similarities with the lenient customs regime established in the Transcaucasian region in the 1840s, which was also understood as a measure to accelerate regional economic development and ensure a quicker integration, however, eventually served to perpetuate the separation of the Transcaucasian region.[13]

In all three cases, it was the real and perceived infrastructural fragmentation of the Russian Empire's space which allowed large territorialized special regimes to co-exist with the stricter customs regime of the core empire without interference. As long as administrators in the Ministry of Finance did not perceive the different customs systems as interlocking, they shied away from establishing costly customs institutions on the empire's peripheries. Considering the hazardous overland trade routes in Russia's Far-East and the lack of a steamship connection, there was little concern over the integrity of Russia's European customs system. Goods imported duty-free into Far-Eastern ports

12 *Turbin:* Dal'nevostochnyi porto-franko, 57–58.
13 See chapter 5.

would have simply lost their competitive edge by the time they reached Russia's core customs space due to the costly and lengthy transportation.

In the debate over the introduction of a Northern porto-franco, which began in the 1880s, the Far-Eastern porto-franco constituted an important point of reference – both for proponents and opponents of a porto-franco in the estuaries of the Ob' and Enisei rivers. The preconditions found in the Far-East, which had initially motivated the establishment of a vast free-trade zone – namely the lack of infrastructural connection to the core empire resulting in a precarious supply situation and the necessity to rely on foreign imports and capital influx – were analogously cited by proponents of a Northern porto-franco. Meanwhile, opponents of the Northern porto-franco referred to the Far-Eastern example as eagerly, citing its negative effects: one of them being the dominance of foreign entrepreneurs, understood to undermine the national cause.

Indeed, it was primarily foreign merchants who could benefit from the porto-franco regime which had developed in the Far-East in the 1860s. They had access to European shipping companies, necessary to meet the demand for European products. Further, they realized the importance of telegraph connections early on and acquired the necessary usage rights. The use of the telegraph decisively increased the speed of monetary transfers and thus increased the turnover speed of their trade operations. Meanwhile, Siberian merchants, despite displaying trade activity, were less successful under the altered conditions as they remained true to their accustomed methods of trade, which were founded in "a traditional feeling of time and lifestyle as they themselves were part of this world in which they had acted for centuries." Foreign companies with a stellar ascent, such as the German Kunst & Albers, also profited from their connections to the London capital flows and banking circles. By the 1880s, Kunst&Albers had transformed into a large enterprise with a capital account of half a million rubles. Despite the introduction of a regular steamship connection between Odessa and Vladivostok, serviced by the Russian voluntary fleet since 1880, foreign shipping companies were still deemed more reliable and cheaper. Even governmental officials resorted to their services rather than those of the voluntary fleet, if transportation was time-sensitive.[14]

Some foreign entrepreneurs, such as Adolph Dattan of Kunst&Albers, even became Russian subjects, hoping to better integrate and conduct their business.[15] This, however, did little to change their perception as agents of large foreign companies. The overpowering position of Kunst&Albers in the Far-East would later be cited as an example for the negative effects of free-trade

14 *Thomas*: Ein deutsches Unternehmen, 612, 615–617, 622–623.

15 Ibid. 621.

regimes and as a decisive argument against the introduction of a porto-franco in the estuaries of the Ob' and Enisei rivers in 1908. Opponents of a free-trade regime cautioned that the Kunst&Albers effect would repeat itself in Western Siberia, as foreign entrepreneurs would benefit most from free-trade regulations, gain ground, and smother Russian competitors. In the case of the Northern porto-franco, German company Gartog&Stang had petitioned for duty-free trade rights, and was suspected of using Siberian merchants as straw men for their endeavors. With its compound name Gartog&Stang, it was strongly reminiscent of Kunst&Albers, making the parallels appear even more striking.[16]

This nexus between nationalist and protectionist demands and the categorical rejection of territorialized duty-free regimes had already begun to develop in the late 1860s and fully unfolded in public debates in the 1880s. Initially, however, porto-franco regimes themselves were interpreted in a more multifaceted manner. This development can be traced well regarding Mikhail Katkov and his "Moskovskie vedomosti", one of the most influential conservative voices of the post-reform period. Turbin argues that in early publications the term "porto-franco" had been used to describe an economic tool, which could have "both a positive or a negative effect on the political process, either weaken or strengthen the unity of the state." While the issue of imperial unity and separatism had gained in importance after the 1863 Polish uprising, this rhetoric initially "cannot be found in debates on the economic development of territories." Initially, "Moskovskie vedomosti" itself had criticized hard-line protectionists and supported territorialized free-trade regimes, where necessary. By the 1880s, however, it had turned to a "systematic ideological critique of the porto-franco" with the term "porto-franco" transforming from a neutral description of an economic instrument into a nationally charged polemical term.[17]

This turn had occurred in the late 1870s, as the Russian Empire was increasingly embarking on a protectionist course.[18] Further, Russian industrial manufacturers began to search for new markets in which they could be competitive. The empire's Far-Eastern markets, if sufficiently protected and connected, appeared promising in this regard.[19] The demands for the closure of the Transcaucasian transit route gained momentum within the same context.[20]

16 RGIA, f. 23, op. 18, d. 169, "Perepiska s chastnymi predprinimateliami i uchrezhdeniiami o zakonoproekte o vvedenii porto-franko v ust'iakh rek Obi i Eniseia; ob ustanovlenii tamozhennykh l'got na tovary, vvozimye v Sibir' Severnym morskim putem", l. 13ob.

17 *Turbin*: Dal'nevostochnyi porto-franko, 60–63.

18 See chapter 1.

19 *Turbin*: Dal'nevostochnyi porto-franko, 60–63.

20 See chapter 6.

In addition to these free-trade regimes introduced by the Russian administration itself, the renegotiation of the Russo-Ottoman peace terms at the 1878 Berlin congress included the mandatory creation of a porto-franco in the annexed city of Batum, which was interpreted by "Moskovskie vedomosti" as the creation of a British trade outpost on the Black Sea. Despite Russia's victory in the Russian-Ottoman war, this peace term was considered a disgrace and further devaluated the term "porto-franco", which was now firmly associated with the unbeneficial treaty.[21]

In practice, much was done by Russia's administration to limit any effects the Batum porto-franco could develop. Its size and specific customs procedures were deliberately designed in a way to render free trade in Batum almost impossible, even if it came at the detriment of the city and its war-torn surroundings.[22] Nevertheless, the existence of the Batum porto-franco regime remained a contested and symbolically charged issue until its closure in 1886, which had been pushed forward by "Moskovskie vedomosti."[23] Similarly, in 1883, the Transcaucasian transit route had been closed down for international trade following a fierce press campaign and strong pressure from Central Russian industrialist interest groups.[24]

In this nationally charged climate under Alexander III, the Far-Eastern porto-franco came under attack as well. In practice, certain limitations on trade in the Far-Eastern porto-franco had already been implemented earlier, such as levying an excise tax on tea, sugar and tobacco, which in effect equaled a customs fee, making it an "'incomplete porto-franco.'" Also, the importation of alcohol was prohibited for public health reasons, although the prohibition could hardly be enforced.[25] Notwithstanding these technicalities, which significantly curtailed the economic impact of the free-trade regime,

21 *Turbin*: Dal'nevostochnyi porto-franko, 63. Initially, the British government had urged that Batum be established as a porto-franco not incorporated into Russia's territory. Eventually, a compromise was found with the city becoming part of the Russian Empire, however, being declared a free port. See *Geiss, Imanuel/Epstein, Fritz T.*: Der Berliner Kongreß 1878. Boppard 1978, 310–319.

22 Senator Dmitrii Aleksandrovich Obolenskii represented one of the few dissenting voices arguing for an expansion of the Batum porto-franco territory, while the majority of the State Council strongly opposed it and strove to "limit the generally negative, in terms of our trade, institution of the porto-franco in Batum to a territory as small as possible." The porto-franco issues in Batum were primarily treated as a foreign political issue, as demonstrated by the fact, that it was discussed in a special commission rather than within the Department of Customs Collection of the Ministry of Finance, see RGIA, f. 1152, op. 9, 1880, d. 434, "Ob utverzhdenie polozheniia o Batumskom porto-franko", l. 106, 115–116; For the dissolution of the Batum porto-franco see AVPRI, f. 144, op. 1886, d. 430, "Po voprosu ob unichtozhenii porto-franko v Batume."

23 *Turbin*: Dal'nevostochnyi porto-franko, 64.

24 See chapter 6.

25 *Beliaeva*: Ot porto-franko k tamozhne, 26; *Urbansky*: Der betrunkene Kosake, 306–307.

the mere existence of a vast free-trade regime in the Far-East acquired the rank of a problem of political symbolism against the backdrop of the contested Batum porto-franco.

In 1884, "Moskovskie vedomosti" picked up an article by Filipp Isaakovich Feigin, who had spent time in the Amur region in 1881, and described a monopolistic advantage of Chinese and other foreign merchants exploiting the region. He advocated limiting duty-free imports and establishing a Russian trade agency, which he suggested to head himself, as well as other protectionist measures. "Moskovskie vedomosti" strongly supported this position, with the "topic of the porto-franco increasingly becoming part of a political discussion, closely intertwined with the question of a new spatial vision of the empire: its unity was guaranteed by a protectionist policy, which was connected to the political body of Russianness." Maintaining only military dominance over the peripheral region without its economic integration into the empire was not considered sufficient anymore. The heterogeneous regulations appeared even less justifiable with regard "to other European empires, foremost Germany, which homogenized and nationalized their space."[26]

This national point of view was met with opposition by the Siberian regional press, which formulated its own vision of administering the imperial economic space, prioritizing the economic development of its peripheral regions. "Vostochnoe obozrenie", founded by the famous oblastnik Nikolai Mikhailovich Iadrintsev, accused Feigin of acting in his own interests only and linked the debate to the closure of the Transcaucasian transit route, which was understood to have been in the interest of a Moscow entrepreneurs lobby only.[27] This juxtaposition between the interests of regional actors and Central Russian entrepreneurs would become a central trope for the Northern porto-franco as well. The first saw the development of their region best served by a territorialized free-trade regime, while the latter cited threats to national unity. They argued that free-trade zones would result in a loss of markets understood as naturally Russian, with foreign entrepreneurs becoming overly dominant.

Baron Andrei Nikolaevich Korf, Governor-general of the Priamur krai (1884–1893), shared a vision of a national homogenization not too dissimilar from Katkov. However, with regard to the accusations brought forward by Feigin Korf rejected the advances of the Ministry of Finance to remove free-trade rights, maintained that foreign entrepreneurs did not enjoy any special privileges and simply dominated trade as there had prior been no stable shipping routes to Russia and Russian merchants suffered from a lack of credit. Removing free-trade privileges would thus have little effect on the dominance

26 *Turbin*: Dal'nevostochnyi porto-franko, 65–66.
27 Ibid. 66–67.

of foreign merchants; meanwhile it would result in increased living expenses in the remote territory. The Governor-general further insinuated that Feigin's proposed project was to the benefit of a few manufacturers from the European part of Russia, whose interests, however, could not outweigh those of the state and the Priamur region.[28]

Thus, even if the conservative press had been successful at devaluing the "porto-franco" concept as detrimental to a national cause and the Ministry of Finance proved willing to act on this notion, both non-governmental regional actors and the empire's own representative on the spot, the Governor-general, maintained its necessity – albeit with different developmental trajectories in mind. Eventually, only minor cosmetic changes were made to the Far-Eastern free-trade regime in the 1880s. Despite the discursive shift against the territorialized free-trade regime, little had changed with regards to the initial local conditions, necessitating its introduction, as the Priamur region remained infrastructurally disconnected from the imperial core customs space.

With the turn towards high protectionism in the 1890s and the construction of the Trans-Siberian railway, which promised to link up the Priamur region to the empire's core economic space, the porto-franco became a point of contention again. Similar to the integration of the Transcaspian region and Bukhara into the Russian customs zone, it was also the infrastructural integration via railway which altered perceptions of space and made the co-existence of protectionist and free-trade customs regimes unacceptable.[29]

With regard to the Far-Eastern porto-franco, a careful step-by-step process had been chosen. By 1899 customs controls had been introduced in the ports of Vladivostok and Nikolaevsk; by January 1, 1901, the Far-Eastern porto-franco was dissolved. The new customs regime, however, only lasted for a short period, as the Russo-Japanese War necessitated its temporary abolishment in 1904 and a return to a porto-franco regime in order to ensure the supply of the region. Despite numerous petitions to maintain the free-trade regime in the post-war period, it was eventually dissolved in 1909.[30]

The Far-Eastern porto-franco constituted the longest lasting and most expansive territorialized free-trade regime in the Russian Empire. Its history demonstrates how territorialized special customs regimes developed from a standard tool used to administer the heterogeneous imperial economic space to a nuisance understood as an impediment to the creation of a unified economic space. This development was rooted both in a growing national discourse, pushing for more homogenization, as well as technological advances, which suggested the malleability of the empire's physical space and effected

28 Ibid. 68–70.

29 See chapter 3.

30 *Beliaeva*: Ot porto-franko k tamozhne, 53–80, 116–154.

changing spatial visions in the central administration. Sharing many pre-conditions, it was an important point of reference in the debate over the introduction of a free-trade regime in the estuaries of the Ob' and Enisei rivers – both for proponents and opponents of such a regime. However, despite certain similarities, the Northern sea route presented sea shipping with very different challenges – first of all, the establishment of a route at all. The Northern sea route itself and a Northern porto-franco had only become viable options after the term and concept of "porto-franco" had become objects of public contestation and acquired a negative connotation.

The following sections outline the early exploratory phase as well as the first phase of commercial seafaring between Great Britain and Western Siberia via the Kara Sea. The governmental policies towards free trade on the Northern sea route are put in relation to the general customs policies and the development of other territorialized free-trade regimes. Further, the interplay between private entrepreneurial and governmental interests, both on the Russian and the British side, are explored, as well as the issue of center-periphery relations, which crystallized around the issue of free trade.

4.2 Exploration, Private Initiative, and the "Nationalization" of the Northern Sea Route

The 1820s and 1830s saw an increased interest in the exploration of the Arctic Ocean. Naval explorer Friedrich Benjamin von Lütke significantly contributed to the knowledge of the Arctic Ocean and Novaia Zemlia by conducting four hydrographic expeditions between 1821 and 1824, however remained unsuccessful in his attempts to enter the Kara Sea.[31]

First attempts to combine commercial and scientific interests were undertaken in 1832, as Arkhangel'sk merchant Wilhelm Brant and *formeister* (forester) P. Klokov petitioned to be granted 25-year privileges for the establishment of trading posts as well as fishing rights and hunting rights and exclusive export and import rights in the Kara Sea region. The Ministry of Finance consulted Arkhangel'sk Military-governor Roman Romanovich Gall on whether such rights could be granted without constraining the rights of other inhabitants involved in fishing and hunting by the shores of Novaia Zemlia and Northern Siberia. The ministry also suggested the establishment of a

31 *Goncharov, Alexander E.*: Istoriia kommercheskikh ekspeditsii severnogo morskogo puti: 1870-e – 1890-e gg. (Dissertation). Kemerovo 2013, 53–54; *Dahlmann, Dittmar*: Torgovoe sudokhodstvo za poliarnym krugom vo vtoroi polovine XIX veka. In: Otechestvennaia istoriia, 5(2001) 21–32, here 22.

stock company, as other interested parties could then partake in the granted privileges. Arkhangel'sk Military-governor Gall supported the petition and did not see any conflict of interest with competitors as Brant's son (Wilhelm Brant had died in the meantime) and Klokov clarified that they petitioned for privileges only in the unexplored and unexploited parts of the Kara Sea. Seeing that the venture was highly risky and promised no quick returns, the Ministry of Finance decided to support the motion and granted the privileges for 25 years, citing that the American company had initially received similar privileges for 20 years as well.[32] An expedition was sent in 1835, however, it was unsuccessful at entering the Kara Sea and one ship went missing.[33]

Scientific exploration continued, but governmental interest in a Northern sea route soon died down, as the authoritative scientist and explorer Karl Ernst von Baer declared the Kara Sea an "Eiskeller" (ice-cellar) following his 1837 expedition to Novaia Zemlia. This wording was picked up and popularized by geographer August Petermann, contributing to the image of the Kara Sea as unnavigable. It would take almost forty years for the route to be proven navigable in 1874. In response, Baer pointed out that he had never declared the route unnavigable, and that his "Eiskeller" concept had merely been misinterpreted by others.[34] Nevertheless, Baer's 1837 dictum had put a temporary halt to exploration attempts in the Kara Sea.

Commercially, however, a new trading route from Western Siberia to Western European ports maintained its allure; yet, no serious ventures were undertaken. Tobol'sk merchant and gold mine owner Vasilii Nikolaevich Latkin explored options to connect the Ob' and Pechora rivers since the 1840s, but did not consider the Kara Sea as a possible route at first. Neither was he successful at attracting governmental support for his endeavors.[35] However, his son-in-law, Mikhail Konstantinovich Sidorov, a wealthy gold mine entrepreneur himself, would go on to become the strongest advocate of a Northern sea route. Already in 1859, Sidorov had turned to the Enisei Governor, arguing that a sea route from Europe to the estuaries of the Ob' and Enisei rivers was possible after all. His advance, however, was not met with any reaction.[36]

32 RGIA, f. 1152, op. 2, 1832, d. 111, "Ob isprashivomoi kuptsom Brandom i chinovnikom Klokovym privilegii dlia ustroistva promyslov i torgovykh snoshenii s Severnoi Aziei po Ledovitomu moriu", l. 1–12.

33 *Goncharov*: Istoriia kommercheskikh ekspeditsii, p 54.

34 *Tammiksaar, Erki/Stone, Ian R.*: Karl Ernst von Baer and the Kara Sea 'Eiskeller'. In: Polar Record, 33(186) (1997), 239–242.

35 *Dahlmann*: Torgovoe sudokhodstvo, 22.

36 Ibid. 22–23; *Goncharov*: Istoriia kommercheskikh ekspeditsii, 60; *Studitskii, Fedor*: Istoriia otkrytiia morskogo puti iz Evropy v sibirskie reki i do Beringova proliva. Part 1. Saint Petersburg 1883, 37–39.

In 1860, a new non-commercial expedition to the Kara Sea was undertaken under the leadership of naval officer Pavel Pavlovich Kruzenshtern. Though he had to return before he could enter the Kara Sea, the expedition discovered that the passage south of Novaia Zemlia had indeed been free of ice, sparking hopes for the establishment of a navigable route. Kruzenshtern's second expedition had found support from the Naval Ministry and in 1862 he again attempted to reach the Kara Sea. Sidorov, who had earlier offered prize money to any captain able to reach the estuaries of the Enisei from Arkhangel'sk, supported Kruzensthern's expedition as well, promising him 5.000 rubles if he reached the Enisei. However, the second expedition failed too, as the ship "Ermak" froze in the ice and the crew had to abandon its vessel, fleeing across the frozen sea for three days till it reached land. Upon his return to Saint Petersburg Kruzenshtern concluded that the establishment of a Northern sea route was not possible.[37]

Despite the failed expeditions seemingly confirming the image of an unnavigable "Eiskeller", Sidorov stood firm in his belief in the possibility and profitability of a Northern sea route, as he hoped to export bulk raw materials, particularly graphite, to Western Europe by sea. The significant support necessary for the exploration and exploitation of a new sea route, however, could not be secured if Latkin and Sidorov argued with their own private commercial interests. Making use of the open debate culture in the wake of the Great Reforms and the formation of numerous entrepreneurial and scientific communities, these two "Zealots of the North", as they were referred to, embarked on a campaign to promote their vision for the infrastructural exploration and economic exploitation of Western Siberia for the sake of Russian national interest.[38]

In order to appeal to a wider audience and detract from their own commercial interests, they "nationalized" their endeavor and invoked a language of patriotism. In their efforts, they received prominent support from publisher Mikhail Katkov, who himself pursued a similar rhetorical strategy of refracting issues through the lens of national-politics. Sidorov and Latkin, on the one hand, promoted the rich economic possibilities of Western Siberia as a national treasury. On the other hand, they played on Anglophobe sentiments virulent since the Crimean War and constructed a theory of a foreign conspiracy to exploit Russia's Northern peripheries, by carefully cropping and miscontextualizing information. A such formulated threat was to appeal to a forming conservative-nationalist audience in order to recruit supporters for the exploration of a Northern sea route. Increasing seafaring activities of other states

37 *Goncharov*: Istoriia kommercheskikh ekspeditsii, 62–63.

38 *Agapov, Mikhail*: 'Zagovor' protiv Severa Rossii: natsionalizatsiia predprinimatel'skogo diskursa v 60-e gg. XIX v. In: Ab Imperio, 4 (2019), 73–96, 77–78.

in the Arctic Ocean did their part to draw attention to the project. Playing on national sentiments, Sidorov called for "self-dependent Russian trade" in Northern Siberia, which implied that the future route would have to be exploited by Russian merchants (specifically excluding naturalized foreigners), financed with Russian capitals, and serviced by a Russian merchant fleet.[39]

But it was not only conservative circles the campaign appealed to. Most notably, Grand Duke Konstantin Nikolaevich, himself a staunch liberal, entertained the notion of equipping an expedition, yet failed against the austerity policies of Minister of Finance Reitern.[40] Sidorov was not able to receive significant support from imperial authorities to equip an expedition, either. The only governmental support his enterprise received was the granting of free-trade and exploitation rights in the Kara Sea region. Against the background of a budgetary crisis, the Ministry of Finance shied away from investing any money into an uncertain expedition. Granting temporary concessions, however, could only do limited harm and at best would present new insights into Arctic seafaring.

While Sidorov's general outlook was clearly protectionist and nationalist, he had petitioned for free-trade rights to stimulate the exploration and exploitation of the Northern sea route. He referred to prior experience in Russia's Far-East, where customs exemptions had been implemented in the 1850s under Governor-general Murav'ev in order to enliven the region. In the Far-East, a number of free-trade regulations had eventually formed a porto-franco system which primarily attracted foreign entrepreneurs.[41] Sidorov, however, did not envision a territorialized free-trade regime, and particularly not one open to international competitors. He petitioned for monopolistic privileges for his company only. In this regard, his suggested tools for regional development had been those of customs exemptions; the underlying doctrine, however, was protectionist and tailored to Sidorov's private commercial interests – a stark contrast to the genesis and functioning of the Far-Eastern porto-franco he referred to.

The prospects of his 1869 petition were good, as the Russian Empire's Asiatic customs policy had recently made a significant shift towards trade-deregulation. Only a year prior, the Orenburg steppe customs border had been dissolved, creating a vast de-facto free-trade zone. Sidorov himself referred

39 Ibid. 77–91; *Renner*: Defining a Russian Nation, 681.

40 *Sukhova, Natalia/Skrydlov, Andrei*: The Russian Geographical Society and the Polar Studies in the Second Half of the 19th Century. In: IOP Conference Series Earth and Environmental Science, 180 (2018), 1–5, 3.

41 *Goncharov*: Istoriia kommercheskikh ekspeditsii, 68–69; *Sidorov, Mikhail Konstantinovich*: Sever Rossii. Saint Petersburg 1870, 515–517; *Turbin*: Dal'nevostochnyi porto-franko, 55–57.

to this measure and contextualized his vision of a Northern sea route as part of an intra-imperial competition between a Northern sea route and Central Asian trade routes for economic relations with "the population of Southern Siberia." His underlying argument was that vast privileges for his company would only level the playing field as trade from Central Asia had been heavily deregulated already. Meanwhile, his endeavor carried the potential of adding another promising access route and upturning the Russian Empire's trading geography.[42]

Indeed, in 1869 his company was granted five-year free-trade privileges for the estuaries of the Ob' and Enisei rivers, which were prolonged for another five years in 1873.[43] The privileges, Minister of Finance Reitern noted, could be granted as the planned expedition was conducted with private funds and carried a great risk, against which the granted privileges appeared "quite insignificant." For the imperial administration, the venture still had an experimental character, as the navigability of the Kara Sea had not even been proven yet. Even if Sidorov drew parallels to free trade in the Far-East, a territorialized free-trade system had not been considered by the Ministry of Finance. Sidorov himself remained dissatisfied with the granted privileges. The free-trade rights were limited to the Turukhansk *okrug*, Surgut *okrug*, and Berezovo *okrug*, which excluded importing duty-free goods to the economically important cities of Tomsk, Krasnoiarsk and Eniseisk. Neither was Sidorov granted rights to exploit gold fields free of duties, if his company discovered any.[44] Sidorov acquired a steamship himself; however, after a first failed expedition he temporarily lost interest in the exploration of the Northern sea route.[45]

Nevertheless, the first decade of Sidorov's and Latkin's (who had died in 1867) attempts to establish a Northern sea route for commercial interest proved to have long-lasting effects. Firstly, it provided a precedent for the granting of short-term customs exemptions to a single entrepreneur or company, which would come to define the future handling of the Northern sea route by the Ministry of Finance. Secondly, Sidorov's and Latkin's campaign to promote their project anticipated argumentative lines which would become dominant in the 1880s, namely the "nationalization" of economic issues. And lastly, they had successfully drawn attention to the economic potential of Siberia's Northern borderlands and a direct sea route. This attention eventually led to the first successful expedition from Western Europe to the estuaries of the

42 *Studitskii, Fedor*: Istoriia otkrytiia morskogo puti iz Evropy v sibirskie reki i do Beringova proliva. Part 2. Saint Petersburg 1883, 34. For the dissolution of the Orenburg customs line see chapter 2.

43 *Goncharov*: Istoriia kommercheskikh ekspeditsii, 69.

44 *Studitskii*: Istoriia otkrytiia morskogo puti iz Evropy v sibirskie reki. Chast' 2, 35–36.

45 *Dahlmann*: Torgovoe sudokhodstvo, 24.

Ob' river in 1874 – albeit not conducted by a Russian crew, as Sidorov had propagated with his visions of a "self-dependent Russian trade" in Northern Siberia.

4.3 The Establishment of the Northern Sea Route

After the devastating Kruzenshtern expedition, Sidorov had run into difficulty finding a Russian crew willing to attempt a passage to the Kara Sea, and in 1868 met with the seafarer and explorer Adolf Erik Nordenskiöld in Tromsø, to discuss a joint expedition. Though Nordenskiöld was enthusiastic about the idea and regularly corresponded with Sidorov, the expedition fell through for financial and administrative reasons. At about the same time, a second central persona for the exploration of the Kara Sea became interested in an expedition. British merchant seafarer Joseph Wiggins formulated a theory for a possible route to the Kara Sea and presented himself to Nordenskiöld in 1872 as a potential crew member for a Swedish expedition. However, as a foreign subject, Wiggins could not be hired. Both men would become definitive for the exploration of the Kara Sea and both stood in contact with Sidorov, as well his new business partner Aleksandr Mikhailovich Sibiriakov, another gold mine entrepreneur, who represented a new generation of "Northern Zealots."[46]

Of the two seafarers, Wiggins would be the first to successfully reach the Kara Sea and the estuaries of the Ob' river in 1874. Wiggins was well aware of both a 2.000-ruble prize money set by Sidorov for a successful passage and of the commercial potential of the new sea route. Using the momentum of the successful voyage, Sidorov spoke before the Society for Aid to Russian Industry and Trade and tried to raise funds for further expeditions. His large private financial investments and campaigning promised to reap results at last. The following year, Nordenskiöld's expedition, financed by Sibiriakov and Swedish industrialist Oscar Dickson, reached the estuaries of the Enisei river. Nordenskiöld continued to Eniseisk, from where he headed for Moscow. His expedition had made an immense impression; he was invited to speak at various societies in Moscow and Saint Petersburg and ultimately offered a sizable donation of 25.000 rubles from Sibiriakov to continue the exploration of the Arctic Ocean. In 1875 and 1876, Wiggins had also been able to repeat his

46 *Skrydlov, Andrei*: N.A. Nordenskiöld's Polar Expeditions and the Russian Society (To the 140th Anniversary of the First Voyage through the Northeast Passage). In: IOP Conference Series Earth and Environmental Science, 302 (2019), 1–6, 2–3; *Goncharov*: Istoriia kommercheskikh ekspeditsii, 65, 96–97; *Dahlmann*: Torgovoe sudokhodstvo, 24–25; *Agapov*: 'Zagovor' protiv Severa Rossii, 75.

voyage, and the Kara Sea began to lose its image as the unnavigable "Eiskeller", inspiring visions of directly linking Western Siberia to global trade currents. This phase of exploration was eventually crowned by Nordenskiöld completely crossing the North-East passage in 1878–1879.[47]

Despite the successful establishment of a Northern sea route, its main advocate Mikhail Sidorov quickly became subject to criticism. The national rhetoric and the promise of a "self-dependent Russian trade", which he had initially used to rally support for his vision, now stood in sharp contrast to the fact that the discoveries were made by British and Swedish subjects. In a note to the Society for Aid to the Russian Merchant Marine (Obshchestvo sodeistviia Russkomu torgovomu morekhodstvu) from 1877, Sidorov defended himself against allegations of unpatriotic behavior:

> Some members of our society accused me of worshipping [preklonenie] foreign merchant skippers by inviting them to voyages to the estuaries of the Siberian rivers! Also, they assured, outside of our society and during our meetings, that we have many of our own skippers and seamen. After my talk to the Society on January 4, they began vigorously helping me in finding Russian skippers and sailors, for which I want to express my sincere gratefulness.[48]

This search, however, produced no experienced sailors suitable for a polar expedition. Further, Sidorov elaborated, the handful of candidates which could be taken into consideration, were not "core Russian [korennye russkie]", but "two Germans from Vindava and a Finn", underlining his understanding of "self-dependent Russian trade" as a *russkii*, not a *rossiiskii* project. Nevertheless, Sidorov argued, he had no other choice than to resort to foreign explorers, as since Kruzenshtern's failed 1862 expedition no Russian seaman was willing to attempt the voyage and neither did he receive the necessary support from either the government or the various societies he was a member of.[49]

If anything, Sidorov's narrative of his personal perseverance at a time when there was no general belief in the possibility of a Northern sea route anymore, aimed at rallying new support, now that the Kara Sea was proven navigable. Society member and later chronologist of the Northern sea route's exploration Fedr Dmitrievich Studitskii jumped to Sidorov's help, reminding the society that the threat of foreign domination on the new route now loomed larger than ever:

47 *Goncharov*: Istoriia kommercheskikh ekspeditsii, 65–66, 97–98; *Studitskii*: Istoriia otkrytiia morskogo puti iz Evropy v sibirskie reki. Chast' 2, 84–88; *Dahlmann*: Torgovoe sudokhodstvo, 25.

48 *Studitskii*: Istoriia otkrytiia morskogo puti iz Evropy v sibirskie reki. Chast' 2, 125.

49 Ibid. 125–135.

> No 583 of "Novoe Vremia" has printed a declaration of the Poznan Committee for Aid to Russian Industries and Trade, stating that "meanwhile in England entrepreneurs have already formed a company with a capital of 20 thousand pounds sterling with the aim of establishing trade relations with Siberia by sea." It is our duty to protect the right of our compatriot to the discovery of the commercial sea route to the Ob' and Enisei rivers, and to make all possible efforts to ensure that trade between Siberia and Europe is in the hands of Russian entrepreneurs.[50]

When the following year two foreign ships chartered by Russian entrepreneurs shipwrecked while ships chartered by British entrepreneurs undertook successful voyages, Studitskii suspected a conspiracy, with "foreigners" resorting to "secret measures", expecting to "scare Russian entrepreneurs with the loss of ships and goods and accidents of ships." The next year, Studitskii speculated, insurance companies would reject insuring Russian goods on these grounds, by which the "secret goal" would be achieved. Thus, Studitskii summarized, it was of utmost importance to create a Russian merchant fleet with Russian ships and Russian sailors to compete on the Northern sea route.[51]

Studitskii's radically protectionist position was indicative of the national-conservative turn which emerged at the end of the 1870s and came to dominate the 1880s under Alexander III. In the same year as the two ships had been lost, the porto-franco of Batum had been introduced as a result of the Berlin Congress. The porto-franco, which was widely received as disgraceful and seen as an "English trading outpost", contributed to the devaluation of the "porto-franco" term and concept.[52] Nevertheless, in 1878 the territorialized porto-franco had not yet entirely vanished from the administrative toolbox. The West-Siberian Governor-general's senior official for special affairs, Nikolai Nikanorovich Balkashin, countered the protectionist demands by suggesting not only to allow foreign ships to use the Northern sea route, but to allow inland navigation on the Siberian rivers as well and grant free-trade rights on both imports and exports to foreigners.[53] The proposition aimed at regional development by stimulating foreign entrepreneurs to invest in the establishment of a regular trade route, which would allow the export of Siberia's natural resources. Unlike the free-trade privileges handed out to Sidorov's company in 1869, Balkashin's proposal resembled more the model of the Far-Eastern porto-franco, as free-trade rights would be universal and extended to a vast territory. However, his proposition was never picked up. Instead, individual companies and expeditions were granted duty-free rights

50 *Studitskii*: Istoriia otkrytiia morskogo puti iz Evropy v sibirskie reki. Chast' 1, 143.

51 Ibid. 231–234.

52 *Turbin*: Dal'nevostochnyi porto-franko, 63.

53 *Goncharov*: Istoriia kommercheskikh ekspeditsii, 121–122.

on a case-to-case basis, rather than within the framework of a stable porto-franco system.

The dispute outlined the two main arguments along which free-trade privileges in the Ob' and Enisei estuaries would be debated in future decades. The Northern sea route could either be understood as a vital connection of Western Siberia to global trade currents and a regional developmental measure – no matter who brokered the trade. Or it could be seen as part of a zero-sum game in which the trade route would have to be protected from foreign encroachment to allow for the development of "self-dependent Russian trade", as Sidorov had formulated it.

However, for the time being, any major decision on the regulation of the Northern sea route was protracted, as the enthusiasm over the nine successful expeditions of 1878 and Nordenskiöl's North-East passage was quickly replaced with disappointment. In 1879, numerous ships failed to reach the Kara Sea, demonstrating that the Northern sea route was still highly risky and far from a regularly navigable trade route. The following year brought about further failed attempts, and despite continuing expeditions, interest in the Northern sea route began to decline. In 1884, Sibiriakov, who had invested large sums into the Arctic exploration, financed his last expedition. He went on to devote his attention to an alternative trade route for Siberian exports – the establishment of a channel between Ob' and Enisei. An aged Sidorov backed out of further ventures before dying in 1887. In the years 1885 and 1886, no expeditions were undertaken on the Northern sea route.[54]

4.4 The Northern Sea Route and the Trans-Siberian Railway

Despite the "Northern Zealots" backing out of commercial trade on the Northern sea route, its discoverer Joseph Wiggins still believed in the commercial potential of the route. In 1887, Henry Sullivan and Joseph Wiggins formed "The Phoenix Merchant Adventurers Ltd." (later "The Anglo-Siberian Trading Syndicate Ltd.") with the intent of establishing regular commercial shipping from England to the Enisei river. In order to compensate for the risks of polar expeditions, they petitioned for seven-year duty-free rights and the right for inland navigation on the Enisei river. The political climate of the late 1880s was strongly protectionist and economic, and particularly trade issues were refracted through a national lens. The proposal was thus met with initial skepticism by the Ministry of Finance and in the Committee of Ministers,

54 Ibid. 119–120, 123–125.

arguing that such free-trade rights could pose a danger to the integrity of the protectionist system of the Russian Empire. The development of new spatial visions in the central administration, which interpreted the economic space of the Russian Empire as increasingly interconnected, constituted the basis for this concern. This effect can be observed for other regions of the empire as well, as demonstrated in other chapters of this book. Initially, it was thus proposed to issue free-trade rights only for a single navigation period. However, the Phoenix Company threatened that they would entirely abandon their endeavor if no long-term concessions were granted. In order to buttress their interests, the entrepreneurs mobilized British ambassador Sir Robert Morier. He proved to be one of the strongest backers of Sullivan's and Wiggin's operation, directly supporting their negotiations for duty-free rights by addressing Russian ministers as well as arranging a meeting between Sullivan and Minister of Finance Vyshnegradskii.[55]

Vyshnegradskii had initially granted a one-year duty-free concession to the company to navigate the Enisei, however, the 1888 expedition was not a success, as the sea vessel and the ship navigating on the Enisei missed each other and goods could not be exchanged. In a letter to the Minister of State Property, Vyshnegradskii explained his frustration with this failure, as his motivation had been the following:

> [...] by allowing the English steamship to navigate the Enisei for one year, we pursued the goal of attracting to this business Russian steamship owners, who in the following years could take upon themselves to ship the goods delivered to the estuaries of the Enisei and along the river. Meanwhile, the actions undertaken by the [Phoenix merchant] company not only were not conducive to this goal, but even had led to the opposite results. One comes to the conclusion that the abovementioned company absolutely did not earn the trust it had received from our government, which had given it exclusive and extraordinary privileges, and that there are no reasons to expand these privileges further.[56]

Despite his protectionist outlooks, Vyshnegradskii had supported and tolerated the British company's endeavors for similar reasons as Sidorov had resorted to foreign-led services in the 1870s. There was no one else willing to navigate the Northern sea route. Nevertheless, experience and information collected during foreign voyages was valued by the Russian government and

55 RGIA, f. 20, op. 5, d. 22, "Ob ustanovlenie prochnykh torgovykh sviazei Anglii s Zapadnoi Sibir'iu posredstvom vodnogo puti cherez Karskoe more i reku Ob'", l. 73,79, 121, 125; *Stone, Ian R.*: Sir Robert Morier and the Sea Route to Siberia. In: Polar Record, 31(178) (1995), 343–346, 343–344.

56 RGIA, f. 20, op. 5, d. 22, l. 158.

successful expeditions were to serve as a role model for Russian entrepreneurs and shipping companies.

Further, within the nationalist political climate of the 1880s, the Minister of Finance was very sensitive to the political implications of such ventures and reassured himself with the Foreign Ministry if the signal sent by duty-free rights granted to a British company was acceptable. On the one hand, the concessions had worried Russian merchants, with industrialist Nikolai Konstantinovich Krestovnikov publicly calling out the measures as "violating the national economic politics promoted by the Ministry of Finance."[57] Even if Vyshnegradskii considered their concern "somewhat exaggerated", public opinion could not be disregarded, as the experience with the closure of the Transcaucasian transit route in 1883 had shown.[58] More importantly, though, he was worried about the foreign political dimension of trade on the Northern sea route, demonstrating the degree to which economic issues were refracted through a national lens in the late 1880s – even at the highest ministerial level. In a letter to Foreign Minister Nikolai Girs, Vyshnegradskii voiced his concern for the political dimensions of duty-free rights for the British company:

> A further granting of the exclusive and extraordinary privileges given to the English company is hardly in the state's interest at a time when a number of English intrigues are coming to light, which are directed against our trade interests in Asia. I attribute special importance to the latter thought and have the honor of addressing you, your Highness, asking whether there would be a possibility of clarifying, through the most widespread press organs abroad, that our government's dismissal of further granting privileges to the English company stands in a known relation to the unwelcomed recent manifestations of English politics in the East.[59]

However, in his response, Girs, who had also been approached on the issue by British ambassador Morier, outright rejected Vyshnegradskii's proposal and himself strongly supported the Phoenix company:

> I would like to note, in this regard, that the question of the Siberian sea route should not be regarded from the point of view of political retaliation: the current issue has no political character. The sea route, at least in a commercial dimension, does not exist. Geographers and seafarers are yet to solve the task of establishing the conditions under which it will be possible to complete a full voyage to the Kara Sea at least once a year. The task is difficult, maybe even unsolvable. Our government has provided, as a prize, the duty-free importation of some goods to all entrepreneurs. Any new trade route,

57 *Krestovnikov, Nikolai*: Angliiskaia konkurrentsiia v Sibiri. Moscow 1889, 4; *Saunders, David*: Captain Wiggins and Admiral Makarov: Commerce and Politics in the Russian Arctic (1874–1904). In: Polar Record, 53(4) (2017), 427–435, 430.

58 RGIA, f. 20, op. 5, d. 22, l. 155ob. See chapter 6 for the Transcaucasian transit route.

59 Ibid. l. 155ob.-156.

even the problematic ones, has opponents. This is absolutely natural. The protests of Siberian merchants had already been heard in the 70s. This did not, however, stop the government from continuing.[60]

In Girs' view, the route was still in an exploratory phase. Essentially, the duty-free privileges granted to the Phoenix Company and also valid for any other interested enterprise created a limited short-term de-facto porto-franco regime on the estuaries of the Ob' and Enisei rivers, which, however, had always been limited to only a few navigation periods and prolonged in a piecemeal fashion, as well as including only a limited list of goods as duty-free. Such a cautious approach promised greater flexibility and has to be seen against the background of the difficulties the Russian government experienced when trying to curtail the Far-Eastern porto-franco's duty-free rights.[61]

By the end of the 1880s, the Ministry of Finance had firmly embarked on the project of creating a unified customs space, and the introduction of any medium- or long-term territorialized free-trade regime would have run contrary to this agenda. Further, the functional basis for any previous duty-free privileges in the Russian Empire's Asiatic territories had always been the infrastructural fragmentation of the imperial economic space. With regards to Western Siberia, the perceived distance to the core economic space, however, was about to change dramatically with the planned construction of the Trans-Siberian railway. In the 1860s and 1870s, the Northern sea route had existed as one of many visions for the infrastructural integration of Siberia; by the end of the 1880s it was now becoming entangled with the Trans-Siberian Railway – both as competitor and enabler.

When the construction of the Trans-Siberian railway had reached Krasnoiarsk in 1893, the idea of delivering the materials for its further construction by the Northern sea route appeared. Initially, the British expedition which delivered the rails had not been planned for this purpose. Met with the task of supplying heavy construction materials in bulk to Krasnoiarsk on the Enisei river, the Russian government saw the time come to make use of the new sea trade route and inquired with Wiggins whether he deemed the delivery of 2000 tons of rails feasible. Apart from the rails, a river flotilla for inland navigation on the Enisei was to be delivered as well. A Russian party took it upon itself to deliver three vessels to the Enisei. Goncharov argues that despite these two parties often being depicted as one expedition, there was indeed little cooperation between the Russian and British seafarers. Russian naval officers complained that they received almost no information from the experienced

60 Ibid. l. 163–164.

61 *Turbin*: Dal'nevostochnyi porto-franko, 68–73; *Beliaeva*: Ot porto-franko k tamozhne, 38–39.

Captain Wiggins. Goncharov suggests that "[…] all these events made the Russians understand that the British are not at all interested in assisting it in the development of the route […]."[62] Conversely, it could be argued that Wiggins was well aware that strong reservations existed against British activities on the Northern sea route, and that by sharing his know-how, he would effectively render his services obsolete in the future. After all, Wiggin's and his company pursued primarily commercial, not scientific, interests.

The voyage to the Kara Sea was successful, however, transshipping the rails onto river boats at the mouth of the Enisei proved difficult due to weather conditions and half of the cargo remained scattered on the riverbanks. Nevertheless, Wiggins was personally rewarded by Alexander III for his service and later approached again to deliver steamships to the Enisei.[63]

The success of the 1893 and 1894 expeditions sparked hope for regular commercial navigation to the estuaries of Ob' and Enisei, but it also highlighted two problems for the future of the Northern sea route. First, the necessary know-how still lay with British seafarers, to whom both the Russian government and private entrepreneurs had to resort. Secondly, the very success of delivering rails from Great Britain to Krasnoiarsk, which contributed to the construction of the Trans-Siberian railway, demonstrated in the most obvious fashion that Western Siberia could no longer be regarded as an economic territory distant from the core economic space. If Western European goods could be shipped right up to the Trans-Siberian railway, the parallel maintenance of a porto-franco regime in the estuaries of the Ob' and Enisei rivers and a highly protectionist core imperial customs space would no longer be bearable. Even if the Northern sea route was not yet reliably navigable, and thus the actual threat of foreign duty-free goods reaching to the core customs space was negligible, the spatial imagination of many imperial bureaucrats had shifted, and Western Siberia appeared to inch closer to the imperial center. The very basis for the institution of territorialized free-trade regimes – the infrastructural fragmentation of the imperial economic space – was lost. Without free-trade privileges or state subsidies, however, shipping on the hazardous Northern sea route was uneconomical.

In order to curtail further foreign navigation and the intrusion of Western-manufactured goods into the core customs zone, a special committee gathered in 1897 and decided to cancel free-trade privileges in the estuaries of the Ob' and Enisei rivers prematurely and introduce the European customs

62 *Goncharov, Alexander E.*: The Trans-Siberian Railway and the Northern Sea Route. In: Journal of Siberian Federal University. Humanities & Social Sciences 6(1) (2013), 31–42, here 35–37.

63 Ibid. 39.

tariff beginning in 1898, effectively terminating any activity for Wiggins' company. This measure, however, was met with resistance from a hitherto less vocal party – Siberian city representatives.[64]

4.5 The Northern Sea Route between Imperial and Regional Interests

Initially, the development of the Northern sea route had been pushed by private entrepreneurs such as Sidorov and Sibiriakov, who hoped for personal profit, even if they cloaked their intentions in national rhetoric. The Russian government had, for the most part, avoided directly investing into the exploration of the route and contented itself with granting duty-free privileges to make the route economically more attractive to risk-averse entrepreneurs, including foreigners such as Wiggins and Sullivan. By the end of the 1890s, however, the Russian government began to take a more serious interest in the Northern sea route, which had by then been proven navigable. At the same time, demands for a porto-franco began to be heard from representatives of Siberian cities, who saw their regional interests disregarded.

First experiments with the importation of tea (one of the most important imported consumer goods in Siberia) via the Northern sea route had demonstrated significant advantages over traditional trade routes from Mongolia or even the sea route to Odessa. Transportation times on the Northern sea route amounted to 1–1½ months, while transportation via Odessa took 7 weeks and, respectively, 1½ years overland through Mongolia. In 1897, Eniseisk merchant Tonkonogov successfully transported a large shipment of brick and non-brick tea from Hankou (today's Wuhan) via London to Eniseisk. The Ministry of Finance had allowed him to do so, applying the special Irkutsk tea tariff of 2 ½ rubles per pud as compared to the 21 rubles per pud which were valid for the European border. With such a significant tariff discrepancy and the swift transportation, the Northern sea route became attractive despite its risks. The introduction of the general European tariff the following year and the decision to institute customs control for goods delivered to the estuaries of Ob' and Enisei, however, put a quick end to such business opportunities.[65]

Apart from potential profits, a duty-free Northern sea route also promised cheaper living costs and higher living standard in the poor Eniseisk gubernia

64 *Redaktsiia Torgovo-Promyshlennoi Gazety*: Severnyi torgovyi put' i khodataistva Sibirskikh gorodov. Saint Petersburg 1898, 9–10.

65 Ibid. 8–10; Polnoe sobranie zakonov Rossiikoi Imperii. Sobranie 3. Volume 11. Saint Petersburg 1894, prilozhenie "Shtaty i Tabeli", 161.

and other regions of Western Siberia. Due to its geographic dislocation in the south, the Trans-Siberian railway could do little to alleviate harsh living conditions and ensure a steady supply, proponents of a porto-franco argued. On the other hand, the possibility of a direct trade route for the exportation of Siberia's natural resources would elevate the economic standard.[66]

To be sure, there was no consensus on the desirability of a porto-franco for the Northern sea route among Siberian merchants. While some merchants, such as Tonkonogov, who had successfully imported tea, saw business potential, others feared foreign competition. Neither did all city duma representatives support a free-trade regime. In Krasnoiarsk, the duma head himself opposed a free-trade regime. Nevertheless, the Krasnoiarsk duma voted 17 to 6 in favor of a porto-franco and joined the petition of the cities of Tomsk, Eniseisk, and Tiumen.[67]

They had entered the special committee with a petition for a prolongation of free-trade rights for at least five years, emphasizing the importation of industrial machinery and goods, as well as consumer goods such as tea. The Tiumen duma argued that regular trade on the Northern sea route was vital for the exportation of the region's grain, while the Enisei duma emphasized the importance of lowering living expenses in the remote region. On the committee they were met with opposition from Central Russian industrialists, who argued that the Northern sea route should serve all-Russian, not regional interests, which they identified as the export function, which however did not outweigh the dangers of duty-free importation of foreign goods, as "the British do not care for exports, but strive to conquer the Siberian market." With regard to the lowering of living costs and the development of Western Siberia through free trade, they argued that the interests of a single region could not outweigh all-imperial interests.[68] While the issue of customs exemptions had prior been the concern of private entrepreneurs, it was now becoming an important point of contention in the negotiation of center-periphery relations and a growing Siberian regionalist self-conception.

The petition for the continuation of free-trade privileges had not been successful. This, however, did not mean that the Russian government had no interests in the exploitation of the Northern sea route, but rather that it was to be nationalized and serve the infrastructural integration of the imperial space as envisioned by Minister of Finance Sergei Vitte under his national economic system. For the first time since the 1870s, the Russian government considered serious investments into the novel trade route. Vitte entrusted the

66 *Redaktsiia Torgovo-Promyshlennoi Gazety*: Severnyi torgovyi put' i khodataistva Sibirskikh gorodov, 12,15.
67 Ibid. 16.
68 Ibid. 17.

project to Vice-Admiral Stepan Osipovich Makarov, who had suggested using ocean-going icebreakers to ensure regular navigation to the Kara Sea. After an expedition in 1897, Makarov concluded that one icebreaker was sufficient, and that it could have smaller dimensions and less power than he had initially assumed. His report convinced Vitte of the undertaking, and the Minister of Finance commissioned the construction of the icebreaker "Ermak", which was to be built at a British shipyard based on the plans provided by Makarov – contrary to Vitte's imperative for state orders to be placed with Russian companies. Vitte had hoped that an icebreaker would allow a fast connection to Russia's Far-East via the Northern sea route and significantly alter the Russian Empire's geopolitical make-up. By 1899, the ship was finished; however, it was troubled with technical problems and never lived up to its envisioned purpose.[69]

Beginning with the debate on the cancelation of free-trade privileges for the Northern sea route, a group of Siberian merchants, industrialists, and city duma representatives began to push forward the issue of a Northern porto-franco in public debate, formulating a regionalist alternative spatial vision to the Trans-Siberian railway project of the central administration. Authors like "Eniseets"[70] appropriated the familiar protectionist rhetoric, however, transferred it to a regional scale. Friedrich List's "national economic system", popularized (in a curtailed and commented version) by now-Minister of Finance Sergei Vitte, built on an evolutionary view which stipulated that nascent industries and developing states required protectionism to grow before they could become competitive internationally. Eniseets picked up this line of argumentation, but translated it from an international to an intra-imperial plane. He argued that Siberia required free-trade privileges to develop its potential in order to be truly integrated into the imperial economic system, rather than become dependent on goods from Central Russia and remain in its economically weak state. The infrastructural integration promised by the Trans-Siberian railway only functioned if intra-imperial economic levels were harmonized. With such an argumentation, he reinterpreted the porto-franco mechanism as a regional protectionist measure conducive rather than disrup-

69 *Saunders*: Captain Wiggins and Admiral Makarov, 431–433; *Makarov, Stepan Osipovich*: Otchet vitse-admirala Makarova ob osmotre im letom 1897 goda, po porucheniiu ministra finansov S.Iu. Vitte, morskogo puti na reki Ob' i Enisei. Saint Petersburg 1898, 70–71.

70 Most likely a pseudonym for Enisei duma representative Stepan Vostrotin, who later published under his real name. As part of their wedding tour, Vostrotin and his wife were on-board the "Stjernen", under the command of Captain Wiggins, in 1894. They were two of only four passengers. "Eniseets" mentions being on-board this ship. See *Eniseets*: Severnyi morskoi put'. Saint Petersburg 1898, 14; *Johnson, Henry*: The Life and Voyages of Joseph Wiggins, F. R.G. S. Modern Discoverer of the Kara Sea Route to Siberia. Based on his Journal & Letters. London 1907, 286.

tive to Vitte's vision of an integrated "national economic system" and thus of all-imperial importance:

We mentioned that the Great Siberian railway could remain without freight – particularly in the space of Eastern Siberia, and thus become a burden to the state budget. This is an issue of huge importance which cannot be disregarded. Only by raising the cultural level and by exploiting the natural riches and productive powers of Siberia, this heavy burden of the Siberian railway can be lifted from Russia's shoulders. An improved agriculture, the sale of agricultural products, and as a result the improvement of the economic state of the agricultural population of Siberia, as well as the appearance of factories and the exploitation of the natural riches of Siberia, the appearance of a wide system of river steamships, which would regulate internal prices, enliven internal trade and elevate trade, the cheapening and unburdening of Siberian life and as a result the increase of wealth in Siberia in a broad sense – only these developments will create freight for the Trans-Siberian railway and give it passengers. This is the reason why, in our opinion, duty-free import of foreign goods to Siberia does not only have a regional, but also an all-imperial importance.[71]

However, raising Siberia's economic level, Vostrotin argued, could not be achieved under the conditions of high customs duties, which weighed disproportionately heavier in distant regions. Russian manufacturers, on the other hand, could not provide the necessary supplies at low prices:

We could be faced with another (narrower) objection. Namely, that by attracting foreigners, we harm the interests of Russian manufacturers and industries. We already stated that as much as navigation on the Kara Sea to the estuaries of the Siberian rivers is not the same as navigation to the ports of the Baltic Sea or the Gulf Finland, the weight of protectionist duties is not felt in the same way on this or the other side of the Ural Mountains: for Siberia the customs are incomparably heavier than for Russia. Further, we can also use the favorite argument of the combative bunch of Russian manufacturers. So far, this combative party of Russian industries has not given birth to cheap prices on sugar and pig iron, on machines and cotton, and on stearin candles; thus, we have all the right to doubt the honesty of their speeches and the technical abilities of Russian industrialists and we say with an even greater right: "give us, Siberia, time to get up on our feet, give us duty-free importation of foreign goods and free us from the weight of your prices, give us the opportunity to grow our agriculture, trade and industries – then close the duty-free import of foreign goods. We dare to think that we will fulfill the promises about our cultural progress faster than the Moscow manufacturers would fulfill their promises of lowering prices on their products and promises on the technical refinement of their manufacture."[72]

Echoing List's argument that protectionism was a temporary measure which would become obsolete on the next evolutionary stage, once international

71 *Eniseets*: Severnyi morskoi put', 34–35.
72 Ibid. 35–36.

competitiveness was achieved, the Northern porto-franco was not framed as a permanent measure. By using the language of contemporary protectionist discourse, Vostrotin attempted to make the proposition of a porto-franco compatible with the Ministry of Finance's larger agenda.

This interpretation of the role of a porto-franco resembled much more the argumentation surrounding the Far-Eastern porto-franco, as well as the customs privileges in the Transcaucasian region, than it did the individualized free-trade privileges once given to Sidorov and other individual entrepreneurs. In both the Far-East and the Transcaucasus it had been argued that temporary free-trade zones contributed to a quicker economic development and harmonization of economic levels between center and periphery, facilitating a quicker integration into the imperial economic space.[73]

Intra-imperial protectionism, however, was not a line of thought solely pursued from a Siberian perspective. Adversely, the infrastructural integration of Siberian grain-producing regions via the Trans-Siberian railway put pressure on Central Russian estate owners, as their production costs were significantly higher. As a measure to protect the already struggling estate owners, the Cheliabinsk tariff break was introduced. In theory, the railway rate system was designed to privilege long-distance transportation by coupling freight rates per ton to transportation distance – the longer the distance covered, the lower the freight rate. Such a system played into the hands of Siberian grain producers shipping westward via railway to the Baltic ports. To decrease intra-imperial competition and protect Central Russian grain producers, in 1896 the Cheliabinsk tariff in break was introduced. It split the freight rate system into two zones, meaning that starting with the city of Cheliabinsk, the calculation of transportation distance, on which the freight rate was based, was zeroed out and transport rates from Siberia westwards were thus artificially raised.[74]

Chances for the establishment of a porto-franco in the estuaries of Ob' and Enisei, however, appeared to shrink, as its prominent model, the contested Far-Eastern porto-franco, was dissolved in 1901. By the turn of the century, the Russian Empire had firmly stepped onto a path of integrating its customs territory, and special territorialized customs regimes were no longer the tool of choice in organizing the imperial economic space. The Far-Eastern porto-franco did have a brief return in 1904, as shortages caused by the Russo-Japanese War called for the incentivization of trade, for which the imperial administration resorted to customs exemptions. In the course of the war, the Northern porto-franco experienced a similar temporary return, as numerous Russian and foreign companies (including Vostrotin's company)

73 See chapter 5.

74 *Mote, Victor L.*: The Cheliabinsk Grain Tariff and the Rise of the Siberian Butter Industry. In: Slavic Review, 35(2) (1976), 304–317, here 304–306.

received duty-free rights to relieve the overloaded Trans-Siberian railway. In 1907, however, the customs privileges were retracted again. In both cases, the short return of free-trade privileges resulted in public debates over the reinstitution of porto-francos. The introduction of the State Duma provided a new opportunity to voice regional interests.[75]

Already in 1906 a special council with 208 participants had been called in by the Governor-general of Irkutsk to discuss means of communication in Siberia. Local industrialists, merchants, shippers, and city duma representatives were invited to participate in the council. Although initially the Northern sea route had not been on the agenda, it soon became clear that an individual subsection had to be created for its discussion. Eventually, an "overwhelming majority" of the council spoke in favor of a Northern porto-franco with city dumas supporting the project and demanding ten-year duty-free privileges to ensure stable growth as well as the infrastructural improvement of the Northern sea route. Subsequently, the issue of a Northern porto-franco was strongly campaigned in public. The language of the articles supporting its institution increasingly emphasized the antagonism of Siberian and Central Russian economic interests. The two great infrastructural projects in Siberia were read as physical manifestations of these differing interests. Had the Northern sea route and the Trans-Siberian railway prior existed as two complementary routes, they were now framed as competing spatial visions.

One of the porto-franco's main advocates, Vostrotin, contested that the Trans-Siberian railway's design did not cater to Siberia's regional needs and did not hold its promise of integrating the imperial economic space and thus demanded the revocation of the Cheliabinsk tariff break, although he doubted that its effect would be sufficient for Siberia's economic rise. Its riches, he envisaged, could only be tapped by directly connecting Western Siberia to global trade currents via the Northern sea route.[76] Similar sentiments resonated in Dunin-Gorkavich's speech in the extraordinary general assembly of the Tobol'sk Duma on April 30th 1907, cited at the beginning of this chapter:

> The construction of the Siberian railway mostly enlivened the space adjacent to the railroad tracks, having only a quite weak impact on the more distant and isolated regions. As a result, the economic condition of Western Siberia today, as before the construction of the railway, is developing weakly. […] At the current time, when the

75 *Beliaeva*: Ot porto-franko k tamozhne, 53–80, 116–154, 133–139; *Goncharov*: Istoriia kommercheskikh ekspeditsii, 93–94.

76 Trudy soveshchaniia 1906g. v Irkutske o putiakh soobshcheniia v Sibiri. Volume 1. Irkutsk 1907, 3, 54, 82–90, 214; *Vostrotin, Stepanov*: Severnyi morskoi put' i Cheliabinskii tarifnyi perelom v sviazi s kolonizatsiei Sibiri. Saint Petersburg 1908, 40–41; *Agapov, Mikhail*: Looking for a Way Out: Trans-Siberian Transportation Projects at the Turn of the 20th Century. In: Quaestio Rossica, 6(3) (2018), 771–783, here 774–778.

question of raising the economic situation of the empire's population is coming up in all its power, the regional question of the development of productive forces in Siberia must be discussed in all its broadness. But fulfilling cultural needs requires large spending and means, which the population cannot provide, and the government does not have. Foreign capitals must be attracted to develop the productive forces of Siberia, which is only possible by instituting a porto-franco.[77]

From a Siberian perspective, the "currently practiced protectionist commercial and industrial policy was to the detriment of Siberia." Dunin-Gorkavich did not necessarily see a closer integration with Central Russia as the remedy, but rather articulated a spatial vision in which the "extension of the porto-franco, which has to encompass all of Western Siberia, as well as the Enisei and Irkutsk gubernias" would allow to include the "rich Semirech'e oblast' into the sphere of influence of the Northern Sea route."[78] A vision which effectively ran counter to the Trans-Siberian railway's design, which was to channel all commercial activity in the empire, rather than allow for autonomous trade relations of peripheral territories. Following a similar logic, the Transcaspian railway had advanced the customs integration of Bukhara and its adjacent territories, increasingly orienting the region's trade towards the Russian Empire as a trading partner.[79]

Along with other economic and political issues, the institution of a Northern porto-franco became a nexus of a Siberian political self-conception. After broad public campaigns, the Siberian duma group eventually entered the State Duma with a draft proposing the institution of a Northern porto-franco in 1908.[80] The proposition, however, encountered strong opposition from the Ministry of Trade and Industry.[81] The ministry argued that the Northern sea route would only serve foreign private interests, arguing that prior duty-free privileges had primarily been used by foreign subjects and cited the unwanted results of the Far-Eastern porto-franco, where foreign merchants had come to dominate. Further, as the Trans-Siberian railway was now operational, any porto-franco would have to be separated by a customs cordon, resulting in the isolation of Siberia. This, the Minister of Trade and Industry suggested, could well be the intention of the draft, insinuating separatism on the side of Siberian duma representatives. In any case, such an internal customs border would neither be practically possible, nor timely, as the Far-Eastern porto-franco

77 *Dunin-Gorkavich*: Neobkhodimost' otkrytiia porto-franko v ust'iach reki Obi i Eniseia, 1.

78 Ibid. 29, 32, 34.

79 See chapter 3.

80 *Stuch, Stephan*: Regionalismus in Sibirien im frühen 20. Jahrhundert (Dissertation). Köln 2003, 62–68.

81 In 1905, key departments of the Ministry of Finance were transferred into the newly founded Ministry of Trade and Industry.

was in the process of being dismantled. Neither did the ministry subscribe to the idea of a customs zone uniting Siberia with Turkestan and Semirech'e, as had been suggested by Dunin-Gorkavich. Any fragmentation of the customs space was seen to undermine trade from Siberia to Central Russia, and even if a Northern porto-franco would be to the benefit of Siberia (which the minister doubted) it would only serve a regional, not an all-imperial, interest.[82] The project was eventually declined by the Council of Ministers as incompatible with the agenda of integrating the Russian Empire's custom space:

> It is without doubt that the opening of a porto-franco on the border of, so to speak, Siberia and European Russia, cardinally undermines the system which Russia pursues based on the example of other states. Precisely, the system of protecting native trade and industries.[83]

The dismissal of a porto-franco regime, which de facto was the only measure which could make the Northern sea route profitable, thus referred to problems in two dimensions: intra-imperial and international. On the one hand, it would have undermined the unity of the economic space, which had been pursued with the removal of special economic zones on the Russian Empire's peripheries since the 1880s. A unity already undermined by the Cheliabinsk tariff break, which was strongly criticized by Siberian actors. On the other hand, the national underpinnings, which had been present in debates on the exploitation of the Northern sea route since the 1860s, when Sidorov and Latkin rallied supporters around a national goal of exploring the new route, were now part of the Russian Empire's highly protectionist agenda, and thus administrative measures favoring foreign entrepreneurs were deemed unacceptable.

During the exploratory phase of the Northern sea route, the Russian government was willing to overlook that most successful expeditions on the Northern sea route had been conducted by foreign crews, with British Captain Wiggins acquiring the reputation as the most knowledgeable seafarer in the Kara Sea. Once the commercial character of voyages on the Northern sea route began to dominate, trade incentives for foreign companies were retracted and the Russian government attempted to take its exploitation into its own hands, as manifested by the construction of the oceanic icebreaker Ermak. Though the track record in the first decade of the 20th century had been poor, the Russian administration's investment into the route and its vital role during the Russo-Japanese War demonstrated that objections against the trade route were primarily refracted through a national lens. On the eve of the World War I, governmental initiatives to establish regular shipping the Northern sea route

82 RGIA, f. 23, op. 18, d. 169, l. 9, 13ob., 14ob.–15, 17–18.

83 *Gosudarstvennaia Duma*: Zakliuchenie po vnesennomu v Gosudarstvennuiu Dumu, za podpis'iu 34 chlenov ee, zakonoproektu o porto-franko v ust'iakh r.r. Obi i Eniseia. Saint Petersburg 1908, 23–24.

intensified. The Naval Ministry showed a particular interest in the route and presented a project on its improvement, constructed telegraph stations, and conducted meteorological observations. However, the route was no longer interpreted as a trade route open to international entrepreneurs, but as a "natural monopoly" of the Russian government.[84]

The problem of disruption to the unity of the imperial customs space, which would have been caused by a Northern porto-franco, could only be solved by creating an all-Russian infrastructure. Russian shipping companies could receive direct governmental subsidies for servicing the route, which would increase the profitability of the route, without having to resort to all-encompassing free-trade regulations, but rather operating with lists of duty-free goods, declared by the Ministry of Trade and Industries. Further, in 1913, the Cheliabinsk tariff break was abrogated as a step towards the integration of Siberia into the economic edifice of the empire. If the Northern sea route would be serviced by Russian companies only, railway and sea route could work in conjunction, without jeopardizing national interests. Thus, at the end of 1913, the Russian government published a call for tender, addressed only to Russian steamship companies. The tender related to regular shipping service on the Northern sea route to the estuaries of the Enisei. The winner would receive direct governmental subsidies worth 120.000 rubles, as well as a zero-interest loan of 500.000 rubles. Thus, the government hoped, the route would finally be serviced by an arctic Russian merchant fleet. However, the onset of World War I forced changes to the government's plans. To ensure supply routes, limited duty-free rights were introduced for the Northern sea route in 1915 for the duration of the war, and foreign companies were incentivized to service the route as well. The list of duty-free goods grew longer over the course of the war, and after the February revolution, the estuaries of the Ob' and Enisei rivers were declared a porto-franco for a further five years.[85]

84 *Agapov*: Looking for a Way Out, 777–778; *Dolidovich, Olesya/Fedorova, Vera/Zhulaeva, Anna*: Conflict of Imperial and Regional Interests on the Introduction of Duty-free Trade Regime in the Mouths of Siberian Rivers during the First World War. In: Bylye Gody, 54(1) (2019), 395–405, 399.

85 *Mote*: Cheliabinsk Grain Tariff, 307–308; RGIA, f. 23, op. 18, d. 169, l. 71; RGIA, f. 23, op. 8, d. 68, "Ob osvoenii Severnogo morskogo puti v Sibiri i o priniatii mer po zaseleniiu Dal'nego Vostoka. Zhurnaly soveshchaniia dlia rassmotreniia khodataistva T-va 'parokhodstvo torgovykh moriakov' ob okazanii emu pravitel'stvennoi podderzhki v dele razvitiia torgovli s Sibir'iu Severnym morskim putem", l. 20; *Dolidovich/Fedorova/Zhulaeva*: Conflict of Imperial and Regional Interests, 400–401; *Pinkhenson, Dmitrii M.*: Istoriia otkrytiia i osvoeniia Severnogo morskogo puti. Volume 2. Leningrad 1962, 656–662, 666–668.

4.6 Conclusion

40 years after Captain Wiggin's first successful passage to the estuaries of the Ob', the Northern sea route had acquired vital importance in the wartime economy, even as it remained dangerous to traverse. Its successful exploration initially owed to the perseverance of adventurers and private entrepreneurs, such as Sidorov and Latkin. The liberal climate of the 1860s facilitated the realization of their ideas, as the creation of new societies and the liberalization of press organs established new forums to debate alternative spatial visions and allowed them to exert influence on public opinion and political decision-making.

In his campaign to rally support for the exploration of the Northern sea route, Sidorov capitalized on these new communicative channels. He also predated the national turn of the 1880s, as he was able to somewhat obscure his private business interests and forge a common denominator for the supporters of his plan by framing his project in a "national" language – a rhetoric strategy which would come to dominate public discourse in the 1880s. In practice, the exploration and exploitation of the Northern sea route relied primarily on the services of foreign explorers and was driven by private business interests.

While Sidorov's visions of a Northern sea route and the belief in its power to reorganize the empire's economic space may appear extravagant against the perils and failures of the early expeditions, it was not unusual for the late 1860s. Bold projects for the geopolitical restructuring of vast spaces enjoyed high popularity, with successful examples such as the Suez Canal bolstering public belief in the malleability of space through technology. The Transcaspian railway brought forward by the Society for Aid to Russian Industry and Trade, discussed in chapter 2, as well as the Trans-Siberian railway or plans to re-route the Amu Darya river originated from the same spirit.[86]

Neither was Sidorov's main demand for the introduction of a free-trade regime in a peripheral region of the Russian Empire unusual for the 1860s. He referred to the Far-Eastern porto-franco as well as the dissolution of the Steppe customs border as successful role models. The establishment of vast territorialized free-trade zones indeed provided the imperial government with an instrument to soften economic hardships in distant peripheries and attract foreign capital, without having allocated funds from the state treasury strained by the budgetary crisis of the 1860s. The idea of a Northern porto-franco was thus a genuine child of the liberal phase of the 1860s, even if, at least rhetorically, Sidorov's proposal already anticipated the nationalist turn of the 1880s.

86 *Pravilova*: River of Empire, 261–263.

However, unlike the Far-Eastern porto-franco, which had established itself successfully in the 1860s, the Northern sea route could only be first navigated in 1874, and it took until the end of the 1880s for commercial shipping to become a viable option. By this time, the "porto-franco" concept had acquired a bad reputation as "non-national" and was thus publicly discredited as an economic instrument. Against the backdrop of competing European states, primarily the German Empire, the Russian Empire had begun to critically reappraise its heterogeneous approach towards the structuring of customs space and reoriented itself towards the integration and unification of its customs territory. With simultaneous efforts to remove the Far-Eastern porto-franco's privileges against local resistance and the dissolution of the politically discredited Batumi porto-franco, the introduction of a new vast porto-franco on the estuaries of the Ob' and Enisei rivers, which could only be serviced by foreign ships, appeared ill-timed and at odds with the general "national" political climate.

For the benefit of naval exploration, temporary concessions were granted to individual companies, but it soon became obvious that the imperial administration was not interested in establishing a permanent direct and duty-free sea trade between Western Siberia and Great Britain, as it ran counter to the goals of the Trans-Siberian railway project.

The Northern sea route and the Trans-Siberian railway were contrary not only in the choice of means of transportation, but primarily in the vision of spatial reorganization they represented. While the Trans-Siberian railway aimed at connecting Russia's Eastern peripheries to the empire's core economic space by channeling their economic activity through the center of the empire, the Northern sea route – if conceptualized as a free-trade route – promised to integrate Western Siberia directly into world trade currents, circumventing the traditional economic centers of the empire. As already observed with the integration of the Russian Empire's Central Asian territories, by the 1890s the Ministry of Finance had firmly embarked on a course of re-orienting peripheral economic activity through the imperial center and raising external protectionist barriers. As long as the Northern sea route could not be serviced by Russian shipping companies and required duty-free concessions to foreign entrepreneurs, it was incompatible with the national economic system.

Paradoxically, though, both the sea route and the British companies servicing it contributed to the construction of the Trans-Siberian railway by delivering materials and thus helping to realize the potential of the new route. This potential was called upon during the Russo-Japanese War, as the Trans-Siberian railway struggled under the logistic demands of warfare. In the course of the war, both the Northern porto-franco and the Far-Eastern porto-franco, which had been reintroduced temporarily, received renewed support. Further, the subsequent introduction of the State Duma provided a new organ to voice regionalist political demands. In both cases, opponents of territorialized free-trade regimes framed the re-institution of porto-francos as a conflict between central and regional interests and an expression of separatist tendencies. The territorialized free-trade regimes were discussed as disruptive to the integrity of the imperial customs space and incompatible with a vision of a nationalizing empire, featuring an integrated administratively homogenous economic space.

The allure of the Northern sea route remained; however, the age of territorialized free-trade zones, which had been a popular administrative tool particularly in the 1860s, had vanished. By the 1910s, the Russian government was not willing to make any customs concessions anymore in order to attract foreign shipping companies. The imperial administration would only support the route if it constituted the monopoly of a Russian merchant fleet. The February Revolution abruptly halted the imperial projects; however, consequent decades of Soviet Arctic exploration continued this legacy, and a clear continuity can be observed with early Soviet exploration of the Northern sea route.[87]

The history of the Northern porto-franco is one of a latecomer. It demonstrates how territorialized free-trade regimes were willingly implemented in the 1860s to compensate for regional economic disbalances between the Russian Empire's peripheral territories, all the while keeping state investments to a minimum. In the 1880s, the context of a nationalizing empire, which emphasized unified economic regimes, shifted attention away from the balancing of regional economic disbalances towards administrative unification and the channeling of economic activity through the imperial center. The imagined and real infrastructural integration of the imperial economic space further complicated the isolation of vast territorialized free-trade zones, which had prior relied on the infrastructural fragmentation of space. Eventually, the Northern porto-franco remained a temporary phenomenon, which had come too late to ever experience full bloom. Nevertheless, for its supporters, it had become – even if much less pronounced and prominent than in the case of the Far-Eastern porto-franco – symbolic for an integration of the imperial economic space at the expense of its peripheries.

87 *Korandei, Fedor*: Ekonomisty v 'pole': Karskaia ekspeditsiia 1924g. i praktiki sozdaniia ekonomicheskogo znaniia. In: Ab Imperio, 2 (2020), 51–56, 53–54.

5. Insular Administration and the Economic Integration of the Caucasian Viceroyalty

The challenge of space fundamentally shaped the Russian Empire's administrative composition. Extending its territory was one thing, but permeating space with administrative power quite another. Rather than advancing its state institutions from the center, various forms of insular institutions were created, which acted as regional power centers and took upon themselves functions usually administered directly from Saint Petersburg. In some areas of administration, regional specificities such as language and religion presented a strong case for an insular approach, but the case was less obvious for customs.[1] After all, it is in the very nature of customs institutions to function on the furthest outside borders and still be responsible to the center. However, until the 1880s the Caucasian Viceroyalty was in full control of its customs institutions. This chapter elaborates on why such privileges were granted initially and which factors inhibited the central administration's attempts to withdraw these prerogatives.

This chapter presents one case of an insular customs administration which was successfully centralized in the 1880s. Simultaneously, however, efforts to dismantle insular customs regimes had been made on other peripheries as well, as part of a larger drive towards the integration of the Russian Empire's customs space. The case of the Grand Duchy of Finland is discussed in chapter 7 of this book. The two cases represent, in many ways, opposing manifestations of the insular principle. The Caucasian Viceroyalty was perceived as economically backwards; meanwhile, the Grand Duchy of Finland had industrialized so successfully by the 1880s, Russian manufacturers perceived it as a threat. While the Caucasian Namestnik was installed to subjugate and weld together his domain – effectively in order to fabricate the region referred to as Transcaucasus – the Grand Duchy of Finland was going through a process of nation-building increasingly suspicious to the imperial center. The first wielded extensive personal rights answering to the Tsar only, in the latter power was divided between the Governor-general of Finland and the Finnish

1 On the functioning of insular administrations, particularly the differences between those in the western and the eastern territories of the Russian Empire see *Matsuzato*: Intra-Bureaucratic Debate.

Senate. As different as both cases are, the long existence of insular structures of administration had a significant impact in shaping the regional economies of both and created peculiarities which were difficult to remove once the issue of integration into the imperial customs space arose.

It is argued that while the creation of a uniform customs space was increasingly regarded as imperative in the late 19th century and appeared as the logical continuation of an increased infrastructural integration and economic approximation between the core economic space and the imperial peripheries, this process was complicated by the entanglements created by insular administrations. The tools of insular administration employed to manage a heterogeneous imperial space fundamentally opposed the creation of a uniform economic space. Superficially, debates revolved around issues of trust, jurisdiction, and efficiency. At the core, however, the reforms constituted a decision between the creation of a unified customs space or a customs union – between the centralization of the empire or the perpetuation of the separateness of its peripheral regions.

The chapter aims to outline the motivation behind both the establishment of an insular customs regime in the Caucasian Viceroyalty (Kavkazskoe Namestnichestvo) and its revocation. It explores how the separate customs regime was defined by asymmetry and a semi-permeable flow of trade between the space of the imperial core and the Transcaucasus, which eventually prompted the integration efforts.[2] The imperial administration understood a semipermeable border as a necessary measure to isolate a peripheral region which it regarded as underdeveloped and a dangerous gateway for the importation of competing foreign produce, in order to prevent it from having negative effects on the core economic space.

The formation of the customs system in the Transcaucasian region is discussed in-depth in this chapter, from its inception in the beginning of the 19th century to its integration into the imperial system in the early 1880s. The chapter highlights how, in the various commissions on customs reform, economic rationale prevailed for a long time over the symbolic and political goal of creating a uniform imperial economic space. Further, it showcases the limitations the empire encountered in trying to remold its economic space due to the effects of a long-lasting, insular administrative setup. The very measures that once allowed for a flexible management of its economic space eventually effected its rigidity.

2 In the Finnish case, discussed in chapter 7, it was also asymmetry – however, under the opposite prefix – which was problematized by the central administration. Here, economic asymmetry increasingly developed to the advantage of the peripheral region since the 1860s.

5.1 The Establishment of the Caucasian Viceroyalty

The 1844 institution of the Caucasian Viceroyalty, which was outfitted with wide-ranging autonomy, should be regarded as the result of a long story of frustration with the administration of the Russian Empire's Caucasian territories – its eventual abolition as the beginning of a phase of administrative centralization.

Georgia's incorporation into the Russian Empire in 1801 was initially followed by a lax oversight on the side of the Russian administrators. In their new domains, they had found a complex traditional system of administration and "either deliberately or in a mood of resignation" left it mostly intact, yet declaring it only a temporary measure. Temporary turned into permanent as the mere Russian presence failed to facilitate the spread of imperial norms. The Saint Petersburg administration grew increasingly irritated and calls for the full integration into a centralized linear administration became louder.[3]

Initial steps had been taken by the chief of the Caucasian military and civil affairs. After militarily re-defining the borders with the Ottoman Empire and Persia in the late 1820s, General Ivan Fedorovich Paskevich had turned his attention to the planning of a comprehensive reform of the civil administration with the aim of making "the inhabitants 'speak, think, and feel Russian.'" His deployment to Warsaw as a strongman to crush the Polish rebellion drew him away from the region, but his reform impulses resulted in the establishment of the first Caucasian Committee in 1833.[4]

While it remained hotly debated whether the Transcaucasian territory was best served with the introduction of the regular linear system of administration used in the empire's internal provinces, armed resistance in the Caucasian highlands accentuated the need for an efficient administration. The imperial voyage through the Caucasus in 1837 quite plainly demonstrated to Tsar Nicholas I the empire's dire stance in the region. Under the auspices of Baron Pavel Vasil'evich Gan, the Caucasian Committee developed a reform package based on the statutes of internal provinces, which became law in 1841. However, within the shortest time it became clear that the reform had failed, as it was met with violent uprising, and already in 1842 General Aleksandr Ivanovich Chernyshev was dispatched to the Transcaucasus for revision.[5]

3 *Rhinelander, L. Hamilton*: The Creation of the Caucasian Vicegerency. In: The Slavonic and East European Review, 59(1) (1981), 15–40, here 20.

4 Ibid. 21–22.

5 *Khodarkovsky, Michael*: Bitter Choices: Loyalty and Betrayal in the Russian Conquest of the North Caucasus. Ithaca 2011, 121–122; *Rhinelander*: Creation of The Caucasian Vicegerency, 22–23.

The efforts to introduce linear rule proved feeble, and Tsar Nicholas shifted his attention to a strong insular administration. Count Mikhail Semenovich Vorontsov appeared to be the ideal candidate, as he had both the military background needed to quell the resistance of the North Caucasian mountaineers and an impressive track record in the civil administration as Governor-general of New Russia. Moreover, he had time and again proven his loyalty to the Tsar. In order to make the difficult assignment palatable to Vorontsov, Nicholas offered him a position as "'viceregent in the Caucasian territory with unlimited plenary powers.'"[6]

Unlike his predecessors, the viceroy would thus not only have supervisory tasks but also be entrusted with the execution of administrative tasks. After the ill-judged prior centralization attempt, the pendulum now swung to the other extreme, and an insular regent with unprecedented powers was to be introduced. Vorontsov was unable to refuse the offer and infighting with the central ministries over the interpretation of "unlimited plenary powers" began. Eventually, he was able to carve out the regulations on the Caucasian Viceroy to his will, and even institutionalized them as transpersonal in 1846. The central ministries found themselves fully sidelined from all affairs in the Transcaucasian territory, except for financial accountability. The Caucasian Viceroy was accountable to the Tsar only, and all contacts with the Saint Petersburg administration were to be conducted via the Caucasian Committee, which represented the Viceroy in the imperial center.[7]

To be sure, insular structures such as governorates-general and the Caucasian Viceroyalty were always understood as temporary measures for the development of a region, preparing it to be properly integrated into the imperial edifice – a notion shared by Vorontsov himself. Extraordinary powers were justified as long as the separation of the Transcaucasian territory persisted – both in terms of geography and local legal base.[8]

The logical consequence of legal equalization and infrastructural integration had thus to be the convergence of peripheral territory with the core empire. However, initiatives for closer integration were not always welcomed by central authorities. The following sections discuss the development, function, and administrative relations of customs institutions in the Transcaucasus linking them to the general political modus-operandi of the region. Ultimately, it is shown how the insular structure intended to accelerate the region's integration eventually perpetuated its exclusion from the imperial economic space.

6 *Rhinelander*: Creation of The Caucasian Vicegerency, 25.

7 Ibid. 23–38; *LeDonne, John P.*: La réforme de 1883 au Caucase. Un exemple d'administration régionale russe. In: Cahiers du Monde Russe, 8(1) (1967), 21–35, here 23–24.

8 *LeDonne*: La réforme de 1883 au Caucase, 23–24; *Rhinelander*: Creation of The Caucasian Vicegerency, 38.

5.2 Early Attempts at Economic Regulation

With regard to the introduction of an imperial customs system in its newly acquired Georgian territories, the Russian administration can hardly be accused of a lack of initial enthusiasm. However, the challenges of practical implementation quickly put them in the "mood of resignation", Rhinelander attests, for the whole of the administration.[9] The three decades until the mid-1830s were characterized by countless administrative initiatives to organize a customs system and as much frustration.

The first introduction of imperial customs in the Georgian territories had been ordered promptly by the Tsar's rescript of September 12, 1801. Already in April 1803, Pavel Dmitrievich Tsitsianov, Governor-general of Georgia, submitted a proposal for the establishment of four shared customs and quarantine stations on the Ottoman and Persian border.[10] This combination of disease control and trade control in one institution became definitive for customs institutions in the Transcaucasus in the following decades. The emphasis in the work of the Quarantine-Customs Institutions (karantinno-tamozhennye uchrezhdeniia) kept shifting between their public health and economic functions. Eventually, this double function proved to have a negative effect on the correct execution of either function and complicated their integration into a ministerial logic of administration, as the two functions combined within one institution were subject to different ministries.

Placed under his personal supervision, these problems were not foreseen by Tsitsianov, who optimistically assumed that his proposed customs system would soon go operational. His premise was to introduce regular imperial customs institutions "from which it becomes obvious that the Mozdok customs and quarantine checkpoints (tamozhenno-karantinnye zastavy), being internal, will have to be abolished."[11] Prior to the annexation of Georgia, Mozdok had constituted the southernmost fortified point on the Caucasus line[12] and the border of the Russian Empire. With the displacement of the imperial state and military border, it appeared "obvious" to Tsitsianov that the economic border would have to follow suit. Unlike Mozdok, which lay north of the Northern Caucasian Mountain ridge on the Georgian military road and thus constituted a bottleneck conducive to the control of traffic, the

9 *Rhinelander*: Creation of The Caucasian Vicegerency, 20.

10 Akty sobrannye Kavkazkoi Arkheograficheskoi Kommissiei. Volume 2. Tiflis 1868, 239.

11 Ibid. 239–240.

12 Russian sources refer to the fortified line north of the Greater Caucasus Mountain range as "Caucasus line", the Transcaucasian region's border with Persia and the Ottoman Empire is usually referred to as "Transcaucasian line." For conciseness, these designations are used by the author as well.

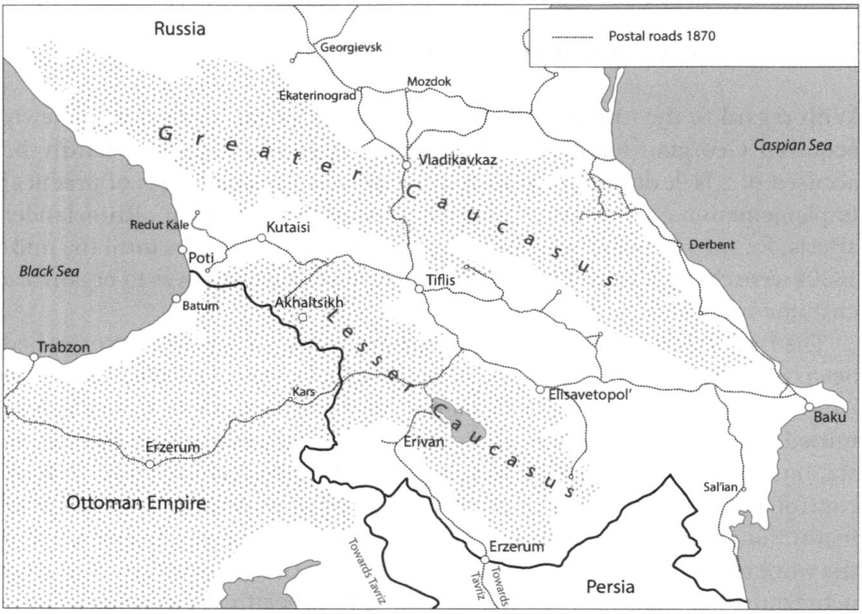

Figure 5: Map of the Transcaucasian region.

proposed new customs line had none of these topographic advantages. It was stretched out along the Ottoman and Persian border, crisscrossed by small routes, topographically challenging and difficult to control.

Effectively treating the new territories on par with the territories north of the Greater Caucasian range, Tsitsianov concluded that the "establishment of customs checkpoints in Georgia based on the general all-Russian laws [obshchimi Vserossiiskimi uzakoneniiami]" implied the "abolition of the now-existent internal customs in Georgia."[13] Here he referred to the *rakhdar*, a traditional road toll rented out yearly, which split the annexed territory into numerous smaller zones.[14] Once the already granted rakhdar rights ran out by the end of 1804, Tsitsianov was keen to remove them, hoping that their revenues would be easily compensated by an increase in trade expected from the connection of Georgia to the Russian Empire and the subsequent customs revenues collected by the imperial administration directly – not by local *rakhdar* collectors.[15]

13 AKAK, vol. 2, 240.

14 "Rakhdar" (sometimes "rakhtar") designates both the toll and the collector of the toll. Rakhdar fees included not only road tolls, but other fees as well. For an overview see ibid. 240–241.

15 Ibid. 240.

Tsitsianov's proposals were met with support by Minister of Commerce Rumiantsev as they promised the "*connection of Caspian and Black Sea trade* [...] which would consolidate Russian sovereignty in this region" and played to his own visions of the Russian Empire as a connecting link in the Europe-Asia trade.[16] The project for the new customs system was approved by the Senate with remarkable dispatch. By October 1803, it was decided that the internal customs line running along the old Caucasian line would be moved south and the traditional rakhdar fees replaced by imperial-style customs. Taking into account the recent annexation and administrative shortages, trade was to be taxed using the lower and simpler Astrakhan tariff.[17] Despite this concession, implementation still proved to be a much more difficult task.

Military conquest of the Ganzha province nullified the planned run of the customs border, while the lack of a highest order from the Tsar precluded Tsitsianov from abolishing the *rakhdar* fees. Further, the prospect of a double taxation of trade – rakhdars and imperial customs – promised to "destroy in Georgia even the slightest shadow of any business [promyshlennost']." Thus, the introduction of the imperial customs system was delayed. New permissions from the center were obtained and new dislocations for the customs stations planned, only to be declared failed by 1805 due to internal "unrests" (bespokoistva) and the lack of officials to man the planned customs stations and a regional customs supervisor (tsolner).[18] Undefined borders, the persistence of traditional laws and administrative incapacity kept delaying the introduction of an imperial customs system in the following years.[19] The new Georgian customs system had looked good on the drawing board, but failed against local realities.

By 1807, the plan to establish customs on the ever-moving external borders was scrapped and the Russian administration settled for the establishment of a main customs station in the city Tiflis, which was deemed "temporary" and operated under the traditional Georgian tariff, rather than introducing the imperial Astrakhan tariff. The traditional rakhdar fees remained in place as well. Eventually, the initial ambitious plan for a customs system was officially relinquished and Tsar Alexander I ordered to halt the implementation of his 1803 ukaz.[20]

The contradiction between treating the Georgian territories as a regular province of the Russian Empire and the failure to integrate them into the customs space did not escape the Ministry of Commerce. Thus, Rumiantsev informed the Georgian Governor-general Ivan Vasilievich Gudovich that

16 Ibid. 241. See also chapter 1.
17 Ibid. 242.
18 Ibid. 243–246.
19 Akty sobrannye Kavkazkoi Arkheograficheskoi Kommissiei. Volume 3. Tiflis 1869, 38–39.
20 Ibid. 40–41.

all goods of Georgian provenience should be treated like goods transported from one Russian port to another and thus allowed for import into the Russian core customs space duty-free. Similarly, foreign goods cleared in the Tiflis customs stations should be allowed free circulation within the Russian Empire.[21] If the new territories could not be administratively integrated by means of delineation from neighboring states and the introduction of linearly organized customs institutions, they could at least be integrated in Saint Petersburg's spatial imaginary by internal deregulation and the dissolution of the now-internal border along the Caucasus line.

Such a concession carried primarily symbolic importance, emphasizing the unity of the Transcaucasian territory with the empire. The central administration was well aware that no significant traffic was to be expected that could endanger the internal Russian markets. Crossing the North Caucasian mountain ridge was both arduous and dangerous, while "Asiatic goods" were hardly considered a threat to the empire's economy.[22] Of course the duty-free regime could hardly paint over the fact that internal rakhdar fees impeding trade circulation within the region and undermining the empire's authority continued to exist. However, without regular imperial customs on the external borders, they could simply not be abolished, as this would have torn a hole in the regional budget.[23] Neither did the Tiflis customs station do much to raise revenues or promote Russian authority, as most goods were smuggled past it into the province's capital.[24]

By the end of the first decade, the Russian Empire's grip on its newly annexed territories' economy remained insignificant. The only notable success had been the opening of the Baku customs station in 1809, which was lavishly celebrated with prayers, dances, feast, and fireworks, and not least a poem dedicated to the introduction of imperial customs.[25] While the Baku customs station was intended to stabilize and further trade with Persia, it quickly proved to do the opposite.

Merchants from Enzeli complained to the Commandant of Baku, Ivan Ivanovich Repin, in 1811 that "they are willing to pay the rakhdar – at any rate you think fit – only not to be burdened by paperwork and undoing the packages, leaving everything as it was. We assure you that the treasury will earn double of what it earns now, as then trade will be renewed in Baku as it

21 Ibid. 45–46.

22 Due to the dangers of crossing the Greater Caucasus Mountain Ridge, it was considered allowing the movement of goods only under military convoys during special designated time frames, AKAK, vol. 2, 243.

23 AKAK, vol. 3, 47.

24 Akty sobrannye Kavkazkoi Arkheograficheskoi Kommissiei. Volume 4. Tiflis 1870, 80.

25 Ibid. 84–86.

was before […].”[26] Such complaints did not die down a decade later, as Persian merchants trading between Enzeli and Sal’ian preferred to leave business altogether rather than take upon themselves a significant detour of at least 280km to clear the goods in Baku customs.[27] But the Ministry of Commerce did not see any leeway with regards to its only functioning customs station in the region.

Only for the western Caucasian mountaineer populations – though for the most part not subjects of the Russian Empire yet – was it deemed possible to make concessions in the customs procedures. They could clear goods at the low-grade customs checkpoints of Derbent and Kuba, rather than at the distant Baku customs. By thus furthering trade turnover, Governor-general Aleksei Petrovich Ermolov hoped that “people who have improved their wealth through trade relations and have become acquainted with some comfort for their lives, become attached to their property and alter their animal nature and habits (zverskii nrav i obychai).”[28] This argumentation essentially echoed the empire’s practice on its south-eastern steppe frontier, where trade was regarded as a conduit of cultural and political influence and an instrument of a Russian civilizational mission.[29]

All things considered, the imperial system, though deemed superior to the traditional rakhdars by the Russian authorities, did more to disrupt trade in the Transcaucasus than to regularize it. Faint proposals to introduce “a special customs guard modeled after the example of the one installed on the European customs sections [of the Russian Empire]” continued to float up in the early 1810s, but the initial optimism for a quick integration had yielded to frustration.[30] The Russian Empire had mostly come to terms with the impossibility and unprofitability of a linear customs border with Persia and the Ottoman Empire – the “long arms” proved to have “weak fingers.”[31]

Nevertheless, for the time being, the Ministry of Finance did not opt to exclude the new territories from the imperial economic zone by re-establishing a customs line on the Caucasus line in the north. Until the 1820s, it was considered that the symbolic capital gained from free trade across the Greater Caucasian Mountain range outweighed the potential economic disruptions from an open Transcaucasian line. Trade with Ottoman and Persian goods across this border was hardly seen as competition to the empire’s economy, while the all-imperial trend towards free-trade doctrine in the late 1810s made

26 Ibid. 92.

27 Akty sobrannye Kavkazkoi Arkheograficheskoi Kommissiei. Volume 6. Part 1. Tiflis 1874, 216.

28 Ibid. 203–204, 215–216.

29 See also chapter 2.

30 Akty sobrannye Kavkazkoi Arkheograficheskoi Kommissiei. Volume V. Tiflis 1873, 35.

31 *Cooper*: Colonialism in Question, 197.

such a solution acceptable, particularly in the "Asiatic" part of the Russian Empire with its own system of tariff and customs regulations introduced in 1817.[32]

The evaluation of the economic relations between the Transcaucasian region and the core empire only shifted in the 1820s. In 1822, the Ministry of Finance adopted a prohibitionist "European" tariff which was at odds with the low-tariff regime introduced in the Transcaucasian region, known as the "Transcaucasian transit route." The latter had led to the establishment of a sizable transit flow of competitive European manufactured goods through the region, and the central administration feared illegal imports into the empire's internal provinces. Once the effect of a borderless regime between the Transcaucasian region and the core empire promised to become economically relevant, its symbolic importance was mostly discarded. The issue of the Transcaucasian transit is discussed separately and in-depth in chapter 6. In the 1810s, however, the economic aspect of the quarantine-customs institutions in the Transcaucasus still took a backseat vis-a-vis challenges to public health presented by plague epidemics.

5.3 Quarantine Control as Function of Customs Institutions

In the 18th century, plague epidemics had been a regular occurrence in the region. When the Russian Empire annexed Georgia in 1801, it did so during an outbreak of the plague in the neighboring Ottoman territory of Akhaltsikh. Despite initially denying the plague epidemic and speaking of a simple "fever [goriachka]", the Russian command installed quarantines on the main roads from the Ottoman Empire. Nevertheless, the epidemic spread to Georgian territories, reaching Tiflis in 1803 and causing high casualties.[33] Tsitsianov was well aware of the regular nature of plague epidemics, as "no 3 years go by without it showing itself somewhere", and pressed for the quick introduction of quarantines.[34] However, due to the joint quarantine-customs framework discussed above, the introduction of permanent quarantine stations was tied to the introduction of regular imperial customs. As the latter kept being delayed, no permanent quarantines were established either.

32 For the debates between protectionist and free-traders in the 1810s see chapter 1. For the development of the Asiatic tariff see chapter 2.

33 *Ermachkov, Ivan A./Koroleva, Larisa A./Svechnikova, Natalia V./Gut, Jasmin*: The Plague in the Caucasus in 1801–1815 years: Part I. In: Bylye Gody, 47(1) (2018), 120–129, here 121–123.

34 AKAK, vol. 2, 242, 246.

Meanwhile, the presence of mobile Russian military units did its part to spread diseases along the Georgian military road and across the Caucasus Mountains. The former customs station of Mozdok had to be reactivated as a quarantine station, yet the epidemic still spread to the adjacent Caucasian gubernia. Through closer exchange from the Transcaucasian region across the Caucasus mountains, the plague began threatening Russia's internal gubernias. As limiting mobility across the mountains was not feasible, channeling traffic through quarantines was the only option. Thus, the introduction of free trade with non-Russian subject mountaineers, who were suspected of harboring contagious diseases, was not only framed as part of a mission civilisatrice, but as a hygienic measure as well. While it did increase direct contact, it also channeled trade through quarantine stations rather than smuggling routes, making it easier to control. By 1809 the plague outbreak in the Caucasus gubernia could be contained.[35]

The next significant epidemic had been caused by the 1810 Russian siege of the Ottoman border city of Akhaltsikh, which proved to be infected with the plague. Despite quarantine measures during the retreat, Russian troops brought back the contagious disease to the Georgian territories and the city of Tiflis.[36] The renewed spread persuaded the local authorities that temporary quarantines were not sufficient and that the border with the Ottoman Empire – considered the "sanctuary of the plague", as the Ottoman Empire had no quarantine system at all – constituted the main public health threat to the Transcaucasian region.[37] While the economic threat of an open Transcaucasian border was deemed acceptable, its potential as gateway for plague epidemics was not.

In 1818, the new commander-in-chief in the Caucasus, Ermolov, determined that the "state of the quarantines leaves one wondering why the plague has not chosen the Caucasian gubernia as its place of residence for all eternity."[38] The new quarantines, both Ermolov and Police Minister Sergei Kuz'mich Viazmitinov agreed, were thus to be constructed by a gubernia architect and from quality materials as well as airtight, to allow for the smoking of goods with "muriatic acid", the latest technology in the field of disease

35 *Ermachkov/Koroleva/Svechnikova/Gut*: The Plague in the Caucasus: Part I, 124–127.

36 *Ermachkov, Ivan A./Koroleva, Larisa A./Svechnikova, Natalia V./Gut, Jasmin*: The Plague in the Caucasus in 1801–1815 years: Part II. In: Bylye Gody, 48(2) (2018), 558–569, here 559–560. For the work of the "Committee for the preservation of the health of the population" established to quell the 1811 epidemic in Tiflis see AKAK, vol. 5, 29–34.

37 For a very balanced and insightful analysis of the development of quarantines in the Ottoman Empire see *Bulmuş, Birsen*: Plague, Quarantines and Geopolitics in the Ottoman Empire. Edinburgh 2012. Quote on 10.

38 AKAK, vol. 6, pt. 1, 202, 205.

control.[39] However, the planned dislocation was along the Caucasian line in the North, not the Ottoman and Persian border. This effectively left the Transcaucasian region outside quarantine protection.

For Viazmitinov, the Caucasian line seemed the only possible quarantine border, "as Georgia, which from all sides is under threat from the plague, can never be considered fully unsuspicious [with regards to the plague]", and an effective quarantine required "at least one strictly controlled quarantine line, where the officials and guards follow all quarantine regulations and are subject to severe liability according to the law in case of neglect."[40] The performance of border control, the minister implied, could not be trusted if it was conducted south of the Greater Caucasus range. This distrust would remain in the central administration's repertoire over the next decades and reappeared in the debate on the dissolution of an internal customs border in the 1870s, discussed later in this chapter.

As the Ministry of Finance planned no customs on this internal line for the symbolic reasons discussed above, the establishment of quarantines could be settled only between the Commander-in-chief and the Police Minister. Thus, the problems caused by the combination of quarantines and customs within one institution were somewhat disentangled. However, it equaled sacrificing the public health of the Transcaucasian region to that of the empire's internal gubernias.

While free trade between the Transcaucasian region and the Caucasus had posed a low economic threat and promised symbolic gains, the issue of disease control was too hazardous to take symbolism into consideration and was solved pragmatically by an internal quarantine border in 1819. Of course, severe quarantine measures and the associated long waiting times for merchants did their part to restrict trade entirely without the introduction of customs tariffs. Thus, the disruption of trade relations between the Transcaucasian region and the Russian Empire's internal provinces began with hygiene measures and the deliberate exclusion of the Transcaucasus from the imperial quarantine space. Its formal exclusion from the imperial customs space soon followed suit.

With the introduction of the Transcaucasian transit route in 1821, the pendulum had swung back again, with customs issues in the Transcaucasus regaining importance for the central administration. Throughout the 1820s, Minister of Finance Kankrin fought hard to abolish the Transcaucasian transit route, as he considered the region a gateway for European manufactured goods

39 Ibid. 203, 205. Viazmitinov most likely refers to the method invented by Louis-Bernard Guyton de Morveau. For the introduction of this method in Spain and its impact on the state-citizen relationship see *Serrano, Elena*: Spreading the Revolution. Guyton's Fumigating Machine in Spain. Politics, Technology, and Material Culture (1796–1808). In: *Roberts, Lissa L./Werrett, Simon* (eds.): Compound Histories. 2018, 106–130.

40 AKAK, vol. 6, pt. 1, 214.

undermining the prohibitionist system. While he was unable to stop the transit privileges granted until 1831, he at least wanted to shield the internal provinces from harmful imports and pushed for the re-establishment of an internal customs border on the Caucasus line, which had been dissolved in 1803. The Mozdok customs stations – reactivated earlier as quarantine station – was to regain its customs function as well.[41]

Until 1821, the Transcaucasian region had been regarded as economically largely negligible. Its linkup to European trade currents via the transit route, however, shifted its assessment in the imperial center. The notion of firewalling Russia's internal provinces from a globally connected gateway on the periphery, introduced by Kankrin, remained one of the main justifications for the exclusion of the Transcaucasus from the imperial customs space until 1881. However, before fully embracing the economic separation of the Transcaucasian region, the central administration had a last attempt at introducing regular custom institutions functioning according to a linear logic of administration.

5.4 Last Attempt for the Introduction of a Linear Logic of Administration

As in many other fields of administration in the Transcaucasian region, the issue of quarantine and customs control was eventually met with a "mood of resignation"[42] by the late 1810s and 1820s. In both cases, the solution proved to be a retreat to the topographically more convenient and stable border on the Caucasian line.

After two decades of shifting borders, the military definition of the Transcaucasian border by General Paskevich in the late 1820s paved the road for comprehensive reforms of the civil administration.[43] This included customs and quarantine reforms, which particularly benefitted from defined borders and significantly reduced troop movement. With the planned expiration of the transit privileges in 1831, the region's short-lived role as a Europe-Asia transit zone was to come to an end as well. Under these favorable preconditions, a regular quarantine-customs border on the Transcaucasian border with the Ottoman Empire and Persia appeared feasible again.

Both Minister of Finance Kankrin and Commander-in-Chief in the Caucasus Paskevich were in agreement on the undesirability of the Transcaucasian

41 Ibid. 223.

42 *Rhinelander*: Creation of The Caucasian Vicegerency, 20.

43 Ibid. 21–22.

transit route. The first regarded it as a disruption to the Russian prohibitionist system, while the latter strove for the normalization of the region and a rollback of region-specific special regulations. By 1831, a project had been presented to the State Council which combined both requirements as "the outlined system has above all the advantage that it quite sufficiently protects our manufacturing industries from foreign competition; that it maintains the unity of the customs administration; that it does not entail any significant deductions from the tariff [...] and finally, that it almost fully destroys any negative effects for our manufacturing industry by the Leipzig transit through Odessa to the Transcaucasus."[44]

The project basically implied the introduction of the imperial European tariff in the Transcaucasian region with only slight deviations.[45] While in the 1810s the Transcaucasus had still been discussed as an "Asiatic" economic region and was subjected to the 1817 Asiatic customs regulations, the 10-year period of the Transcaucasian transit had effected a shift in the perception of the region – now it was interpreted within a European context and thus had to receive the European tariff.

Nevertheless, its status remained hybrid, as it could hardly be disregarded that the region shared its land borders with Persia and the Ottoman Empire, clearly considered "Asiatic" states. In a special act on trade, signed on the same day as the 1828 Treaty of Turkmanchai, a 5 % flat-rate duty had been agreed upon for Persian goods, which was later applied to Turkish goods as well, for the sake of uniformity.[46] Had the 1821 transit route regulations taxed all goods indiscriminately, regardless of their provenience, "European" goods were now subject to significantly higher duties, while "Asiatic" goods retained the 5 % tariff.

While such a differentiation in taxation was not unusual, the dualism between "European" and "Asiatic" goods was to extend to the import regulations into the empire's core economic space as well. "Asiatic" goods cleared with the 5 % fee in the Transcaucasus were allowed to freely circulate within the whole empire, while "European" goods imported and cleared under the "European tariff" in the Transcaucasian region were forbidden for import beyond the Caucasian line altogether.[47] Again, "Asiatic" goods were regarded as negligible, while all of the potential risk to subvert the empire's prohibitionist system was seen with "European" manufactured goods.

44 Akty sobrannye Kavkazkoi Arkheograficheskoi Kommissiei. Volume 12. Tiflis 1904, 147.

45 Akty sobrannye Kavkazkoi Arkheograficheskoi Kommissiei. Volume 7. Tiflis 1878, 148–149.

46 *Iuzefovich, Trofim Pavlovich*: Dogovory Rossii s Vostokom. Politicheskie i torgovye. Saint Petersburg 1869, 223–227. These trade regulations are sometimes mistakenly attributed to be part of the Treaty of Turkmanchay itself.

47 AKAK, vol. 7, 148–149.

Essentially, the Ministry of Finance distrusted local customs authorities to conduct clearance procedures correctly. Thus, it opted to firewall the imperial core from the Transcaucasian region altogether before taking any risks. The distrust formulated here persisted and was likely deepened by the insular administration of the Transcaucasian customs beginning in 1846. It would reappear as a main point of contention during the integration debates of the 1870s.

Despite this exclusion of the Transcaucasian customs space – even if limited to goods of European provenance – it was to receive some form of regular customs protection system based on the western border. Also, after three decades of Russian rule, the traditional internal rakhdar fees were to be finally abolished.[48] Paskevich's deployment to Warsaw in 1831 somewhat complicated the cooperation between the Ministry of Finance and the Caucasian administration, as the newly appointed Commander-in-Chief Baron Grigorii Vladimirovich Rozen categorically opposed Kankrin's view on the Transcaucasian transit route. He argued against the application of the European tariff, as he did not deem the Transcaucasus ready for the severity and complexity of the regular tariff yet.[49]

But to no avail. Rozen's objections went unanswered, and the implementation of the planned reform proceeded. By 1836, the rakhdar fees were indeed abolished – as had been first planned in 1803/04 – and some quarantine-customs stations had gone operational.[50] However, it appears that the maintenance of an internal customs border on the Caucasus line and the import prohibition for "European" goods from the Transcaucasus had appeased the Ministry of Finance and slowed its interest in the establishment of a regular quarantine-customs line on the border with Persia and the Ottoman Empire. Rozen proposed fundamentally reforming the Transcaucasian quarantine institutions. Besides a tighter net, he suggested giving up the combination of quarantine and customs functions within one institution. The advantage might have been cost efficiency, but it came at the expense of quality, as the two functions interfered with one another, he argued. However, his proposals were dismissed as too costly. The Ministry of Finance argued that the internal provinces would be protected better and cheaper on the Caucasus line with its limited roads.[51] Pressed for a decision, the Ministry of Finance subordinated the symbolic importance of an integrated economic space to fiscal considerations. The topographic advantages of the Caucasus line could not be argued

48 Ibid. 152–153.

49 Akty sobrannye Kavkazkoi Arkheograficheskoi Kommissiei. Volume 8. Tiflis 1881 157–158.

50 Ibid. 186.

51 Ibid. 139–141, 159–160, 167–168; Akty sobrannye Kavkazkoi Arkheograficheskoi Kommissiei. Volume IX. Tiflis 1884, 683.

with, while the all-imperial economic importance of the Transcaucasian region was still doubtful.

Throughout the 1830s and 1840s, the Ministry of Finance maintained protectionist intentions in its reorganization of the Transcaucasian customs administration with a pronounced view for the interests of Central Russia's manufacturing industries. Once it had accepted that a regular and reliable quarantine-customs border with Persia and the Ottoman Empire was neither feasible nor profitable, it retreated to the Caucasian line as the main border of the imperial customs space. By firewalling the Transcaucasian region – both by way of economic regulations and by physical delineation with an internal customs border – the ministry's main goals seemed satisfied and reform fervor died down. As in other areas of administrative reform in the Transcaucasus, attempts to implement a linear administration in quarantines and customs had failed by the early 1840s. The 1845 restructuring of the Transcaucasian region as Viceroyalty according to the insular principle made way for a reversal of the 1830s and 1840s attempts to introduce the imperial "European" tariff and regulations and renewed the emphasis on special regional solutions.

5.5 Insular Administration as Accelerator for Integration

With the introduction of the insular administration of the Namestnichestvo, the Ministry of Finance found itself fully sidelined from any quarantine-customs affairs in the Transcaucasian region. Almost immediately, in 1846, Vorontsov reintroduced the Transcaucasian transit route with its flat-rate 5% tariff valid for both "European" and "Asiatic" goods.[52] This rollback towards low tariffs and trade procedures with low bureaucratic hurdles was not only conceived as an economic measure, but also put in the context of hygienic control.

Vorontsov argued that the prior attempted implementation of a complicated and tight net of quarantine stations was impossible due to the length and topography of the Transcaucasian border and that he would not strive to replicate the experience. Rather, he subscribed to the notion that the empire's internal provinces were best protected by the Caucasian line, which could be controlled more effectively with the limited cross-mountain roads. For the Transcaucasian region, however, trade regulation was the key to epidemic prevention. As long as high tariffs incentivized illegal trade on countless uncontrollable smuggle routes from the Ottoman Empire, the introduction of contagious diseases could hardly be controlled. By reducing tariffs and

52 For more detail see chapter 6.

bureaucratic hurdles, trade could be channeled through a few existing quarantine stations, ensuring better quarantine control.[53]

While all these measures emphasized the separateness of the Transcaucasian region from the core economic space of the Russian Empire, they were conceptualized as measures to elevate the region's economic and public health situation and eventually facilitate its integration. The raison d'être for the Namestnichestvo was to eventually make itself obsolete.[54]

The two reasons for the delineation of the Transcaucasian region from the empire's core space were quarantine control and a prohibitionist customs policy in the core empire, which could not be upheld on the region's borders. Once these two factors lost their importance, integration could succeed, Vorontsov's successor Aleksandr Ivanovich Bariatinskii hoped.[55] Indeed, the plague problematic had disappeared in the Transcaucasian region in the 1840s.[56] However, it is hard to gauge whether Vorontsov's reform played a significant role. It is more likely that the 1838 introduction of quarantines in the Ottoman Empire – the main gateway for plague epidemics in the Transcaucasus – gradually reduced the carrying-over of diseases across the border.[57] Thus, the internal border on the Caucasus line had lost its relevance as quarantine line and was abolished in 1857.[58]

The 1857 tariff revision of the "European" tariff now promised an opportunity to resolve the customs aspect as well. The long-standing prohibitionist system associated with Minister of Finance Kankrin had already received its first liberalization with the 1850 tariff. The post-Crimean revision of 1857 was expected to go even further and allow for a convergence between the "European" tariff and the extremely liberal "Caucasian" tariff.[59]

A proposal for such a convergence brought forward by Bariatinskii, however, was dismissed by Minister of Finance Brok, for he argued that it would be "impossible to achieve such harmonization [sorazmernost'] between the general tariff and the Transcaucasian tariff, which would be required to remove

53 Akty sobrannye Kavkazkoi Arkheograficheskoi Kommissiei. Volume 10. Tiflis 1885, 214–217.

54 *LeDonne*: La réforme de 1883 au Caucase, 23–24; *Rhinelander*: Creation of The Caucasian Vicegerency, 38.

55 AKAK, vol. 12, 145–146.

56 Ibid. 147.

57 *Bulmuş*: Plague, Quarantines and Geopolitics, 104. It is noteworthy that the nexus of quarantines and customs had a significant role in the Ottoman Empire as well, although played out in a wholly different way. In order to limit the impact of free-trade arrangements imposed by European states on their own manufacturers, the Ottoman Empire made use of quarantine regulations as pretense to limit imports and complicate foreign trade and shipping see ibid. 98,109.

58 AKAK, vol. 12, 151.

59 For the 1850s tariff revisions see chapter 1.

the [internal customs] line without damage to the customs revenue or the internal industries."[60] Above all, such an integration would be irreconcilable with the insular administration of the customs institutions in the region and would require "the subjugation of Transcaucasian customs institutions to the general imperial customs administration, similarly as had been done when the customs line between the Empire and the Kingdom of Poland was removed."[61]

Lacking insight into the tariff commission's work, Bariatinskii could hardly argue with the first point, however he categorically objected the comparison with the Kingdom of Poland:

This measure [the integration of the Kingdom of Poland into the imperial customs space] was political, not administrative. Under no circumstances could it be allowed that the main authority in the Kingdom [of Poland], which administered the customs institutions prior to the removal of the customs line, would prove itself incapable of having it under its command after its removal. On the contrary, with regard to the Caucasian and Transcaucasian regions, the government had adopted a wholly different system. For its stable and quick merging [sliianie] with Russia, and with regard to its remoteness and the special characteristics of its popula3tion, it was recognized as the best measure to fully subject it to the main local authority, even with the admission of some divergence from the general administrative rules existing in the Empire. The customs institutions, along with all others, were subjected to the Namestnik, based precisely on these general considerations and not because when this measure was implemented the Caucasus had a weak, almost non-existent customs line, which, as it seems to me, was not even taken into consideration.[62]

For Bariatinskii, the comparison of his domain with the Kingdom of Poland implied a questioning of his ability to effectively administer the Transcaucasian region and ensure its customs security – the very reason for his appointment. If this – and not the incompatibility of customs tariffs – was the real reason to dismiss the integration of the Transcaucasus into the imperial customs zones, the Ministry of Finance made a serious logical mistake, he argued.

[...] if this is based on some sort of suspicion towards the rigor of control on the part of the main local authority with regard to the execution of customs regulations, then this suspicion should be even bigger at the moment, as this weak [customs] line, which under the different tariffs constitutes the only protective customs wall [tamozhennuiu ogradu] between the Empire and the Transcaucasian region, is fully under the control of the Namestnik.[63]

60 AKAK, vol. 12, 148.
61 Ibid. 148.
62 Ibid. 149.
63 Ibid. 149.

Bariatinskii had anticipated the major contradiction and point of contention which would eventually lead to the full integration and centralization of the Transcaucasian customs administration in 1881: The Ministry of Finance could firewall the region, but the firewall could not be trusted if it was not under central control, but in the hands of the Namestnik.

The Ministry of Finance's fears were based on the assumption that high-duty European goods would be imported through the Caucasus, where customs controls would be weak, and reach the core provinces of the Empire at a loss for the treasury. Bariatinskii doubted that such a wide dissemination was realistic at all. Instead, he proposed his vision of an integrated region from which both the Transcaucasus and the provinces north of the Greater Caucasus Range would profit. By removing the internal customs line, the Transcaucasian ports would become gateways to supply Ekaterinodar, the Stavropol' gubernia and the lands of the Don Cossacks, he argued.[64]

Eventually, the State Council decided to abolish the internal quarantine border on the Caucasian line, however, maintaining its function as an internal customs line. If anything, the economic separation was accentuated even more, as the same State Council decision also renamed the Tiflis customs station into the Transcaucasian customs stations, emphasizing the region's insularity. It was argued that the 1857 tariff revision maintained tariff privileges for the Transcaucasian region, resulting in irreconcilable tariff differences.[65] The next general tariff reform of 1868, however, would prove Bariantiskii's suspicions right, as the Caucasus indeed received the all-imperial "European" tariff, yet the internal customs line was maintained.

The 1868 revision of the European tariff conducted under Minister of Finance Reitern had been a balancing act between accommodating the general European trend towards tariff liberalization, set off by the Cobden-Chevalier treaty, and the maintenance of protectionist measures through the unsteady phase of the Great Reforms.[66]

These new reductions in tariff stakes promised to allow for the convergence of the "Caucasian" tariff with the imperial European tariff. The initiative for rapprochement again came from the Caucasus Namestnik, now Grand Duke Mikhail Nikolaevich. In 1869, he proposed to the State Council to introduce the European tariff in the Transcaucasian Black Sea ports, with only a few deductions for specific goods, such as Turkish tobacco. The Caspian Sea ports and the landed border with Persia and the Ottoman Empire were to maintain the prior 5 % flat-rate regulations for "Asiatic" goods, both due to the low-price nature of goods traded there and for the sake of maintaining the

64 Ibid. 150.
65 Ibid. 151.
66 For the 1868 tariff revision see chapter 1.

local population's cross-border relations.[67] The Ministry of Finance did not object this exception as it believed the "landed border from the Black Sea to the Caspian Sea constituted, so to speak, one whole."[68] This caveat was by no means unusual, as the Russian customs administration differentiated goods and the application of either the "European" or "Asiatic" tariff by origin of manufacture. In the late 1860s, neither the Caspian Sea nor Northern Persia were yet conceived as a gateway for European-manufactured goods by the Ministry of Finance, and thus the resources for installing complicated customs procedures could be saved on both the shore and the landed border.[69]

The greater goal of tariff revision was not disturbed by these exceptions, as the focus lay with the trade relations of the Transcaucasus to other European states and the import of European-manufactured goods. If their discounted importation into the Transcaucasian region came to an end, the ultimate goal of convergence of the Transcaucasian customs space with the imperial core customs space could be achieved, as the State Council pointed out:

> [...] the exclusion from the general customs tariff, which was allowed for foreign goods imported into the Transcaucasian region, was motivated in prior times by the exclusive position of this region prior to its final pacification. Now such an isolation, which resulted in inevitable customs procedures complicating relations between this region and the other parts of the Empire, is no longer justified by local circumstances. On the contrary, the greatest possible vitalization of relations to the mutual benefit of both is required. In consequence, it is desirable to strive for a gradual abolition of the exceptions granted to the Transcaucasian region, and for the introduction of a customs tariff identical to that of the other parts of the Empire.[70]

By the late 1860s, the Transcaucasian region was no longer seen as being in a state of exception, and its economic normalization and integration hinged on tariff equalization. Beginning in May 1870, the Transcaucasian Black Sea ports were subject to the European tariff and were put on an equal footing with all other "European" regions of the Russian Empire.[71] However, the intended dissolution of the internal customs border on the Caucasus line did not follow suit.

The initiative for tariff convergence had come from the Caucasus Namestnik, with the intent of fulfilling the prerequisites for the Transcaucasian

67 RGIA, f. 1268, op. 14, d. 134, "O primenenii k Zakavkazskomu kraiu evropeiskogo tamozhennogo tarifa, Vysochaishe utverzhdennogo 5-go iiulia 1868 goda", l. 1–1ob., l. 5ob.

68 Ibid. l. 10.

69 For the development and dissemination of new spatial imaginaries of the Caspian Sea and Transcaspian region see chapter 6.

70 RGIA, f. 1268, op. 14, d. 134, l. 1ob.

71 Polnoe sobranie zakonov Rossiikoi Imperii. Sobranie 2. Volume 45. Section 1. Saint Petersburg 1874, no. 48113.

region's integration into the empire's core customs space, strengthening the region's role as a trade hub. This rapprochement would seem to be to the "mutual benefit of both", as the State Council had formulated it.[72] In practice, the following decade demonstrated that despite all unificatory rhetoric, the exclusion of the Transcaucasian region was perpetuated by the Ministry of Finance due to the insular principle of administration inherent to the Namestnichestvo and its incompatibility with the workings of the central customs administration.

5.6 The Customs Integration of the Transcaucasus

The two main fields of conflict between the Namestnik and the Ministry of Finance obstructing the region's integration had been the control over the fiscal incomes and over the execution of customs control as such.

Since Bariatinskii had made an advance to merge the Transcaucasian customs space in 1857, the region's budgetary rights had changed and the Namestnichestvo had gained an even higher degree of insularity. Already in 1847, a project giving full budgetary autonomy to the Transcaucasian Namestnichestvo had been discussed, although it had eventually been dismissed.[73] Bariatinskii resurrected the project, and in 1858 the Transcaucasian Namestnichestvo gained full authority over all incomes of the region.[74] This included customs revenues and gave a new spin to the trade relations between the region and the core imperial economic space: As customs duties are collected in the customs station of first contact, the development of the Transcaucasus into an important trade gateway and hub would have meant that important revenues went into the Namestnik's treasury and were detracted from the all-imperial treasury. Had the Ministry of Finance actively promoted the region's role as a trade hub by removing the internal customs border, it would have thus effectively undermined its own stream of revenue.

On the other hand, control over the execution of customs procedures in the Transcaucasus was fully in the hands of the Caucasian Namestnik. The Ministry of Finance feared that it would not be performed to its standards. The Caspian Sea trade – split between the jurisdiction of the ministry and the Namestnik – already served as an example for the detrimental nature of an insular customs organization, the Ministry of Finance argued. It claimed that the port city of Astrakhan suffered from the lax controls in Baku:

72 RGIA, f. 1268, op. 14, d. 134, l. 1ob.
73 *Pravilova*: Finansy Imperii, 111–115.
74 Ibid. 115–116.

Asiatic goods imported to customs stations in the Transcaucasian ports and to Astrakhan are both subject to a 5 % ad valorem duty. The same goods are evaluated differently in the Caspian customs of the Transcaucasian region than in the Astrakhan customs [under centralized control]. Our experience proves that the estimation is much lower in the first than in the latter, thus the owners of the goods find it more convenient to clear them in the quarantine-customs institutions of the Transcaucasian region, at the expense of the customs incomes of the Astrakhan customs and to the detriment of the trade with equivalent products there, which are cleared with a higher estimation in Astrakhan. Above all, it should also be pointed out that one reason why goods destined for Astrakhan are cleared in the quarantine-customs institutions of the Transcaucasian region, and then – already cleared – are shipped via cabotage ships further to Astrakhan, is that goods destined for Astrakhan, according to shippers and merchants [tovarokhozaiev], are not only paid for without any control in the Caspian quarantine-customs stations and without the execution of any formalities, but even without unloading them at all. The clearance is done based solely on the price declared by the owners of the goods [tovarokhozaieva]. The result of such a state of things is a yearly loss of 49.155 rubles in customs revenues for the Astrakhan customs [and thus the all-imperial treasury].[75]

Above all, the ministry claimed that the Transcaucasian customs stations lacked expertise in the evaluation of critical goods, "apparently following their own considerations in such cases", rather than consulting the central customs administration. Such "a difference in the actions of the Transcaucasian customs and the imperial customs can have nothing but harmful effects."[76]

Neither was the complicated multi-stage hierarchy of customs institutions established on the empire's European borders maintained. On the "European" customs border, only first-class customs stations received the right to seal cleared goods, as their personnel were trained and paid better than that of lesser customs posts. In the Transcaucasus, such rights were granted even to the smallest customs checkpoints (zastavy) on the border with Persia and the Ottoman Empire.[77] The ministry's verdict was that customs control under the Namestnik was subpar and undermined its own efforts of protecting the Russian customs space:

Under the current relations of the Ministry of Finance to the customs control in the Transcaucasian region, the treasury of the Empire does not receive the appropriate revenue from foreign goods consumed within its confines, as it goes to the treasury of the Caucasian Namestnichestvo. Also, it does not have any control over the correct

75 RGIA, f. 21, op. 11, d. 292, "Zapiska neustanovlennogo avtora o sostoianie tamozhennykh uchrezhdenii i primenenii ustava v Zakavkazskom krae", l. 9ob.-10.

76 Ibid. l. 8.

77 Ibid. l. 5ob-6.

> clearance of these goods and over the execution of the goals of the tariff by the Transcaucasian customs institutions at all. Removed from any participation in the monitoring of smuggling on the landed border [on the Caucasus line] between the Transcaucasian region and the Empire, it is left without the possibility of fulfilling its obligations. The detrimental consequences of such non-normal conditions, in which the Transcaucasian region currently finds itself with regard to its customs relations to the Empire, can no longer be tolerated without harm to the state [...][78]

The insular institution of the Namestnichestvo, which had been introduced to accelerate the region's development and prepare it for integration, now perpetuated its exclusion. Both the Ministry of Finance and the Namestnik shared the basic premise that the Transcaucasian customs space should be merged with that of the core empire; however, neither wanted to relinquish control or revenues. Under these conditions only two solutions were feasible: either the Transcaucasian customs institutions were fully remodeled to follow the linear logic of administration, giving the Ministry of Finance both budgetary and executive rights. Or the region was firewalled further along the Caucasus line. The first solution was beyond the immediate influence of the Ministry of Finance, as it could only be implemented in agreement with the Namestnik or under the highest orders. Reliance on the latter soon led to the escalation of the conflict, specifically because border control had been under the control of the Namestnik – a fault line already pointed out by Bariatinskii in 1857.

The Ministry of Finance had made a first attempt at proposing a restructuring of Transcaucasian customs, bringing them under full central control in 1873; however, this was met with a flat refusal by Grand Duke Mikhail Nikolaevich.[79] The Namestnik reacted by surging ahead with an attempt to both retain control over customs in the region and ease trade relations with the empire's core customs space. Misusing a bureaucratic loophole, he single-handedly dissolved the internal customs border. His autonomous status granted him the right to determine the staffing plan (shtaty) for each customs station within his authority. In November 1874, he declared a new staffing plan, which simply did not include any personnel for the customs stations in Prokhladinsk, Mozdok and Kizliar – incidentally all located on the internal customs border north of the Greater Caucasus range.[80] The Ministry of Finance was presented with a fait accompli.

78 Ibid. l. 11ob.-12.

79 RGIA, f. 1152, op. 9, 1881, d. 84, l. 3.

80 RGIA, f. 1268, op. 20, d. 102, "Ob izmenenii i dopolnenii sushchestvuiushchikh zakonopolozhenii po karantinno-tamozhennoi chasti na Kavkaze i za Kavkazom", l. 25–25ob.

Of course, the Ministry of Finance protested this bureaucratic trick and brought it before the State Council, which agreed that:

> [...] the existence of the Caucasus [customs] surveillance [nadzor] is conditioned by the paragraphs 2224, 2368–2370 of the customs regulations on the prohibition of the landed import of European goods from the Transcaucasian region into the Empire, and that through the dissolution of this surveillance in an indirect way, the validity of said paragraphs would be canceled. The General Assembly of the State Council acknowledges that the new staffing plan cannot serve as a predetermining solution to issues which do not immediately concern the staffing plan.[81]

Nevertheless, the move succeeded in putting the Ministry of Finance under pressure to react. It could either accept the factual dissolution of the internal customs border and bring a legislative proposal on the way to legalize it, or take the burden of administering customs control upon itself. The two main issues, however, remained: control over customs incomes and the ministry's distrust towards customs controls not under its own auspices.

The Caucasus Namestnik was well aware of this distrust and pointed out the archaic nature of the customs border as such. He argued that the customs function on the Caucasian line had been introduced in the mid-1830s only as an additional function on top of the more important quarantine function. Initially, customs control had been justified by differential tariffs, which had existed prior to 1868.[82] Now, it "had lost any significance and only serves as an obstacle to the establishment of firmer trade relations with the internal gubernias of Russia."[83]

Meanwhile, the "constant complaints of local merchants about the halting of their transports on the Caucasian line"[84] led him to dissolve the line. Fears of smuggling, he argued, were unsubstantiated, as the costs of transportation within the Transcaucasian region and across the border were too substantial, while the contraband trade in the region was mostly aimed at fulfilling the needs of the local population and had no relation to the empire's internal gubernias.[85]

Basically, the Namestnik subscribed to the notion that natural barriers and the infrastructural weakness of the Russian Empire made the internal customs border obsolete. In many ways, his logic followed that of the Ministry of Finance in other regions, where administrative costs were weighed against

81 Ibid. l. 22–22ob.
82 Ibid. l. 24ob.
83 Ibid. l. 25.
84 Ibid. l. 25.
85 Ibid. l. 25.

potential losses through smuggling.[86] However, in the case of the Transcaucasus, the Ministry of Finance saw the potential for much greater losses. Leaving the border open and customs control in the hands of the Namestnik could potentially develop the Transcaucasian region into a preferred first point of entry for merchants attracted by the allegedly laxer and beneficial clearance procedures – just as had been alleged for the Baku customs. Meanwhile, customs revenues would remain in the regional treasury. For the Ministry of Finance, the Transcaucasus' connection to regional and global trade currents posed a threat to the empire's tariff protection edifice, which could only be guaranteed by centralized control.

The Ministry of Finance argued that without the control of the ministry "over the correct application of the tariff in uniformity with the customs stations of the Empire", there would be "serious fears" that contraband could enter the core imperial customs space.[87] Instead of a relaxation on import regulations, aspired by the Namestnik, the Ministry of Finance proposed a tightening of controls. It suggested establishing a specific internal customs guard on the Caucasus line and allowing imports exclusively via the Rostov-Vladikavkaz railway, transferring the import regulations used on the Finnish railway. In practice, this meant that train cars with goods destined for import into the core customs space would have had to be sealed on the last station within the Transcaucasian region and checked upon arrival in Rostov by the local imperial customs.[88] Such sharpened controls were bound to disrupt trade across the border.

To the Namestnik, the struggle over competence lay at the core of the decision:

> Thus, it seems that the main reasoning in this issue lies foremost not with the development of trade relations between the internal gubernias and the Transcaucasian region, only by which internal trade within the region can grow, but with the administrative competence (podvedomstvennost') over the quarantine-customs institutions.[89]

The Ministry of Finance took an "all or nothing at all" stance. Either the Transcaucasian customs territory was fully integrated into a linear logic, with the ministry in charge of border control and collecting revenues, or the region was strictly excluded from the empire's core customs space.

It was a decision over the role of the Transcaucasus within the imperial regional hierarchy. The first solution followed the blueprint for the integration

86 The dissolution of the south-eastern customs border is a case in point, see chapter 2.

87 RGIA, f. 1268, op. 20, d. 102, l. 27–27ob.

88 Ibid. l. 27ob.-28.

89 Ibid. l. 28.

of the Kingdom of Poland into the imperial customs territory in 1851. The Transcaucasian region would have been normalized and made a regular unit of the economic space, while the loss of incomes would be compensated to the Namestnik's treasury based on the average customs incomes of previous years.[90] Obviously such a solution assumed a static economy and would not account for any foreseeable growth in imports and revenues. The latter solution was modeled after the Finnish case, or the status of the Kingdom of Poland prior to its 1851 integration. Goods cleared in the Transcaucasus would not be considered eligible for importation into the core customs space and would have to be cleared again at an imperial customs station.[91] Thus, it was an issue of redefining the Transcaucasian Namestnichestvo as either a full part of the empire or an economic unit of its own.

A decision had been delayed by the outbreak of the Russo-Ottoman War of 1877–1878. However, the enormous fiscal toll of the war saw the Ministry of Finance switch customs collection to gold currency, thus effectively raising the imperial tariff by 30 %. Such a significant increase necessarily incentivized smuggling. In the case of the Transcaucasus, with its almost non-existent internal and external customs borders, the flat-rate tariff increase exacerbated the potential for smuggling and pushed for a quick solution to the region's customs status vis-a-vis the core customs space.[92]

Further, the perpetuation of the region's separateness would have sent off the wrong political signal, as State Comptroller and future Minister of Finance Samuil Greig pointed out in 1878:

> [...] the financial history of other countries provides us with examples of the unification of the customs of different states under one administration. However, examples of several independent customs administrations within one state cannot be found anywhere.[93]

By the late 1870s, the tailor-made territorialized solutions to organizing customs space had lost their appeal. The Russian Empire's peripheries were increasingly envisioned as connected to one whole by the central administration. The Transcaucasus had once been seen as "populated by hostile tribes and devoid of good ways of communication, which constituted a natural barrier to contraband"[94], by the Ministry of Finance. Now, infrastructural developments seemed to move the empire closer together in the central administration's imaginary.[95] The Namestnik agreed with this point:

90 RGIA, f. 21, op. 11, d. 292, l. 13.
91 Ibid. l. 12.
92 RGIA, f. 1152, op. 9, 1881, d. 84, l. 3ob.
93 Ibid. l. 3 ob.
94 RGIA, f. 21, op. 11, d. 292, l. 3ob.-4.
95 Ibid. l. 3ob.-4.

In recent times, the remoteness of the Caucasus from the central administration of the state has lost its importance, due to the convergence of railway roads with Black Sea ports and the connection of the Northern Caucasus by the same ways with the internal gubernias of Russia, as well as with the establishment of the telegraph.[96]

With physical distance increasingly losing its importance in the administrative imaginary, the differential treatment of economic spaces no longer signified administrative efficiency but rather backwardness vis-a-vis other states and empires, which succeeded at forming strong integrated economic spaces.

Against all expectations, railway construction in the Transcaucasus proceeded much slower, and Namestnik Mikhail Nikolaevich complained about the "unsubstantial results achieved in regard to the development and strengthening of the economic and spiritual unification of this region with Russia."[97] He prepared an array of reforms for which he tried to secure additional funding; however, the state budget had been in deep disarray after the recent war, leaving only little leeway. The administrative insularity of the Caucasian Namestnichestvo and the high costs associated with it increasingly prompted criticism within governmental circles.[98]

This weakened position of the Namestnik and the establishment of a porto-franco in Batum, which required an official commission from the Department of Customs Collection on the spot, presented a convenient opportunity to renegotiate the status of the Transcaucasian customs. The new Minister of Finance and former State Comptroller Greig pushed to resolve the issue via the State Council.[99]

In 1878, the department's director, Nikolai Aleksandrovich Kachalov, traveled to the Transcaucasian Namestnichestvo to propose a plan for full customs-integration of the region under the auspices of the Ministry of Finance. He first met with Count Dmitrii Ivanovich Sviatopolk-Mirskii, assistant to the Caucasian Namestnik. In his memoirs, Kachalov describes almost threatening Sviatopolk-Mirskii:

I asked Mirskii to regard the project and discuss whether they had any objections or counter-measures to the unification. If that was not the case, would it not be better for the Caucasian command to yield voluntarily, without awaiting that the issue is solved by an order from higher authorities? The scrutiny of the project significantly softened the Caucasian separatism.[100]

96 RGIA, f. 1152, op. 9, d. 84, l. 4.

97 Cit. *Volkhonskii, Mikhail*: Uprazdnenie namestnichestva na Kavkaze v 1881–1882gg. In: Rossiiskaia istoriia, 3 (2018), 171–189, here 171.

98 Ibid. 172–175.

99 *Kachalov, Nikolai Aleksandrovich*: N. A. Kachalov. Zapiski tainogo sovetnika. Moscow 2012, 539.

100 Ibid. 540–541.

Despite Kachalov's self-confident description, it was likely the content of the project which had Sviatopolk-Mirskii and eventually Namestnik Mikhail Nikolaevich agree. The Ministry of Finance had abandoned its rigid stance and proposed to retain numerous special rights for the Caucasian Namestnik with its revised project.

The integration of the Kingdom of Poland in 1851 presented the model for the integration. The local authorities would retain rights to intervene in urgent issues; take part in the selection of high customs authorities assigned to the region, control quarantine institutions, and finally the local budget was compensated for the loss in customs income. By 1881 – twelve years after the tariff equalization – the unification of the Transcaucasian customs region with the empire's European customs space had been decided.[101] This restructuring of the customs administration according to a linear logic of administration constituted only the first departure from the insularity principle. Within a short time, the insular administration of the Namestnichestvo as such was fully dismantled.

The debate over a dissolution of the Caucasus Committee in the late 1870s, which would have put legislative proposals concerning the Transcaucasus on the same footing as those of any other regular region in the empire, proved that a closer integration of the Namestnichestvo was hardly possible without encroaching on the Namestnik's rights. Namestnik Mikhail Nikolaevich insisted on the maintenance of the Caucasian Committee, despite maintaining the importance of closer relations with the imperial core.[102] The basic problems encountered during the attempts to integrate the Transcaucasus into the imperial customs space transferred to a larger scale as well.

Eventually, the assassination of Alexander II gave the decisive impulse to the transformation of the Transcaucasus' administrative status. Alexander III had "nurtured a personal dislike for 'Uncle Kostia' [Grand-Duke Konstantin Nikolaevich]" and wanted to remove him as quickly as possible from the posts he occupied."[103] In 1881 he decided to replace him by appointing Caucasus Namestnik Mikhail Nikolaevich as chairman of the State Council.[104] With the powerful personality of Mikhail Nikolaevich gone, the institution of the Namestnik was open for renegotiation. It was clear that the extensive autonomy of the Namestnik would be curtailed; the degree of change, however, was up for debate. Alexander III showed himself open to keeping the title of Namestnik if a suitable person could be found. Disagreeing with the reactionary change of course signified by the April Manifesto, the Tsar's favored candidate Dmitrii

101 RGIA, f. 1152, op. 9, 1881, d. 84, l. 5–6, 55.

102 *Volkhonskii*: Uprazdnenie namestnichestva na Kavkaze, 176–177.

103 Ibid. 178.

104 Ibid. 178.

Alekseevich Miliutin refused. Eventually, the title of Namestnik was abolished, and replaced by the less imposing title "Head of Civil Administrative Affairs in the Caucasus" (Glavnonachal'stvuiushchii po grazhdanskoi chasti na Kavkaze) in 1882, whose rights were curtailed substantially and basically equaled those of other governors-general in the Russian Empire.[105] For the administration of the Transcaucasian customs, this effected little de-facto change, as it had proven avant-garde in introducing the linear principle of administration in the Transcaucasian region and only needed to re-formalize its rights accordingly.

5.7 Conclusion

Over the first three decades of Russian rule in the Transcaucasus, various attempts to introduce a linear ministerial logic of administration had proven feeble. Be it for the overlap with preexisting administrative and economic traditions, the lack of administrative resources, or the instability of a frontier region. The introduction of the Namestnichestvo and the resolute decision for an isolated insular administration had been the logical consequence of this struggle. If the region was not yet ready for centralized administration, it could be brought there quicker with a more immediate and powerful administration. The basic premise was that deviance and distance were best resolved by an insular administration.

However, as the case of the Transcaucasian customs regime showed, neither the equalization of tariffs, nor the approximation – both physical and imaginary – of the region to the center were sufficient for full integration. Three decades of insularity had produced too many peculiarities and had strengthened the local power center too much, precluding an easy integration. Thus, the flexible tailored customs solutions, once employed to manage a heterogeneous imperial space in preparation for its integration, eventually proved rigid and obstructive to this very goal.

In the Transcaucasus, the imperial administration had never envisioned such a separate development, but solely accepted it as a transitory stage. Its perpetuated separateness was increasingly problematized in the late 1870s and framed as archaic in comparison with competing strong centralized states. The trajectory of the Transcaucasian customs space had been understood as one of convergence throughout, with the eventual goal of its integration into a unified customs space.

105 Ibid. 182–189.

In this regard, the case of the customs space of the Grand Duchy of Finland strongly differs, as it had initially been conceived as part of a customs union, not a unified customs space. Finland, too, featured an insular administration, which, however, followed a wholly different logic than that of the Namestnichestvo. Nevertheless, its status as a separated customs space came under pressure in the 1880s as well. However, its long history of insular administration proved to be more difficult to overcome for the central administration than that of the Transcaucasian Namestnichestvo, as is discussed in chapter 7.

6. The Transcaucasian Transit: Stepping Stone to the World or the Empire's Backyard Market?

The unique geographic position of the region wedged between the Greater Caucasus Mountains in the north, the lesser Caucasus Mountains in the south, and the Black and the Caspian Sea, has for the longest time held and still holds today an attraction for global trade. Located at the intersection of European and Asiatic trade currents, the Transcaucasus promised to provide a convenient link.[1] Visions of trade across the Caspian Sea had already occupied the minds of Ivan IV and of Peter I.[2] In the 1780s – before the region was annexed by the Russian Empire – Armenian merchants in control of the Russo-Persian trade had shared with a French traveler their vision of a transit route through the region, which would be quicker and safer than the Cape Route or the declining Silk Road. However, they lacked both capital and political power for an implementation.[3] Little did they know that it would be a combination of Russian political dominance and the impulse from an entrepreneurial Frenchman which would give life to their vision 40 years later.

The Transcaucasian transit route discussed in this chapter primarily constituted a set of customs regulations which enabled a regular flow of European goods with heavily discounted customs tariffs from Black Sea ports in the Transcaucasus across the region to the northern provinces of Persia. These provinces were both an important production center for silk as well as Persia's largest consumer markets, promising to become markets for European-manufactured goods. Prior existent trading routes such as the Tabriz-Trabzon route

1 The Russian Empire's administrative description of the region as *Zakavkaz'e* implies a view from Saint Petersburg over the Greater Caucasus Mountain range as well as a negation of previous cultural and political constellations in the region by using a topographic feature for its definition. However, as the term *zakavkazskii tranzit* (Transcaucausian transit) is used consistently throughout the sources, this chapter will also utilize said toponym to facilitate readability.

2 For Peter's failed attempts to conquer the Kazakh steppe in order to secure trade routes with India see chapter 2.

3 *Van Regemorter, Jean-Louis*: Le mythe génois en Mer Noire: la France, la Russie et le commerce d'Asie par la route de Géorgie (1821–1831). In: Annales. Histoire, Sciences Sociales, 19(3) (1964), 492–521, here 492–493.

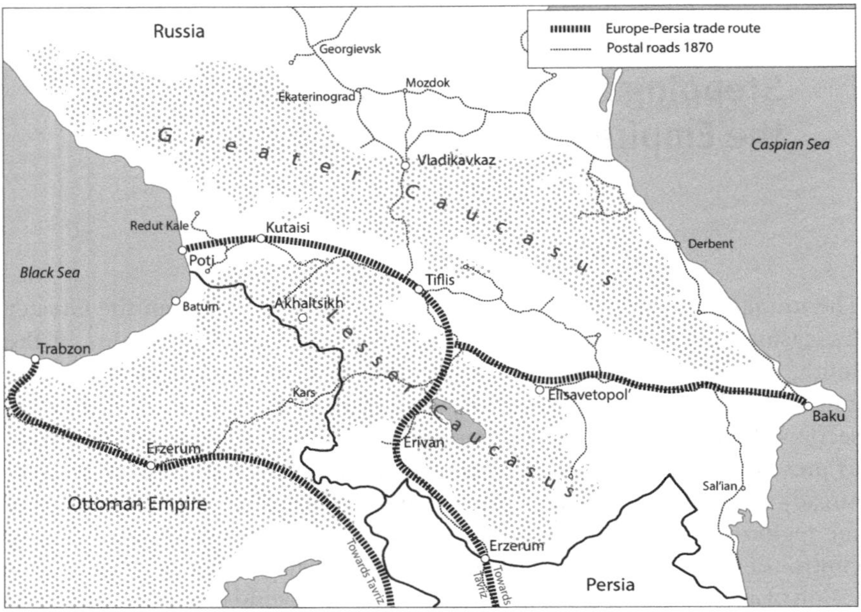

Figure 6: Map of transit routes to Tavriz.

had fallen dormant by the 19th century.[4] The granting of customs privileges by the Russian administration for transit trade through its Transcaucasian territories promised to revive trade between western Europe and northern Persia. Infrastructural features and the safety of transport played an important role in the success of the new transit route as well as in its decline. However, it was primarily the legal framework of customs regulations enabling or prohibiting discounted trade of European goods, not the physical properties of the route, which sparked heated debates in the 19th century. This chapter attempts to trace the unstable development of these special customs regulations throughout the 19th century and to contextualize them within larger trends in the Russian Empire's management of its economic space.

It is argued that the Transcaucasian transit route presented a focal point for the negotiation of the role of the Transcaucasian region within the framework of the Russian Empire. Depending on the political context, its function was either interpreted as a developmental measure serving a quicker integration of the Transcaucasus, as a tool to alter international trade geographies, or as

4 *Issawi, Charles*: The Tabriz-Trabzon Trade, 1830–1900: Rise and Decline of a Route. In: International Journal of Middle East Studies, 1 (1970), 18–27, here 18.

an unacceptable violation of national interests. Thus, in a broader sense, the "Transcaucasian transit question" can be regarded as an issue of delineation, manipulation, and creation of economic and political space, and constitutes one of the most contested issues in the integration of the Russian Empire's economic space.

The trajectory of the transit route's development allows us to gauge the changing spatial visions within different branches of the imperial administration, as views on the interconnectedness of the Transcaucasus with the core imperial space and Russia's Central Asian territories informed decisions on the transit route's fate. Its evolution provides insights into the decision-making processes within the imperial administration as the transit route issue saw the collision of different ministries with one another as well as with the Caucasian Namestnik. Ultimately, the transit route's end had been brought about by the rise of new interest groups outside the imperial administration, demonstrating a new quality to the negotiation of the empire's economic policies, as they were increasingly nationalized and discussed with a new degree of publicity.

6.1 The Introduction and the First Prohibition of the Transcaucasian Transit

The realization of the Transcaucasian transit route was the result of the shifting geopolitical composition on the south-eastern borders of the Russian Empire, the spread of liberal economic thought, as well as individual initiative. Armand-Emmanuel de Vignerot du Plessis, duc de Richelieu, was one of the strongest supporters of the Black Sea trade in early 19th century Russia and instrumental to the establishment of the Transcaucasian transit route. The duke, who had emigrated to the Russian Empire after the French Revolution, had risen through the ranks of the Russian army to eventually become the Governor of Odessa in 1803 and Governor-general of the newly annexed territories of Novorossiia in 1805. An adamant proponent of Black Sea trade, he facilitated the rapid ascension of Odessa as an international port by granting trade incentives and lowering fees and regulations during his service, and is credited for the original plan to establish a porto-franco in Odessa.[5] Thus it is little surprising that upon his return to Bourbon France in 1814, the Duke of Richelieu would become an advocate for a new trade route to Persia and India via the Black Sea. Alongside Louis XVIII, he attempted to solicit a

5 *Herlihy*: Odessa, 21–48; See Richelieu's entrance in the Russian biographical dictionary: Russkii biograficheskii slovar'. Volume 16. Saint Petersburg 1913, 256–259.

permission for free transit, at first, however, suggesting a route from Taganrog to Astrakhan. His advocacy of the Transcaucasian transit route, which will be regarded in this chapter, was the result of a historic coincidence.[6]

The political conditions to implement such a scheme only occurred after the Russian annexation of Kartli and Kakheti in 1801 and the consequent subjugation of the remaining Georgian principalities by waging warfare with the Ottoman and Persian Empires.[7] The origins of the Transcaucasian transit route can be traced back to the initiative of the Transcaucasian Governor Aleksei Ermolov, who envisioned the attraction of Europe-Asia trade to this war-torn region as a measure for local economic development. By sharing his idea with the Caucasus traveler and future French consul in Tiflis, Jacques François Gamba, in 1818, the plan eventually reached the Duke of Richelieu, who backed it up. Returning to Georgia in an official capacity in 1819, with the Duke of Richelieu's support, Gamba advanced the design of the Transcaucasian transit. His proposal was brought forward during a brief phase in which free-trade policies, including lower European tariffs and the opening of the Odessa porto-franco in 1819, were favored by the Russian government, as is discussed in detail in chapter 1. The transit was eventually permitted by the government in 1821 for a period of ten years.[8] The initial institution of the Transcaucasian transit route was thus the result of a lucky convergence of personal transnational interconnections, the acquisition and merging of the southern Caucasian region under one administration, and the vogue of free-trade thought in the empire's Ministry of Finance. The latter was only short-lived and would soon lead the concept of the transit route to become a political battlefield, giving its development throughout the 19th century a highly unstable trajectory marked by numerous abrupt changes.

Technically, the establishment of the Transcaucasian transit route meant little more than the introduction of strongly discounted tariffs for European goods imported through the Black Sea port of Redut-Kale and transited to Tabriz in Persia, incentivizing merchants to favor this route over the traditional Trabzon-Tabriz route. While the Russian Empire's customs system differentiated between European and Asiatic products – as was codified with the introduction of an Asiatic tariff in 1817 – the Transcaucasus received an exemption to these rules and European goods were subject to the same flat 5 % customs duties as were negotiated for Asiatic products in the 1813 Treaty

6 *Van Regemorter*: Le mythe génois en Mer Noire, 493–494; See Gamba's entrance in the Russian biographical dictionary: Russkii biograficheskii slovar'. Volume 4. Saint Petersburg 1914, 196; *Kislovskii*: Istoriia tamozhennogo dela, 189–190.

7 *Forsyth, James*: The Caucasus. A History. Cambridge 2013, 270–272.

8 *Van Regemorter*: Le mythe génois en Mer Noire, 494; Russkii biograficheskii slovar'. Volume 4, 196; *Kislovskii*: Istoriia tamozhennogo dela, 189–190.

of Gulistan.[9] Further, the Transcaucasian route featured a recently completed military road from Redut-Kale to Tiflis, making it attractive to merchants.[10]

However, the introduction of these trade privileges in 1821 came at a peculiar timing, as they constituted one of the last measures of a free-trade-inspired customs policy, before the Russian Empire's economic policy wholeheartedly swung back to a strictly prohibitive policy with the issuing of the new 1822 tariff.[11]

As tariff stakes rose to double digits for the core empire, the flat 5% customs in the Transcaucasus, which did not differentiate between European and Asiatic produce, created a glaring example of misbalance between the economic regimes of the empire. While the transit route was particularly designed to facilitate Europe-Persia trade and thus benefit the regional development of the Transcaucasus via the collection of customs and the attraction of entrepreneurs, Kankrin regarded the route through a strictly protectionist lens, addressing the Committee of Ministers in 1825:

> The unclarity of the Gulistan treaty has given birth to many difficulties for trade in Russia, particularly the thus eased trade through Redut-Kale serves, and in the future will serve even more the destruction of our trade and particularly our factories. Foreigners, especially the French, as can be seen from various reports, try to open up, and have already been successful at doing so, a route to deliver their goods to Persia. These goods have begun to squeeze out our products. Such a competition is even more dangerous given that the Asiatic people have so far not had such objects and replaced them with ours, or, if they had had them, acquiring them had been of great difficulty before the opening of the transit through Georgia.[12]

However, with the ten-year guarantee of the privileges, the new protectionist financial administration, embodied by the Minister of Finance Egor Kankrin, had to be patient before it could revoke the privileges. Kankrin had started numerous attempts at prematurely retracting the transit privileges in favor of a protectionist policy. In 1827, he argued before the State Council that Russia's manufactured goods were not competitive either in Europe or in America, and thus capturing Asiatic markets was both of utmost importance. Further, he stated that "Russia's location" gave it "a privileged right to own it [the Asiatic trade]."[13] However, his attempts to prematurely retract the ten-year privileges remained unsuccessful.

9 For the development of the differentiation between "European" and "Asiatic" customs see chapter 2.

10 *Issawi*: Trabzon-Tabriz Trade, 22.

11 *Kislovskii*: Istoriia tamozhennogo dela, 195–197; *Lodyzhenskii*: Istoriia russkogo tamozhennogo tarifa, 197–241. For details on this change in customs policy see chapter 1.

12 AKAK, vol. 6, pt. 1, 243.

13 Ibid. 246–247; AKAK, vol. 7, 120–125.

Meanwhile, the transit route gained popularity and, as envisioned by the Duke of Richelieu, attracted Europe-Asia trade that would use Odessa, operating as porto-franco since 1819, as its hub. Particularly textile goods from Leipzig benefited from the new route, finding easy access to the Persian market.[14] Thus, transit facilitated the coalescence of the Black Sea region. Once the ten-year period had expired in 1831, however, the Ministry of Finance was quick to scrap the virtually duty-free and unregulated transit, expanding the general "European" tariff to the Transcaucasus, although with certain deductions, taking into account its weak economical position.[15]

Had the regional administration remained under the auspices of Count Ivan Paskevich, Commander-in-chief of the Caucasus from 1827 onwards, this action would have gone unrivalled, as he explicitly opposed the transit route he had inherited during his reign and sided with Minister Kankrin on the issue.[16] The newly appointed Commander-in-chief Baron Grigorii Rozen, however, assumed a contrary position, arguing that turbulences in the Ottoman Empire's Black Sea trade operations presented a window of opportunity to attract most of the Europe-Asia trade to the Transcaucasian route, promising regional capital accumulation and prosperity, which would benefit the whole empire as well as arguing from a plainly practical point of view: the low-barrier transit required only minimal expenditures on border protection.[17] However, Rozen's efforts were to no avail. Minister of Finance Kankrin argued from a strictly protectionist perspective, and envisioned a quick bounce back of the Russian industry under the umbrella of high tariffs; thus, markets, particularly ones formally within the empire, could not be surrendered to foreign produce.[18] As customs and trade regulations in the Transcaucasian region were an exclusive domain of the Ministry of Finance and its departments in the 1830s, little could be done about the decision.

When opportunity arose again to discuss broader issues of Transcaucasian trade in 1835–1836, Rozen put the transit route up for discussion again. Now, with a track record of four years in office and the benefit of retrospection, he hoped for a more favorable position. His 1831 predictions had come true: the region's Black Sea ports fell idle and into decline; customs income, which constituted one of the region's few income sources, had plummeted, while expenditures for border control had increased. Most importantly, the conquest

14 RGIA, f. 1152, op. 2, 1831, d. 122, "O predlozheniiakh Barona Rozena kasatel'no Zakavkazskoi torgovli", l. 7.

15 Polnoe sobranie zakonov Rossiikoi Imperii. Sobranie 2. Volume 6. Section 1. Saint Petersburg 1832, no. 4622.

16 RGIA, f. 1152, op. 2, 1831, d. 122, l. 3–6.

17 Ibid. l. 7–11.

18 Ibid. l. 2.

of northern Persian markets, which had been one of Kankrin's main arguments for the transit prohibition, had been unsuccessful. Instead, trade currents had moved to the less convenient and more dangerous Trabzon-Erzerum-Tabriz route and along with them the Armenian merchants, who had previously conducted the Transcaucasian trade, now "putting themselves in the service of the English trade." Thus, in the interest of the Transcaucasian region and the empire itself, as Rozen duly noted, the route should be reopened for a guaranteed period of twenty years, allowing the transit of all European and colonial goods with a flat tariff rate of 10 %.[19] The Ministry of Finance reacted in its habitual way, discarding the proposition. It was backed by the State Council:

In the opinion of the State Council, the private benefit and profit of a few local traders and even the benefit of the region, even if it could be proven, cannot serve as a persuasive argument for the establishment of trade privileges to the benefit of one region, if this trade, which is to the exclusive benefit of foreign industries, destroys the own industries, squeezes domestic produce out of distribution and establishes foreign influence without positively influencing the overall trade volume of the whole state, and, contrary to political views, serves to separate the region from the other parts of the Empire, a development which does not require detailed enunciation here, but is regarded as distinctively important.[20]

The issue of the Transcaucasian transit combined in it itself aspects of foreign policy, domestic economy, and the cohesion of the empire. The central administration's argument was built upon an understanding of both the Transcaucasus and northern Persia as markets for Russia's developing industries, which could not be shared with other countries. Further, in the 1830s the Ministry of Finance had still hoped for the establishment of a regular customs regime in the Transcaucasian region, thus the introduction of long-standing exemptions seemed untimely.[21]

Kankrin envisaged the region's trade in firm Russian hands in the future, as one "cannot expect much participation in trade transactions from the Transcaucasian traders. Their means are limited, their knowledge about trade is weak and their greed knows no bounds. The Transcaucasus and the Russian industry does not await such brokers for their trade with Asia, but much rather Russian capitalists."[22] With his zero-sum game understanding of trade and his rejection of Smithian economic theory he also discarded the possibility of any synergetic effects, arguing that although some believe "that Russian

19 RGIA, f. 21, op. 11, d. 289, "Delo ob izmenenii tamozhennogo upravleniia v Zakavkazskom krae", l. 10–11.

20 Ibid. l. 45.

21 For the development of the Transcaucasian customs regime see chapter 5.

22 RGIA, f. 21, op. 11, d. 289, l. 18.

trade will increase if free import of foreign goods through the Transcaucasus is allowed" these ideas are based on a "quite superficial thinking about free trade that is wide-spread nowadays."[23]

In Kankrin's reading, the role of the Transcaucasus as a peripheral region vis-a-vis the Russian Empire was to be a subordinate one, as the protectionist domestic policy and his understanding of international trade as belligerent condemned special customs regimes to the benefit of a single region as disruptive to the unity of the empire. Albeit, he did not offer any solutions to balance the blatant economic imbalances, which left little doubt that the Transcaucasus was by no means a well-integrated territory of the empire's economic space.

This spatial vision of a centralized and hermetically sealed empire was challenged by actors on the "periphery", or, in less centrist terms, by well-informed imperial administrators on the spot. Baron Rozen's twenty-year development plan was not formulated in separatist or aggressively regionalist terms, but much rather envisioned integration through economic convergence with the core empire.[24] Further, it was based on a realistic assessment of the region's means to enforce prohibitive measures, soberly stating that the task would hardly be easier even if the current number of 166 border guards was doubled.[25]

Meanwhile, moderate transit fees could benefit the regional budget without requiring additional expenditures. The discussion, however, should not be regarded as a dialogue between the central administration and the Transcaucasian Commander-in-chief only. Count Mikhail Vorontsov, Governor-general of Bessarabia and Novorossiisk, came to the aid of Rozen, supporting both his conclusions on the growing importance of the Trabzon-Erzerum-Tabriz transit route and the usefulness of the Transcaucasian transit via Redut-Kale and Poti ports, arguing that this would serve both the quick development of Mingrelia's shoreline, as well as the region's inner provinces.[26] Vorontsov's support carried the initial spirit of the transit's design, which was to benefit both the Transcaucasus and the rising city of Odessa. This cooperative approach did not work along the spokes of the empire but developed between the two regions, forging an alternative territorial vision with an emphasis on synergetic effects that did not reduce the Transcaucasus to a mere outlet market for central industries.[27]

23 Ibid. l. 19.

24 For the idea of economic convergence and integration of the Transcaucasus by means of special economic regulations see also chapter 5.

25 RGIA, f. 21, op. 11, d. 289, l. 9.

26 Ibid. l. 13.

27 Jana Osterkamp proposes to look beyond the assumed radial structure of empires and pay more attention to cooperative phenomena see *Osterkamp, Jana*: 'Kooperatives Imperium'. Loyalitätsgefüge und Reich-Länder-Finanzausgleich in der späten Habsburgermonarchie. In: Geschichte und Gesellschaft, 42(4) (2016), 592–620.

Under Egor Kankrin's Ministry of Finance, however, such plans had only a slim chance and thus transit remained prohibited.

6.2 The Rise of the Transit Route under the Namestnichestvo

The second iteration of the Transcaucasian transit route was established quickly after Kankrin's resignation in 1844 and his death the following year. It has to be viewed against the general backdrop of the region's development with the creation of the *Namestnichestvo* that vested the regional administration with extensive autonomy.[28] Count Vorontsov was the first to assume the new office, and thus it is little surprising that the Transcaucasian transit was placed on the agenda quickly and permitted in 1846, becoming operational in 1848.[29]

However, as Rozen had predicted, by 1846 the Trabzon route had established itself fairly well, and the new Transcaucasian route, following from Redut-Kale via Tiflis crossing the Persian land-border at Julfa and ultimately leading to Tabriz, was hardly a competitor. Although statistical data for the period and region should be regarded with caution, in this case the imbalance between the two transit routes is more than obvious:

Table 2: Trade volume on Transcaucasian transit route and Trabzon transit route (1848–1851).

Trade volume in pud per year towards Persia		
	Transcaucasian transit route	Trabzon transit route
1848	746	213.000
1849	5.386	218.000
1850	8.677	236.000
1851	7.712	236.000

Data extracted from: RGIA, f. 40, op. 1, d. 31, "Vysochaishe utverzhdennyi Zhurnal Osobogo komiteta po voprosu o Zakavkazskom tranzite ot 19 aprelia 1879g.", l. 146.; one *pud* equates to 16,38 kg.

28 *Sidorko, Clemens P.*: Die Eroberung Tschetscheniens und Dagestans als Fallbeispiel kolonialer Expansion des Zarenreichs im 19. Jahrhundert. In: Jahrbücher für Geschichte Osteuropas, 47(4) (1999), 505–511, here 510. For the discussion of customs policy under the Namestnichestvo see chapter 5.

29 RGIA, f. 40, op. 1, d. 31, l. 145.

At this rate, the Transcaucasian transit route was not bound to have any significant impact either on the region's economic development or on the empire's domestic industry, reducing it to one of many administrative oddities of the Viceroyalty. However, almost two decades after its reopening, external factors facilitated a drastic increase in its trade volume. Stricter quarantine laws introduced by the Ottoman Empire in 1863 urged the Persian government to consider alternative routes to export its goods. Further, neither the Trabzon port nor the roads in the Ottoman Empire were maintained well and security was an issue complicating transportation on this route.[30]

Unlike 1831, when Rozen unsuccessfully tried to persuade the central government to take advantage of the Ottoman Empire's difficulties with their Black Sea trade, this time Namestnik Mikhail Nikolaevich made use of his autonomous position and fully embraced the opportunity presented. He permitted an additional transit route via Tiflis to Baku, effectively linking the Black Sea to the Caspian Sea.[31] It was due to this sea access that the appeal of the Transcaucasian route quickly increased. Funds were also allocated in 1865 to improve the existing route, turning the road section between Erivan and Julfa into a chaussee.[32] These changes quickly increased the appeal of the Transcaucasian route, and trade from Europe towards Persia jumped from 27 thousand pud for the year 1863 to 130 thousand pud after the opening of the new Baku-route in 1864, reaching 224 thousand pud by 1870.[33] As a new budgetary law issued in 1858 had established that all revenues collected in the Transcaucasus would be put at the Namestnik's disposal, this transit trade was purely to the benefit of the region.[34]

The revival of the Transcaucasian route underscored the departure from Kankrin's attempts to interpret the Transcaucasus as an exclusively Russian trading zone, as well as a general shift in the relationship between the center and the Transcaucasian region. Under the Namestnichestvo, regional development and the direct and indirect economic gains from the transit route were emphasized, rather than the region's role as an outlet market for the industries of the core empire. This shift, however, was not conceptualized by the Namestnik as a separatist measure, but rather understood as part of a strategy to enable economic convergence with the empire's core economic space and allow for an eventual integration. Despite these intentions, special solutions

30 *Issawi*: Trabzon-Tabriz Trade, 20–21; *L'vovskii, Silvestr*: Zakavkazskii Tranzit. Iz V otd. otcheta D. S. S. L'vovskogo o komandirovke, po vysochaishemu poveleniiu, na Kavkaz, v 1881–1882 g. Saint Petersburg 1883, 5–6.

31 *L'vovskii*: Zakavkazskii Tranzit, 5–6.

32 *Nachtigal*: Verkehrswege in Kaukasien, 241.

33 RGIA, f. 40, op. 1, d. 31, l. 148.

34 *Pravilova*: Finansy Imperii, 116; RGIA, f. 21, op. 11, d. 292, l. 2. See also chapter 5.

such as the transit regulations also created administrative incompatibilities with the core economic zone, prolonging the exclusion of the Transcaucasian region, as discussed in chapter 5. Paradoxically, the permission for transit trade from the Black Sea to the Caspian Sea, which enlivened the route, also created a new territorial perspective that would turn out to cause the transit route's eventual shutdown.

6.3 Central Asia and the Caspian Sea – A New Spatial Vision

The 1860s and early 1870s saw large military campaigns in Central Asia pushing the state border further to the south. For the financial administration, this posed the question of whether these new territories should be incorporated into the empire's customs line. As shown in chapter 2, in 1868, the decision was reached to dissolve the previously existent Orenburg customs line without moving it southwards, effectively leaving trade at the new border unguarded. Assuming a low impact of the "Asiatic trade" conducted in the region and the unlikeliness that any goods would reach the empire's core economic space due to the region's topography and infrastructural weakness, the central administration opted for a de-facto free-trade zone, yet stopped short of calling it such. Making use of topographic features to reduce administrative costs was a common strategy, and the dissolution of the Orenburg line was modeled after the establishment of the Far Eastern porto-franco.[35] It could be argued that the initial permission for the Transcaucasian transit route followed a similar logic, seeing that the northern Caucasus mountain range effectively separated the region from the core empire, which even allowed temporary free trade between the core customs zone and the Transcaucasian region, without the latter having an effective outside customs border.[36]

The introduction of the Baku transit route in 1864 in conjunction with the territorial gains in Central Asia, however, undermined this logic, as the route was not merely providing access to the Northern Persian markets anymore, but came to be seen as a potential gateway for European commerce into Russia's Central Asian dominions. Shortly after Russia defeated the Khanate of Bukhara in 1868, the Society for Aid to Russian Industry and Trade put forward a petition for linking the Transcaucasus with Central Asia. They

35 RGIA, f. 1152, op. 7, 1868, d. 172, l. 23.

36 Nachtigal argues that roadlessness was particularly problematic in the Transcaucasus, and that the interest for infrastructural integration of the region only came to prominence in the mid-19th century. *Nachtigal*: Verkehrswege in Kaukasien, 9,14. See also chapter 5 for the internal customs border on the Caucasus line.

formulated a vision of an integrated, Russian-dominated economic space linked by roads and eventually railways. However, at this moment the space the society proposed to remodel was not under Russian control, as the Transcaspian region had not been conquered yet, and the Khanate of Bukhara enjoyed significant autonomy.[37] The fulfillment of their vision would have to wait until 1895, when the Central Asian economic space was fully integrated into the empire's customs zone. The Transcaucasian transit, the society quickly added in an 1869 supplement, would have to be banned as well, as it undermined any plans for Russian dominance on these new markets.[38]

Such a new spatial vision was also articulated by governmental representatives on the Caspian Sea commission established in 1870. Representatives from the Ministry of Foreign Affairs and the Ministry of War conceived the adjacent territories as closely interlinked. The Ministry of Foreign Affairs made clear that "the primary political and trade interests of the whole empire cannot be sacrificed to the interests of a single province" and argued for a shutdown of the Baku transit route, depicting it as harmful to Russia's commercial and political interests in the newly acquired territories. Though the committee eventually decided in favor of retaining the transit route, as it would stimulate the development of the Transcaucasian railway and shipping on the Caspian Sea – arguments also brought forward by the Caucasus Namestnik – the endorsement was not overly enthusiastic, leaving plenty of room for future contestation. In 1872, the Persian Shah granted Baron Julius de Reuter an extensive concession, which included the construction of a railway, providing a first opportunity to renegotiate the transit route.[39]

For the Namestnik much was on the line, as the Transcaucasian region had opened its first railway following from Poti to Tiflis the same year and required the goods of the transit route to cover the costs of its operation. Thus, admitting to certain shortcomings of the transit route, he proposed a revision of the regulations rather than a shutdown:

37 *Obshchestvo dlia sodeistviia russkoi promyshlennosti i torgovle*: Zapiska o torgovykh putiach v Sredniu Aziiu; *Obshchestvo dlia sodeistviia russkoi promyshlennosti i torgovle*: Materialy po voprosu o torgovykh putiakh v Sredniiu Aziiu. For a detailed discussion of the society's proposal see chapter 3.

38 *Obshchestvo dlia sodeistviia russkoi promyshlennosti i torgovle*: Dopolnitel'naia Zapiska o torgvykh putiach v Sredniiu Aziiu.

39 RGIA, f. 1152, op. 8, 1876, d. 559, "Ob izmenenii pravil o tranzite cherez Zakavkazskii krai evropeiskikh tovarov v Persiiu i Turtsiiu i aziatskikh iz Persii i Turtsii v Evropu", l. 216–217; For the Reuter concession and the Russian government's reaction see *Kazemzadeh, Firuz*: Russia and Britain in Persia. Imperial Ambitions in Qajar Iran. London 2013, 101–147. Quote from AVPRI, f. 144, op. 488, 1870, d. 383, "Po povodu vysochaishe uchrezhdennogo komiteta dlia obsuzhdeniia voprosov, kasaiushchikhsia politicheskogo i torgovogo znacheniia Kaspiiskogo moria. Tranzit tovarov v Persiiu i Sr. Aziiu", l. 76.

> [...] the revision of the current regulations does not imply fully squeezing the Europe-Persia transit from the region, the benefit of which is fact-proven by now, but it means the implementation of rather strict controls and penalties with the aim of introducing via these temporary measures the full existing rules of the Empire in a near future, for which the time has not yet come.[40]

The perspective of introducing uniform regulations between the core empire and the Transcaucasian region was accepted by both the ministries pushing for a transit prohibition and the Namestnik; however, the time frames envisioned differed.

Both the ministries as well as the Namestnik tried to make use of the Transcaucasus' unique topography, either as a locking bolt for an envisioned zone of influence in Central Asia and northern Persia, or as a way to tap into global trade currents to the benefit of the Transcaucasian region. Effectively, both approaches hinged on the question of infrastructure. With underdeveloped infrastructure, the transit route could hardly become a serious threat to Russian dominance in Central Asia, while on the other hand, the development of both the Transcaucasian railway and the Caspian shipping depended on the transit cargo. This contradiction was essentially unresolvable and a decision could only be protracted. For the time being, it seemed to play out to the advantage of the Namestnik.

A last charge had been initiated by the Foreign Ministry in 1878, based on a complaint by the Russian Consul General in Tabriz about the dominance of Western European products on the Northern Persian markets. However, the special commission initiated to inquire into the issue deemed the previous experience of transit prohibition unsuccessful and inefficient, arguing that other, less convenient routes were available to international commerce. Essentially, the commission backed the Namestnik's position, endorsing the further development of the route's competitiveness by means of "granting it any possible facilities."[41] Since the opening of the Baku route, transit volume towards Persia had grown significantly, from 27 thousand pud per year in 1863 to almost 450 thousand pud in 1876, making it a pillar of the region's economy and its infrastructural development.[42]

40 RGIA, f. 1152, op. 8, 1876, d. 559, l. 54.
41 RGIA, f. 40, op. 1, d. 31, l. 139,165–168.
42 Ibid. l. 148.

6.4 The Transcaucasian Transit in a Nationally Charged Discourse

In many ways, the region's development was gaining momentum in the 1870s, as the emerging Baku oil industry was freed from taxation in 1877 to facilitate its growth.[43] The Russian victory over the Ottoman Empire further enlarged the Transcaucasian region by Kars, Ardahan, and Batumi provinces, opening up an additional Black Sea port. Both military and economic considerations prompted the decision to extend the railway system from Tiflis to Baku, with its exploitation to be guaranteed by the state.[44] In terms of the Transcaucasian transit route, any facilitation of shipping could only make it more attractive. Had it not been for an essential shift in the political landscape of the empire, the transit route, re-accredited by a special commission as recently as 1879, would have been likely to experience continual growth. However, debate about a possible transit prohibition flared up with the accession of Alexander III after his father's assassination.

While previous attacks on the transit route had been initiated by the Ministry of Foreign Affairs and the War Ministry, the renewed debate emanated from a private group of individuals for whom Alfred Rieber coined the term "Moscow Entrepreneurial Group." This loosely defined group of entrepreneurs had already attempted to influence the empire's economic policy throughout the 1860s, during the formative period of the Great Reforms, featuring a strictly protectionist and nationalist outlook. However, as Rieber points out, they "counted too heavily on the appeal of their patriotic motives and paid too little attention to financial considerations which were uppermost in the minds of both the Tsar and his Finance Minister, M. Ch. von Reutern."[45] Despite these initial failures, they did manage to secure the attention of Tsesarevich Aleksandr Aleksandrovich, making it "only a matter of time before the trade and tariff policies supported by the Moscow group would become the law of the land."[46] The conflict about the Transcaucasian transit route is a point in case.

The prospective opening of the new Transcaucasian railway branches was taken as a pretense to open a public debate about the transit route in 1882. The mouthpiece of a campaign for the shutdown of the Transcaucasian transit route had been Mikhail Katkov's "Moskovskie vedomosti." Throughout the

43 *McKay*: Baku Oil and Transcaucasian Pipelines, 607.

44 Ibid. 610.

45 *Rieber*: Emergence of a New Form in Autocratic Politics II, 177–178.

46 Ibid. 186.

years 1882 and 1883, the conservative editor and his newspaper published regular pieces on the transit route, branding it as unpatriotic and proliferating the separation of the Transcaucasian region from the Russian Empire. Katkov's discussion of the transit route fell well in line with a concept of nation-building based on "a modern, unified state, whose responsibility for the rule of law lay with a politically aware civil society."[47] The distinctly deviant customs regime in the Transcaucasus would not fit this description, and "Moskovskie vedomosti" set out to increase pressure against the route. Renner argues that Katkov's success was founded not in the "winning of arguments", but in "the supply of argumentative categories" and refracting issues through the lens of national-politics.[48] In the case of the Transcaucasian transit Katkov was explicitly called out for lobbying the economic interests of a small group of Russian manufacturers as national interests. However, Katkov's rhetorical strategy of insinuating the unpatriotic motives of his critics deflected such attacks:

> Some of the latter [supporters of the transit], by the way, just compromise their own cause by trying to depict all those in disagreement with them as know-nothings [nevezhda], who should not be listened to and as representatives of the "interests of the Zamoskvorechie [district]" and people "masking self-interests by the use of patriotic rhetoric", paying attention to whom is considered a joke. Nothing is worse than a rhetoric which is trying to argue that in the discussion of trade interests, self-interest should not be taken into consideration. On the contrary, the side should win the argument on the transit which can prove that its decision promises the most gain for Russia's industries; obviously, from a Russian perspective, even the largest gains of foreign trade are less important than the petty interests of the Zamoskovorechie.[49]

The polemic discreditation of his opponents also extended to the work of the Ministry of Finance's council called in to scrutinize the transit issue. "Moskovskie vedomosti" insinuated that the composition of the council was inadequate, questioned the statistical basis of the Ministry of Finance, and sowed doubt about incorrect procedures within the counsel by circulating rumors on its work.[50]

> We do not take it upon us to judge in how far these rumors are true. We do not know if the "Journal of the council, taking place at the Ministry of Finance on the question of the Transcaucasian transit on 25 October 1882", was composed correctly or not,

47 *Renner*: Defining a Russian Nation, 661.

48 Ibid. 681.

49 *Katkov, Mikhail Nikiforovich*: Sobranie peredovykh statei Moskovskikh Vedomostei. 1882 god. Saint Petersburg 1898, 568.

50 Ibid. 610,628. *Katkov, Mikhail Nikiforovich*: Sobranie peredovykh statei Moskovskikh Vedomostei. 1883 god. Saint Petersburg 1898, 4, 50.

or whether it was signed by all in attendance; but we can say with certainty that this journal is printed in the "Materialy" [Materials on the Transcaucasian Transit published by the Ministry of Finance].[51]

The accumulation of numerous such small commentaries on the council's work created an image of a flawed decision-making process within the Ministry of Finance, suggesting that the outcome of the council was already pre-determined to be in favor of the transit and to the loss of Russian entrepreneurs, without however crossing the line of acceptable critique.

At the same time, "Moskovskie vedomosti" presented themselves as the representatives of Russian interests, citing hundreds of entrepreneurs – with and without stakes in the Transcaucasian business – down to the peasant whose economic future would allegedly depend on the shutdown of the transit route.[52] Seeing that the trade volume on the Transcaucasian transit route was still marginal compared to the Russian Empire's production, the gravity of the suggested repercussions is very doubtful. Nevertheless, the narrative of a financial administration out of touch with the real economic needs of Russian subjects brought forward in "Moskovskie vedomosti" put the Minister of Finance, who found himself increasingly in trouble fending off the attacks with the accustomed bureaucratic means, under pressure.

Owning up to his reputation as "minister-professor", the former professor of economics and now Minister of Finance Nikolai Bunge commissioned Silvestr L'vovskii of the Department of Customs Collection to conduct an on-site investigation of the transit's effects on trade in the Transcaucasian region. In his report, L'vovskii concluded that the existence of alternative transit routes through the Ottoman Empire would eventually cancel out any envisioned protectionist effect of a transit prohibition through the Transcaucasian region – as had been the case after the prior prohibition. Rather than consolidating Russia's political influence in northern Persia and Central Asia a prohibition might even have a negative foreign political effect, as it would put control and initiative over the trade route into the hands of other European powers:

Taking into account the existence of finished British projects for a Europe-India railway, the heaviness and irreversibility of the blow that Britain could exert on our trade, political influence, and role in the East, as well as the fact that the implementation of this plan could be a possible consequence of a shutdown of the Transcaucasian transit, one has to come to the conclusion that latter measure endangers our political standing much more than the existence of the Persian and Transcaucasian transit, which, according to many indicators, has already reached the limits of its development.[53]

51 *Katkov*: Sobranie peredovykh statei Moskovskikh Vedomostei. 1883 god, 50

52 Ibid. 2.

53 *L'vovskii*: Zakavkazskii Tranzit, 29–30.

By all means, transit was understood as an instrument in the Great Game, and the Ministry of Finance, as opposed to the Ministry of Foreign Affairs and the Ministry of War, was determined to keep a firm hold of it, rather than discarding it to stand by the side line. The firmness of the grip, however, was a problem acutely addressed in L'vovskii's report. He admitted that the lax border protection was not only commercially dangerous but potentially enabled the smuggling of "advanced firearms to Persia and Central Asia."[54] He proposed a catalog of stricter formal controls, but essentially the problem of smuggling could only be solved by a significant and costly increase in the number of border guards.[55] An according project had even been drafted in 1881 but shelved due to the enduring budgetary crisis.[56]

From the start on, opinions on the future of the transit route were split in the special council convening on the issue on February 25, 1883. Particularly the Ministry of War, the Ministry of Transportation, the Ministry of State Property as well as the Russian Envoy to Persia took an unyielding stance against the transit route, claiming that it undermined state interests in Central Asia and Persia and that the Transcaucasian region was sufficiently developed to subordinate its interests to those of the empire.[57] The majority of members, however, preferred a compromise, be it the shutdown of just the Baku-route while keeping the Julfa-route open or the introduction of a transit fee.[58]

The Minister of Finance Bunge tried to steer clear of extreme measures and proposed a solution both moderately protectionist as well as fiscally sensible. Rather than shutting down the route and facilitating the rise of the Trabzon-route, he proposed the introduction of a transit fee that would even out the production costs between Russian manufacturers and their more efficient Western competitors. While maintaining the benefits of transit for the region, this would both cater to the protectionist demands of the entrepreneurial groups as well as secure increased fiscal income of several hundred thousand rubles. He also proposed a formal ban on the transportation of transit goods from Baku to Krasnovodsk to ease the War Ministry's fear of foreign influence in the recently annexed Transcaspian region.[59]

54 Ibid. 38.

55 Ibid. 39–40.

56 Zapiska departamenta tamozhennykh sborov po voprosu o Zakavkazskom tranzite. In: Dopolnenie k materialam po voprosu o Zakavkazskom tranzite. Saint Petersburg 1883, 1–20p. 12.

57 RGIA, f. 40, op. 1, d. 35, "Vsepoddaneishii doklad ministra finansov N. Kh. Bunge, utverzhdennyi 25 fevralia 1883g., o rezul'tatakh osobogo soveshchianiia po Zakavkazskomu tranzitu s prilozheniem zasedanii soveshchaniia i mnenii chlenov ego", l. 65, 82.

58 Ibid. l. 28–30.

59 Ibid. l. 39–42.

It is telling that the former Minister of Finance (1862–1878) Mikhail von Reitern, who was also part of the council and responsible for the recent success of the transit route since 1864, supported Bunge's proposal.[60] It was a continuation of his policy that acknowledged the practical impossibility of sealing the Transcaucasian border, resisted nationalist demands, and opted for a low-budget trade regulation that allowed the region to benefit from international trade. Additionally, for Bunge, who had inherited a severe budgetary crisis, the fiscal argument was of particular importance, as he had only recently implemented a flat-rate 10 % increase in the general customs tariff. A prohibition of transit promised higher expenditures on border control as well as a slump in the Transcaucasian railways transport volume, which would have to be covered by the state as its guarantor. A moderate transit fee, on the other hand, could compensate, if not increase, the state's income.

In the shifted political framework of Alexander III's reign, this technocratic solution had to compete against more extreme public voices, such as "Moskovskie vedomosti", to obtain the Tsar's approval. As early as December 18, 1882, two months before the special counsel convened on the issue, Alexander's gray eminence Konstantin Petrovich Pobedonostsev had already addressed the issue of the Transcaucasian transit in a letter to the Tsar, pointing out the increasing public pressure:

> At the moment, there is a strong commotion and aggravation in Moscow and all over the trade world due to the heated question of the Caucasian transit on the newly opened Tiflis-Baku railway. [...] Unfortunately, this heated question came up at the most critical time for Russian trade and manufacture. Trade is in a deadlock, there is a horrible lack of money, the exchange rate is dropping, after the unsuccessful trade fair, there are more bankruptcies, debtors from out of town are not paying, there is no demand for grain, and public banks, left with no control, are bursting. Under these circumstances, the opinion has spread, and is further supported by rumors and articles in Petersburg newspapers, that the government intends to open free transit just for the sake of free-trade principles. [...] I do not allow myself to judge on the subject matter as such, but would like to comment on the following aspect. When there is commotion in the liquid layer of the intelligentsia or in the sphere of journalists or liberal bureaucrats [...] one can afford not to pay too much attention. But this time the commotion is happening in the sphere that is the most Russian, most conservative, most loyal to the Emperor for the sake of Russian and national interests. For the government, particularly at times as such, it would be very harmful if these people had reason to complain that they have not been heard, and that the interests of Russian trade have been left without attention, and that the issue has been decided by one-sided bureaucrats in the chancellery. It is vital to make sure they have no reason for that. But there will surely be reason if this important question will be handled similarly to previous important questions such

60 Ibid. l. 123–124.

as peasant land purchases, the peasant bank or alcohol production, etc. These issues entered the State Council directly without a prior general discussion in a meeting with all ministers. Therefore, there was a fundamental and even irritating disagreement between the ministers – a disagreement that is no secret to anyone. I believe that the issue of the peasant bank, which in my opinion has been decided completely wrong, would have been decided differently if it had not been handed to the State Council at all, but discussed in advance by the Council of Ministers.[61]

It is noteworthy that Pobedonostsev did not claim to judge the content of the issue, but much rather the political signal that a decision would send. His appeal seems to have rung through to Alexander III, as can be seen from Aleksandr Polovtsov's diary:

He [the Grand Duke Mikhail Nikolaevich] tells me that the Tsar wishes that the issue of the transit through the Caucasus should not be handed to the State Council and finally decided by a special counsel under the Grand Duke's chairmanship, and that the Tsar has decided to close the transit. In these words, the Grand Duke sees a success of the Moscow agitation and the Petersburg intrigue against Bunge.[62]

Bunge himself had been informed on the decision by the Tsar as well, being told that the transit question was treated as an "internal politics" issue. Nevertheless, he did receive permission to invite experts to investigate a special tariff on goods such as sugar.[63] It is hard to judge whether the Minister of Finance truly believed in the persuasiveness of his rational argumentation, but his solutions for the transit presented in the special counsel on February 25, 1883, cited above, were an indication that he was not willing to just give in to the demands of a conservative press campaign, but treated the Transcaucasus as an economic issue, rather than one of only symbolic politics.

Met with resistance in the council, Bunge adjusted this initial plan and handed it into the State Council on March 14, 1883. His new plan included a shutdown of the Baku transit route, generally considered more problematic due to the Caspian Sea access, however, retaining the Julfa transit route with a transit fee.[64] This slimmed-down solution and its submission to the State Council may well have been a last attempt to prevent the full shutdown of the Transcaucasian transit and eventually was accepted by the general assembly of

61 *Pobedonostsev, Konstantin*: Pis'ma Podenostseva k Aleksandru III. Volume 1. Moscow 1926, 397–399.

62 *Polovtsov, Aleksandr*: Dnevnik Polovtsova. 1883–1886. Volume 1. Moscow 2005, 40.

63 Ibid. 40. Sugar export subvention, particularly to Asiatic countries, was of great importance due to sectoral overproduction and political imperatives to bail out sugar producers, many of whom where gentrymen and constituted the loyal basis for tsarist rule see *Munting*: Russian Beet Sugar Industry. Also see chapter 3 for its Central Asian dimension.

64 RGIA, f. 1152, op. 10, 1883, d. 169, "O rassmotrenie v Gosudarstvennom Sovete voprosa o Zakavkazskom tranzite", l. 309.

the State Council with 28 votes in favor and 18 against. Yet it was only a pyrrhic victory, as the Tsar made his determination clear by confirming the minority opinion instead and effectively ending the existence of the Transcaucasian transit route with the ruling of May 13, 1883.[65]

The visions of an inherently Russian zone of influence in Central Asia and Persia, which had already been articulated by the Ministry of War and the Foreign Ministry during the 1870s, had been enforced by a large-scale press campaign and a group of industrialists which previously had only limited access to policy making. Unlike the 1870s, when the debates surrounding the Transcaucasian transit were primarily an interministerial affair and attacks on the transit route could be kept in check by rational technocratic argumentation, the situation in 1883 placed the Ministry of Finance into a wholly new setting. Despite commissioning an on-site investigation that refuted the envisioned benefits of a transit prohibition by pointing out its practical impossibility and the existing alternative routes, its argumentation was unsuccessful. The issue of the Transcaucasian transit was ultimately resolved following an internal political logic, rather than an economic rationale.

Neither can the notion of a ministry set on "free transit just for the sake of free-trade principles" be accepted, which had been brought forward by Bunge's opponents, as the minister's overall policies are much better described as cautiously, yet explicitly protectionist.[66] His proposition to levy a transit fee is a case in point. Ultimately, a new dynamic had been introduced into the policy-making process, as Alexander III was much more receptive to nationally-framed demands. Refracted through a national lens, regional special economic regimes, such as the Transcaucasian transit route, appeared as a challenge to the empire's interests if equated to the interests of a small group of merchants and traders from Central Russia.

Ultimately, the 1883 transit prohibition demonstrated that both in the imperial administration as well as in the public spheres, a new vision of the territorial interconnectedness of the empire had asserted itself – both grounded in infrastructural development as well as a new spatial imaginary. This new understanding of the empire's cohesion induced a shift in the relationship between the core imperial space and its peripheral regions, as special territorial regimes were now increasingly understood to have repercussions in the core economic space, and thus became less viable options for the ordering of the imperial economic space. This entailed the curtailment of flexible adminis-

65 Otchet po deloproizvodstvu gosudarstvennogo soveta za 1883g. Saint Petersburg 1884, 153–165; Polnoe sobranie zakonov Rossiikoi Imperii. Sobranie 3. Volume 3. Saint Petersburg 1883, 234. Alexander III increasingly made use of his right to overrule decisions of the State Council see *Mosse*: Aspects of Tsarist Bureaucracy, 283–285.

66 See also chapter 1 for Bunge's economic policies.

trative mechanisms tailored to the specificities of peripheral regions, and a shift towards the prioritization of universal solutions and the unification of the empire's custom space. Ultimately, this introduced the new argumentative line of regional sacrifice for the good of the empire as well.

6.5 The Aftermath of the 1883 Transit Route Closure

Unlike after its first prohibition (1831–1846), the Transcaucasian transit route would not be reinstated until the fall of the Russian Empire. However, its memory appears to have been vivid enough to occasionally spark controversy. Most notably, the years 1908–1911 saw a debate including the Batum city council. It is beyond the scope of this chapter to trace it closely; however, a few words should be said on it, as it provides an additional time layer that is marked by a retrospective evaluation of the intentions and outcomes of the 1883 transit prohibition.

The renewed discussion had been started by an article published in "Torgovo-promyshlennaia gazeta" (Newspaper of Trade and Industry) claiming that the German project of the Baghdad railway once again endangered Russian interests on Persia's markets, and that it would be timely to make use of the available infrastructure in the Transcaucasus to attract trade, while also generating substantial profits from possible railway and transit fees.[67] These arguments, echoing the 1880s debate, had been quickly dismissed by both the Ministry of Trade and Manufacture and the Department of Customs Collection, arguing that, on the one hand, international trade treaties prohibited the institution of transit fees and that, on the other hand, protectionism was still of highest priority.[68]

Nevertheless, the new initiative inspired the Batum City Council to enter a petition with the Namestnik, who forwarded it to the Minister of Finance on March 27, 1911. To back up their demand for the reopening of the transit, they even commissioned local tax inspector I. K. Mulin to conduct a specific study, evaluating the results of the transit prohibition. The final report of the Batum city council invoked a language of sacrifice of regional interests for the benefit of the empire:

> With this prohibition [of the transit in 1883], the government pursued two goals: 1) curtailing contraband business developing due to the transit of foreign goods and 2) creating a privileged position for Russian industrialists on the Persian and

67 *Treskinskii, A.*: K voprosu o zakavkazskom tranzite v Persiiu. In: Torgovo-promyshlennaia gazeta, 221, 3.10.1908, 107–109; RGIA, f. 560, op. 45, d. 76, l. 35.

68 RGIA, f. 560, op. 45, d. 76, l. 36, 45.

Central Asian markets. These goals were considered to be of such importance by the government that it was decided in advance that to attain them, the damage would have to be accepted, which the prohibition of the transit would cause our region, which had enjoyed great benefits from the transportation of foreign goods from the Black Sea to the Caspian Sea and from Tiflis to Erivan or Akhaltsikh and further. The May 13, 1883 law also caused Batum a heavy loss, as the city lost its role as the main transit point right at the start of its development.[69]

However, the city council questioned the economic rationale behind the prohibition and its eventual results. The study conducted by Mulin deemed the effects of the prohibition limited, as the success Russian produce was enjoying on the Persian markets was not monocausal. Although Russia's share in Persian imports had reached an impressive 48 %, almost half of this was made up of sugar. With an 83,3 % share in Persia's sugar imports, Russia had achieved the almost monopolistic position the supporters of a transit prohibition had envisioned. However, the impressive numbers are somewhat misleading as they could only be achieved by substantial export subventions from the Russian state.[70]

To soften the negative effects of sugar overproduction in the 1880s, manufacturers received export premiums from the government. Further, a law had been introduced in 1893 that limited the volume of sugar which could be released on the internal Russian market to help stabilize prices. Any additional produce was punished with a special tax, if sold within the empire. Exports, however, were freed of excise tax, thus making them almost mandatory. As only limited markets were available, it was no surprise that Persia was flooded with Russian sugar.[71] The appeal of the Batum city council to correct what it deemed an unwarranted discrimination of their region's interests was not met with support by the Ministry of Finance. The last decade of the Russian Empire saw similar debates over the return of regional economic customs privileges in other peripheral regions, such as was the case with the Far-Eastern porto-franco, which, however, did not result in their reinstitution.[72] Since the 1880s, the Russian Empire had firmly pursued the unification of its heterogeneous customs space, and special regional customs regimes increasingly fell out of favor as administrative tools.

How does the success of a symbolically strong protectionist measure, such as the prohibition of the Transcaucasian transit, tie in with the general customs policies of the Russian Empire from the 1880s onwards? One of the most cited and in-depth analyses of the Russian tariff system, written by Mikhail

69 Ibid. l. 78.
70 Ibid. l. 75–83.
71 Ibid. l. 132. See also *Munting*: Russian Beet Sugar Industry.
72 *Beliaeva*: Ot porto-franko k tamozhne, 133–148.

Sobolev, led him to conclude that despite an often-articulated protectionist rhetoric, the Russian tariff policies would be more rightly described as fiscally motivated rather than purely protectionist. He argues that the budgetary crisis of the late 1870s and 1880s and Russia's heavy reliance on customs duties as source of income (second only to the alcohol excise) led the government to significantly increase its tariffs; however, never to an extent that would severely reduce imports. On paper, protectionist demands would be met, while customs incomes rose consistently throughout the 1880s and 1890s. However, Sobolev cautioned that his study only applied to the western border and disregarded "special regimes" such as the Transcaucasian customs territory.[73]

The analysis of the Transcaucasian transit shows that Sobolev's thesis of a narrow fiscalism masked as protectionism does not hold true for the Transcaucasus. The measures taken in 1883 were in many respects to the fiscal detriment of the Russian Empire, as on the one hand, the transit incomes for the region dropped significantly, while border protection had to be ramped up anyway. Further, the expenditures for the Transcaucasian railway, before at least partially covered by the transport of transit goods, fell on the state as guarantor. Lastly, the transit prohibition, if evaluated for its proclaimed protectionist intention, was not sufficient to guarantee a significant market share in Persia and was followed by a number of additional export subsidies and excise-tax-exemptions, which reduced fiscal gains. It could thus be argued that the Transcaucasian region and its adjacent territories fulfilled a different function within the economic system of the empire. Rather than being import and fiscally oriented like the western borders, the transit prohibition allowed to utilize them as outlets or "valves" to regulate the internal market and counterbalance overproduction problems. This helps explain why an institution such as the Transcaucasian transit, which was import-oriented and generated regional fiscal income, came to be seen as potentially dangerous to the core empire's interests, which lay with the development and regulation of its central industries as well as with the safeguarding of internal political support from conservative spheres.

6.6 Conclusion

The markedly unstable history of the Transcaucasian transit demonstrates well the development of the relationship between the imperial center and the Transcaucasian region. It allows us to observe different interpretations of the region's function within the empire, ranging from semi-autonomous territory

73 *Sobolev*: Tamozhennaia politika Rossii, 823.

to subordinate outlet market and eventually as strategic device in the Great Game. The specific form the transit took reflected current political balances between the center and the region and changing spatial visions within the central and the regional administration. Visions of an integrated Black Sea territory and global transit competed with an understanding of the Transcaucasus as an emerging market of the Russian Empire. The conquest of Central Asia and the infrastructural development significantly impacted the spatial imagery of Saint Petersburg administrators, who increasingly understood the imperial space as interconnected and feared the repercussions of special economic regimes found on its peripheries. While the Ministry of Finance remained skeptical about the actual significance of the Transcaucasian transit route on the all-imperial economy throughout the 1870s, the Ministry of War and the Ministry of Foreign Affairs problematized it as a liability in an international competition for influence south of Russia's borders.

These interministerial conflicts could be kept in check, as the Ministry of Finance argued, with local expertise and implementation difficulties on-site that were not accounted for in the designs of the War Ministry and the Foreign Ministry. The political shift of Alexander III's reign, however, introduced a new dynamic into the negotiation of economic "special regimes" as a nationally charged public debate on the transit route, and the public discreditation of the Ministry of Finance's usual decision-making process put Bunge under pressure. Eventually, the 1883 prohibition of the transit was decided directly by the Tsar, who had given in to public pressure and overruled the State Council decision. The decision ushered in the dismissal of flexible regional solutions in favor of a uniform administration of the imperial customs space, which would become the dominant approach in customs politics over the following decades.

Despite the introduction of the same import tariffs as on the empire's western borders, the Transcaucasian region nevertheless assumed a different function within the economic system. Its borders were fiscally less important; the maintenance of border protection, however, became relevant for a system of external protectionism based on export subsidies that required a strong demarcation between internal and external markets.[74]

The prohibition of the Transcaucasian transit route marks a watershed in the history of the administrative regulation of the Russian Empire's economic space, as it constituted the first instance in which the political demand for a uniform economic space in a nationalizing empire, brought forward in public debate, was preferred over a pragmatic and fiscally motivated solution.

74 For details on the operating mode of this mechanism see chapter 3.

7. The Finnish Customs Space: Nation-Building within a Nationalizing Empire

Of the many territories of the Russian Empire endowed with special autonomous rights, the Grand Duchy of Finland enjoyed the broadest autonomy and was able to retain it for the longest time. In terms of customs, it remained the only larger territorial unit outside of the imperial customs space when the Russian Empire collapsed in 1917. Attempts had been made to integrate its economic space since the late 1880s; however, the complicated harmonization of political and economic interests eventually proved unsuccessful. The main line of tension ran between the controversial status of Finnish statehood with the associated allegations of separatism and the difficulty of integrating an economically well-developed region with significant trade relations to other European states.

At first glance, the relationship of Finland's customs space to that of the Russian Empire shares traits with the setup found in the Caucasian Viceroyalty, as in both cases an insular administration had been put in place to better accommodate regional specificities. However, unlike in the Transcaucasus, the installation of an insular customs administration in the Grand Duchy of Finland did not initially pursue the long-term goal of integration.[1] Rather, the change of course in the late 1880s was the empire's reaction to a nation-building process that was picking up pace in Finland, at the same time as politics in the Russian Empire were increasingly refracted through the prism of "nationality" by both press organs and the imperial administration itself.

The following chapter gives an overview of the development of Finland's relation to the Russian Empire in general, outlines its customs status until the 1880s, and eventually discusses the imperial administration's integration attempts and the factors precluding its success.

This chapter argues that the insularity of Finland as a customs territory had promoted its economic rise and created cross-border imbalances between the peripheral economic space and the core customs space to the advantage of Finland, which makes it the "odd man out" within this study, as the relationship was the opposite for the empire's "Asiatic" peripheries. When demands for a customs integration flared up, this peculiar relationship presented the

1 For the integration of the Caucasian Viceroyalty see chapter 5.

authorities with a "nationalist" dilemma, as both the politically symbolic unification within one customs space as well as the protection of the core economic space from an overdeveloped periphery by means of an internal customs border were put forward as "national" policies.

Further, due to the long existence as an insular customs system deeply entangled with the Grand Duchy's state structure, a customs integration into the Russian Empire would not be possible without encroaching on other autonomy rights and causing political repercussions. Unlike in other territories discussed in this study, Finland was not only administratively separated, but also went through a nation-building process within a nationalizing empire, making changes to its customs status politically delicate.

Thus, it was for both macroeconomic and political reasons that the Grand Duchy of Finland remained the only autonomous customs space when the Russian Empire collapsed.

7.1 The Autonomous Status of the Grand Duchy of Finland

The large degree of autonomy the Grand Duchy of Finland enjoyed originated as an appeasement policy after the Treaty of Tilsit in 1808. In its initial phase of rule, the Russian Empire aimed at demonstrating the benefits of Russian rule over the prior Swedish rule. To this end Finland was allowed to retain its previous civil and political laws, the Finnish Senate received a strong standing vis a vis the Russian Governor-general and other privileges were introduced. The return of the "Old Finland" province, conquered by the Russian Empire in the 18th century, constituted the ultimate sign of good-will. The strategy proved successful, with the higher estates in the Grand Duchy positioning themselves loyally towards the Russian Empire.[2]

Against often-cited accusations, the installation of a Russian Governor-general did not limit Finnish autonomy either. The early Governor-generals successfully protected their domains and the insular principle of administration from the encroachment of the imperial ministries. Nevertheless, the course had initially been one of rapprochement with the Russian Empire in many domains. It was only with Russia's defeat in the Crimean War and a generational change that a shift away from the Russian Empire could be perceived.[3]

The short-lived period of press freedom following the war opened up space for debate in the Grand Duchy of Finland over its status as either an

2 *Jussila, Osmo*: Velikoe kniazhestvo Finliandskoe. 1809–1917. Helsinki 2009, 105–106.

3 Ibid. 181, 266; *Jussila, Osmo*: Die russische Reichsgesetzgebung in Finnland in den Jahren 1809–1898. In: Jahrbücher für Geschichte Osteuropas, 33(3) (1985), 345–365, here 364.

imperial province or a sovereign state in union with the Russian Empire. Osmo Jussila regards this period, and particularly the year 1861, as crucial for the development of a national imaginary. Soon de-jure changes granting the Grand Duchy broader autonomy followed. Unlike the Kingdom of Poland, which lost its autonomous status after the unsuccessful 1863 uprising and was subjected to harsh Russification measures, the Grand Duchy of Finland successfully capitalized on the liberal period of the 1860s. For the first time since 1809, the Estate Diet of Finland convened in 1863, meeting regularly henceforth. Further, the introduction of a separate currency, the Finnish Markka, and an own army emphasized Finland's autonomous status.[4]

Finland's autonomous status had been questioned by the conservative press, particularly by Mikhail Katkov, since 1863. However, the debates were quickly shut down by the government. Only in the 1880s, under the reign of Alexander III, did "the Finnish question" regain prominence.[5] Though the new Governor-general of Finland, Fedr Logginovich Geiden, did not have a clear-cut Russification program when he took office in 1881, by the turn of the decade all major aspects of Finnish autonomy were up for debate. It was on Alexander III's personal initiative that the separate postal system, currency and customs zone, as well as the question of legislative authority as a whole, were renegotiated.[6]

Despite serious investigations into the issue of Finland's legislative status and its possible subjugation to imperial law by the 1891 committee, headed by Nikolai Bunge, eventually a cautious course of action was chosen and the committee's results were shelved. The new Tsar Nicholas II initially continued his predecessor's course; however, by the late 1890s demands for imperial unity from the conservative nationalist press began to rise against the backdrop of a general destabilization of the autocracy.[7]

The appointment of Nikolai Ivanovich Bobrikov as Governor-general of Finland in 1898 marked a turning point in Russo-Finnish relations. The choice

4 *Jussila*: Velikoe kniazhestvo Finliandskoe, 267–271, 287, 407–437; *Lundin, Leonard*: Constitutional and Historical Background of the Russification Dispute in Finland. In: *Thaden, Edward C.* (ed.): Russification in the Baltic Provinces and Finland, 1855–1914. Princeton 1981, 357–372, 367–369. In the Grand Duchy of Finland, Russification primarily took the form of administrative Russification, which Thaden differentiates from unplanned and cultural Russification see *Thaden, Edward C.*: Russification in the Baltic Provinces and Finland, 1855–1914. Princeton 1981, 7–10. For a discussion of the ambiguity of the term "Russification", its use and the differing actions it implied see *Weeks, Theodore R.*: Russification: Word and Practice, 1863–1914. In: Proceedings of the American Philosophical Society, 148(4) (2004), 471–489.

5 *Polvinen, Tuomo*: Imperial Borderland: Bobrikov and the Attempted Russification of Finland, 1898–1904. Durham, North Carolina 1995, 28.

6 *Jussila*: Velikoe kniazhestvo Finliandskoe, 478, 528–537.

7 *Polvinen*: Imperial Borderland, 23–27.

of Bobrikov originated from Minister of War Aleksei Nikolaevich Kuropatkin's suspicion of Finland's separate army. The introduction of imperial conscription regulations in Finland was to quell separatist tendencies and increase security in a region so close to the capital. Making such staunch inroads on the Grand Duchy's autonomous rights required a resolute Governor-general, which could be found in Bobrikov. After initial hesitations, Bobrikov, whose career had been solely in the military until then, agreed to take the post and firmly committed himself to the dismantling of Finnish autonomy. He initially succeeded in strengthening the position of the Governor-general of the Grand Duchy of Finland[8] and pursued a ten-point program doing away with almost all special rights of the Grand Duchy.[9]

If the issue of conscription had already indicated a change of course, the February Manifesto of 1899 left no doubt about it. From a Finnish perspective, it was understood as a coup d'état, shifting legislative initiative towards Saint Petersburg. De-jure little had changed; however, in practice the Finnish Diet had been actively involved in the enactment of numerous imperial laws since 1863. With the February Manifesto and its vague definition of what constituted an "imperial law", the backdoor was open to circumvent the Diet and impose legislation forcefully from the center. It marked the end of a period of flexibility on the side of the central administration. The Finnish public took it as an aggressive encroachment on the Grand Duchy's autonomous status.[10]

The following years saw a sharpening of the conflict between demands to retain Finnish autonomous rights and Bobrikov's push for integration. Both Finland's separate army and postal system had been dissolved and repressive measures increased, with the Governor-general acquiring quasi-dictatorial rights. In 1904, Bobrikov was assassinated, yet against the backdrop of the Russo-Japanese war and internal unrest in Russia the reaction was not a tightening of the grip on Finland, but rather an interruption of the imperial government's attempts at integrating the Grand Duchy.[11]

The results of the revolutionary year 1905 had been a significant rollback of the measures impinging on Finnish autonomous rights. The repressive measures of the Bobrikov period had resulted in a bolstering of the Finnish self-conception as a separate state, and resulted in progressive parliamentary and suffrage reform. Further, Finnish statesmen, led by Leopold Mekhelin, attempted to use the empire's weakened position to secure more autonomy for the Grand Duchy and renegotiate its relation to the Russian Empire.[12]

8 He also had the letterhead of his office changed to simply "Finnish Governor-general", symbolically discounting the Grand Duchy's special status.

9 *Polvinen*: Imperial Borderland, 51–70.

10 Ibid. 82–86; *Jussila*: Reichsgesetzgebung in Finnland, 351.

11 *Polvinen*: Imperial Borderland, 240–267.

12 *Jussila*: Velikoe kniazhestvo Finliandskoe, 692–693, 700–709.

The respite, however, did not last long and was followed by a "second period of oppression", with a roll-back of the granted concessions and a renewed fervor to fully integrate the Grand Duchy into the Russian Empire. The foundation of a Special Council for Finnish Affairs in 1907 and a new general order of reporting brought the Grand Duchy under increased control of the Council of Ministers. Laws of "all-imperial relevance" were subject to the approval of the council. The vague definition of "all-imperial relevance", however, allowed it to rule even into detailed internal affairs of the Grand Duchy. The beginning of the First World War brought upon a further curtailment of Finnish autonomy and a sharpening of political repression.[13] After the collapse of the Russian Empire, the Grand Duchy of Finland declared its independence as a sovereign state in December 1917.

The development of the relations between the Grand Duchy of Finland and the Russian Empire can be very roughly divided into three phases. Between 1809 and 1863, it constituted a Governorate-general which remained mostly unimpaired by unificatory measures, as it was considered a trouble-free region of the empire; its trajectory, however, was one of gradual rapprochement with the Russian Empire. Between 1863 and the late 1880s, the Grand Duchy acquired a larger degree of autonomy, with its Senate and Diet claiming significant rights for themselves. This phase demonstrates well how insular administrations "renewed the integrity of macro-regions, glorified the historical power centers, and reproduced memories of the former independent polities"[14] – or in the case of Finland gave rise to the development of an imagined community. The final phase, beginning in the late 1880s, saw the imperial administration increasingly problematizing the Grand Duchy's autonomous status, which was curtailed in a number of more or less intense waves of unificatory measures.

7.2 Finnish Customs Policies before the 1890s

With regard to the customs relations between the Grand Duchy and the core empire, the Ministry of Finance mainly followed the above-mentioned periodization. Finland's continual exclusion from the Russian Empires customs territory demonstrates well how the application of an insular logic of administration initially allowed for a flexible management of the imperial economic space and turned out highly obstructive when integration attempts began in the late 1880s. Ultimately, an integration into the imperial customs zone was never effected, as the long-term separate development of the Finnish economic

13 Ibid. 692–693, 710–724, 734–739.
14 *Matsuzato*: Intra-Bureaucratic Debate, 86.

space had created too many peculiarities. The initial flexible regime ultimately effected the rigidity of the division between both economic spaces. As will be demonstrated, economic and functional considerations eventually outweighed political and symbolic ones in the ministerial debates over integration.

As in other administrative areas, after 1809, the Grand Duchy's customs regulations initially followed previous Swedish law. From the start, however, responsibility for customs had been placed with the Government Council (Pravitel'stvennyi sovet)[15] and the Governor-general, establishing the insular principle in the customs administration. A customs line separating the Grand Duchy from the core empire was drawn between Vyborg and Käkisalmi in 1811, aimed at counteracting contraband transited from Sweden via the Grand Duchy, which included English goods banned under the Continental Blockade. In 1812, Finland received a separate Customs Direction (Glavnaia tamozhennaia direktsiia), and soon a first separate Finnish tariff was published, modeled after the first post-Napoleonic-War tariff in the core empire. Likewise, the Finnish tariff followed the liberalization brought about by the 1816 Russian tariff soon after. Only with the 1819 tariff a first departure from Russia's general customs policy can be observed. However, this deviation was soon reeled in as the Russian prohibitionist tariff of 1822 did not fare well with more lenient tariff regimes on its borders.[16]

In this regard, the situation was similar to that of the Transcaucasian region. Regional economic requirements were weighted against the threat to the integrity of a prohibitionist system constituted by lower tariffs in bordering regions. Unlike the Transcaucasian region, however, the border with the Grand Duchy was in immediate proximity of the imperial capital and could not be easily discounted by just relying on distance and infrastructural fragmentation as deterrents to smuggling.

The concern was rooted in a distrust for the efficiency of border protection. In the case of the Grand Duchy, inquiries into the revocation of customs autonomy to bring border protection under Saint Petersburg's ministerial control had already been made in 1816, however, the project failed against the protests of the Finnish Senate and a lack of support from the Tsar. The basic issue nonetheless persisted into the 1830s, with the central financial administration trying to secure revision rights for Finnish customs institutions, which was again opposed by the Finnish Senate, citing the autonomous character of its customs institutions.[17] However, there seems to be no indication of attempts

15 Since 1816: Imperial Finnish Senate.

16 Materialy po delu o tamozhennom ob"edinenii Velikogo Kniazhestva Finliandskogo i Imperii, 1890–1892 g. Saint Petersburg 1901, 33; *Jussila*: Velikoe kniazhestvo Finliandskoe, 396–397; *Suni*: Finliandsko-Russkie torgovye otnosheniia, 31–32.

17 *Jussila*: Velikoe kniazhestvo Finliandskoe, 398–400.

by the Ministry of Finance to fully integrate the Finnish customs system from the 1820s on. It seems likely that the ministry followed a strategy observed in other peripheral regions for the same period: lowering administrative expenditures whenever possible, without damaging the integrity of the main customs zone's protection. The comparatively short customs border with the Grand Duchy, running from Vyborg to Käkisalmi, was simply easier to protect efficiently than the outside borders of the Grand Duchy with its topographically challenging coast line.

Although the customs administration was organized according to the insular principle and under Finnish autonomous control, trade agreements and tariffs themselves were not. They remained the exclusive domain of the emperor, though the Finnish Senate did provide its input. It is therefore little surprising that Finnish tariff policy in the 1820s and 1830s followed the main lines of the imperial tariff. The economic preconditions, however, were quite different in the Grand Duchy. Thus, the Finnish customs administration complained that such a tariff policy did not match the region's needs. The strict prohibitions crippled the potential of customs as important state revenue and increased costs of living, without having any positive effect on Finland's economy.[18]

First reductions in the import tariff for consumer goods and in export duties were made in 1839, soon followed by the Haartman tariff reform of 1841, which further significantly lowered tariffs on consumer goods and entailed a strengthening of border control with both Norway and Sweden, as well as the Russian Empire's core customs zone. It was framed as a temporary exception from the basic tariff that was otherwise still in force, but marked a trend towards tariff liberalization which would be picked up in the core empire a decade later. Indeed, the lowering of tariffs succeeded in raising Finland's state revenues from customs, a strategy later adopted for the Russian Empire's core customs zone.[19]

This overall lowering of the general tariff had been in part motivated by the integration of the Kingdom of Poland into the imperial customs zone, which required an adaptation to the lower Polish tariff. Although the Grand Duchy of Finland was considered a loyal territory and the repercussions of the revolutionary year 1848 played a lesser role than in the case of the Kingdom of Poland, Tsar Nicholas I nevertheless considered analogously integrating the Grand Duchy into the core customs space. Eventually, it was the topography

18 *Heikinnen, Sakari/Heinonen, Visa/Kuusterä, Antti/Pekkarinen, Jukka*: The History of Finnish Economic Thought, 1809–1917. Tammiisaari/Ekenäs 2000, 171–172, 175–176.

19 Ibid. 175–176; *Jussila*: Velikoe kniazhestvo Finliandskoe, 400–401. For the changes in the general tariff and the resulting increase of customs revenue see chapter 1.

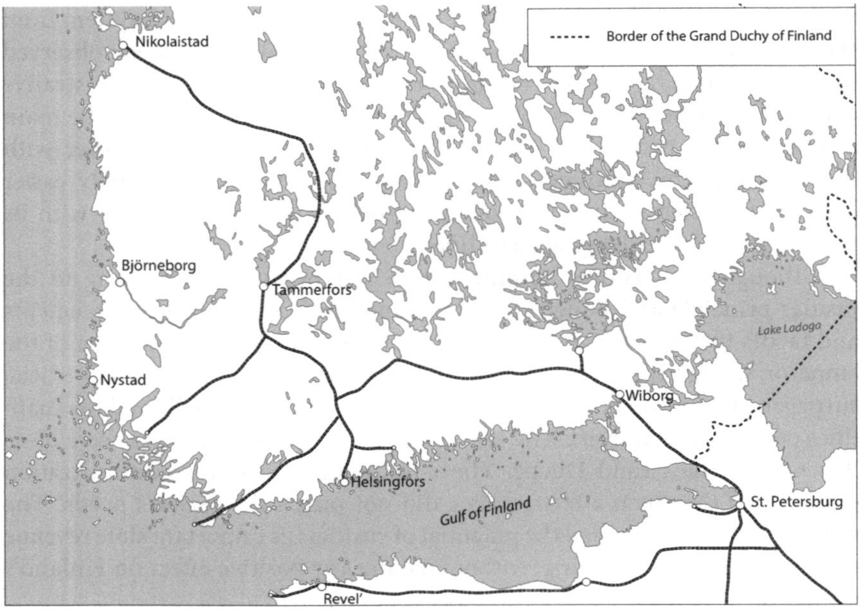

Figure 7: Map of Finno-Russian border and Finnish skerries.

of the Finnish coast with its many skerries which precluded the integration effort – efficient border control would have been too complicated and costly. The onset of the Crimean War eventually had the project sink into oblivion.[20]

Thus, for the Nicholaen period, Finno-Russian customs and trade relations were informed by an appeasement policy towards the Grand Duchy as well as the Russian Empire's prohibitionist tariff policy, which made the exclusion of Finland from its customs space convenient from the perspective of imperial customs. The Finnish tariff followed the general lines of the imperial tariff; however, when regional requirements demanded its softening, the Russian Empire showed itself to be flexible and granted concessions. The existence of a linear customs border separating both economic spaces was the precondition for such flexible measures.

The ascent of Alexander II marked a trend towards tariff liberalization in the Russian Empire with the tariffs of 1858 and 1868. This extended to the Grand Duchy as well, which received significantly more moderate tariffs in 1859 and 1869. Further, the autonomous status of its customs administration

20 *Borodkin, Mikhail:* Istoriia Finliandii. Tom V. Vremia Imperatora Nikolaia I. Saint Petersburg 1915, 216–220; *Jussila*: Velikoe kniazhestvo Finliandskoe, 226–228, 401–402.

was strengthened as it was allowed to set up its own customs guard on the Finnish side of the Russo-Finnish border.[21]

Trade relations between the Grand Duchy and the imperial core customs space were put on a more equal basis as well. Had the customs border been mostly semi-permeable since the 1830s, with Russian products coming into the Grand Duchy mostly duty-free, but not vice-versa, Russian import tariffs were now adjusted to facilitate more trade inflow from the Grand Duchy. Nevertheless, certain restrictions and quotas for the importation of Finnish goods were retained for fear of a strong internal competition. These considerations were also cited by the State Council as the main reason for dismissing a proposed full integration of the Grand Duchy into imperial customs territory, which was favored by Foreign Minister Gorchakov for political reasons.[22]

These reforms effected a double-opening for the Finnish economy. It could tap into global trade currents, profiting from cheaper raw material imports and the opening of markets in the course of an international wave of trade liberalization. On the other hand, Finnish products received preferential treatment when exported to the nearby Russian imperial market. This constellation facilitated a quick industrialization. The timber industry constituted the main staple of Finland's economy. However, the Grand Duchy did not solely remain an exporter of raw materials but also acquired an important position as an exporter of metal and textile manufactured goods to the Russian Empire.[23] Thus, while the Russian customs policy during its first 50 years of rule did indeed effect a strong re-orientation of the Grand Duchy of Finland towards the Russian imperial economic zone, it was by no means an exclusive relationship but stood next to extensive trade relations of Finland to various Western European states.

During the late-1850s to mid-1870s trade relations between the Grand Duchy and the core empire intensified, while the Finnish and the imperial tariff were on a path of convergence, making Minister of Finance Reitern confident that both economic zones would soon be on an equal footing customs-wise. Thus, he discarded any plans for full customs integration of the Grand Duchy.[24]

Finno-Russian customs relationships until the 1880s can thus be broken up into two phases. In the Nicholaen period, the exclusion of the Grand Duchy from the imperial customs space had presented an opportunity to avoid the burden of protecting a topographically challenging customs border and had

21 *Jussila*: Velikoe kniazhestvo Finliandskoe, 402–403. See also chapter 1.

22 *Heikinnen/Heinonen/Kuusterä/Pekkarinen*: History of Finnish Economic Thought, 176–180; *Suni*: Finliandsko-Russkie torgovye otnosheniia, 33–38; O tamozhennom ob"edinenii Velikogo Kniazhestva Finliandskogo i Imperii, 42–45.

23 *Suni*: Finliandsko-Russkie torgovye otnosheniia, 41–42; *Alapuro, Risto*: State and Revolution in Finland. Leiden 2019, 30–34.

24 *Suni*: Finliandsko-Russkie torgovye otnosheniia, 64.

been part of a larger appeasement policy during the transitional period from Swedish to Russian rule. The early Alexandrian period saw an expansion of Finnish customs autonomy, which gave a competitive edge to Finnish products. However, by the late 1870s, Finland's economic privileges and its nation-building process, which had begun in the 1860s, were increasingly regarded as problematic, and so was its insular customs administration.

The general crisis of Russia's industry in the 1880s caused a drift towards protectionism, exacerbating tariff differences with the Grand Duchy, and resulted in demands for a re-negotiation of Finno-Russian customs relations. Further, against growing conservative-nationalist thought under Alexander III, the separate and privileged status of Finland's economy became increasingly politicized and brought the question of full integration back on the agenda. The long separate economic development of the Grand Duchy and the political sensitivity of the revocation of autonomous rights, however, complicated a transition of the customs administration from an insular to a linear principle.

7.3 Finno-Russian Relations during the 1880s-Industrial Crisis

When the Russo-Finnish trade relations had been substantially renegotiated in 1858, the import quotas set for Finnish goods by far exceeded its production capacities and were not problematized by either party. By the mid-1870s, however, Finnish production had increased sufficiently to require a raising of the import quotas, which the Finnish Senate and the State Secretary petitioned for. On the other hand, the turn in Russia's customs policy towards increased protectionism, which began with the 1877 switch to customs collection in gold, and a beginning industrial crisis, raised demands from Central Russian manufacturers for increased protection of the imperial core customs zone. Finnish manufacturers were on the one hand regarded as enjoying a preferential treatment, since the Finnish tariff had not risen along with the imperial tariff, thus keeping raw material prices low. On the other hand, Finland was regarded as a gateway for Western European goods to circumvent the high tariff barriers established in the Russian Empire by importing semi-finished goods into Finland, where they would receive a final touch before being imported as tariff-favored Finnish goods into the Russian Empire.[25]

In 1883, the Ministry of Finance set up a commission to discuss means to curtail the import of materials for metal manufacturing which were transited through Finland into the core customs zone. This initial commission was

25 Ibid. 51–57.

followed by a general revision of the Russo-Finnish trade agreement, aiming to reduce the preferential position imports from Finland enjoyed.[26] This has to be seen against the background of an increasing industrial crisis in the Russian Empire, which sharpened the awareness for its peripheries as contested markets or internal competitors. This pattern can be observed with regard to other regions of the Russian Empire as well. In a similar vein, the Transcaucasian transit route was claimed to have surrendered Russian markets to European contenders and was eventually abolished in 1883.[27]

In the late 1860s, the Finnish customs policy had been regarded as firmly on the way to rapprochement with the Russian Empire, as both were liberalizing. 20 years later, the rift could not have been bigger. The Grand Duchy of Finland profited from conducting foreign trade with low tariffs on its own borders, as the Russian Empire became increasingly protectionist towards other states, while maintaining lenient tariffs towards the Grand Duchy. The revision of tariff relations in the mid-1880s thus had larger implications. It implicitly asked as which kind of political and economic unit Finland would be treated by the Russian Empire henceforth.

Minister of Finance Bunge discussed three possible scenarios. The first was full customs integration. The Grand Duchy would receive the same tariff as the Russian Empire and control over the customs borders would be centralized. Apart from the political implications of encroaching on Finland's autonomous rights, the minister also cited hard economic reasons. By then, Finnish production chains were strongly connected to other western economies and the Finnish economy would likely suffer from the imposition of Russia's high-protectionist tariff. Creating an additional economic crisis amid the one he already had to deal with was not in Bunge's interest.[28]

The second option was a thorough separation of the two economies. The Grand Duchy of Finland could have been placed in the same position as any foreign state vis-a-vis Russia, being subjected to the same high import duties.[29] Though in this case both the interests of Russian and Finnish manufacturers would have been served, the political implications were unacceptable. Such a separation would not only have undone prior efforts to reorient the Finnish economy towards the Russian Empire, but also underlined its autonomous status, which was increasingly perceived as politically undesirable.

Ultimately, the Ministry of Finance opted for a third option, which allowed it to avoid sending any sharp political signals. Import tariffs for the Grand

26 Ibid. 66–71.

27 See chapter 6.

28 *Suni*: Finliandsko-Russkie torgovye otnosheniia, 78.

29 Ibid. 79.

Duchy were significantly increased in 1886, yet kept at a level lower than the general tariff for foreign states. The compromise was in every way unsatisfactory, as it was neither strict enough to appease Russian manufacturers' calls for protectionism, nor did it sufficiently soften the impact on Finland's industries. Mutual trade plummeted from 47,3 (1881–1885) to 34,1(1886–1890) Million Finnish Mark, the output of the Finnish metallurgic industry shrank by three times, and the Finnish economy began to increasingly reorient itself towards Western European trading partners.[30] Thus, the pragmatic solution chosen only temporarily postponed the underlying conflict, while exacerbating it in the long-term.

7.4 The 1890s Geiden Commission on Full Customs-Integration

The Finnish Senate unsuccessfully attempted to petition for a softening of these new terms of trade with Tsar Alexander III. On top of the detrimental effects of the new tariff on its industries, the decrease in trade also affected the state revenues of the Grand Duchy, which was heavily reliant on customs collection. The Senate's proposal to introduce Finnish import tariffs on Russian goods to compensate for these fiscal losses was also met with stern refusal by the Tsar.[31] The semi-permeability of the imperial customs border, which allowed the regulation of undesired imports while maintaining unrestricted exports of Russian goods, was symptomatic for the Russian Empire's core customs zone and can be observed on the Caucasian customs line as well. Reciprocal customs duties, which would have strengthened the impression of the Grand Duchy acting as a separate and equal state, would have sent the wrong political signal in a heated nationalist climate.

Rather than with concessions, the Senate's propositions were met with a commission for the full integration of the Finnish customs zone into the imperial customs zone, which began its work in 1890. However, it did not originate from the Ministry of Finance, which was aware of the difficulties implied and had already discarded such an option in 1885, but was a personal initiative of Tsar Alexander III. His Finland policy had been under constant attack from nationalist-conservative newspapers, foremost Katkov's "Moskovskie vedomosti." An integration of the postal, customs, and currency system of the Grand Duchy promised quick and visible results. If the average Saint Petersburg *dachnik* (cottager) would have been harassed no further when

30 *Kornilov*: Russko-finliandskie tamozhennye otnosheniia, 55–63; *Suni*: Finliandsko-Russkie torgovye otnosheniia, 79–82.

31 *Kornilov*: Russko-finliandskie tamozhennye otnosheniia, 62–63.

crossing the border to go on holiday and could have paid with his accustomed rubles while on vacation, this would send a palpable signal.[32]

Obviously, the Finnish Senate harshly opposed the prospect of integration, and even Governor-general Geiden, who generally favored a course of cultural Russification, perceived the initiative as rushed. Schweitzer argues that it might have been the vehemence with which the Finnish Senate insisted on its rights that further agitated Alexander III. The Senatorial memorandi presented to him tried to argue that the proposed reforms would require the consent of the Finnish Diet, which, however, would be unlikely to be granted.[33] Essentially, this highlighted the constitutional rights to question and limit the Tsar's autocratic power in the Grand Duchy, which the Finnish Senate believed to hold. Alexander III took this as an affront, leaving an infamous marginal note on the memorandi:

> I have read all these memorandi and am astounded what they are talking about, a part of the Russian Empire or a foreign state? So, after all, does Russia belong to or constitute a part of Finland or does the Grand Duchy of Finland belong to the Russian Empire? I find that the customs unification is necessary, that the issue is not easy and that it requires a lot of work, but can be done. With regards to the post, currency and monetary part it is unforgivable that the separation still exists and the unification with the all-imperial system is necessary.[34]

Schweitzer argues that it had been the radicalism with which the Finnish Senate had framed its objection which aggravated the situation. More moderate voices in the Senate had been muted, leaving no leeway for a compromise solution which would allow the Tsar to save face and accommodate Finnish interests.[35] The issue of customs integration and its technical and macroeconomic details were thus superseded by political logic.

In 1890, a commission headed by Governor-general Geiden with both Finnish and Russian representatives was established to work out the project of the Grand Duchy's customs integration. It was clear from the get-go, that the aims of the two parties were irreconcilable. Senator Clas Herman Molander and Vice Minister-Secretary of State for Finland Vladimir Aleksandrovich von Den spoke for the Grand Duchy, demonstrating a will to adjust the low Finnish tariffs as long as the basic autonomous position of the Grand Duchy remained untouched, while Geiden clearly pointed out that the declared

32 *Schweitzer, Robert*: Autonomie und Autokratie. Die Stellung des Großfürstentums Finnland im russischen Reich in der zweiten Hälfte des 19. Jahrhunderts (1863–1899). Gießen 1978, 227–229. For a comprehensive discussion of the imperial Russian dacha see *Lovell, Stephen*: Summerfolk. A History of the Dacha, 1710–2000. Ithaca 2003, 58–117.

33 *Schweitzer*: Autonomie und Autokratie, 233–235.

34 Quoted after ibid. 236. Highlights are in the original.

35 Ibid. 233, 236–238.

goal of the commission was the administrative integration of the Finnish customs system.[36]

These two positions were essentially irreconcilable, and as the project had been initiated on the direct initiative of the Tsar, it would appear that the outcome of the commission was to be the full integration of the Grand Duchy's customs system. However, it became clear within the commission that the long existence of an insular administration in the Grand Duchy of Finland greatly complicated its integration.

The Finnish Senate had addressed the Governor-general with a long memorandum on customs unification, which was discussed in the committee. The memorandum sketched out the detrimental effects the "radical measure presented by a full so-called customs union" would constitute. They pointed out the Grand Duchy's high dependence on imports, which was five times higher per capita than that of the core empire. Further, the fiscal capacity of the Grand Duchy would have been affected in unexpected ways. The important alcohol excise could not be levied anymore if it remained unclear which amounts of Russian alcoholic beverages were imported, thus making the maintenance of an internal border necessary anyway.[37] The latter argument demonstrates well the difficulty of transferring only one administrative structure to the linear principle. If anything, excise collection would have had to be centralized as well, which however would have been another considerable encroachment on Finnish autonomy rights.

The maintenance of an internal border solely for alcohol imports, however, would "not accord to the system, usually implied under the name of a customs union." Neither were the preconditions for such a union given, which the Senate saw in the "unity of the natural conditions of production and in the general structure of the economies of the respective countries." The second precondition would have been reciprocity, meaning that "the tariff and other laws required by the union were *joint* measures, established by mutual agreement." The Senate was quick to point out that "there can be no talk of any demands on the Finnish side for the Empire to change its tariff according to the requirements of Finland."[38] Aware of the political sensitivity of the issue, the Senate thus attempted to accentuate that it did not claim the status of a sovereign state for the Grand Duchy and that it simply regarded the construction of a customs union as not appropriate for the situation.

The Senate sees it as its duty to point out that this way not a *customs union*, but a merging [sliianie] will be realized, by which the preparation and direction over most important financial and economic issues of Finland will be taken away from the con-

36 O tamozhennom ob"edinenii Velikogo Kniazhestva Finliandskogo i Imperii, 62, 65.
37 Ibid. 3–7.
38 Ibid. 7–8.

trol of Finnish authorities, which, due to the main laws and the HIGHEST regulations issued based on them, have to manage these issues and enter with HIS IMPERIAL HIGHNESS with a most loyal presentation.[39]

While not claiming the status of a sovereign state, the passage clearly emphasized the autonomous rights of the Grand Duchy, which the Senate sought to maintain. The emperor, so the Senate chose to interpret it, had not intended such a full merging – *sliianie* – and it would be sufficient to raise Finnish tariffs "to the necessary level of compliance with the imperial [tariffs]" without altering the general administrative setup.[40] This reading of the Tsar's intentions was surely a conscious misinterpretation, as it was clear that Alexander III was particularly interested in the symbolic value of said *sliianie* rather than pursuing a purely economic agenda.

The memorandum was trying to drive the point that an integration of the Finnish customs system would not be possible as it would require the control of the imperial Ministry of Finance over issues subject to Finnish authorities as guaranteed by Finnish law.[41] As such, the issue of customs unification found itself right in the middle of a large on-going debate over the legal status of the Grand Duchy and the codification of its laws.[42] To buttress this controversial point, the Senate also proposed very practical reasons against a unification.

The Finnish customs institutions had developed differently than the Russian ones and carried more varied functions. They collected other fees, such as different shipping fees, monitored the adherence to maritime regulations, and were charged with initiating legal action as well. Customs were thus in many ways entangled with other institutions, complicating their subjugation to the imperial Ministry of Finance.[43] Basically, the long development as an insular administration had made the Finnish customs system incompatible with the all-imperial system.

Ultimately, the Senate addressed a concern the Ministry of Finance held, which had long precluded the inclusion of the Grand Duchy, arguing that the Finnish skerries would greatly increase the risk of foreign contraband entering the imperial customs space, leading to a proliferation of smuggling and an ensuing "moral deterioration" of the population as well as economic losses. Thus, the Senate argued that a full integration was neither feasible nor beneficial. The aim of the Tsar, as the Senate read it, was "to allow a free circulation in the whole territory of the Russian Empire for goods produced

39 Ibid. 8.

40 Ibid. 8–9.

41 Ibid. 9.

42 For the various codification proposals and commissions see *Jussila*: Velikoe kniazhestvo Finliandskoe, 465–527.

43 O tamozhennom ob"edinenii Velikogo Kniazhestva Finliandskogo i Imperii, 9–10.

by the labor of the subjects of HIS HIGHNESS both in the Empire and in the Grand Duchy." To this end, the Senate was willing to take any measures which "could be taken by administrative way", meaning without any alteration to Finland's autonomous status.[44] This idiosyncratic solution would, it argued, be more suitable and beneficial than "the superficial imitation of foreign types of customs unions"[45], calling for a continuation of the traditional flexible approach towards Finland's economic space.

In practice, the Senate proposed to raise the tariffs on raw materials, which were significantly lower in the Grand Duchy, equalizing the production costs between Finnish and Russian manufacturers, which would allow for a free flow of domestic goods between the two parts of the empire. Exclusions should only be made for a number of foodstuffs, to keep living costs low in the Grand Duchy.[46]

Despite its openness to tariff change, the senatorial memorandum still pointed out that it understood the proposed measures as a "sacrifice" to the interests of the Russian Empire.

> As far as Finland is concerned, the Senate would like to deliberate that it could not go without weighing the gains from extending the right of selling goods from the region [of the Grand Duchy] to the Empire against, on the other hand, the effects which can be expected from the increase of the Finnish tariff necessary to allow the facilitation of trade. The Senate cannot omit the fact that a switch to a customs system adjusted to an economic structure significantly differing from the Finnish and absolutely not matching the local production requirements will very likely impair the economic activity of the Grand Duchy so much, that the difficulties caused by this will outweigh the gains from the right of free trade with the Empire. [...] The Senate hopes that with view to the significant sacrifices, which the projected changes will require from Finland, it will be regarded as reasonable to take the reasoning and rules proposed by the Senate into consideration as far as possible during the preparation of the final projects.[47]

Above all, the Senate was aware that a general revision of the imperial tariff was being prepared, which could have meant even further repercussions.[48] The members of the Senate were likely unfamiliar with the details of this new tariff, but it would have been clear to them that the trajectory was towards more protectionist tariff stakes. The new 1891 tariff, often labeled "Mendeleev-tariff" for the famous chemist central to its creation, would indeed turn out to

44 Ibid. 10–11.
45 Ibid. 9.
46 Ibid. 12–13.
47 Ibid. 31.
48 Ibid. 32.

be highly protectionist and caused the Russian and German Empire to spiral into a tariff war.[49]

Naturally, debate within the commission broke out over the interpretation of the intentions of the Tsar's orders. The commission members from the Ministry of Finance insisted that it implied a full integration of the Grand Duchy into the imperial customs system and pointed out that "achieving full equity of conditions on the borders of both Finland and the Empire obviously could only be achieved by a full uniformity of the customs administration there and with us, concentrated under the authority of our Ministry of Finance."[50] The Finnish representatives von Den and Molander reacted accordingly, citing the Finnish Senate's reading of the Tsar's will, and emphasizing the autonomy rights secured behind the Grand Duchy, which would preclude its customs integration.[51]

Further, von Den pointed out that a customs integration would be met with a public outcry:

> It is known that the public does not have much regard for the collection of customs duties, and that the public sees itself in the right to conduct all types of tricks to circumvent this tax. This negative attitude of the public, without doubt, will grow, if it will look on the powers collecting it as foreign ones, and on the money collected as going to a foreign treasury. This feeling might be inappropriate and wrong, but it is hard not to account for it in practical legislation, as it is factual.[52]

Though paying lip service to the "inappropriateness" of such feelings, von Den clearly sketched out the antagonistic attitude towards the reform, which would be seen as a political attack, and pointed out the political sensitivity of the proposed customs unification. Eventually, the situation escalated as he accused the customs commission of serving as a backdoor to dismantle Finland's autonomous status.

> Pertaining to the demand to merge the Finnish customs incomes with the all-imperial, it is so little motivated by the representatives of the Ministry of Finance, and formulated so unclearly, that it is difficult to understand what its aim is, and consequently even more difficult to object. If the goal is to completely destroy any regional administration in Finland, then this measure truly is very effective, but then even broader measures would have to be taken than those entrusted to some commission on customs.[53]

Indeed, discontent within the Finnish public vis-a-vis the numerous reform programs had been growing and Alexander III found himself stuck between

49 See chapter 1.

50 O tamozhennom ob"edinenii Velikogo Kniazhestva Finliandskogo i Imperii, 63–64.

51 Ibid. 65.

52 Ibid. 84–85.

53 Ibid. 86–87.

demands of the Russian-nationalist public and the necessity to calm Finnish public opinion.[54] With regards to the customs issue, the Tammerfors privileges presented an ideal escape from this predicament.

The Tammerfors privileges constituted an import customs exclusion granted in 1821 to manufacturers in the city of Tammerfors as a developmental measure valid until 1855.[55] Alexander II had prolonged these privileges until 1905. They included the duty-free import of raw materials and machinery required for industrial production and had substantially aided the development of the city, which accounted for 10 % of the Grand Duchy's total industrial output. This extremely privileged position gave Tammerfors manufacturers too much of a competitive edge to allow them free access to the all-imperial market, and thus the commission argued that the integration of the Finnish customs space could not be conducted as long as the Tammerfors privileges were valid.[56] Generally, certain Finnish industries, foremost the paper producers, were in such an advantageous position with regard to Russian manufacturers that the Ministry of Finance feared the ruin of the latter if the semi-permeable internal customs border was lifted, undermining the highly protectionist course.[57] With the Tammerfors privileges in place, however, a merging was simply economically unimaginable.

The guaranteed run-time of the Tammerfors privileges until 1905 allowed to postpone any substantial changes while saving face. In its conclusion on the project, the Ministry of Finance reiterated its intention to fully integrate the Grand Duchy. It would, however, only proceed after the Tammerfors privileges were no longer valid. It proposed that the Finnish Senate attempt to convince the concerned manufacturers of accepting a buy-out to surrender said privileges prematurely.[58] Unsurprisingly, the offer of waiving their duty-free import rights within an increasingly protectionist surrounding was declined by most manufacturers.[59]

The other impediment to full integration, namely the issue of authority over this legislative change, had meanwhile been discussed by the Justice Ministry and the Codification Department of the State Council, with both ruling that there was no legal basis for the claim that the Finnish Diet had to approve of the reform putting it under the full authority of the Tsar.[60]

54 *Polvinen*: Imperial Borderland, 22–23.

55 Notably the same year as the Transcaucasian transit route had been established, see chapter 6.

56 O tamozhennom ob"edinenii Velikogo Kniazhestva Finliandskogo i Imperii, 94–96.

57 Ibid. 92.

58 Ibid. 114–119.

59 Ibid. 147.

60 Ibid. 122, 130–131.

By 1891, however, Alexander III found himself compelled to order a manifest known as the "Reassurance Manifest", which discarded worries about the reforms in Finland as unsubstantiated and grounded in wrong interpretations and rumors. He also reiterated the historically grown special status of the Grand Duchy. Despite the conciliatory phrasing, Jussila argues that the essence of the manifest lay with its middle section, which emphasized the unification of Finnish and all-imperial legislation as it was prepared at the time.[61] For the time being, plans for customs unification, however, were halted due to the fragile political situation in the Grand Duchy.

The project for a full integration of the Finnish customs system thus failed against a number of factors strongly associated with its separate development and insular administrative setup. Political sensitivity played a paramount role, as the integration plans were met by public backlash in Finland. Its political institutions had attained a strong standing since the early 1860s, and the issue of customs unification was interpreted as a considerable encroachment by the imperial authorities on the Grand Duchy's autonomy. Unlike in the Transcaucasus, customs relations with the core empire were not simply an issue of distribution of power debated within governmental circles, but met with an ongoing nation-building process and a vigilant public.

Further, throughout decades of a flexible policy towards Finland's economic space, many peculiarities and misbalances had developed, which complicated its integration into the imperial economic space. The Tammerfors privileges were only the most visible instance; however, the Finnish economy had developed around its intermediary position, entertaining relations both to other western States and to the Russian Empire. This development had been at times deliberately, at times unintentionally promoted by the Russian Empire's tariff policy.

Lastly, the Grand Duchy's customs administration had functioned autonomously since 1812 and was not modeled after the imperial customs administration. Unlike in the Transcaucasus, the ultimate goal of establishing an insular customs administration had not initially been to achieve its integration into the imperial system, but to secure the loyalty of the Grand Duchy. The customs system was organized differently, with a broader sphere of activity and interlinked with other branches of administration, thus complicating its disentanglement and centralization.

61 *Jussila*: Velikoe kniazhestvo Finliandskoe, 536–537; O tamozhennom ob"edinenii Velikogo Kniazhestva Finliandskogo i Imperii, 159–161.

7.5 Renewed Attempts at Customs Integration

Although customs unification had been temporarily shelved, Finnish customs kept being debated throughout the 1890s with regard to two dimensions: international relations and the domestic imperial market. The highly protectionist 1891 imperial tariff had provoked a tariff war with the German Empire, and the Finnish customs tariff had been one important point of contention. In the late 1880s, the German Empire had become a significant importer for the Grand Duchy, surpassing the Russian Empire in categories such as grain and sugar. In the 1894 trade negotiations to end the Russo-German tariff war, the maintenance of a low Finnish import tariff for the German Empire had been one of the main demands. Though it was perceived as an unacceptable challenge to the unity and indivisibility of the Russian Empire, it was eventually agreed that the Finnish tariff would be raised only incrementally over the duration of the German-Russian commercial treaty.[62] The long separate development of the Grand Duchy's economy, with its strong trade ties to other states, became an impediment to the equalization of the Finnish and Russian tariff.

Nevertheless, the first round of tariff increases already began in 1895, with a commission headed by Nikolai Petrovich Langovoi. Its aim was to account for the rift in tariffs exacerbated by the 1891 imperial tariff. While the leeway on Finland's foreign tariff was limited by the trade agreement with Germany, the commission concentrated on increasing the stakes for Finnish imports into the imperial core customs space. Similarly, attempts were made to improve import conditions for Russian sugar, wine, and tobacco to Finland, in order to give them a competitive edge over foreign products and widen the market for Russian manufacturers.[63] Instead of pursuing a convergence, as intended by a customs union, it was effecting the opposite and strengthening the semi-permeability of the border in a protectionist effort in the interests of Central Russian manufacturers. By 1897, a new Finnish tariff had been worked out and published which increased the barrier for Finnish exports to Russia while promoting Russian exports to Finland, effectively inverting the prior trade dynamic between the two customs zones.[64]

Though the 1890 commission had not effected an immediate customs-integration, the reprise was only temporary. With the appointment of Bobrikov as Governor-general of the Grand Duchy, centralization was the key agenda and now had a strong enforcer as well. The primary focus was on the integration of the Finnish army, but the customs issue soon appeared on the agenda as well.

62 *Kornilov*: Russko-finliandskie tamozhennye otnosheniia, 88–89.

63 Ibid. 100, 113–115.

64 Ibid. 118–120.

Minister of Finance Sergei Vitte also pushed for a quicker resolution of the issue, as the Russo-German commercial treaty was running out in 1904, and he wanted to avoid for Finnish tariffs to become the subject of bargaining again. If the Grand Duchy of Finland was fully integrated, no separate demands on its tariffs could be made during negotiations with the German Empire.[65]

A new commission was established in 1900 with the aim, set out by Vitte, of accomplishing customs integration by 1903. However, the commission members were split. Naturally, the Finnish representatives continued to oppose an integration and showed themselves even less willing to compromise than in 1890. Members of different imperial authorities were split as well, though, arguing that Russian manufacturers profited from the internal customs border and that an overhasty removal of the border would jeopardize their business vis-a-vis the Finnish competition. Again, the Tammerfors privileges, still valid until 1906, were cited as the main deterrent to integration. Ultimately, it was the fragile political situations in the Grand Duchy which resulted in the temporary slowdown of the centralizing reforms – customs integration included.[66]

After a short respite following the revolutionary year of 1905, the issue of customs integration resurfaced in 1912. In the meantime, a law on "the order of issuing laws and decrees regarding Finland with all-imperial importance"[67] had been passed in 1910, which strongly extended the central administration's grasp on Finnish affairs. The role of the Finnish Senate was reduced to a solely consultative one, if legislative initiatives had "all-imperial importance" – the definition of this status, however, was left wide-open for interpretation.[68]

In 1912, a customs commission headed by Sergei Fedorovich Veber was established, which once again revealed the same tensions. The Finnish delegates reiterated the distinctive characteristics of the Finnish economy, which required separate tariffs, while representatives from the Moscow Exchange Committee emphasized that Russian manufacturers profited from the internal customs border. Eventually, the commission closed without achieving any results.[69]

Since the first serious efforts at implementing the full customs integration of the Grand Duchy into the imperial customs space, this tension between the political and economic aspects of integration had existed. While national-conservative newspapers demanded Finland's economic integration for

65 Ibid. 127–128.

66 Ibid. 129–133.

67 "Zakon o poriadke izdaniia kasaiushchikhsia Finliandii zakonov i postanovlenii obshchegosudarstvennogo znacheniia", Polnoe sobranie zakonov Rossiikoi Imperii. Sobranie 3. Volume 30. Saint Petersburg 1913, no. 33795.

68 *Kornilov*: Russko-finliandskie tamozhennye otnosheniia, 196.

69 Ibid. 200–207.

political and symbolic reasons, reading the separation as a sign of separatism, the no less nationally motivated Russian protectionist tariff program would have been undermined by a unification. Both the asymmetric economic development, which made the two economic units incompatible, as well as the stern resistance of the Finnish Senate against the integration resulted from a longstanding insular administration, not intended to achieve the integration of the Finnish customs into the Russian. The flexible approach chosen by the Russian Empire in the early 19th century ultimately effected the rigidity of the division between both economic spaces.

By the time the Russian Empire collapsed in 1917, the Grand Duchy of Finland had remained the only larger economic unit not integrated into the Russian imperial customs space. With its declaration of independence on December 6 1917, Finland regained full control over its economic policies.

7.6 Conclusion

Despite the fundamentally different political and economic preconditions of the Caucasian Viceroyalty and the Grand Duchy of Finland, both were administered according to an insular logic for a significant part of the 19th century. The customs relation of these two economic spaces to the imperial core economic space was informed by this decentralized approach, which, however was motivated differently. The first required a regional administration to increase administrative permeation and efficiency in a remote area with customs institutions primarily performing quarantine functions. The latter was initially conditioned by an appeasement policy for a strategically important region close to the imperial center and allowed for prior relations of the Grand Duchy to Sweden to continue during a transitional phase.

The Russian Empire's highly protectionist tariff policy, beginning in the 1820s and only loosening in the 1850s, required efficient control of customs borders. As both regions shared a complicated topography on their external borders, the central administration opted to retreat to more convenient internal customs lines in both cases. The need for efficient control of the core economic space was paramount to administrative unity in the first half of the 19th century. The resulting exclusion of both regions from the core customs space allowed for the introduction of deviant flexible customs regimes tailored to regional requirements. This resulted in stark tariff differences to the "European" tariff, conditioning the semipermeable nature of the internal customs borders with the imperial core customs space. The Russian Empire exported duty-free to its peripheral territories but maintained high tariff barriers on imports into the core customs space.

The liberalization of the all-imperial tariff in the 1860s alleviated this tariff discrepancy with the Transcaucasian and Finnish tariff, almost fully matching the "European" tariff. However, tariff convergence was not followed up by administrative integration of either peripheral insular customs system. While the Namestnik had actively petitioned for an integration, no such impulses had come from the Grand Duchy. Despite tariff convergence, the entanglement of the respective customs systems with other administrative branches, organized under an insular logic complicated full integration. Further, the central customs administration mistrusted the local customs authorities in both regions. Only a full-integration – in terms of tariffs and executive control – was deemed acceptable and thus the separation of customs zones was maintained, rather than using a shared-power approach between the central and regional authorities.

Economically, the two regions stood in diametrically opposite relation to the imperial core economic zone. The Transcaucasian region was regarded as an underdeveloped region and a potential gateway for smuggling. The Grand Duchy of Finland, on the other hand, had developed strongly due to its intermediary position between the Russian Empire and foreign trading partners, which was achieved by its separate customs policy. Maintaining the exclusion from the imperial customs space, as in the first case, equaled keeping a bad apple from the proverbial barrel. In the latter case, potentially dangerous internal competition to Russian manufacturers was isolated.

The protection of domestic industries and markets was a staple of nationalist argumentation in the 1880s. In the case of the abolition of the Transcaucasian transit route in 1883, discussed in chapter 6, politically nationalist demands and the interests of central Russian industrialists overlapped. In the debate over the customs integration of the Grand Duchy, however, tension built up between demands for the symbolic unity of the Russian Empire and the fears of Russian manufacturers over strong Finnish competition. The issue demonstrates well the contradictions erupting in a nationalizing empire.

The long application of flexible heterogeneous approaches to its different territories had created peculiarities and developmental trajectories, complicating the integration of the two economic zones. In the case of the Namestnichestvo, the conflict was mostly over the distribution of power and played out between different branches of the imperial administration. In the case of the Grand Duchy, customs integration attempts had much larger political repercussions. The insular customs status of the Grand Duchy had promoted its economic rise and symbolized its autonomous status. Customs were one focal point of Finnish nation-building, along with the separate postal system and the Finnish marka introduced in 1860. Within the context of a nationalizing empire, the project for Finland's customs integration was thus perceived as an attack on Finnish autonomy and a watershed for defining the relation of the Grand

Duchy to the Russian Empire. Ultimately, integration failed against a mix of both political and macroeconomic factors.

In both cases, the imperial administration had initially opted for flexible approaches towards structuring its heterogeneous economic space. However, the established insular regimes exacerbated the deviance over time. As the unified nation-state became the new benchmark, the imperial mode of managing Russia's heterogeneous economic space by installing idiosyncratic local customs regimes was challenged. The flexibility the imperial administration had initially exhibited to accommodate the specificities of the Grand Duchy of Finland eventually effected administrative rigidity, as the legacies of the insular administration ultimately limited the empire's leeway in reshaping its economic space.

Epilogue

State Comptroller Samuil Greig's resolute dismissal of the Russian Empire's fragmented customs space as a deviant path, quoted in the introduction to this book, exemplifies a transitional moment in the management of the Russian Empire's economic space. By 1877, the model of a unified economic space had asserted itself as the benchmark internationally. The Russian reality, however, was still one of infrastructural and administrative fragmentation as well as heterogeneous customs regimes. Spatial imaginaries in the imperial administration had already begun to drift from an approach of managing the "space of empires" to the creation of a "space of states."[1] However, decades of particularistic regional regulations could not be undone quickly. Neither were the local peculiarities necessitating special regimes in the first place overcome. Greig's statement thus has more to say about his vision for a new imperial economic space and his belief in the malleability of economic geographies than about the complex local and inter-imperial constellations which had shaped the Russian Empire's economic space in the previous decades. This book attempted to approach various *situations of economic territoriality* from the historic context of their inception, asking not whether the tools chosen by the imperial administration to structure its economic space were successful, but rather inquiring their creators' motivation and the factors which necessitated certain solutions, which resulted in future path-dependencies as well as the contradictions criticized by Samuil Greig.

At the start of the 19th century, the Russian Empire still lacked a systematic approach to its economic space in the east. Although the label "Asiatic" had already been in use in the late 18th century, it did not signify a specific system of its own, but was only used to mark deviance. The economic tools employed on the steppe border in the late 18th century mimicked the mercantilist policies used on the Russian Empire's Western borders, albeit with very different results. The beginning 19th century ushered in a reconceptualization of the imperial economic space as a dualistic system – "European" and "Asiatic." It was not simply geographic labeling but introduced a completely different approach to structuring customs space with differing underlying motivations and goals. While in its "European" section, Nicholaen Russia clung to highly protectionist policies and intensified its border control along a linear border, the Empire's "Asiatic" space featured free-trade policies and fluid borders.

1 *Maier*: Once Within Borders, 15.

The "Asiatic" system, formalized in 1817, was still deemed deviant from the regular "European" customs; yet it was not understood as inferior anymore, but rather as a more suitable solution for the conditions found on site and the goals pursued with Russia's south-eastern trade. Customs in the "European" part followed a strict fiscal and protectionist logic, as they constituted an essential source of state revenue, and Russian industries were unable to compete with foreign competitors without considerable protection. In Russia's "Asiatic" peripheries and beyond their borders, these arguments played a much smaller role, as trade regulations were primarily influenced by issues arising from imperial expansion. Here, political motives dominated over fiscal and macroeconomic considerations.

In its Georgian territories the Russian Empire had attempted the introduction of regular customs early on, only to find that its available administrative resources were insufficient to transfer its own "European" model. The customs management of the Transcaucasian region fluctuated between centralizing attempts and deregulation. Initial enthusiasm for the introduction of Russian trade regulations, which were regarded as more progressive and rational, was quickly replaced by frustration. Where imperial regulations were introduced they proved unsuitable and disruptive to local trade and were criticized by merchants demanding a return to the old system. The programmatic changes in customs policy in the 19th century reflected the central imperial administration's changing attribution of the Transcaucasian Region to either the "European" or the "Asiatic" economic – and by extension – cultural space.

On the steppe border, a linear customs line had been discussed as well, yet never effectively been implemented. Administrative incapacity was, however, only one factor for the vast deregulation which characterized the "Asiatic" customs regime. The openness of borders promised an extension of the Russian Empire's sphere of influence. Trade was conceptualized as a conduit of cultural and political influence and an essential tool of a "mission civilisatrice." Russian-manufactured goods were to convince Caucasian mountaineers and subjects of the Central Asian Khanates of the advantages of Russian subjecthood. Strict customs controls were understood as an impediment to this exchange. Even worse, strict customs controls, which could not be upheld with rigidity, had the potential to damage the Russian Empire's prestige. Thus, the "Asiatic" customs system, which sharply contradicted the protectionist arrangement in the "European" parts of the empire, promised both a way to avoid admitting administrative shortcomings and to generate symbolic capital from proclaiming benevolent free-trade policies.

The establishment of an "Asiatic" system, did not necessarily mean the exclusive assertion of imperial regulations. Quite the contrary, previous trade regulations such as the *rakhdar* continued to exist. Issues of imperial rule, prestige, and public hygiene were paramount to fiscal and macroeconomic concerns in the Transcaucasus and on the steppe border. Thus, it is little surprising that the Russian Empire resorted to decentralization measures, putting insular administrators such as Governors-general or the Namestnik in charge and side-lining the Ministry of Finance. "Men on the spot" were trusted with finding tailored solutions for trade regulations in "their region." However, the laxer trade regulations chosen reflected not only an accommodation of established economic practices, but were also conceptualized as regional developmental measures. A lower degree of trade regulations was considered a temporary privilege which would allow a specific territory to close the economic gap to the core imperial economic space quicker. Thus, decentralizing measures were to implicitly contribute to an eventual harmonization of the empire's regions, allowing for a re-centralization.

However, in the long run these insular customs administrations often bred distrust against peripheral institutions within the Ministry of Finance and created idiosyncrasies and entanglements which proved hard to resolve once the integration of a peripheral territory came on the agenda. The prolonged existence of insular customs administrations effectively complicated their integration into the imperial customs space. Nevertheless, these autonomous customs arrangements did not create sufficient pressure for integration as long as the fiscal relevance of a territory remained small and the integrity of the "European" customs system in the core empire was not endangered by the deviant regimes on the periphery. The basis for this co-existence of contradictory customs systems was an understanding of the Russian Empire's economic space as infrastructurally fragmented, with its particular customs systems not interlocking with one another – a basis challenged in the 1870s by a growing belief in the malleability of physical space through technology and the prospect of shrinking the imperial space.

The Transcaucasian transit route presented a notable exception to this laissez-faire attitude towards peripheral economic spaces at an early stage. It represented not merely another deregulation in "Asiatic" trade, but became a canvas for competing visions of the empire's economic space. The vision of an integrated Black Sea region connected to global trade currents, brought forth from the Caucasus administration, collided with the central administration's fear of losing internal markets and political influence to Western European competitors, with whom Russia's industries could not compete. Just as Russian goods were understood as conduits of Russian influence, so could foreign goods become a liability to Russia's imperial rule on its own peripheries. Nevertheless, the weak infrastructural connection of the Transcaucasian region to core imperial markets precluded the full termination of the Transcaucasian transit route for the time being. However, already in the early Nicholaen period, this issue highlighted a potential fault line which would reemerge in other constellations in the late 1870s: special customs regimes could serve as tools for the development of peripheral regions, but they were also suspect of nurturing separatist tendencies and alienating peripheral regions from the empire.

In the early 1860s, this concern still took the back seat to austerity measures in the administration and the necessities of maintaining and supplying distant peripheral regions. The establishment of a vast free-trade zone in Russia's Far-East was such an attempt at alleviating the region's economically weak position while avoiding large administrative costs. The empire had found itself in the predicament of not being able to sufficiently support its Far-Eastern territories, meanwhile allowing the region to forge relations with global trade partners to overcome these shortcomings held the potential of alienating said region from the empire. Only the increased infrastructural integration of the imperial space promised to eventually solve this contradiction. The Far-Eastern porto-franco had been one of the most prominent changes brought about by the Great Reforms in terms of separate customs arrangements. It matched the global free-trade trend of the 1860s and continued the dualistic system of "European" and "Asiatic" customs systems established in 1817. However, it was the general liberalizations brought about by the Great Reforms, which eventually undermined the basis of this dualistic customs system, albeit not at the pace set by the Ministry of Finance.

Although much more reluctantly and with fiscal concerns as a central focus, the Russian Empire still followed the global tariff liberalizations of the 1860s in its "European" tariff, which saw significant changes during the Great Reforms. Effectively, these tariff reductions implied an approximation with the "Asiatic" tariffs and were understood as a transitory phase towards a future harmonization of the two tariff systems by Minister of Finance Mikhail Reitern. His tentative approach stemmed not least from an aversion to engaging in costly undertakings on Russia's "Asiatic" peripheries under the conditions of a fiscal crisis. Neither did he evaluate integrative measures as necessary, seeing that the parallel functioning of a borderless economic space in Central Asia and the Far-East did not interfere with the internal markets, for lack of infrastructural connections. The phase of the Great Reforms, however, had introduced two new factors, which began to increasingly exert pressure on the Ministry of Finance: the empowerment of new interest groups which gained weight in economic debates, and the rise of the railway as a tool to shrink the imperial space – both in reality and in the spatial imaginary.

Had the Ministry of Finance so far mostly demonstrated a pragmatic approach towards its eastern peripheral regions and confidently relied on territorial fragmentation as a tool to protect its core customs space, it now found itself confronted with new territorial visions inspired by the transformative potential of the railway, which were brought forward in the public as well as picked up by other ministries, putting the Ministry of Finance in a position to react. In the 1870s, the Ministry of Finance mostly still managed to operate as before and ward off attacks on its heterogeneous customs system with the means of administrative reports and the debunking of claims about widespread smuggling that would endanger the core customs territory. The ascent of Alexander III, however, empowered a nascent nationalist press and a group of Central Russian entrepreneurs which were increasing pressure to integrate. Politically nationalist demands were formulated in the realm of the economy, while economic demands were increasingly framed as nationalist concerns. Though an amorphous "national course" constituted the focal point under Alexander III's rule, its application to the imperial customs space constituted a contradictory conundrum for the Ministry of Finance.

The attempted integration of the Grand Duchy of Finland is a point in case. Symbolically, a nationalist course of Russification would have necessitated its integration into the Russian customs space, as vehemently demanded by Mikhail Katkov and his "Moskovskie vedomosti." However, for Central Russian manufacturers – all too willing to demand the protection of Russian industries – a "national" solution constituted the exact opposite: firewalling them as strongly as possible from intra-imperial Finnish competition. A unified customs space might have been accepted as the benchmark by the 1880s, as exemplified by Greig, its creation however was complicated by the long existence of separate customs regimes which had created imbalances, such as Finland's strong industrial position relative to the core empire or administrative entanglements with insular administrations, as observed in the Caucasian Viceroyalty. The imperative of creating a uniform customs space limited the empire's leeway in resorting to its previous flexible solutions. If, however, the highly protectionist customs system developing in the late 1880s and peaking in the 1890s was to be extended to all of the empire's borders, the Ministry of Finance would find itself in a double bind. Under the conditions of a well-connected imperial space, openness and fluidity on any of its borders would be disruptive to the protectionist bulwark; on the other hand, air-sealing the Russian Empire's vast borderline would be practically impossible. Further, the fluidity of borders satisfied economic necessities in peripheral regions, which could not be easily compensated by a better integration into intra-imperial trade.

Both in the Central Asian khanates and the Far-Eastern region, substantial trade currents were oriented globally, profiting from low customs rates and simple trade regulations in circumvention of the core empire's customs space. The enforcement of strict protectionist customs measures thus endangered these regions' subsistence. On the other hand, a stable supply from the empire's core economic space required solid infrastructural integration. Such an integration, in turn, threatened to dismantle the longstanding practice of relying on spatial fragmentation as means of customs protection, thus necessitating tight and efficient border control along long, topographically challenging and distant borders, which could hardly be protected in an economical way.

The railway promised to be the tool to drastically reshape the imperial economic geography and Minister of Finance Sergei Vitte embodied the new agenda of creating a national customs space. Bold territorial visions of an integrated imperial market brought forward in the 1860s, such as the integration of the Central Asian khanates, now appeared tangible. Alternative visions brought forth from peripheral actors requiring territorialized free-trade regimes, on the other hand, were increasingly regarded with suspicion. The establishment of a free-trade zone on the Ob' and Enisei rivers promised to link Western Siberia to global trade currents making use of the Northern sea route, in an arrangement similar to the Far-Eastern porto-franco established in the 1860s. However, by the late 1890s such setups following the logic of the "space of empires", as defined by Maier, were not consequently stimulated by the Ministry of Finance anymore, fearing that special regional regulations were hard to take back once established, and could alienate regions from the core empire.[2] Although the Trans-Siberian railway promised to create an integrated imperial market, peripheral actors such as Dunin-Gorkavich remained disappointed with the results, and demands for regional free-trade zones regularly reappeared until the end of the Russian Empire.

By the 1890s, the Russian Empire had firmly embarked on the project of creating a unified customs space, leaving behind its dualistic system established in the early 19th century, even if in practice numerous special regulations continued to exist. The rearrangement of economic relations also prompted a renegotiation of political relations. The Khanate of Bukhara, a protectorate of the Russian Empire, lost its hitherto guaranteed autonomy in trade regulation, as it was included into the customs zone of the Russian Empire. The decision was motivated by practical issues of border protection, as the Bukharan territory was wedged between the Transcaspian Region and the Governorate-general of Turkestan, making effective customs border control almost impossible and very costly. The redefinition of Bukhara's economic relation to the Russian Empire obviously implied a foreign political component and exemplified the increasing encroachment of the Ministry of Finance on the Foreign Ministry's domain, which had begun in the 1890s.

Apart from rearranging relations with the Emir of Bukhara, the drawing of a customs line also equaled a settling of the Russo-Afghan border. With regards to Bukhara's trade, the inclusion into imperial customs territory meant both a break with long-standing trade practices as well as the opportunity to capitalize on it being part of the Russian Empire. The implementation of modern Russian customs procedures unlocked hitherto unavailable trade

2 Ibid. 15.

routes. While imperial trade regulations were supposed to improve market access for Russian merchants, Bukharan merchants also quickly reoriented themselves under the new conditions and capitalized on the railway and telegraph technologies linking them to global trade currents.

For the Grand Duchy of Finland, the planned customs integration became a contested issue of national self-assertion. Unlike with other special customs territories, the Grand Duchy's customs authority had not initially been conceptualized as a measure to accelerate its integration into the Russian economic space. Neither was its economic development inferior to that of the core economic space, as in other cases. Finland's trade and industries profited from the granted privileges, such as the Tammerfors customs privileges, as well as the intermediary position between foreign partners and the Russian Empire. The long existence of a separate customs regime resulted in a situation in which the integration of Finland was economically undesirable for the imperial Ministry of Finance. For the Grand Duchy of Finland, on the other hand, customs autonomy had constituted one pillar of its nation-building process, which had accelerated significantly since the 1860s.

Under the nationalist turn of the 1880s the economic relations of the Grand Duchy of Finland with the Russian Empire were charged politically by a Russian nationalist press and the decision for integration was eventually made by the Tsar himself, defying economic rationale. However, the deep entanglement of the Finnish customs administration with other administrative branches and the maintenance of a separate budget made an integration extremely complicated and could not be implemented without an outright attack on what were considered secured autonomy rights by the Finnish parliament. The political implications were considered too dangerous by the Saint Petersburg administration and eventually the decision was protracted, citing economic reasons. Despite further attempts, Finland eventually remained the Russian Empire's only significant customs territory outside the imperial customs space in 1917.

Throughout the 19th century, the Russian Empire had gradually transitioned from imagining and subsequently managing its economic space as a "space of empires" towards adopting a "space of states" approach.[3] The many idiosyncratic solutions implemented to accommodate the heterogeneous preconditions in the vast empire were initially founded on the infrastructural fragmentation of the imperial space. The radically different customs systems found in the empire could only co-exist as long as they did not significantly interact with one another and disrupt the functioning of the other systems. Unlike with the British Empire, however, the Russian Empire's domains were not separated by bodies of water, but by infrastructural deficits. Overcoming

3 Ibid. 15.

this insufficiency was considered a raison d'état, and railway technology promised to deliver the necessary tools. However, the intended shrinking of the imperial space also undermined the hitherto existing mode of managing the empire's heterogeneous economic territories as independent customs systems, resulting in an increased pressure to integrate the Russian Empire into a unified customs space as well.

This trend, which picked up pace in the 1870s and 1880s, is telling of two significant shifts in the spatial imaginary of the Russian imperial administration. On the one hand, Saint Petersburg ministerial bureaucrats began to share visions of connectedness enabled by technological advancement and reimagined the Russian Empire as a tightly knit space. On the other hand, this spatial conceptualization increasingly limited the administration's leeway in resorting to previous cost-efficient and flexible solutions. The Ministry of Finance found itself before the challenge of structuring its borders according to the model of smaller nation-states, yet facing the world's longest border and a lack of resources to saturate this vast space administratively.

Starting with the 1890s, the Russian Empire had confidently embarked on the goal of unifying its customs space, even at the expense of its own peripheral territories' interests. By the time of its collapse, it had – with the exclusion of Finland – successfully implemented Samuil Greig's 1877 dictum of "the unification of the customs of different states under one administration."[4] To the outside, the Russian Empire appeared as a monolithic and protectionist customs space. Internally, the regional economic disbalances, for the alleviation of which special territorialized customs regimes had been introduced in the first place, persisted.

4 RGIA, f. 1152, op. 9, d. 84, l. 3 ob.

Bibliography

I. Archival Sources

Rossiiskii Gosudarstvennyi Istoricheskii Arkhiv (RGIA),
Russian State Historical Archive, Saint Petersburg (Russia)

Fond 20	Departament torgovli i manufaktur MF
Fond 21	Departament tamozhennykh sborov MF
Fond 23	Ministerstvo torgovli i promyshlennosti
Fond 40	Vsepoddanneishie doklady po chasti torgovli i promyshlennosti i materialy k zakliucheniiu torgovykh dogovorov s inostrannymi gosudarstvami
Fond 560	Obshchaia kantseliariia ministra finansov
Fond 563	Komitet finansov
Fond 1152	Departament gosudarstvennoi ekonomii Gosudarstvennogo Soveta
Fond 1263	Komitet ministrov (1802–1906)
Fond 1268	Kavkazskii komitet

Rossiiskii Gosudarstvennyi Voenno-istoricheskii Arkhiv (RGVIA),
Russian State Historical Military Archive, Moscow (Russia)

Fond 400	Glavnyi shtab

Arkhiv Vneshnei Politiki Rossiiskoi Imperii (AVPRI),
Archive of the Foreign Policy of the Russian Empire, Moscow (Russia)

Fond 144	Persidskii stol
Fond 147	Sredneaziatskii stol

II. Newspapers, Journals, Reference Works and Legislative Texts

Adres kalendar'. Obshchaia rospis' nachal'stvuiushchikh i prochikh dolzhnostnykh lits po vsem upravleniiam v Rossiiskoi imperii

Akty sobrannye Kavkazkoi arkheograficheskoi kommissiei

Arkhiv Gosudarstvennogo Soveta

Imperatorskoe Russkoe istoricheskoe obshchestvo. Biograficheskii slovar'

Entsiklopedicheskii slovar' Brokgauza i Efrona

Gosudarstvennaia vneshniaia torgovlia v raznykh ee vidakh

Istoricheskii vestnik
Obzor vneshnei torgovli Rossii po evropeiskoi i aziatskoi granitsam
Orenburgskie gubernskie vedomosti
Otechestvennye zapiski
Polnoe sobranie zakonov Rossiiskoi Imperii
Severnaia pchela
Sibirskie vedomosti
Moskovskie vedomosti
Russkii vestnik
Torgovo-promyshlennaia gazeta
Trudy obshchestva dlia sodeistviia Russkoi promyshlennosti i torgovle
Turkestanskie vedomosti
Vostochnoe obozrenie

III. Published Sources

Dogovor mezhdu Rossiei i Bukharoi. Shaar, 28 sentiabria/10 oktiabria 1873g. In: *Adamov, E.A.* (ed.): Sbornik dogovorov Rossii s drugimi gosudarstvami. 1856–1917. Moscow 1952, 135–139.

Obshchestvo dlia sodeistviia russkoi promyshlennosti i torgovle: Dopolnitel'naia Zapiska o torgvykh putiach v Sredniiu Aziiu i o vliianii na nashu sredneaziatskuiu torgovliu sushchestvuiushchego tranzita tovarov chrez Kavkaz. Saint Petersburg 1869.

Gendemianskii mirnyi dogovor mezhdu Rossiei i Khivoi. In: *Sazonov, A.A./Gerasimova, G.N./Flushkova, O.A./Kisterev, S.K.* (ed.): Pod stiagom Rossii: Sbornik arkhivnykh dokumentov. Moscow 1992, 347–352.

Materialy po delu o tamozhennom ob"edinenii Velikogo Kniazhestva Finliandskogo i Imperii, 1890–1892 g. Saint Petersburg 1901.

Obshchestvo dlia sodeistviia russkoi promyshlennosti i torgovle: Materialy po voprosu o torgovykh putiakh v Sredniiu Aziiu. Saint Petersburg 1869.

Ekspeditsiia zagotovleniia gosudarstvennykh bumag: Ministerstvo Finansov. 1802–1902. Volume 1. Saint Petersburg 1902.

Otchet po deloproizvodstvu gosudarstvennogo soveta za 1883g. Saint Petersburg 1884.

Redaktsiia Torgovo-Promyshlennoi Gazety: Severnyi torgovyi put' i khodataistva Sibirskikh gorodov. Saint Petersburg 1898.

Tamozhennyi ustav po aziatskoi torgovle. Saint Petersburg 1817.

Trudy soveshchaniia 1906g. v Irkutske o putiakh soobshcheniia v Sibiri. Volume 1. Irkutsk 1907.

Gosudarstvennaia Duma: Zakliuchenie po vnesennomu v Gosudarstvennuiu Dumu, za podpis'iu 34 chlenov ee, zakonoproektu o porto-franko v ust'iakh r.r. Obi i Eniseia. Saint Petersburg 1908.

Zapiska departamenta tamozhennykh sborov po voprosu o Zakavkazskom tranzite. In: Dopolnenie k materialam po voprosu o Zakavkazskom tranzite. Saint Petersburg 1883, 1–20.

Obshchestvo dlia sodeistviia russkoi promyshlennosti i torgovle: Zapiska obshchestva dlia sodeistvia russkoi promyshlennosti i torgovle, o torgovykh putiakh v Sredniu Aziiu. Saint Petersburg 1868.

Baev, Mikhail Georgievich: Otchet chinovnika Ministerstva Finansov General'nogo Shtaba General-Maiora Baeva po komandirovke dlia issledovaniia nashei granitsy s Persiei i Avganistanom v predelakh Zakaspiiskoi oblasti. Saint Petersburg 1888.

Borodkin, Mikhail: Istoriia Finliandii. Tom V. Vremia Imperatora Nikolaia I. Saint Petersburg 1915.

Bunge, Nikolai Kh.: Promyshlennost' i ee ogranichenie vo vneshnei torgovle. (Stat'ia vtoraia) Obshchee obozrenie vneshnei torgovli Rossii. In: Otechestvennye zapiski, June (1857), 473–508.

Dunin-Gorkavich, Aleksandr Aleksandrovich: Neobkhodimost' otkrytiia porto-franko v ust'iach reki Obi i Eniseia. Tobol'sk 1907.

Eniseets: Severnyi morskoi put'. Saint Petersburg 1898.

Fisher, Konstantin: Zapiski Senatora K.I. Fishera. Chast' 1. In: *Shubinskii, S.N.* (ed.): Istoricheskii vestnik. Tom CXI. Saint Petersburg 1908, 43–70.

Grigor'ev, Vasilii Vasilievich: Razbor sochineniia P.I. Nebol'sina: Ocherki torgovli Rossii s Srednei Aziei. In: *Veselovskii, K.S.* (ed.): Dvadtsat' piatoe prisuzhdenie uchrezhdenykh P.N. Demidovym nagrad. 26 Maia 1856 goda. Saint Petersburg 1856, 109–182.

Gubarevich-Radobyl'skii, Anton: Chai i chainaia monopolia. Opyt issledovaniia osnov oblozheniia chaia v Rossii. Saint Petersburg 1908.

Gubarevich-Radobyl'skii, Anton: Ekonomicheskii ocherk Bukhary i Tunisa. Opyt sravnitel'nogo issledovaniia dvukh sistem protektorata. Saint Petersburg 1905.

Gubarevich-Radobyl'skii, Anton: Kakie dorogi sleduet stroit' v Turkestane i v Zakavkaz'e. Saint Petersburg 1914.

Gubarevich-Radobyl'skii, Anton: Znachenie Turkestana v torgovle Rossii s sopredel'nymi stranami Azii. Saint Petersburg 1912.

Herz, Johann: Noch ein Wort über Tęgoborski's Werk: Die Finanzen, der öffentliche Kredit, die Staatsschuld, und das Besteuerungssystem des österreichischen Kaiserstaates, mit vergleichendem Hinblick auf Preussen und Frankreich. Vienna 1844.

Il'in, A.: Obshchaia karta fabrichno-zavodskoi promyshlennosti Rossiiskoi Imperii. In: *Mendeleev, D.* (ed.): Fabrichno-zavodskaia promyshlennost' i torgovlia Rossii. Saint Petersburg 1893.

Iuzefovich, Trofim Pavlovich: Dogovory Rossii s Vostokom. Politicheskie i torgovye. Saint Petersburg 1869.

Johnson, Henry: The Life and Voyages of Joseph Wiggins, F.R.G.S. Modern Discoverer of the Kara Sea Route to Siberia. Based on his Journal & Letters. London 1907.

K-shev, M.: Sredneaziatskaia torgovlia v 1859 godu. In: Orenburgskie gubernskie vedomosti, 9, 27.2.1860, 39–41.

Kachalov, Nikolai Aleksandrovich: N.A. Kachalov. Zapiski tainogo sovetnika. Moscow 2012.

Kalinovskii, Bal'tazar Fomich: O razvitii i rasprostranenii idei svobodnoi torgovli i o primenenii ikh k polozhitel'nym zakonodatel'stvam v glavnykh zapadno-evropeiskikh gosudarstvakh. Saint Petersburg 1859.

Katkov, Mikhail Nikiforovich: Sobranie peredovykh statei Moskovskikh Vedomostei. 1882 god. Saint Petersburg 1898.

Katkov, Mikhail Nikiforovich: Sobranie peredovykh statei Moskovskikh Vedomostei. 1883 god. Saint Petersburg 1898.

Kokorev, Vasilii A.: Vzgliad Russkogo na evropeiskuiu torgovliu. In: Russkii vestnik, 14 (1858), 29–64.

Krestovnikov, Nikolai: Angliiskaia konkurrentsiia v Sibiri. Moscow 1889.

L. V.: Svobodnaia torgovlia i pokrovitel'stvennaia sistema v Rossii. Doklad Moskovskomu Otdeleniiu Obshchestva dlia sodeistvia Russkoi Promyshlennosti i Torgovle. Moscow 1891.

L'vovskii, Silvestr: Zakavkazskii Tranzit. Iz V otd. otcheta D. S.S. L'vovskogo o komandirovke, po vysochaishemu poveleniiu, na Kavkaz, v 1881–1882 g. Saint Petersburg 1883.

Lodyzhenskii, Konstantin N.: Istoriia russkogo tamozhennogo tarifa. Cheliabinsk 1886.

Makarov, Stepan Osipovich: Otchet vitse-admirala Makarova ob osmotre im letom 1897 goda, po porucheniiu ministra finansov S.Iu. Vitte, morskogo puti na reki Ob' i Enisei. Saint Petersburg 1898.

Mendeleev, Dmitrii: Tolkovyi tarif, ili issledovanie o razvitii promyshlennosti Rossii v sviazi s ee obshchim tamozhennym tarifom 1891 goda. Saint Petersburg 1892.

Nebol'sin, Pavel I.: Ocherki torgovli Rossii s stranami Srednei Azii, Khivoi, Bukharoi i Kokanom: so storony Orenburgskoi linii. Saint Petersburg 1856.

Nikol'skii, Sergei: O vneshnikh tamozhennykh poshlinakh. Moscow 1865.

Pobedonostsev, Konstantin: Pis'ma Podenostseva k Aleksandru III. Volume 1. Moscow 1926.

Polovtsov, Aleksandr: Dnevnik Polovtsova. 1883–1886. Volume 1. Moscow 2005.

Reutern, Mikhail Kh./Barnett, Vincent: Memorandum on Tariff Reform in Russia (1867). In: Œconomia. History, Methodology, Philosophy, 4(1) (2014), 29–34.

Rumiantsev, Nikolai Petrovich: Kratkoe vvedenie v razum proektov Astrakhanskogo i Orenburgskogo tarifov. In: Arkhiv Gosudarstvennogo Soveta. Tom 3. Chast' 1. Saint Petersburg 1878, 385–391.

Rumiantsev, Nikolai Petrovich: Zapiska ministra kommertsii o razume tarifa. In: Arkhiv Gosudarstvennogo Soveta. Tom 3. Chast' 1. Saint Petersburg 1878, 369–380.

Shavrov, Nikolai: Put' v Tsentral'nuiu Aziiu po napravleniiu ukazannomu Petrom Velikim. Saint Petersburg 1871.

Sidorov, Mikhail Konstantinovich: Sever Rossii. Saint Petersburg 1870.

Skach'kov, Petr Emel'ianovich: Russko-kitaiskie otnosheniia, 1689–1916. Moscow 1958.

Sobolev, Michail Nikolaevich: Tamozhennaia politika Rossii vo vtoroi polovine XIX veka. Tomsk 1911.

Studitskii, Fedor: Istoriia otkrytiia morskogo puti iz Evropy v sibirskie reki i do Beringova proliva. Part 1. Saint Petersburg 1883.

Studitskii, Fedor: Istoriia otkrytiia morskogo puti iz Evropy v sibirskie reki i do Beringova proliva. Part 2. Saint Petersburg 1883.

Subbotin, A. P.: Rossiia i Angliia na Sredneaziatskikh rynkakh. Saint Petersburg 1885.

Tęgoborski, Ludwik: De l'instruction publique en Autriche, par un diplomate etranger: qui a long-temps résidé dans ce pays. Paris 1841.

Tęgoborski, Ludwik: Des finances et du crédit public de l'Autriche de sa dette, de ses ressources financières et de son système d'imposition. Paris 1843.

Tęgoborski, Ludwik: Études sur les forces productives de la Russie. Volume 1. Paris 1852.

Tęgoborski, Ludwik: Études sur les forces productives de la Russie. Volume 2. Paris 1852.

Tęgoborski, Ludwik: Études sur les forces productives de la Russie. Volume 3. Paris 1853.

Tęgoborski, Ludwik: Études sur les forces productives de la Russie. Volume 4. Paris 1855.

Terent'e v, M. A.: Kak ustranit' torgovoe sopernichestvo anglichan v Srednei Azii? In: Trudy obshchestva dlia sodeistviia russkoi promyshlennosti i torgovle. Volume 2 (1873), 154–186.

Terent'ev, M. A.: Rossiia i Angliia v bor'be za rynki. Saint Petersburg 1876.

Ustav Obshchestva dlia sodeistviia russkoi promyshlennosti i torgovle. Saint Petersburg 1867.

Treskinskii, A.: K voprosu o zakavkazskom tranzite v Persiiu. In: Torgovo-promyshlennaia gazeta, 221, 3.10.1908, 107–109.

Ushinskii, A.: O znachenii manufakturnoi promyshlennosti v Rossii i ob okhrannoi sisteme, s izlozheniem mnenii raznykh pisatelei v zashchitu-i-protiv ucheniia o svobodnoi mezhdunarodnoi torgovle. Saint Petersburg 1858.

Vernadskii, Ivan Vasil'evich: O vneshnei torgovle. In: Russkii vestnik, 2 (1856), 603–624.

Vitte, Sergei: Natsional'naia ekonomika i Fridrikh List. Kiev 1889.

Vitte, Sergei: Printsipy zheleznodorozhnykh tarifov po perevozke gruzov. Kiev 1883.

von Cancrin, Georg: Weltreichthum, Nationalreichthum und Staatswirthschaft, oder, Versuch neuer Ansichten der politischen Oekonomie. Munich 1821.

Vostrotin, Stepanov: Severnyi morskoi put' i Cheliabinskii tarifnyi perelom v sviazi s kolonizatsiei Sibiri. Saint Petersburg 1908.

Wiesner, Adolf: Russisch-politische Arithmetik. Streiflichter auf was Werk des russischen Geheimrathes M-L. von Tegoborski: Ueber die Finanzen, den Staatskredit, die Staatsschuld, die Hülfsquellen und das Steuersystem Oesterreichs. Leipzig 1844.

IV. Secondary Literature

Aaslestad, Katherine B.: Introduction. Revisiting Napoleon's Continental System. Consequences of Economic Warfare. In: *Aaslestad, K. B./Joor, J.* (eds.): Revisiting Napoleon's Continental System. Local, Regional and European Experiences. Houndsmill, Basingstoke 2015, 1–22.

Abashin, Sergei/Arapov, Dmitrii/Bekmakhanova, Nailia: Tsentral'naia Aziia v sostave Rossiiskoi Imperii. Moscow 2008.

Adelsgruber, Paulus/Cohen, Laurie/Kuzmany, Börries: Getrennt und doch verbunden. Grenzstädte zwischen Österreich und Russland 1772–1918. Wien 2011.

Agapov, Mikhail: Looking for a Way Out: Trans-Siberian Transportation Projects at the Turn of the 20th Century. In: Quaestio Rossica, 6(3) (2018), 771–783.

Agapov, Mikhail: 'Zagovor' protiv Severa Rossii: natsionalizatsiia predprinimatel'skogo diskursa v 60-e gg. XIX v. In: Ab Imperio, 4 (2019), 73–96.

Alapuro, Risto: State and Revolution in Finland. Leiden 2019.

Anan'ich, Boris: Banking Firms in the Russian Empire, 1860–1914. In: Russian Studies in History, 35(1) (1996), 6–61.

Andreeva, E. A. (ed.), Upravlencheskaia elita Rossiiskoi Imperii. Istoriia ministerstv, 1802–1917. Saint Petersburg 2008.

Bairoch, Paul: Economics and World History. Myths and Paradoxes. New York 1993.

Barkey, Karen/Von Hagen, Mark: After Empire. Multiethnic Societies and Nation-Building. The Soviet Union and the Russian, Ottoman, and Habsburg Empires. Boulder 1997.

Barnett, Vincent: D. I. Mendeleev, Russian Protectionism and German Political Economy. In: *Rieter, H./Shirokorad, L./Zweynert, J.* (eds.): Deutsche und russische Ökonomen im Dialog. Wissenstransfer in historischer Perspektive. Marburg 2005, 169–184.

Barnett, Vincent: Economics in Russia. Studies in Intellectual History. Aldershot, Hampshire 2008.

Barnett, Vincent: A History of Russian Economic Thought. New York 2005.

Barnett, Vincent: M. Kh. Reutern and Tariff Reform in Russia. In: Œconomia. History, Methodology, Philosophy, 4(1) (2014), 17–27.

Bassin, Mark: Imperial Visions: Nationalist Imagination and Geographical Expansion in the Russian Far East, 1840–1865. Cambridge 1999.

Becker, Seymour: Russia's Protectorates in Central Asia: Bukhara and Khiva, 1865–1924. London 2004.

Beliaeva, Natal'ia: Ot porto-franko k tamozhne. Ocherk regional'noi istorii Rossiiskogo protektsionizma. Vladivostok 2003.

Blackwell, William L.: Beginnings of Russian Industrialization, 1800–1860. Princeton 1968.

Blanchard, Ian: Russian Railway Construction and the Urals Charcoal Iron and Steel Industry, 1851–1914. In: The Economic History Review, 53(1) (2000), 107–126.

Bobrovnikov, Vladimir/Babich, Irina: Severnyi Kavkaz v sostave Rossiiskoi Imperii. Moscow 2007.

Brisku, Adrian: Political Reform in the Ottoman and Russian Empires. A Comparative Approach. London 2017.

Bulmuş, Birsen: Plague, Quarantines and Geopolitics in the Ottoman Empire. Edinburgh 2012.

Burbank, Jane/von Hagen, Mark: Coming into the Territory: Uncertainty and Empire. In: *Burbank, J./von Hagen, M./Remnev, A.* (eds.): Russian Empire. Space, People, Power. 1700–1930. Bloomington 2007, 1–29.

Cooper, Frederick: Colonialism in Question. Theory, Knowledge, History. Berkeley 2005.

Cvetkovski, Roland: Modernisierung durch Beschleunigung. Raum und Mobilität im Zarenreich. Frankfurt am Main 2006.

Dahlmann, Dittmar: Torgovoe sudokhodstvo za poliarnym krugom vo vtoroi polovine XIX veka. In: Otechestvennaia istoriia, 5(2001) 21–32.

Dameshek, Lev/Remnev, Anatolii: Sibir' v sostave Rossiiskoi Imperii. Moscow 2007.

Divall, Colin: Railway Imperialisms, Railway Nationalisms. In: *Burri, M./Elsasser, K. T./Gugerli, D.* (eds.): Die Internationalität der Eisenbahn. Zürich 2003, 195–210.

Dolbilov, Mikhail/Miller, Aleksei: Zapadnye okrainy Rossiiskoi Imperii. Moscow 2006.

Dolidovich, Olesya/Fedorova, Vera/Zhulaeva, Anna: Conflict of Imperial and Regional Interests on the Introduction of Duty-free Trade Regime in the Mouths of Siberian Rivers during the First World War. In: Bylye Gody, 54(1) (2019), 395–405.

Ermachkov, Ivan A./Koroleva, Larisa A./Svechnikova, Natalia V./Gut, Jasmin: The Plague in the Caucasus in 1801–1815 years: Part I. In: Bylye Gody, 47(1) (2018), 120–129.

Ermachkov, Ivan A./Koroleva, Larisa A./Svechnikova, Natalia V./Gut, Jasmin: The Plague in the Caucasus in 1801–1815 years: Part II. In: Bylye Gody, 48(2) (2018), 558–569.

Etges, Andreas: Wirtschaftsnationalismus: USA und Deutschland im Vergleich (1815–1914). Frankfurt/Main 1999.

Forsyth, James: The Caucasus. A History. Cambridge 2013.

Ganelin, Rafail/Anan'ich, Boris: Sergei Iul'evich Vitte i ego vremia. Saint Petersburg 1999.

Ganzenmüller, Jörg/Tönsmeyer, Tatjana: Einleitung: Vom Vorrücken des Staates in die Fläche. Ein europäisches Phänomen des langen 19. Jahrhunderts. In: *Ganzenmüller, J./Tönsmeyer, T.* (eds.): Einleitung: Vom Vorrücken des Staates in die Fläche. Ein europäisches Phänomen des langen 19. Jahrhunderts. Köln/Weimar/Wien 2016, 7–31.

Gatrell, Peter: The Russian Fiscal State, 1600–1914. In: *Yun-Casalilla, B./O'Brien, P. K.* (eds.): The Rise of Fiscal States: A Global History, 1500–1914. Cambridge 2012, 191–212.

Gatrell, Peter/Anan'ich, Boris: National and Non-National Dimensions of Economic Development in Nineteenth- and Twentieth-Century Russia. In: *Teichova, A./Matis, H.* (eds.): Nation, State and the Economy in History. Cambridge 2003, 219–236.

Geiss, Imanuel/Epstein, Fritz T.: Der Berliner Kongreß 1878. Boppard 1978.

Gerasimov, Ilya/Kusber, Jan/Mogilner, Marina/Semyonov, Alexander: New Imperial History and the Challenges of Empire. In: *Gerasimov, I./Kusber, J./Semyonov, A.* (eds.): Empire Speaks out? Languages of Rationalization and Self-Description in the Russian Empire. Leiden 2009, 3–32.

Gerasimov, Ilya/Glebov, Sergey/Kaplunovski, Alexander/Mogilner, Marina/Semyonov, Alexander: In Search of a New Imperial History. In: Ab Imperio, 1 (2005), 33–56.

Gerschenkron, Alexander: Economic Backwardness in Historical Perspective. A Book of Essays. Cambridge, Massachusetts 1962.

Golbeck, Matthias: (Selbst)beschreibungen vom Rand des Imperiums. Die Briefe des russischen Beamten und Amateurwissenschaftlers N. F. Petrovskij aus dem Generalgouvernement Turkestan und Kaschgar 1870–1895. In: *Aust, M./Schenk, F. B.* (eds.): Imperial Subjects. Autobiographische Praktiken in den Reichen der Romanovs, Habsburger und Osmanen. Köln 2015, 291–323.

Goncharov, Alexander E.: Istoriia kommercheskikh ekspeditsii severnogo morskogo puti: 1870-e – 1890-e gg. (Dissertation). Kemerovo 2013.

Goncharov, Alexander E.: The Trans-Siberian Railway and the Northern Sea Route. In: Journal of Siberian Federal University. Humanities & Social Sciences 6(1) (2013), 31–42.

Gordin, Michael D.: A Well-ordered Thing. Dmitrii Mendeleev and the Shadow of the Periodic Table. New York 2004.

Grant, Jonathan A.: Big Business in Russia. The Putilov Company in Late Imperial Russia, 1868–1917. Pittsburgh 1999.

Hahn, Hans-Werner: Geschichte des Deutschen Zollvereins. Göttingen 1984.

Hahn, Hans-Werner/Kreutzmann, Marko (eds.): Der deutsche Zollverein. Ökonomie und Nation im 19. Jahrhundert. Köln 2012.

Heikinnen, Sakari/Heinonen, Visa/Kuusterä, Antti/Pekkarinen, Jukka: The History of Finnish Economic Thought, 1809–1917. Tammiisaari/Ekenäs 2000.

Heller, Klaus: Der russisch-chinesische Handel in Kjachta: Eine Besonderheit in den außenwirtschaftlichen Beziehungen Rußlands im 18. und 19. Jahrhundert. In: Jahrbücher für Geschichte Osteuropas, 29(4) (1981), 515–536.

Heller, Klaus: Der russisch-chinesische Handel von seinen Anfängen bis zum Ausgang des 19. Jahrhunderts. Erlangen 1980.

Herlihy, Patricia: Odessa: A History, 1794–1914. Cambridge, Massachusetts 1986.

Hildermeier, Manfred: Das Privileg der Rückständigkeit. Anmerkungen zum Wandel einer Interpretationsfigur der Neueren Russischen Geschichte. In: Historische Zeitschrift, 244(3) (1987), 557–603.

Issawi, Charles: The Tabriz-Trabzon Trade, 1830–1900: Rise and Decline of a Route. In: International Journal of Middle East Studies, 1 (1970), 18–27.

Ivanov, Kirill: Razvitie tamozhennogo dela v Rossii v kontse XIX-nachale XX veka: ot avtonomnogo zapretitel'nogo tarifa k torgovym konventsiiam. Saint Petersburg 2012.

Joffe, Muriel: Autocracy, Capitalism and Empire: The Politics of Irrigation. In: The Russian Review, 54(3) (1995), 365–388.

Joffe, Muriel: Regional Rivalry and Economic Nationalism: The Central Industrial Region Industrialists' Strategy for the Development of the Russian Economy, 1880s-1914. In: Russian History, 11(4) (1984), 389–421.

Jussila, Osmo: Die russische Reichsgesetzgebung in Finnland in den Jahren 1809–1898. In: Jahrbücher für Geschichte Osteuropas, 33(3) (1985), 345–365.

Jussila, Osmo: Velikoe kniazhestvo Finliandskoe. 1809–1917. Helsinki 2009.

Kappeler, Andreas: Rußland als Vielvölkerreich. Entstehung – Geschichte – Zerfall. München 2008.

Kaschuba, Wolfgang: Die Überwindung der Distanz. Zeit und Raum in der europäischen Moderne. Frankfurt am Main 2004.

Katajala, Kimmo: Cross-Border Trade in Karelia from the Middle Ages to the October Revolution 1917. In: *Lähteenmäki, M.* (ed.): The Flexible Frontier. Change and Continuity in Finnish-Russian Relations. Helsinki 2007, 70–87.

Kazemzadeh, Firuz: Russia and Britain in Persia. Imperial Ambitions in Qajar Iran. London 2013.

Khalfin, Naftula A.: Obshchestvo dlia sodeistviia russkoi promyshlennosti i torgovle i Sredniia Aziia. In: Voprosy Istorii, 8 (1975), 45–63.

Khalfin, Naftula A.: Rossiia i khanstva Srednei Azii. Moscow 1974.

Khodarkovsky, Michael: Bitter Choices: Loyalty and Betrayal in the Russian Conquest of the North Caucasus. Ithaca 2011.

Kipp, Jacob W.: M. Kh. Reutern on the Russian State and Economy: A Liberal Bureaucrat during the Crimean Era, 1854–60. In: The Journal of Modern History, 47(3) (1975), 437–459.

Kislovskii, Iurii: Istoriia tamozhennogo dela i tamozhennoi politiki Rossii. Moscow 2004.

Konovalov, Iurii Petrovich: Morskoi torgovyi flot Rossii v period promyshlennogo kapitalizma. 60-e - seredina 90-ch gg. XIX v. (na materialakh Chernomorsko-Azovskogo basseina). Odessa 1981.

Korandei, Fedor: Ekonomisty v 'pole': Karskaia ekspeditsiia 1924g. i praktiki sozdaniia ekonomicheskogo znaniia. In: Ab Imperio, 2 (2020), 51–56.

Kornilov, Genrikh: Russko-Finliandskie tamozhennye otnosheniia v kontse XIX – nachale XX v., 1885–1914. Leningrad 1971.

Krikhunov, Vladimir: Protektsionizm ili Fritrederstvo: vybor puti. Moscow 2002.

Krikhunov, Vladimir: Tamozhennaia politika Rossii i ee ekonomicheskaia effektivnost', 1877–1914 gg. Moscow 1999.

Kupriianova, Liubov': Tamozhenno-promyshlennyi protektsionizm i Rossiiskie predprinimateli (40–80-e gody XIX veka). Moscow 1994.

Lähteenmäki, Maria: Cows, Guns and Bolsheviks: Smuggling in the Borderland Between South-East Finland and St. Petersburg. In: *Katajala, K. L., Maria* (eds.): Imagined, Negotiated, Remembered. Constructing European Borders and Borderlands. Münster 2012, 119–140.

Laverychev, Vladimir: Russkie kapitalisty i periodicheskaia pechat' vtoroi poloviny XIX v. In: Istoriia SSSR, 1 (1972), 26–47.

LeDonne, John P.: La réforme de 1883 au Caucase. Un exemple d'administration régionale russe. In: Cahiers du Monde Russe, 8(1) (1967), 21–35.

Lieven, Dominic: Empire. The Russian Empire and its Rivals. London 2000.

Lincoln, Bruce W.: The Great Reforms. Autocracy, Bureaucracy, and the Politics of Change in Imperial Russia. Dekalb 1990.

Lincoln, Bruce W.: In the Vanguard of Reform. Russia's Enlightened Bureaucrats, 1825–1861. DeKalb 1982.

Lovell, Stephen: Summerfolk. A History of the Dacha, 1710–2000. Ithaca 2003.

Lundin, Leonard: Constitutional and Historical Background of the Russification Dispute in Finland. In: *Thaden, E. C.* (ed.): Russification in the Baltic Provinces and Finland, 1855–1914. Princeton 1981, 357–372.

Maier, Charles S.: Once Within Borders. Territories of Power, Wealth, and Belonging since 1500. Cambridge, Massachusetts 2016.

Maier, Charles S.: Transformations of Territoriality. 1600–2000. In: *Budde, G./Conrad, S./Janz, O.* (eds.): Transnationale Geschichte. Themen, Tendenzen, Theorien. Göttingen 2006, 32–55.

Martin, Thomas: Baumwollindustrie in Sankt Petersburg und Moskau und die russische Zolltarifpolitik (1850–1891). Eine vergleichende Regionalstudie. Giessen 1998.

Matsuzato, Kimitaka: Intra-Bureaucaratic Debate on the Institution of Russian Governors-General in the Mid-Nineteenth Century. In: *Uyaka, T.* (ed.): Asiatic Russia. Imperial Power in Regional and International Contexts. Abingdon, New York 2012, 83–101.

McCaffray, Susan P.: The Politics of Industrialization in Tsarist Russia. The Association of Southern Coal and Steel Producers, 1874–1914. DeKalb 1996.

McCaffray, Susan P./Melancon, Michael: Introduction: A Member of the Family – Russia's Place in Europe, 1789–1914. In: *McCaffray, S. P./Melancon, M.* (eds.): Russia in a European Context, 1789–1914. A Member of the Family. New York 2005, 1–10.

McKay, John P.: Baku Oil and Transcaucasian Pipelines, 1883–1891: A Study in Tsarist Economic Policy. In: Slavic Review, 43(4) (1984), 604–623.

Miller, Aleksei: Imperiia Romanovykh i natsionalizm. Esse po metodologii istoricheskogo issledovaniia. Moscow 2006.

Morrison, Alexander: Introduction: Killing the Cotton Canard and Getting Rid of the Great Game: Rewriting the Russian Conquest of Central Asia, 1814–1895. In: Central Asian Survey, 33(2) (2014), 131–142.

Morrison, Alexander: 'Nechto Eroticheskoe', 'Courir Après L'ombre'? – Logistical Imperatives and the Fall of Tashkent, 1859–1865. In: Central Asian Survey, 33(2) (2014), 153–169.

Mosse, W. E.: Aspects of Tsarist Bureaucracy: The State Council in the Late Nineteenth Century. In: The English Historical Review, 95(375) (1980), 268–292.

Mote, Victor L.: The Cheliabinsk Grain Tariff and the Rise of the Siberian Butter Industry. In: Slavic Review, 35(2) (1976), 304–317.

Munting, Roger: The Russian Beet Sugar Industry in the XIXth Century. In: The Journal of European Economic History, 2 (1984), 291–309.

Nachtigal, Reinhard: Verkehrswege in Kaukasien. Ein Integrationsproblem des Zarenreiches 1780–1870. Wiesbaden 2016.

Noda, Jin: Russo-Chinese Trade Through Central Asia. In: *Uyaka, T.* (ed.): Asiatic Russia. Imperial Power in Regional and International Contexts. Oxon 2012, 153–173.

Olcott, Martha Brill: The Kazakhs. Stanford 1995.

Osterkamp, Jana: 'Kooperatives Imperium'. Loyalitätsgefüge und Reich-Länder-Finanzausgleich in der späten Habsburgermonarchie. In: Geschichte und Gesellschaft, 42(4) (2016), 592–620.

Pahre, Robert: Politics and Trade Cooperation in the Nineteenth Century. The "Agreeable Customs" of 1815–1914. Cambridge 2008.

Paine, Sarah C. M.: Imperial Rivals. China, Russia, and their Disputed Frontier. Armonk 1996.

Pinkhenson, Dmitrii M.: Istoriia otkrytiia i osvoeniia Severnogo morskogo puti. Volume 2. Leningrad 1962.

Pintner, Walter M.: Government and Industry during the Ministry of Count Kankrin, 1823–1844. In: Slavic Review, 23(1) (1964), 45–62.

Pintner, Walter M.: Russian Economic Policy under Nicholas I. Ithaca 1967.

Plekhanov, Aleksandr/Plekhanov, Andrei: Otdel'nyi Korpus Pogranichnoi Strazhi na granitse Rossii, 1893–1919. Moscow 2012.

Polunov, Aleksandr Iur'evich: Russia in the Nineteenth Century. Autocracy, Reform and Social Change, 1814–1914. Armonk, N. Y. 2005.

Polvinen, Tuomo: Imperial Borderland: Bobrikov and the Attempted Russification of Finland, 1898–1904. Durham, North Carolina 1995.

Pravilova, Ekaterina: 'Cena' Imperii: centr i okrainy v Rossiiskom biudzhete XIX-nachala XX vv. In: Ab Imperio, 4 (2002), 115–44.

Pravilova, Ekaterina: Finansy imperii. Den'gi i vlast' v politike Rossii na natsional'nykh okrainakh, 1801–1917. Moscow 2006.

Pravilova, Ekaterina: From the Zloty to the Ruble: The Kingdom of Poland in the Monetary Politics of the Russian Empire. In: *Burbank, J./Von Hagen, M./Remnev, A.* (eds.): Russian Empire: Space, People, Power, 1700–1930. Bloomington 2007, 295–319.

Pravilova, Ekaterina: River of Empire: Geopolitics, Irrigation, and the Amu Darya in the Late XIXth Century. In: Cahiers d'Asie centrale, 17/18 (2009), 255–287.

Pyziur, Eugene: Mikhail N. Katkov: Advocate of English Liberalism in Russia, 1856–1863. In: The Slavonic and East European Review, 45(105) (1967), 439–456.

Remnev, Anatolii: Rossiia dal'nego vostoka. Imperskaia geografiia vlasti XIX – nachala XX vekov. Omsk 2004.

Remnev, Anatolii: Stepnoe general-gubernatorstvo v imperskoi geografii vlasti. In: *Sugorova, N.* (ed.): Aziatskaia Rossiia: Liudi i struktury Imperii. Omsk 2005, 163–222.

Renner, Andreas: Defining a Russian Nation: Mikhail Katkov and the 'Invention' of National Politics. In: The Slavonic and East European Review, 81(4) (2003), 659–682.

Rhinelander, L. Hamilton: The Creation of the Caucasian Vicegerency. In: The Slavonic and East European Review, 59(1) (1981), 15–40.

Rieber, Alfred J.: The Moscow Entrepreneurial Group: The Emergence of a New Form in Autocratic Politics. In: Jahrbücher für Geschichte Osteuropas, 25(1) (1977), 1–20.

Rieber, Alfred J.: The Imperial Russian Project. Autocratic Politics, Economic Development, and Social Fragmentation. Toronto 2017.

Rieber, Alfred J.: The Moscow Entrepreneurial Group: The Emergence of a New Form in Autocratic Politics: II. In: Jahrbücher für Geschichte Osteuropas, 25(2) (1977), 174–199.

Rolf, Malte: Einführung: Imperial Biographien. Lebenswege imperialer Akteure in Groß- und Kolonialreichen (1850–1918). In: Geschichte und Gesellschaft, 40 (2014), 5–21.

Rozhkova, Mariia K.: Ekonomicheskie sviazi Rossii so Srednei Aziei, 40–60-e gody 19. veka. Moscow 1963.

Saunders, David: Captain Wiggins and Admiral Makarov: Commerce and Politics in the Russian Arctic (1874–1904). In: Polar Record, 53(4) (2017), 427–435.

Schenk, Frithjof Benjamin: Das Zarenreich als Transitraum zwischen Europa und Asien: Russische Visionen und westliche Wahrnehmungen um die Jahrhundertwende. In: *Aust, M.* (ed.): Globalisierung imperial und sozialistisch: Russland und die Sowjetunion in der Globalgeschichte 1851–1991. Frankfurt am Main 2013, 41–63.

Schenk, Frithjof Benjamin: Mastering Imperial Space? The Ambivalent Impact of Railway-Building in Tsarist Russia. In: *Leonhard, J./von Hirschhausen, U.* (eds.): Comparing Empires. Encounters and Transfers in the Long Nineteenth Century. Göttingen 2011, 60–77.

Schenk, Frithjof Benjamin: Russlands Fahrt in die Moderne. Mobilität und sozialer Raum im Eisenbahnzeitalter. Stuttgart 2014.

Schimmelpenninck van der Oye, David: Paul's Great Game: Russia's Plan to Invade British India. In: Central Asian Survey, 33(2) (2014), 143–152.

Schweitzer, Robert: Autonomie und Autokratie. Die Stellung des Großfürstentums Finnland im russischen Reich in der zweiten Hälfte des 19. Jahrhunderts (1863–1899). Gießen 1978.

Semyonov, Alexander: Empire as a Context Setting Category. In: Ab Imperio, 1 (2008), 193–204.

Serrano, Elena: Spreading the Revolution. Guyton's Fumigating Machine in Spain. Politics, Technology, and Material Culture (1796–1808). In: *Roberts, L. L./Werrett, S.* (eds.): Compound Histories. 2018, 106–130.

Shepelev, Leonid E.: Sud'by Rossii. Problemy ekonomicheskogo razvitiia strany v XIX-nachale XX vv. Dokumenty i memuary gosudarstennykh deiatelei. Saint Petersburg 2007.

Sheptun, Alla: The German Historical School and Russian Economic Thought. In: Journal of Economic Studies, 32(4) (2005), 349–374.

Sheptun, Alla: Russian Monetary Reformers: Speransky, Mordvinov and Bunge. In: *Barnett, V./Zweynert, J.* (eds.): Economics in Russia: Studies in Intellectual History. Abingdon 2016, 41–56.

Sidorko, Clemens P.: Die Eroberung Tschetscheniens und Dagestans als Fallbeispiel kolonialer Expansion des Zarenreichs im 19. Jahrhundert. In: Jahrbücher für Geschichte Osteuropas, 47(4) (1999), 505–511.

Simms, J. Y.: The Economic Impact of the Russian Famine of 1891–92. In: The Slavonic and East European Review, 60(1) (1982), 63–74.

Simms, James Y.: The Crop Failure of 1891: Soil Exhaustion, Technological Backwardness, and Russia's 'Agrarian Crisis'. In: Slavic Review, 41(2) (1982), 236–250.

Simpson, Brian P.: Money, Banking, and the Business Cycle, Volume II: Remedies and Alternative Theories. New York 2014.

Skrydlov, Andrei: N. A. Nordenskiöld's Polar Expeditions and the Russian Society (To the 140th Anniversary of the First Voyage through the Northeast Passage). In: IOP Conference Series Earth and Environmental Science, 302 (2019), 1–6.

Smith-Peter, Susan: Sweet Development. The Sugar Beet Industry, Agricultural Societies and Agrarian Transformation in the Russian Empire 1818–1913. In: Cahiers du monde russe, 57 (2016), 101–124.

Sokolov, A.Ia.: Torgovaia politika Rossii v Srednei Azii i razvitie Russko-Afganskikh torgovykh otnoshenii. Tashkent 1971.

Solonchenko, Ekaterina: Tamozhennaia politika na iugo-vostoke Rossii i ee realizatsiia v Orenburgskom krae v 1752–1868 gg. Orenburg 2007.

Solonchenko, Ekaterina A.: Preobrazovanie Orenburgskogo tamozhennogo okruga v 1862–1868gg.: ot reformirovaniia k rasformirovaniiu. In: Reformy i reformatory v Rossii. Orenburg 2003, 72–93.

Solov'ev, A. G./Sennikov, A. A.: Rossiia i Turkmeniia v XIX veke. Ashkhabad 1946.

Soucek, Svat: A History of Inner Asia. Cambridge 2000.

Stadelbauer, Jörg: Bahnbau und kulturgeographischer Wandel in Turkmenien: Einflüsse der Eisenbahn auf Raumstruktur, Wirtschaftsentwicklung und Verkehrsintegration in einem Grenzgebiet des russischen Machtbereichs. Berlin 1973.

Stadelmann, Matthias: Großfürst Konstantin Nikolaevič. Wiesbaden 2012.

Stepanov, Valerii: Ivan Alekseevich Vyshnegradskii. In: Russian Studies in History, 35(2) (1996), 73–103.

Stepanov, Valerii: Mikhail Khristoforovich Reitern. In: Russian Studies in History, 35(2) (1996), 8–41.

Stepanov, Valerii: N. Kh. Bunge. Sud'ba reformatora. Moscow 1998.

Stepanov, Valerii: Nikolai Khristianovich Bunge. In: Russian Studies in History, 35(2) (1996), 42–72.

Stone, Ian R.: Sir Robert Morier and the Sea Route to Siberia. In: Polar Record, 31(178) (1995), 343–346.

Strakhova, Natalia P.: Rossiiskii tamozhennyi tarif 1822 goda. In: Vestnik Volgogradskogo gosudarstvennogo universiteta. Seriia 4: Istoriia. Regionovedenie. Mezhdunarodnye otnosheniia, 11 (2006), 15–22.

Stuch, Stephan: Regionalismus in Sibirien im frühen 20. Jahrhundert (Dissertation). Köln 2003.

Sukhova, Natalia/Skrydlov, Andrei: The Russian Geographical Society and the Polar Studies in the Second Half of the 19th Century. In: IOP Conference Series Earth and Environmental Science, 180 (2018), 1–5.

Sunderland, Willard: Taming the Wild Field. Colonization and Empire on the Russian Steppe. Ithaca 2004.

Suni, Lev: Finliandsko-Russkie torgovye otnosheniia vo vtoroi polovine XIX veka, 1858–1885. Tartu 1963.

Suny, Ronald Grigor: The Empire Strikes Out. Imperial Russia, 'National' Identity, and Theories of Empire. In: *Suny, R. G./Martin, T.* (eds.): A State of Nations. Empire and Nation-Making in the Age of Lenin and Stalin. Oxford 2001, 23–66.

Surnina, Irina: Tsenzura i "Ekonomicheskii ukazatel'" I. V. Vernadskogo 1857–1861 godov. In: Filologicheskie nauki. Voprosy teorii i praktiki, 2(80) (2018), 244–249.

Taki, Victor: Tsar and Sultan. Russian Encounters with the Ottomann Empire. London and New York 2016.

Tammiksaar, Erki/Stone, Ian R.: Karl Ernst von Baer and the Kara Sea 'Eiskeller'. In: Polar Record, 33(186) (1997), 239–242.

Taranovski, Theodore: Alexander III and his Bureaucracy: The Limitations on Autocratic Power. In: Canadian Slavonic Papers/Revue Canadienne des Slavistes, 26(2/3) (1984), 207–219.

Taylor, Norman W.: Adam Smith's First Russian Disciple. In: The Slavonic and East European Review, 45(105) (1967), 425–438.

Tchoudinov, Alexandre: Russia and the Continental System: Trends in Russian Historiography. In: *Aaslestad, K. B./Joor, J.* (eds.): Revisiting Napoleon's Continental System. Local, Regional and European Experiences. Houndsmill, Basingstoke 2015, 56–68.

Thaden, Edward C.: Russification in the Baltic Provinces and Finland, 1855–1914. Princeton 1981.

Thomas, Ludmila: Ein deutsches Unternehmen im russischen Fernen Osten (1864–1921). Zwänge und Grenzen der Anpassung. In: *Dahlmann, D./Scheide, C.* (eds.): '... das einzige Land in Europa, das eine große Zukunft vor sich hat.' Deutsche Unternehmen und Unternehmer im Russischen Reich im 19. und 20. Jahrhundert. Göttingen 1998, 611–635.

Thomas, Ludmila: Streben nach Weltmachtpositionen. Russlands Handelsflotte, 1856 bis 1914. Berlin 1995.

Torp, Cornelius: The Challenges of Globalization. New York 2014.

Torp, Cornelius: Die Herausforderung der Globalisierung. Wirtschaft und Politik in Deutschland, 1860–1914. Göttingen 2005.

Tovpeka, Andrei: Razvitie sistemy sviazi i upravleniia v pogranichnoi strazhe Rossiiskoi imperii, 1827–1917 gg. Saint Petersburg 2014.

Turbin, Aleksandr: Dal'nevostochnyi porto-franko v iazykakh i praktikakh modernizuiushcheisia imperii. In: Ab Imperio, 1 (2019), 45–78.

Urbansky, Sören: Der betrunkene Kosake. Schmuggel im sino-russischen Grenzland (circa 1860–1930). In: *Aust, M.* (ed.): Globalisierung imperial und sozialistisch. Russland und die Sowjetunion in der Globalgeschichte 1851–1991. Frankfurt am Main 2013, 301–329.

Van Regemorter, Jean-Louis: Le mythe génois en Mer Noire: la France, la Russie et le commerce d'Asie par la route de Géorgie (1821–1831). In: Annales. Histoire, Sciences Sociales, 19(3) (1964), 492–521.

Vinkovetsky, Ilya: Russian America: An Overseas Colony of a Continental Empire, 1804–1867. Oxford 2011.

Voerkelius, Mirjam: Russland und die Sowjetunion auf den Weltausstellungen. In: *Aust, M.* (ed.): Globalisierung imperial und sozialistisch: Russland und die Sowjetunion in der Globalgeschichte 1851–1991. Frankfurt am Main 2013, 207–224.

Volkhonskii, Mikhail: Uprazdnenie namestnichestva na Kavkaze v 1881–1882gg. In: Rossiiskaia istoriia, 3 (2018), 171–189.

Von Laue, Theodore H.: Sergei Witte and the Industrialization of Russia. New York 1963.

Wcislo, Francis William: Tales of Imperial Russia. The Life and Times of Sergei Witte, 1849–1915. Oxford 2011.

Wcislo, Frank: Rereading Old Texts: Sergei Witte and the Industrialization of Russia. In: *McCaffray, S.P./Melancon, M.* (eds.): Russia in the European Context, 1789–1914. A Member of the Family. New York 2005, 71–83.

Weeks, Theodore R.: Russification: Word and Practice, 1863–1914. In: Proceedings of the American Philosophical Society, 148(4) (2004), 471–489.

Weiss, Claudia: Wie Sibirien "unser" wurde. Die Russische Geographische Gesellschaft und ihr Einfluss auf die Bilder und Vorstellungen von Sibirien im 19. Jahrhundert. Göttingen 2007.

Wendler, Eugen: Die List-Rezeption in Rußland. In: *Wendler, E.* (ed.): "Die Vereinigung des europäischen Kontinents." Friedrich List – Gesamteuropäische Wirkungsgeschichte seines ökonomischen Denkens. Stuttgart 1996, 473–490.

Wenzlhuemer, Roland: Connecting the Nineteenth-Century World. The Telegraph and Globalization. Cambridge 2013.

Wortman, Richard S.: Scenarios of Power: From Alexander II to the Abdication of Nicholas II. Princeton 2000.

Zlotnikov, Mikhail F.: Kontinental'naia blokada i Rossiia. Leningrad 1966.

List of Illustrations

Figures

Graphics

Tables

All maps, graphics and tables created by author.

Index